SECOND EDITION

W9-ARO-993

DB2

for the

PART 2

COBOL

Programmer

Curtis Garvin

Anne Prince

MIKE MURACH & ASSOCIATES, INC.

Authors:	Curtis Garvin
	Anne Prince
Editor:	Mike Murach
Cover design:	Zylka Design
Design and production:	Tom Murach

Related Murach books:

DB2 for the COBOL Programmer, Part 1
Murach's Structured COBOL
Murach's CICS for the COBOL Programmer
The CICS Programmer's Desk Reference
IMS for the COBOL Programmer, Parts 1 and 2
MVS TSO, Parts 1 and 2
MVS JCL

Printed in the United States of America.
10 9 8 7 6 5

ISBN: 1-890774-03-0

Library of Congress Cataloging-in-Publication Data
Garvin, Curtis, 1961-
    DB2 for the COBOL programmer: version 4.1/Curtis Garvin, Steve
Eckols. -- 2nd ed.
       p. cm
   ISBN 1-890774-02-2 (pbk.: v. 1)
   ISBN 1-890774-03-0 (pbk.: v. 2)
   1. Database management.   2. IBM Database.   3. COBOL (Computer
program language)   4. SQL (Computer program language)   I. Eckols,
Steve. II Title.
QA76.9.D3G385   1998
005.75'65--dc21   98-40935
                                                      CIP

Contents

Introduction

DB2 is the primary database management system (DBMS) for IBM mainframe computers that run under the MVS operating system. Although you can use several different methods to work with DB2 databases, most DB2 work on a mainframe is done through COBOL programs. So *Part 1* of this series covers the DB2 features that every COBOL programmer needs to know for just about every program. Then, this book expands on what is covered in *Part 1* by presenting material that goes beyond the basics. When you complete this book, you'll have the skills you need to be a senior programmer or programmer/analyst.

4 ways this book differs from other DB2 books

- This is the only DB2 book that's designed just for COBOL application programmers. In contrast, most other DB2 books focus on ad hoc processing or database administration that's beyond what programmers need to know to the exclusion of many of the DB2 features for COBOL programming.

- Most of the chapters in this book are self-contained, so you can learn the skills you need when you need them. If you want to learn about working with distributed data, for example, you can go directly to chapter 4 without reading the first three chapters. And if you want to learn about using DB2's commands and utilities, you can go directly to chapter 11. The only exceptions are that you should read chapter 1 (on data sharing) before you read chapter 2 (on locking), and you should read chapters 6, 7, and 8 (on CICS programming) in order.

- To help you learn more easily, this book presents 7 complete COBOL programs run under the MVS operating system using DB2 version 4.1. These programs let you clearly see how the DB2 code you're learning fits in with your COBOL code. And once you've used these programs for training, they become time-saving models for the programs you develop on the job.

- After you use this book to learn DB2 programming and database administration, it becomes the best reference guide you've ever used. Why? Because all the content is logically organized by function under headings that clearly identify the information chunks, so it's easy and fast to find what you're looking for. And all of the essential information for each function is summarized in the illustrations, so you read less to get the information you need.

What's new in this edition

The first edition of this book was based on DB2 version 2. With the release of DB2 versions 3, 4, and 5, though, some significant enhancements became available. As a result, the primary purpose of this second edition is to present the new language and features that became available with those versions. That means every chapter has been thoroughly revised and updated to reflect these versions.

In addition, two new chapters have been added to this book to cover the major new features that weren't available with version 2. Specifically, this book now includes a chapter on OS/390 and the data sharing features it provides, and it includes a chapter on stored procedures. In addition, we added a chapter on advanced locking concepts that expands on what was presented in *Part 1* of this series. And we added a chapter that covers the most useful DB2 commands and utilities. With these new chapters, you'll have all the information you need to develop any COBOL program that accesses DB2 data and to manage the data you need to test those programs.

What this book teaches

This book assumes that you already have the skills presented in *Part 1* of this series. Specifically, it assumes that you know how to develop COBOL programs that retrieve and modify DB2 tables; how to code embedded SQL statements that use unions and joins, advanced selection conditions, column functions, data manipulation features, and subqueries; how to work with variable length data and nulls; how to use the DB2 features for error processing; how to use the COBOL constructs that affect locking; how to prepare and run programs; how to use SPUFI; and how to use QMF to update tables. If you don't have some of these skills, you'll want to get *Part 1* of this series before you proceed with *Part 2*.

With that as background, this book raises you to the next professional level. To start, the two chapters in section 1 present advanced DB2 concepts that will increase your understanding of how DB2 works. In chapter 1, you'll learn about the various System/390 configurations and how these systems provide for sharing data. Then, chapter 2 expands on the locking concepts you learned in *Part 1*. In particular, it explains how locking works in a data sharing environment. Although the information in this section isn't mandatory for reading the other chapters in this book, it gives you a perspective on data sharing and locking that can help you write more efficient programs. That's why we recommend that you read these chapters at some point in your DB2 training.

Section 2 of this book teaches you some advanced programming techniques that weren't presented in *Part 1*. In chapter 3, you'll learn how to develop programs that issue SQL statements dynamically. In chapter 4, you'll learn how to write programs that access distributed data. And in chapter 5, you'll learn how to write programs that execute stored procedures and how to develop stored procedures in COBOL. When you complete this section, you'll have all the skills you need to develop COBOL programs that access DB2 data in a batch environment or under TSO.

Since most interactive programs run under CICS, though, you need to learn how to use CICS facilities. So that's what you'll learn in section 3 of this book. In chapter 6, you'll learn basic CICS concepts and terminology. In chapter 7, you'll learn basic CICS programming techniques. And in chapter 8, you'll learn how to browse DB2 data in a CICS program. Although these chapters introduce you to the concepts and skills for developing programs that run under CICS, they don't present everything you need to know about CICS. For a complete course on CICS, we recommend our CICS books: *CICS for the COBOL Programmer*, *Part 1* and *Part 2*.

The last section of this book presents the least you need to know about database administration. In chapter 9, you'll learn how to design your own database. In chapter 10, you'll learn how to use the SQL DDL statements to create and manage DB2 objects. And in chapters 11, 12, and 13, you'll learn how to use the database administration features that let you set up a quality assurance environment for testing DB2 programs. Specifically, you'll learn how to use the most important DB2 commands and utilities in chapter 11; you'll learn how to look at the information in the DB2 catalog tables in chapter 12; and you'll learn how to use the EXPLAIN statement to get performance analysis data in chapter 13.

How to download the 7 example programs and other files from our web site

As we mentioned earlier, the 7 programs in this book not only teach you DB2 processing, they're also time-saving models for your own programs. That's why we make them available to you on our web site, along with some other useful files that you can use for program development tasks (there are JCL job streams, for example). By downloading these files to your system, you'll save hours of entry time.

To download the files, go to the Downloads portion of our web site (*www.murach.com/downloads*). From there, you can download the zip file for this book to a default folder on your system. Then, from your Windows Explorer, you can double-click on the name of the downloaded file to expand it into its component files in this folder: C:\Murach\DB2\Part2. Since all of the files are in ASCII (text) format, you can then open them with a word processor or a text editor.

Please let us know how this book works for you

If you have any comments about this book, we would enjoy hearing from you. That's why there's a postage-paid comment form at the back of this book. And if this book helps you learn what you wanted to know, we'd be especially delighted to hear about it. That's what makes it all worthwhile.

Curtis Garvin
Author

Anne Prince
Author

Section 1

Advanced DB2 concepts

The two chapters in this section present some advanced DB2 concepts that will take you to the next step in your understanding of how DB2 works. Specifically, chapter 1 describes the various System/390 system configurations and one of OS/390's integral features: the ability to share data. Then, chapter 2 presents some advanced locking concepts. If you read *Part 1* of this series, the information in this chapter will expand on what you learned in chapter 11 of that book.

Although it's not critical that you read the chapters in this section before you read the other chapters in this book, we recommend that you read them at some point. If you do, they'll give you a perspective and understanding of data sharing and locking that most application programmers don't have. And that knowledge will not only help you write more efficient programs, but it may also help you get that new job or advancement you've been looking for.

When you read the chapters in this section, be sure to read chapter 1 first. Because some of the locking concepts presented in chapter 2 have to do with data sharing, you'll want to understand how data sharing works before you read that material.

1

OS/390 and data sharing concepts

DB2 version 4.1 made it possible for applications running on separate DB2 subsystems to share data. That means that these applications can read and update the data in the same data sets at the same time.

Because the techniques you use to share data depend in large part on the operating system and system hardware you're using, this chapter starts by describing some of the common System/390 configurations. Then, it summarizes the various techniques for accessing shared data. Finally, it describes DB2 data sharing on one of the most advanced System/390 configurations, the parallel sysplex.

The evolution of System/390 computers

In the early 1990's, many mainframe shops began looking at the possibility of replacing their mainframes with PC-based networks. However, several factors prevented many of those companies from making this move. The most critical factor was the inability of PC-based networks to manage large volumes of data.

Because it was clear that more and more companies were looking for networking capabilities, IBM developed a new architecture, called the *System/390*, or just *S/390*. This system provides many of the same features as a PC-based network, but can manage large volumes of data that those systems can't. Because of that, it has quickly become one of the most popular IBM systems ever built.

How the first System/390 computers were configured

Figure 1-1 presents two of the first System/390 configurations. The first configuration, called a *single system uniprocessor*, consists of a single *central processor* (*CP*). This processor, along with the other system hardware such as channels and storage, make up what is known as a *central processor complex*, or *CPC*. The idea of a central processor complex is common to all System/390 configurations.

The second configuration shown in this figure is a *tightly coupled multiprocessor*. This configuration is made up of two or more central processors that share the same storage. The main advantage of this system over the single system uniprocessor is its increased capacity. However, its capacity is still limited by the maximum number of CPs it can contain.

In addition to the system hardware, each of these systems require an operating system that provides its basic functions. Today, the most popular operating system is *MVS/ESA*. In the two configurations in this figure, a single copy, or *image*, of MVS controls the system operations. In the case of the tightly coupled multiprocessor, one of the functions of the operating system is to distribute the work among the CPs. That way, the CPs can perform work simultaneously, providing a function called *multiprocessing*.

Before I go on, you should know that in 1995, the MVS/ESA operating system was superseded by a new operating system called *OS/390*. OS/390 provides a complete package that includes the MVS/ESA operating system, along with other products that are typically required in today's mainframe environments. Throughout this chapter, though, we'll refer to the MVS/ESA operating system since it's still at the center of OS/390.

A single system uniprocessor

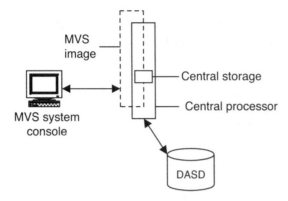

A tightly coupled multiprocessor

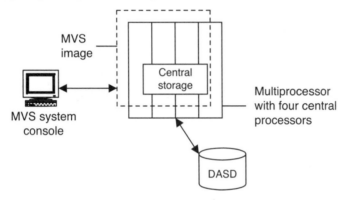

Concepts

- A *System/390*, or *S/390*, computer consists of one or more *central processors* (*CPs*). The CPs, along with other system hardware such as channels and storage, make up a *central processor complex* (*CPC*).

- A *single system uniprocessor* consists of a single CP that's managed by an MVS/ESA operating system. Because the system is controlled by a single copy of the operating system, it has a single MVS *image*.

- A *tightly coupled multiprocessor* consists of two or more CPs that share central storage. The CPs are managed by a single MVS/ESA operating system. The operating system can distribute work among the CPs so that multiple program instructions can be processed simultaneously.

- When a system that's managed by a single operating system fails, the entire system fails. The entire system must also be taken down to implement software or hardware changes. However, these systems are easy to manage because they have a single image.

Figure 1-1   The first System/390 configurations

How a loosely coupled system is configured

Figure 1-2 presents the next major step in the evolution of the System/390. In this *loosely coupled configuration*, two or more central processor complexes are connected using *channel-to-channel communications*. Then, components of the job entry subsystem, along with a feature of the MVS/ESA operating system called *global resource serialization*, manage the sharing of data, printers, and consoles among the CPCs. JES2 or JES3 provides for the sharing of a work input queue across two or more CPCs and for distributing work via a shared job queue. And global resource serialization provides for the sharing of data at the data set level across those same CPCs.

Although a loosely coupled configuration lets you coordinate some of the work of the CPCs, it does not provide a way for a product or application running on one CPC to communicate with a product or application running on another CPC. To do that, the product or application must provide its own communication mechanism. In addition, each CPC has its own MVS image that must be managed separately from the other images, often by a human operator who monitors product-specific messages on a set of consoles. Both of these shortcomings are addressed by the sysplex configuration.

A loosely coupled configuration

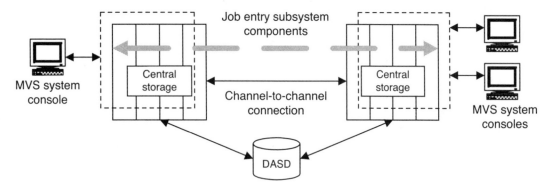

Concepts

- A *loosely coupled configuration* consists of two or more CPCs connected by *channel-to-channel communications*. Usually, the CPCs are tightly coupled multi-processors, but they can also be single system uniprocessors.

- The CPCs in a loosely coupled configuration can share data, printers, and consoles. The components used to accomplish this sharing are JES2 or JES3 and *global resource serialization*. These components provide a way of sharing a work input queue across the MVS images.

- Because a loosely coupled configuration includes multiple CPCs, it provides increased system capacity and system availability over single system uniprocessors and tightly coupled multiprocessors. However, the management of a loosely coupled configuration is more difficult because each CPC must be managed separately.

- Although the job entry subsystem and global resource serialization provide a way of sharing data and a work input queue, they do not provide for communication between products and applications running on different CPCs. These products and applications must establish their own mechanism for communicating with each other.

Figure 1-2   A loosely coupled configuration

How a base sysplex is configured

In September of 1990, IBM introduced the MVS *systems complex*, or *sysplex*. A sysplex is similar to a loosely coupled configuration in that it consists of two or more CPCs that can share data and work. Unlike a loosely coupled configuration, though, the programs running on separate CPCs in a sysplex can communicate with each other to coordinate their work.

The product that provides this functionality is called the *cross-system coupling facility*, or *XCF*. XCF became available with version 4 of MVS/ESA, and it's the facilitating component of a base sysplex system. This is illustrated in the configuration shown in figure 1-3.

You should notice in this figure that although each CPC has its own copy of MVS and therefore its own MVS image, all of the CPCs in the complex can be viewed through a single system image. This makes managing a sysplex significantly easier than managing a loosely coupled system. Also notice that this configuration includes a *Sysplex Timer*. The Sysplex Timer ensures that the time-of-day clocks on all the CPCs in the sysplex are synchronized.

Another feature that was made available with MVS/ESA version 4 is the support of *Enterprise Systems Connection* (*ESCON*) *I/O channels*. These channels use fiber optic cables that carry light pulses rather than electrical signals like the bus and tag cables used with parallel channels. Because they use light, fiber optic cables aren't susceptible to external disturbances such as electromagnetic and radio-frequency interference. They can also transmit data at much faster speeds than bus and tag cables. In addition, fiber optic cables are smaller than bus and tag cables and can be used over greater distances.

A recent improvement to ESCON channels are *FICON* (*Fiber Connection*) *channels*. These channels provide an increased data transfer rate and maximum throughput rate over ESCON channels. In addition, they can be used over even greater distances than ESCON channels.

A base sysplex configuration

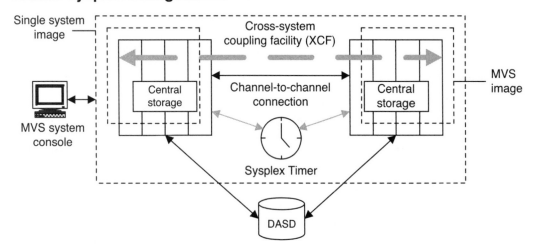

Concepts

- A systems complex, or *sysplex*, consists of a group of two or more CPCs that communicate and work cooperatively with each other. The CPCs in a sysplex are connected by channel-to-channel communications supported by a shared data set and can be viewed as a single logical entity from a system console.

- In a *base sysplex*, the *cross-system coupling facility* (*XCF*) provides the mechanism for authorized programs (such as DB2) on the same system or on different systems to communicate with each other so they can coordinate their work. XCF is a component of MVS that became available with MVS/ESA version 4.

- A *Sysplex Timer* is a hardware unit that is used to synchronize the time-of-day clocks for all of the CPCs in the sysplex. It ensures that the time stamping for transactions, logs, and messages are consistent across the entire sysplex.

- The capacity and availability of a base sysplex are the same as for a loosely coupled system. However, XCF improves communication among the CPCs of the sysplex and makes system management easier.

Figure 1-3   A base sysplex configuration

How a parallel sysplex is configured

In 1994, IBM announced version 5 of MVS/ESA. This version supports a new System/390 configuration called a *parallel sysplex* that can currently support up to 32 CPCs. Figure 1-4 illustrates a parallel sysplex configuration.

The most significant new feature of a parallel sysplex is the *Coupling Facility*. This feature provides for the integrity and serialization of data that's shared across the sysplex. For mission-critical applications, two or more Coupling Facilities may be employed. Then, if a failure occurs in the main Coupling Facility, a backup Coupling Facility can be employed to provide uninterrupted processing of data. Later in this chapter, you'll learn how DB2 uses the Coupling Facility to share data.

When it was first introduced, the Coupling Facility had to be implemented on a separate hardware device as indicated in this figure. More recent System/390 computers, however, can support the Coupling Facility internally. This optional feature is called the *Internal Coupling Facility*.

Another new feature of MVS/ESA version 5 is the *Workload Manager* (*WLM*). The main function of the Workload Manager is to balance the workload across the sysplex. In other words, the Workload Manager determines which CPC work is assigned to. It performs that task based on processing goals established by the system administrator. Those goals are defined in terms of business needs and objectives rather than system-related parameters as in the past.

Before I go on, you should know that the CPCs in a parallel sysplex configuration are typically referred to as *servers*, and the workstations that are used to initiate programs that run on the servers are typically referred to as *clients*. In other words, this is the mainframe implementation of a client/server system. You'll see this terminology used in later chapters of this book.

A parallel sysplex configuration

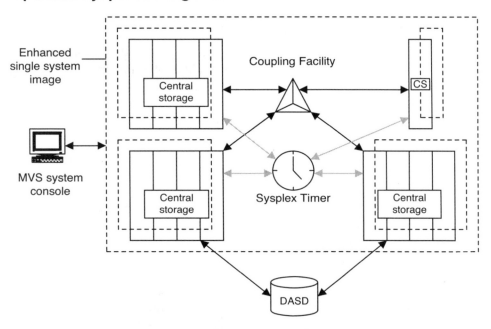

Concepts

- In a *parallel sysplex*, the CPCs communicate through the *Coupling Facility*. The Coupling Facility is a combination of hardware, software, and licensed internal code that manages the data integrity and serialization needed for data sharing. The support for the Coupling Facility became available with MVS/ESA version 5.

- The CPCs in a parallel sysplex communicate with the Coupling Facility over high-speed fiber-optic links called *coupling links*. MVS/ESA provides the services needed for authorized applications (including DB2) to use the Coupling Facility services.

- A component of MVS/ESA version 5 called the *Workload Manager* (*WLM*) manages the workload of a parallel sysplex based on goals established by the system administrator. The WLM provides for balancing the workload across the CPCs of the sysplex.

- Because a parallel sysplex can support more CPCs than a base sysplex, it provides additional capacity and increased availability. It also provides improved data sharing capabilities through the Coupling Facility, and it provides improved workload balancing through the Workload Manager.

Figure 1-4   A parallel sysplex configuration

How parallel processing is implemented on a parallel sysplex

As its name implies, a parallel sysplex also provides for *parallel process-ing*. Parallel processing is similar to multiprocessing, but implies that in addition to processing work simultaneously on two or more processors, the same type of work is being processed. For example, batch, query, and online transaction processing workloads can all be made to run in parallel. As you can imagine, parallel processing can dramatically improve processing efficiency in a data sharing environment. In particular, parallel processing can increase the throughput for an online workload, and it can decrease the processing time for a long-running application. Figure 1-5 illustrates how this works.

The first diagram in this figure illustrates how two or more CPCs can process online transactions simultaneously. To accomplish this, the Workload Manager works in conjunction with a transaction manager like CICS to distrib-ute the applications to the available CPCs. Note that the transactions that are processed in parallel can be the same transactions, or they can be different transactions.

The second diagram in this figure illustrates how a long-running applica-tion can be split into smaller units of work that can run in parallel. For ex-ample, an application that updates data based on a table of transactions and then prints a listing of the transactions could be divided into two programs: one that performs the update function and one that prints the listing. Then, these two programs could run in parallel. As an application programmer, you can take advantage of parallel processing by not combining related functions into a single program.

In both of the diagrams in this figure, you'll notice that all the CPCs have access to the same data. If they didn't, they wouldn't be able to process the same applications or applications that used the same data. Parallel processing, then, depends in large part on the ability of the CPCs to share data. In the following topics, you'll learn more about how DB2 data is shared on a parallel sysplex.

How parallel processing increases throughout for an online workload

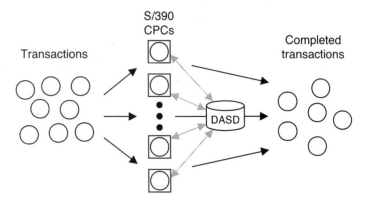

How parallel processing decreases processing time for long-running applications

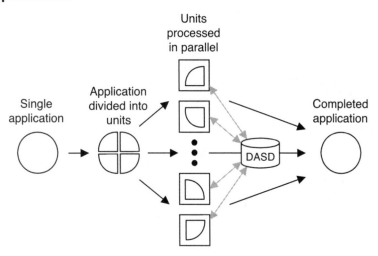

Description

- *Parallel processing* refers to the processing of a specific type of work on two or more processors at the same time. Batch, query, and online transaction processing (OLTP) workloads are the most common types of work to be run in parallel.

- If the number of online transactions exceeds the processing capabilities of the system, the processing of those transactions can be delayed causing response times to increase. To address that problem, additional CPCs can be added to the sysplex so that the transactions can run in parallel as illustrated in the first diagram above.

- If a program is written so that it performs two or more related tasks, it can be rewritten so that each task is performed by a separate program. Then, those programs can be run in parallel as illustrated in the second diagram above. This technique is particularly appropriate for programs that take a long time to execute.

Figure 1-5   How parallel processing is implemented on a parallel sysplex

How to share DB2 data

The term *data sharing* refers to the sharing of data on a parallel sysplex using the Coupling Facility. However, you don't necessarily need this configuration to share DB2 data. Before I describe how data sharing is implemented on a parallel sysplex, then, I'll present some alternatives for sharing DB2 data.

Alternatives for accessing shared DB2 data

Figure 1-6 summarizes some of the alternatives for sharing DB2 data across two or more DB2 subsystems. The first alternative is to use a single server that's responsible for processing all requests for the data. Although this technique eliminates data integrity problems, the communication between systems can be inefficient. In addition, a failure of the server makes the data inaccessible to all systems.

Another alternative is to partition the data among two or more servers so that each server manages a portion of the data. Then, data requests must be sent to the appropriate server. This technique provides for sharing of the workload across two or more servers, thereby increasing overall system efficiency. To keep the workload in balance, however, the servers and the data they control must be managed continually. And, if a server fails, the data it manages is no longer accessible.

A third alternative is to distribute the data among two or more servers. This technique is similar to partitioning the data, except that the servers are connected over a network. Because the routing of data over a network can be inefficient, it's appropriate when data must be stored at remote locations. You'll learn more about working with distributed data in chapter 4.

The final alternative presented in this figure is to implement data sharing. When you use data sharing, the workload can be spread out across the servers since each server can access the required data directly. You'll learn how data sharing is implemented in the next two topics.

Use a single server

- A single server controls and manages the data. Other systems must send their data requests to that server.
- Data integrity problems don't occur since a single server updates the data.
- The communication between systems can reduce performance.
- Data access relies on a single server. If that server goes down, data is no longer accessible.

Partition the data among two or more servers

- Each server controls a portion of the data, and requests for data must be sent to the server that controls it.
- Data integrity problems don't occur since a single server updates the data.
- Data must be split across the servers and managed continually so that the workload is balanced.
- If a system fails, the data it controls can't be accessed.

Distribute the data among two or more servers

- Data is distributed among two or more servers connected over a network.
- To access distributed data, application programs must specify the location of the data (see chapter 4). Then, the request is routed to that location.
- Routing data requests over a network can have a significant effect on response times.

Implement data sharing

- Each server has direct access to the data.
- The workload can be spread out across the servers.
- If a server fails, its workload can be assigned to another server.

Figure 1-6   Alternatives for accessing shared DB2 data

How DB2 data sharing groups are implemented

Figure 1-7 illustrates the basic data sharing concepts. Here, the sysplex consists of five CPCs and six DB2 subsystems that are divided into two *data sharing groups*. These groups, which are defined by the DBA, have access to specific data. Notice that each DB2 subsystem can be a *member* of one, and only one, group.

One of the advantages of data sharing is that data can be accessed by any member of a data sharing group. Because of that, the Workload Manager can balance the workload among the members of the group. In addition, if a DB2 subsystem or an entire CPC in the group goes down, its work can be routed to another subsystem or CPC. In other words, data access doesn't depend on a single subsystem or server like it does when you use any of the other techniques for sharing data that were presented in figure 1-6.

To implement data sharing, the DB2 subsystems in a data sharing group communicate with each other through the Coupling Facility. You'll learn more about the Coupling Facility in the next topic. For now, just realize that it provides the services necessary for two or more DB2 subsystems to access the same data at the same time.

Once data sharing groups are established, they are transparent to the application programs that use them. That means that no special coding is required to identify the location of the data or the data sharing group that has access to it. That also means that changes to the system configuration or the data sharing groups have no effect on existing applications. Even so, it makes sense for application programmers to have a basic understanding of how data sharing works.

DB2 data sharing groups

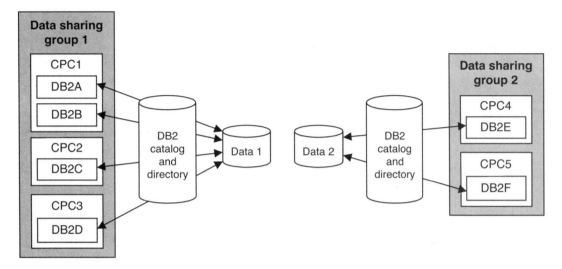

Description

- To implement data sharing on a parallel sysplex, DB2 subsystems are organized into *data sharing groups*. The *members* of each group can reside on the same CPC or on different CPCs. Each DB2 subsystem can be a member of a single data sharing group.

- The DB2 subsystems in a data sharing group communicate with each other through the Coupling Facility. Although two or more groups can use the same Coupling Facility, a member of one group can't communicate with members of another group.

- In addition to the actual data, the members of a data sharing group also share the DB2 catalog and directory that store information about the plans and packages that access the data.

- If a DB2 subsystem or an entire CPC in a data sharing group shuts down, work can be routed to another subsystem or CPC in the group since all the members of the group can access the same data.

- Because the DB2 subsystems in a data sharing group appear to application programs as a single subsystem, no special programming is required to access shared data.

Figure 1-7   How DB2 data sharing groups are implemented

How DB2 uses the Coupling Facility to share data

An integral part of the data sharing environment is the Coupling Facility. The main function of the Coupling Facility is to maintain the integrity of the data that's shared by the members of a data sharing group. To do that, it implements the structures shown in figure 1-8.

To insure that two or more DB2 subsystems don't update the same data at the same time, the Coupling Facility includes a *lock structure*. The lock structure provides for shared and exclusive locking capabilities like those that are provided by DB2. If you understand DB2 locking, then, you won't have any trouble understanding the function of the lock structure. In the next chapter, you can learn more about how the Coupling Facility manages locking.

The Coupling Facility also provides a *list structure*, also called the *shared communications area* (*SCA*). As its name implies, the list structure contains information that's stored in lists. That information can then be accessed by any of the members of the data sharing group.

When an application reads data, the data is stored in the buffer pool of the DB2 subsystem that requests it. If that data is subject to sharing, it is also registered with the Coupling Facility. Then, if the data is updated, it is written to a *group buffer pool* that's part of the Coupling Facility's *cache structure*. When that happens, any other member of the data sharing group that has accessed the same data is notified that the data has changed, and the copy of the data in that member's buffer pool is invalidated. That member can then retrieve the current data from the group buffer pool.

The coupling facility and its structures

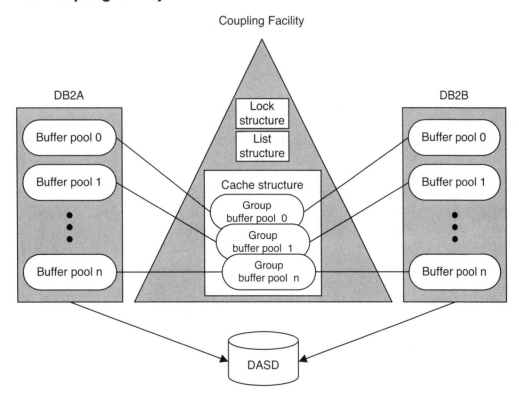

Description

- The *lock structure* provides the shared and exclusive locking capabilities that prevent more than one application from changing the same data at the same time.

- The *list structure* is DB2's *shared communications area* (*SCA*). It's used to store data such as work queues, directories, and status information that's organized in lists.

- The *cache structure* provides a *buffer invalidation* mechanism that tracks the data accessed by the members of a data sharing group and notifies those members when the data changes. The changed data is stored in the *group buffer pools* so it's available to all the members of the group.

Figure 1-8   How DB2 uses the Coupling Facility to share data

Perspective

Now that you've completed this chapter, you should be able to see why data sharing is critical to a System/390 parallel sysplex configuration. Without the ability to share data, each central processor complex would have to access its own data or copies of the same data, causing an administrative nightmare. That's why data sharing is considered one of the most significant improvements ever made to DB2.

When data sharing is implemented in a parallel sysplex environment, special locking capabilities are required to maintain the concurrency and integrity of the shared data. Those capabilities are provided by the DB2 subsystems in a data sharing group and the lock and cache structures of the Coupling Facility that were introduced in this chapter. To learn more about how locks are managed in a data sharing environment, you can read the next chapter.

2

Advanced locking concepts

Chapter 11 in *Part 1* of this series presented the basic locking concepts that all COBOL programmers need to know to use locking efficiently. But there's a lot more to locking than what's presented in that chapter. This chapter, then, expands on what you learned in *Part 1*. In case you didn't read *Part 1*, though, this chapter starts by reviewing the basic locking concepts.

A review of the basic locking concepts

DB2 uses locking to prevent one program from accessing data that has been changed, but not committed, by another program. Because locking can affect the *concurrency* of a system (the number of programs and users that can access the data in shared tables at the same time), it's important for you to understand how locks work and how you can affect locking using bind parameters and COBOL constructs. That's what you'll learn in the following topics.

DB2 table spaces and lock sizes

Each DB2 table is stored in a *table space*. This space defines the physical structure of the VSAM data sets that are used for storing the tables. Figure 2-1 presents the three types of table spaces DB2 provides and describes the size of the locks it can acquire on each type.

All three types of table spaces are divided into equal-sized units called *pages*, and each page contains rows of table data. In a *segmented table space*, the pages are grouped into units called *segments* where each segment contains data from a single table. That makes it possible to lock data at the table level as well as at the row, page, and table space level. For most applications, this is the most efficient type of table space because it maximizes concurrency.

A *partitioned table space* can only contain data from a single table. In this type of table space, the pages that contain the rows of the table are grouped into units called *partitions*. Prior to DB2 version 5, the data in a partitioned table space could be locked only at the row, page, or table space level. Now, with DB2 version 5, you can also lock data at the partition level. To do that, the table space must be defined with the LOCKPART option set to YES. Partitioned table spaces are most appropriate for large tables that contain one million or more pages.

A *simple table space* is divided into pages without any higher level structure, which means that it can be locked only at the row, page, and table space levels. Like a segmented table space, a simple table space can contain data from more than one table. Unlike a segmented table space, though, each page in a simple table space can contain data from more than one table. Because this type of table space is inefficient, it's typically not used for new applications.

One of the factors that determine the lock size used in a table space is the LOCKSIZE option that's set when the table space is defined. Although this option can be set to ROW, PAGE, TABLE, or TABLESPACE, the ANY option is used for most table spaces. Then, DB2 selects the optimum lock size for each processing situation. In most cases, that size is a page, which means that less data is locked and more concurrency is possible. If too many locks are held at the page or row level, though, DB2 can *escalate* the locks to the next level. By increasing the lock size, DB2 reduces the overhead that's required for managing the locks, but this also reduces the concurrency.

A segmented table space

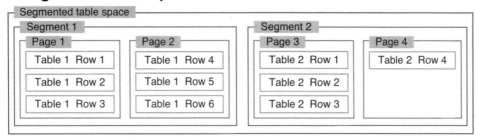

A partitioned table space

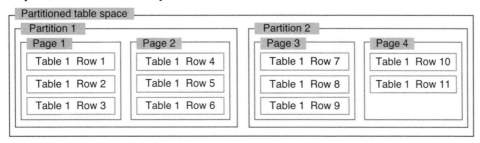

A simple table space

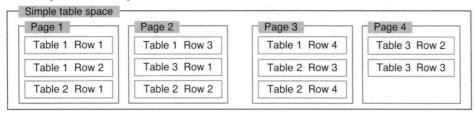

Description

- A *segmented table space* is divided into equal-sized groups of pages called *segments* that can contain rows from only one table. DB2 can take locks at the row, page, table (segment), or table space level of a segmented table space.

- A *partitioned table space* contains rows from a single table that are divided into components called *partitions*. DB2 can take locks at the row, page, partition, or table space level of a partitioned table space. For a lock to be acquired at the partition level, the table space must be defined with the LOCKPART = YES option.

- A *simple table space* is divided into pages that can contain rows from different tables. DB2 can take locks at the row, page, or table space level of a simple table space.

- A table space can be defined with a default lock size of ROW, PAGE, TABLE, TABLESPACE, or ANY. If ANY is specified, DB2 selects the optimum lock size, which is usually a page.

- If locks are held at the page or row level and the number of locks that are held exceeds an installation default, DB2 *escalates* the locks to the next highest level.

- Before a lock can be taken at the page or row level, a compatible lock must be taken at the table, partition, or table space level. And before a lock can be taken at the table level, a compatible lock must be taken at the table space level. See figures 2-5, 2-6, and 2-7 for details.

Figure 2-1   DB2 tables spaces and lock sizes

Before DB2 can take a lock at one level, it must take a lock at the higher levels. Before it can take a lock at the page level in a segmented table space, for example, it must take a lock at the table level. And before it can take a lock at the table level, it must take a lock at the table space level. Note that row and page locks are considered to be at the same level, so it's not necessary to take a page lock before taking a row lock. Similarly, partition and table space locks in a partitioned table space are considered to be at the same level. You'll learn more about the locks that are acquired in various situations later in this chapter.

DB2 lock modes and lock promotion

Figure 2-2 presents the six *modes* of locks that DB2 can acquire. As you can see, DB2 can take a Share (S), Update (U), or Exclusive (X) lock on any lockable object. The Intent Share (IS), Intent Exclusive (IX), and Share with Intent Exclusive (SIX) locks can be taken only on tables, partitions, and table spaces. These are the locks that DB2 takes automatically before taking a lock at a lower level.

The mode of a lock determines what the program that owns the lock and concurrent programs can do with the locked data. If, for example, DB2 applies an IX lock to a table space, both the lock owner and concurrent programs can read and change the data in the tables in that space. This lasts until one of the programs acquires a U lock on a page or row, indicating that the data will be updated. But even then, the other programs can read, but not change, the data in that page or row. Before the data can be updated, though, the U lock must be *promoted* to an X lock. Then, the other programs can't update the data until the X lock is released. In fact, they can't even read the data unless they're bound with the UR isolation level as explained in the next figure. But that's not common.

The modes of table, partition, and table space locks

Lock mode	Lock owner can	Concurrent program can	Promotion possibilities
IS (Intent Share)	Read but not change data	Read and change data	S, X, or IX lock
IX (Intent Exclusive)	Read and change data	Read and change data	X or SIX lock
S (Share)	Read but not change data	Read but not change data	X lock
U (Update)	Read but not change data until the lock is promoted to an X lock	Acquire S lock and read data, but can't acquire a U lock	X lock
SIX (Share with Intent Exclusive)	Read and change data	Read but not change data	X lock
X (Exclusive)	Read and change data	Read data, but only if the program uses UR isolation	

The modes of page and row locks

Lock mode	Lock owner can	Concurrent program can	Promotion possibilities
S (Share)	Read but not change data	Acquire S lock or U lock, or read data without acquiring a lock	X lock
U (Update)	Read but not change data until the lock is promoted to an X lock	Acquire S lock and read data, but can't acquire a U lock	X lock
X (Exclusive)	Read and change data	Read data, but only if the program uses UR isolation	

Description

- DB2 sets and *promotes* locks automatically based on the options that were used when the table space and table were defined, the options that were used when the program package and plan were bound, and the processing that's being performed.
- The mode and size of locks that are acquired determine what locks other programs can acquire on the same data and what they can do with that data.
- Before data that's held for update can be updated, the U lock on that data must be promoted to an X lock. That can happen only after all other programs that have locks on the data release those locks.

Note

- A concurrent program that's bound with cursor stability (CS) and CURRENT-DATA(NO) can also read data that's held with an X lock if DB2 can tell that the data has been committed.

Figure 2-2   DB2 lock modes and lock promotion

Bind parameters that affect lock duration

The *duration* of a lock is the length of time that the lock is held, which is measured from the time the lock is acquired to the time it's released. This is affected by three parameters that are set when a program is bound into a plan or package. Figure 2-3 describes these parameters: ACQUIRE, RELEASE, and ISOLATION.

For a batch program, you normally use the ALLOCATE option for the ACQUIRE parameter and the DEALLOCATE option for the RELEASE parameter. Then, the table, partition, or table space lock is acquired when the bind plan is allocated, and the lock is released when the bind plan is terminated. These options will improve the run-time of most batch programs without degrading concurrency.

In contrast, the USE and COMMIT options are better for interactive programs. With those options, a table, partition, or table space lock is acquired when it's needed and released when a commit occurs. This maximizes concurrency with minimal effect on program performance.

The ISOLATION options affect the page and row locks that are acquired by a program. In general, the various levels offer more or less concurrency at the cost of more or less protection from other application programs. The one that should be used for most programs is CS, or Cursor Stability, which should maximize concurrency at the same time that it insures data integrity. When this isolation level is used, read-only page locks are released as soon as another page is accessed.

Bind parameters that affect table, partition, and table space locks

Parameter	Locks are acquired or released	Recommendation
ACQUIRE(ALLOCATE)	When the plan is allocated	Use for batch processing
ACQUIRE(USE)	As they are needed	Use for online processing
RELEASE(DEALLOCATE)	When the plan is terminated	Use for batch processing
RELEASE(COMMIT)	When a commit occurs	Use for online processing

Bind parameters that affect page and row locks

Isolation level	Description
RR (Repeatable Read)	Ensures that your program doesn't read a row that another program has changed until the other program releases the row, and that other programs don't change a row that your program has read until your program commits the change or the program ends.
RS (Read Stability)	Ensures that your program doesn't read a row that another program has changed until the other program releases the row. Also ensures that other programs don't change qualifying rows (those that satisfy the search condition specified in your program) until your program commits the changes or ends. However, other programs can insert new rows or update non-qualifying rows.
CS (Cursor Stability)	Ensures that your program doesn't read a row that another program has changed until the other program releases the row, but doesn't prevent other programs from changing rows that your program reads before your program commits changes or ends. This option should be used for most packages and plans.
UR (Uncommitted Read)	Lets other programs change any row your application reads during the unit of work, and lets your program read any row that another program has changed even if the change hasn't been committed. This option can be used only with read-only operations and should be used for working with tables that are changed infrequently.

Note

* The isolation levels are in sequence from the one offering the most isolation (and least concurrency) to the one offering the least isolation.

Figure 2-3   Bind parameters that affect lock duration

COBOL constructs that affect locking

In general, DB2 handles locking and concurrency automatically based on the options that are set when a table space is defined and when a program package or plan is bound. In addition, though, COBOL provides three constructs that affect locking. These are the WITH clause, the WITH HOLD clause, and the LOCK TABLE statement shown in figure 2-4.

You use the WITH clause to override the isolation level that the plan or package was bound with. The SELECT statement shown at the top of this figure, for example, specifies the UR isolation level. Note that the isolation level you specify is in effect only for the statement in which it appears.

If you request RR or RS isolation, you can also code the KEEP UPDATE LOCKS clause. This clause causes DB2 to acquire an X lock on the selected pages or rows instead of an S or U lock. To use KEEP UPDATE LOCKS, you must also code the FOR UPDATE OF clause.

The second example in this figure is a DECLARE CURSOR statement that uses the WITH HOLD clause. When that clause is specified, the cursor position is maintained past a commit point, even if the plan was bound with ISOLATION(CS) or RELEASE(COMMIT). Then, you can access the next row in the cursor-controlled table by issuing a simple FETCH statement. Although this can simplify the coding in your COBOL program, it also increases lock duration, which can lead to suspensions and timeouts. A *suspension* occurs when a program requests a lock that is already held by another program and can't be shared. And a *timeout* occurs if the program is suspended for longer than a preset time interval. If you use the WITH HOLD clause, then, you should monitor your program and the programs that run with it to determine whether response times are satisfactory.

You can use the LOCK TABLE statement presented in this figure to override the initial lock that DB2 takes. Note that if you use this statement for a table in a simple table space, the lock is applied to the entire table space since individual tables can't be locked. Also notice that you can lock a single partition in a partitioned table space by including the PART clause. This clause became available with DB2 version 5 and can be used only if the table space is defined with the LOCKPART = YES option.

The mode of the lock DB2 acquires when you use the LOCK TABLE statement depends on whether you include the SHARE MODE or EXCLUSIVE MODE clause and whether on not a lock is already held on the table, partition, or table space. If you request an exclusive lock on a table in a segmented table space, for example, an X lock is taken on the table and an IX lock is taken on the table space. And if you request a share lock on a table in a segmented table space, an S lock is taken on the table and an IS lock is taken on the table space unless an IX lock is already held on the table. In that case, an SIX lock is taken on the table.

An SQL statement that uses the WITH clause

```
SELECT MAX(SALARY) AS MAX_SAL,
       MIN(SALARY) AS MIN_SAL,
       AVG(SALARY) AS AVG_SAL
    FROM MM01.EMPLOYEE
       WITH UR
```

Description

- The WITH clause can be used to override the isolation level of a bound plan or package. It can be used in SELECT and SELECT INTO statements and in IN-SERT, UPDATE, and DELETE statements that don't use a cursor.

- If you specify RR or RS isolation, you can also code the KEEP UPDATE LOCKS clause. Then, an X lock is acquired for the affected rows instead of an S or U lock. To use this clause, the FOR UPDATE OF clause must also be specified.

- The isolation level in the WITH clause is in effect only for that statement.

An SQL statement that uses the WITH HOLD clause

```
EXEC SQL
    DECLARE EMPLCURS CURSOR WITH HOLD FOR
        SELECT EMPNO, DEPTNO, LNAME, FNAME, EXT
        FROM MM01.EMPLOYEE
            WHERE DEPTNO = 'B12'
        ORDER BY EMPNO
END-EXEC.
```

Description

- When you code the WITH HOLD clause, the cursor position is maintained past a commit point. Thus, the locks needed to maintain that position aren't released, even if they were acquired with ISOLATION(CS) or RELEASE(COMMIT).

- You should code the WITH HOLD clause only for cursors that need to be accessed after a COMMIT has been taken.

- If the WITH HOLD clause reduces concurrency to an unsatisfactory level, you can remove the clause and rewrite the code so it uses a second cursor that maintains the location of the last row that was processed when the first cursor is closed.

The two forms of the LOCK TABLE statement

```
LOCK TABLE table-name [PART n] IN SHARE MODE
LOCK TABLE table-name [PART n] IN EXCLUSIVE MODE
```

Description

- The LOCK TABLE statement requests a lock on the specified table or partition. You can lock a partition only in a partitioned table space that was defined with LOCKPART = YES. If you request a lock on a table in a simple table space, the entire table space is locked.

- The size and mode of the lock that's acquired depends on the type of table space and whether or not a lock is already held on the data.

Figure 2-4   COBOL constructs that affect locking

Expanding the basic concepts

Now that you understand the basic locking concepts, you're ready to learn how locks are acquired for various operations and how the two types of indexes you can use affect locking. That's what you'll learn in the following topics.

How locks are acquired for SELECT operations

The locks that are acquired for various DB2 operations depend on several factors, including the LOCKSIZE option that was specified for a table space, the ISOLATION option that was specified for a plan or package, and the type of table space that the data is stored in. In figure 2-5, for example, you can see the locks that are acquired for a SELECT operation based on these factors. As you can see, different locks are taken depending on whether or not the data will be updated.

Notice in the second table that if page- or row-level locking is used and the isolation level is RR or RS, DB2 can lock the page or row with an S, U, or X lock. An X lock is used if the KEEP UPDATE LOCKS clause is included on the SELECT statement. Otherwise, an S or U lock is used depending on the setting of the U LOCK FOR RR/RS installation option. This option is set by the database administrator.

The sample table in this figure shows the locks that are acquired for a SELECT operation on a segmented table space. In this case, the data is locked at the table level and is retrieved for updating. Because of that, the table is locked with a U lock. In addition, the entire table space is locked with an IX lock. That way, other programs can read and change the data in other tables in the table space, but they can only read data in the locked table.

Locks acquired for a SELECT FOR READ ONLY statement

LOCKSIZE	ISOLATION	Lock mode		
		Table space/partition	Table	Page or row
TABLESPACE	CS, RS, or RR	S	None	None
TABLE	CS, RS, or RR	IS	S	None
PAGE, ROW, or ANY	CS, RS, or RR	IS	IS	S

Locks acquired for a SELECT FOR UPDATE OF statement

LOCKSIZE	ISOLATION	Lock mode		
		Table space/partition	Table	Page or row
TABLESPACE	CS, RS, or RR	U	None	None
TABLE	CS, RS, or RR	IS or IX	U	None
PAGE, ROW, or ANY	CS	IX	IX	U
	RS or RR	IX	IX	S, U, or X

A segmented table space with table-level locking

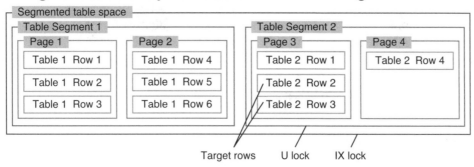

Target rows   U lock   IX lock

Notes

- If a cursor is ambiguous or no cursor is used, DB2 acquires locks as shown in the first table above.

- If UR isolation level is specified, no locks are taken.

- If LOCKSIZE is set to PAGE, ROW, or ANY, the locks may differ from those shown above if a type 1 index is used or if an index or table space scan is performed.

- A lock can be acquired at the partition level only if the table space is defined with the LOCKPART = YES option. When locks are acquired at the partition level, a lock is not taken at the table space level.

- If data is locked at the page or row level and RS or RR isolation is used, an X lock is acquired if the KEEP UPDATE LOCKS clause is specified on the WITH clause. Otherwise, an S or U lock is acquired depending on the setting of the U LOCK FOR RR/RS installation option.

Figure 2-5   Locks acquired for SELECT operations

How locks are acquired for UPDATE and DELETE operations that use a cursor

Figure 2-6 shows the locks that are acquired when a cursor is used to perform UPDATE or DELETE operations. As you can see, an X lock is taken at the lowest level regardless of the isolation level. Then, an IX lock is taken at any higher levels. Keep in mind that when you update or delete a row from a cursor-controlled results table, the row has already been retrieved and locked for updating as described in figure 2-5. So the locks are simply promoted to those shown in this figure.

The first example in this figure shows the locks that are acquired for an UPDATE or DELETE operation on a partitioned table space that allows partition-level locking. Here, the page that contains the row to be updated or deleted is locked with an X lock, and the partition that contains that page is locked with an IX lock. Because UR isolation can't be used at the page level, no other program can access the data in the locked page until the lock is released. However, they can read and change the data in other pages of the partition and in other partitions in the table space.

Notice in this example that the table space itself is not locked. When you use partition-level locking, partitions can be locked independently of the other partitions in the table space. In contrast, the entire table space is locked if partition-level locking isn't allowed.

The second example in this figure shows the locks that are acquired for the same operation in a segmented table space. In this case, row-level locking is used, so an X lock is acquired for the target row. Then, IX locks are acquired on the table and table space.

Locks acquired for an UPDATE or DELETE statement that uses a cursor

LOCKSIZE	ISOLATION	Lock mode Table space/partition	Table	Page or row
TABLESPACE	Any	X	None	None
TABLE	Any	IX	X	None
PAGE, ROW, or ANY	CS, RS, or RR	IX	IX	X

A partitioned table space with page-level and partition-level locking

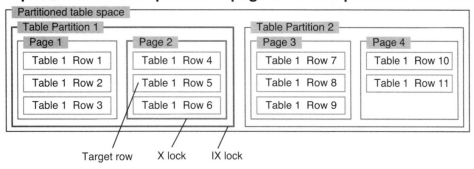

A segmented table space with row-level locking

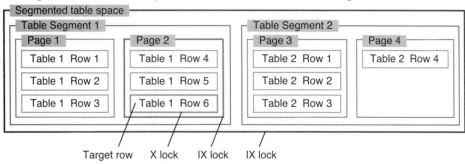

Note

- UR isolation can be used only if data is locked at the table or table space level.

Figure 2-6   Locks acquired for UPDATE and DELETE operations that use a cursor

How locks are acquired for INSERT, UPDATE, and DELETE operations that don't use a cursor

Figure 2-7 shows the locks that are acquired for INSERT, UPDATE, and DELETE operations that don't use a cursor. Notice here that if you perform an UPDATE operation with row- or page-level locking, the type of lock DB2 acquires depends on the isolation level. If the isolation level is CS, DB2 takes a U lock when it retrieves the row. Then, it promotes the U lock to an X lock when it updates the row. If the isolation level is RR or RS, DB2 takes an S or a U lock when it retrieves the row depending on the setting of the U LOCK FOR RR/RS installation option mentioned earlier.

DB2 acquires similar locks for a DELETE operation with row- or page-level locking. If the isolation level is CS, DB2 takes an X lock if the qualifying rows can be identified using just the index. Otherwise, it can take a U lock and promote it to an X lock when it updates the data. If the isolation level is RR or RS, DB2 takes an X lock if the KEEP UPDATE LOCKS clause is specified. Otherwise, DB2 takes an S or a U lock and updates it to an X lock later.

The example in this figure shows the locks acquired for an UPDATE or DELETE operation on a simple table space. Because the rows to be updated or deleted can reside in two or more pages of the table space, the entire table space is locked with an X lock. Then, no other program can access any of the tables in this table space until the lock is released.

Locks acquired for an INSERT statement

LOCKSIZE	ISOLATION	Lock mode		
		Table space/partition	Table	Page or row
TABLESPACE	CS, RS, or RR	X	None	None
TABLE	CS, RS, or RR	IX	X	None
PAGE, ROW, or ANY	CS, RS, or RR	IX	IX	X

Locks acquired for an UPDATE statement that doesn't use a cursor

LOCKSIZE	ISOLATION	Lock mode		
		Table space/partition	Table	Page or row
TABLESPACE	CS, RS, or RR	X	None	None
TABLE	CS, RS, or RR	IX	X	None
PAGE, ROW, or ANY	CS	IX	IX	U to X
	RS, RR	IX	IX	S to X or U to X

Locks acquired for a DELETE statement that doesn't use a cursor

LOCKSIZE	ISOLATION	Lock mode		
		Table space/partition	Table	Page or row
TABLESPACE	CS, RS, or RR	X	None	None
TABLE	CS, RS, or RR	IX	X	None
PAGE, ROW, or ANY	CS	IX	IX	X or U to X
RS,RR	IX	IX		X, S to X, or U to X

A simple table space with a lock at the table space level

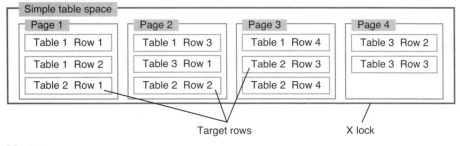

Notes

- If LOCKSIZE is set to PAGE, ROW, or ANY, the locks may differ from those shown above if a type 1 index is used or if a table space scan is performed.

- If the data for a DELETE operation is locked at the page or row level, the type of lock that's taken depends on the ISOLATION setting and whether qualifying rows can be identified by the index alone.

- If an S or U lock is acquired on a table or row, the lock is promoted to an X lock when the data is updated.

Figure 2-7   Locks acquired for INSERT, UPDATE, and DELETE operations that don't use a cursor

How type 1 and type 2 indexes affect locking

An *index* is an ordered set of pointers to the data in a DB2 table. Each index is based on the values of data in one or more columns of that table. Indexes are used most commonly to improve performance and ensure uniqueness. However, just because a table has an index doesn't mean DB2 will use it. In general, DB2 uses an index only if it provides the most efficient access to a table.

Although it's not important for you to understand all the details of how indexes work, you should have a general idea of how indexes are structured and how they can affect locking. Figure 2-8 summarizes this information.

The diagram at the top of this figure presents the basic structure of an index. In this case, the index consists of three levels, but an index can consist of one or more levels depending on the number of entries it contains. At the least, an index must include a *root page*. If the root page is the only page in the index, its structure is like that of the leaf pages shown in this figure. The *leaf pages* contain the information necessary to identify individual rows in the table.

If an index consists of two or more pages, the root page contains information that points to the pages in the next level of the index. If the index consists of just two levels, the second level consists of the leaf pages. If the index consists of three or more levels, though, the root page points to the first level of *nonleaf pages*. Then, the nonleaf pages can point to additional levels of nonleaf pages. The last level of nonleaf pages point to the leaf pages.

Before version 4.1 of DB2 became available, DB2 provided a single type of index structure, now known as a *type 1 index*. Version 4.1 introduced a new type of index, called a *type 2 index*. Although both types of indexes use the same basic structure shown in this figure, the actual structure and contents of the pages for the two indexes differ. For example, each page in a type 1 index can be divided into smaller units called *subpages*. Type 2 index pages don't have subpages.

What's more important than the structure or content of the indexes is how these two types of indexes affect locking. With type 1 indexes, pages or subpages are locked when locks are acquired on the related data in the table space. Because row-level locking can't be used with type 1 indexes, that means that at the least, all of the subpages in the index that contain entries that point to rows in a locked page must be locked. And if data is locked at the table or table space level, the entire index is locked. Because of that, timeouts and suspensions frequently occur when type 1 indexes are used.

In contrast, type 2 indexes don't take locks on index pages. Instead, only the key for each row that's locked in a table space is locked in the index. Because of that, these indexes virtually eliminate timeouts and suspensions.

Type 2 indexes also provide functions that weren't available with type 1 indexes. I've already mentioned one: row-level locking. You must also use type 2 indexes to use UR isolation, data sharing, and a number of other features. Because of the improved performance and concurrency that type 2 indexes provide, type 1 indexes are rarely used. In fact, they won't be supported in future releases of DB2.

The general structure of an index

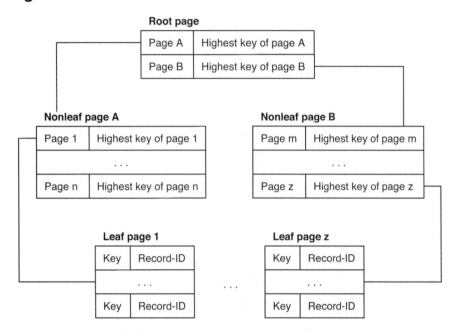

Description

- An *index* is a DB2 object that contains a set of pointers to data in a related DB2 table. These pointers are organized into a hierarchy of pages as shown above.

- At the bottom of the index structure are one or more *leaf pages*. The entries in these pages point directly to rows in the table.

- *Nonleaf pages* contain entries that point to the leaf pages. Nonleaf pages can be organized into one or more levels depending on the number of entries in the index.

- At the top of the index structure is a *root page*. The root page points to the first level of nonleaf pages.

- Each leaf page of a type 1 index is divided into *subpages*. A subpage is the smallest unit of locking for this type of index and is used when page locks are acquired on a table space. If a table or table space lock is acquired, the entire index is locked, which can cause timeouts and suspensions.

- Type 2 indexes use a technique called *data-only locking*. With this technique, only the key and the data it points to are locked. The index pages themselves are never locked, which provides increased concurrency and performance.

- Type 2 indexes also provide the following functions: row level locking, UR isolation, duplicate null values in unique keys, data sharing, full partition independence, and CPU and sysplex parallelism.

Note

- Type 2 indexes became available with DB2 version 4.1. Type 1 indexes will no longer be available with version 6.

Figure 2-8   How type 1 and type 2 indexes affect locking

How locks are used in a data sharing environment

When you access data in a data sharing environment, additional locks are required to maintain data concurrency and data integrity, or *coherency*, among the members of a data sharing group. Specifically, *logical locks*, also called *transaction locks*, are used to maintain data concurrency, and *physical locks* are used to maintain data coherency. In the following topics, you'll learn how these locks are used in a data sharing environment.

How logical locks are used

Logical locks, or *L-locks*, are used in both data sharing and non-data sharing environments. These are the locks you've learned about throughout this chapter. When L-locks are used in a non-data sharing environment, they're called *local locks* because they're used only by the local DB2 subsystem. In a data sharing environment, the local locks must be propagated to the locking structure of the Coupling Facility (part of the parallel sysplex infrastructure you learned about in chapter 1). That way, other members of the data sharing group know what level of access they have to the data. This process of propagating locks is called *global lock propagation*, and the locks that are propagated are called *global locks*.

Figure 2-9 describes the *explicit hierarchical locking* that's used to determine which locks held by a member of a data sharing group are propagated to the Coupling Facility. In this hierarchy, the locks at the top level are referred to as *parent locks*, and the locks at the lower level are referred to as *child locks*. In a partitioned table space, for example, the lock that's held on a table space or partition is the parent lock, and the locks held on individual pages or rows are the child locks.

Almost all parent locks are propagated to the Coupling Facility. The only time a parent lock isn't propagated is when another program running in the same DB2 subsystem already has the same lock, or a more restrictive lock, on the same data. To understand why that is, you need to understand that global locks are owned by the subsystem and not by individual programs.

In contrast, child locks are propagated only when two or more subsystems have parent locks on the same data and one or more of those subsystems intends to update the data. In that case, child locks must be propagated so the subsystems know what level of access they have to each row, page, or table in the partition or table space.

Explicit hierarchical locking for global lock propagation

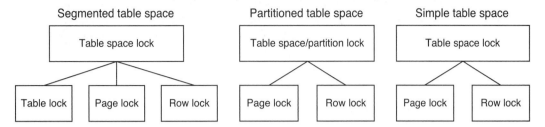

How child locks are propagated in a data sharing environment

| Parent lock held | | Child locks propagated | |
DB2A	DB2B	DB2A	DB2B
S, IS	None, S, IS	None	None
S, IS	IX, SIX	S	X
IX	IX	All	All
IX, SIX	None	None	None
IX, SIX	S, IS	X	S

Description

- DB2 uses *global locks* to communicate information about *local locks* to other members of a data sharing group. Global locks are propagated to the lock structure of the Coupling Facility so they're available to all the members of the data sharing group.

- A subcomponent of OS/390 called *Cross-System Extended Services*, or *XES*, provides for global lock management. XES uses *logical locks*, or *L-locks*, to provide for data concurrency.

- A hierarchy of parent locks and child locks are used for global lock propagation. The locks at the top level of the hierarchy are the *parent locks*, and the locks below them are the *child locks*.

- Parent locks are almost always propagated to the Coupling Facility. Because XES recognizes only S and X locks, IS locks are propagated as S locks and IX and SIX locks are propagated as X locks. This can cause *XES lock contention*, which must be resolved by the MVS systems requesting the locks and *IRLM* (*Intersystem Resource Locking Manager*).

- Child locks are propagated only if two or more DB2 subsystems have interest in the same data and at least one holds a parent IX or SIX lock. See the table above and the scenario in the following topic for more information.

- XES uses a hashing algorithm to assign each lockable object (row, page, table, partition, or table space) to a *hash class* in the lock structure. Because two or more objects can map to the same hash class, *false contention* can occur. False contention can be resolved by the MVS systems requesting the locks.

- If any subsystem holds a parent X lock, no other subsystem can propagate locks since no other locks are compatible with X locks. If another subsystem requests a lock, it must wait until the X lock is released.

Figure 2-9   How logical locks are used in a data sharing environment

DB2 uses a subcomponent of OS/390 called *Cross-System Extended Services*, or *XES*, to propagate locks to the Coupling Facility. XES uses a hashing algorithm to assign the object that's being locked to a *hash class* in the lock structure of the Coupling Facility. Because there are fewer hash classes than there are lockable objects, more than one object can map to the same hash class. When two different objects map to the same hash class, *false contention* occurs. As its name implies, false contention refers to contention that doesn't really exist. Fortunately, false contention can be resolved by the MVS systems involved.

Although the table in figure 2-9 indicates that intent locks can be held on parent objects, these lock modes can't be propagated to the Coupling Facility. That's because XES recognizes only S and X locks. So IS locks are propagated as S locks, and IX and SIX locks are propagated as X locks. This can cause a problem when a subsystem requests a lock on a table or object that another subsystem holds an X lock on. Then, another type of contention, called *XES contention*, can occur. To resolve this contention, the *Intersystem Resource Locking Manager* (*IRLM*) for the subsystem that holds the lock is used to detect that the lock is actually an intent lock and is in fact compatible with the lock requested by the other subsystem.

One final type of contention that can occur with global locks is *IRLM contention*. This type of contention occurs when a subsystem requests a lock and another subsystem holds a lock that really is incompatible. Then, the second subsystem can't acquire the requested lock until the first subsystem releases its lock.

An L-lock scenario

Figure 2-10 presents a scenario that will give you a better idea of how L-locks work in a data sharing environment. Here, two DB2 subsystems in the same data sharing group are accessing a table space named TS1. To start, a program running in the first subsystem, DB2A, requests an X lock on page 1 of the table space so it can update the data in that page. DB2A acquires that lock as well as an IX lock on the entire table space, and then propagates the lock information to XES (1). Because the IX lock is a parent lock and DB2A doesn't currently hold a lock on that table space, XES propagates the lock to the Coupling Facility as an X lock (2). Because no other subsystem is accessing the table space at this point, the child lock on the page isn't propagated.

Next, a program running on DB2B acquires an S lock on another page in the same table space and acquires an IS lock on the table space. Then, DB2B propagates the lock information to XES (3). When XES tries to propagate the IS lock to the Coupling Facility as an S lock, it receives a contention signal because the S lock is incompatible with the X lock that's held on the table space by DB2A (4). However, the MVS system on which DB2A is running, MVS1, recognizes that the contention is caused by the IX lock having been propagated as an X lock and is able to resolve the contention. At that point, the S lock requested by DB2B is propagated to the Coupling Facility (5).

A scenario that requires L-lock propagation

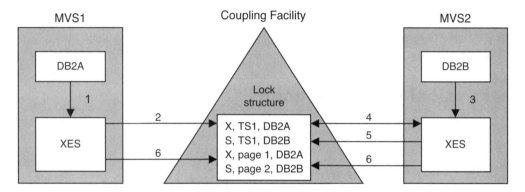

Description

1. A program running in DB2A requests an X lock on page 1 in a partitioned table space named TS1. DB2A acquires an X lock on the page and an IX lock on the table space, then passes the information on to XES.

2. XES assigns the table space lock to a hash class in the lock structure of the Coupling Facility. Since XES doesn't recognize IX locks, though, the lock is propagated to the Coupling Facility as an X lock.

3. A program running on DB2B requests an S lock on page 2 of table space TS1. DB2B acquires an S lock on the page and an IS lock on the table space, then passes the information on to XES.

4. XES attempts to propagate the IS lock on the table space to the Coupling Facility as an S lock. Because the lock structure contains an incompatible lock request from DB2A (an X lock), a contention signal is sent back to DB2B.

5. When it's determined that the contention is due to the IX lock from DB2A being propagated as an X lock (XES lock contention), the contention is resolved and the lock request from DB2B is propagated to the Coupling Facility.

6. Because both subsystems now have an interest in the table space and DB2A is updating the data, the child locks on the two retrieved pages are propagated to the Coupling Facility.

Figure 2-10   An L-lock scenario

Because two subsystems now have an interest in the same table space and because one of those systems is holding the data for updating, child locks must be propagated (6). DB2A propagates the X lock it holds on page 1 so that DB2B can't read that page until the lock is released. And DB2B propagates the S lock it holds on page 2 so that DB2A can't change the data in that page.

How physical locks are used

In chapter 1, you learned that the cache structure of the Coupling Facility provides a buffer invalidation mechanism that tracks the data accessed by the members of a data sharing group and notifies those members when the data changes. That mechanism is implemented using physical locks, or *P-locks*. P-locks ensure that each subsystem always has access to the most current copy of the data.

Figure 2-11 describes the five P-lock modes and how they interact with the group buffer pool in the cache structure. Notice that if none of the members of a data sharing group are updating data, there is no interaction with the group buffer pool. In that case, each member can store a copy of the data in its local buffer pool and not have to worry about the data changing. The same is true if only one member is updating data and no other members are accessing the data. The member that's updating the data can store the updated copy in its local buffer pool and not have to worry about communicating the changes with other members of the group.

In contrast, if one or more members are updating data and other members are accessing the same data, information must be stored in the group buffer pool so that each member has access to the most current data. In that case, the data is said to be *GBP-dependent*. The information that's stored in the group buffer pool for GBP-dependent data depends on whether the member is reading or updating the data.

Any time a member updates data that's GBP-dependent, it stores a copy of the page that contains the data in the group buffer pool. Then, if another member reads the page, it retrieves it from the group buffer pool rather than from DASD. The page remains in the group buffer pool until the program that updated the page commits the change and releases its lock.

If a member is reading the data, it registers each page read in the group buffer pool. Then, if another member changes the data in that page, the first member's page is marked as invalid. That way, if the member accesses the page again, it will know to retrieve an updated version of the page from the group buffer pool.

If a member requests a P-lock and another member holds a lock that's not compatible with the requested lock, *P-lock negotiation* occurs. The negotiation process usually involves changing the existing P-lock to a less restrictive lock so that the new lock can be acquired. For example, an S lock held by one DB2 subsystem can be changed to an IS lock so that another subsystem can update the shared data. The negotiation process also includes the registering and writing of pages to the group buffer pool as necessary.

Physical locks and group buffer pool interaction

P-lock held	Description	Effect on group buffer pool
S	This member has the table space or partition open for reading and no members are updating the data.	None. The data is not GBP-dependent.
IS	This member has the table space or partition open for reading and another member is updating the data.	Each page that's read is registered in the GBP. The GBP is checked for a page before it's retrieved from DASD and when it becomes invalid in the local buffer due to another member updating it.
X	This member has the table space or partition open for updating and no other members are accessing the data.	None. The data is not GBP-dependent.
SIX	This member has the table space or partition open for updating and another member has it open for reading.	Each page that's changed is written to the GBP.
IX	This member and another member have the table space or partition open for updating.	Each page that's read is registered in the GBP, and each page that's changed is written to the GBP. The GBP is checked for a page before it's retrieved from DASD and when it becomes invalid in the local buffer due to another member updating it.

Description

- *Physical locks*, or *P-locks*, provide for data coherency when two or more subsystems in a data sharing group have an interest in the same table space or partition. P-locks are held by each member that has an interest in a table space or partition and indicates that members level of interest.

- When two or more members have an interest in the same table space or partition, information about that table space or partition is stored in the group buffer pool (GBP). In that case, the data is said to be *GBP-dependent*.

- Each page that's read from a GBP-dependent table space or partition is registered in the GBP. This ensures that members are informed when their copy of the page in the local buffer pool becomes invalid as a result of another member updating the page.

- Each page that's updated in a GBP-dependent table space or partition is written to the GBP. Then, other members can retrieve the updated page from the GBP before it's committed.

- If a member requests a P-lock that's not compatible with a P-lock held by another member, *P-lock negotiation* occurs. During this process, the existing P-lock can be changed to a less restrictive mode so that the other member can acquire the needed lock. In addition, pages can be registered in or written to the GBP.

- P-locks can also be held on individual pages. In particular, these P-locks, called *page P-locks*, are used when two members attempt to update the same page of data with row-level locking in effect.

Figure 2-11   How physical locks are used in a data sharing environment

Although P-locks are normally taken at the table space or partition level, they can also be taken at the page level. *Page P-locks* are used, for example, when row-level locking is in effect and two subsystems are updating the same data. Because of the increase in locking activity that row-level locking causes in a data sharing environment, you should use it with caution.

A P-lock scenario

Figure 2-12 presents a P-lock scenario that will help you understand how P-locks work. In step 1, two members of a data sharing group (DB2A and DB2B) request read-only access to two different pages (page 1 and page 2) of the same table space (TS1). Because the pages haven't been updated, it isn't necessary to store any information about the pages in the group buffer pool.

In step 2, DB2A tries to acquire a lock that will let it update the data in page 1. Because it can't do that while DB2B holds an S lock on the table space, P-lock negotiation occurs. During this negotiation, the S lock held by DB2B is changed to an IS lock, and the S lock held by DB2A is promoted to an SIX lock. In addition, the page that was already read by DB2B (page 2) is registered in the group buffer pool. That way, if DB2A changes this page, DB2B will be notified that its copy of the page is invalid.

Once DB2A acquires the SIX lock, it can update the data in page 1. When it does, the updated page is stored in the group buffer pool. Then, if DB2B or another subsystem tries to access that page, it can retrieve the current data from the group buffer pool.

Step 1: Two DB2 subsystems retrieve shared data

A program running in DB2A reads page 1 from table space TS1, and a program running in DB2B reads page 2 from the same table space. Both members acquire a P-lock with mode S on the table space, and the pages are written to the local buffer pool for each member.

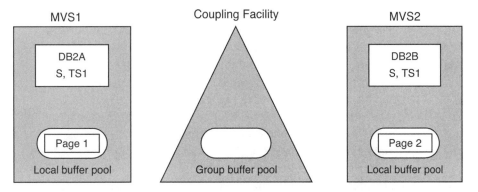

Step 2: One DB2 subsystem updates the shared data

DB2A tries to update the data in page 1. Because it can't do that while DB2B is holding an S lock on the table space, P-lock negotiation occurs. As a result of the negotiation, the S lock on DB2B is changed to an IS lock, and DB2B registers page 2 in the group buffer pool. Then, the S lock on DB2A is changed to an SIX lock and the page is updated. A copy of the updated page is written to the group buffer pool so it's available to other members.

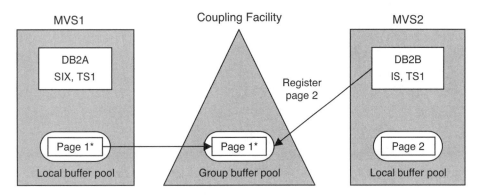

Additional operations

- If DB2B, or any other member of the data sharing group, tries to retrieve page 1 after it's been updated, the page is retrieved from the group buffer pool rather than from DASD.

- If DB2A retrieves and updates page 2, DB2B's registration of page 2 is marked as invalid. Then, before DB2B accesses page 2 again, it copies the updated record from the group buffer pool to its local buffer pool.

Note

- The * in the second diagram above indicates that the page has been updated.

Figure 2-12   A P-lock scenario

Perspective

My colleagues here at Mike Murach & Associates have asked me several times, "Do COBOL programmers really need to know all this locking stuff?" And my answer has always been, "You bet!" The fact is, if you don't know how locking works, you won't know when or how to use the bind parameters and COBOL constructs that affect locking.

But does this chapter present more than you need to know to use these features? Maybe. Nevertheless, the more you know about locking, the better you'll be at developing programs that use locks efficiently.

Even though this chapter has presented a lot of detailed information about locking, it could have presented a lot more. Since this book is written for application programmers, though, and not systems programmers or DBAs, that wasn't necessary. So if you understand the information in this chapter, you should know all an application programmer needs to know about locking.

Section 2

Advanced DB2 programming techniques

This section consists of three chapters that present advanced DB2 programming techniques. These techniques weren't included in *Part 1* of this series because they're not essential to basic DB2 training. As a professional DB2 programmer, however, you'll want to at least have a basic understanding of how you use these techniques so you can apply them in the appropriate situations.

Chapter 3 covers dynamic SQL, an advanced feature that lets programs execute SQL statements they generate as they execute. Chapter 4 covers distributed processing, a feature that lets you access data on a remote system that you can connect to over a network. And chapter 5 shows you how execute stored procedures from your DB2 programs and how to create stored procedures written in COBOL. All three of these chapters are independent of one another, so you can read them in any order you like.

3

How to use dynamic SQL

Dynamic SQL is an advanced feature you can use in your programs to create and prepare SQL statements while the programs run. This chapter introduces you to dynamic SQL and presents four different approaches to using it.

Introduction to dynamic SQL

In the first part of this chapter, you'll learn what dynamic SQL is and how it differs from static SQL. You'll also learn about the various techniques you can use to process SQL statements dynamically. Then, the rest of this chapter will expand on those techniques.

How dynamic SQL and static SQL are different

All of the programs in *Part 1* of this DB2 series use *static SQL.* That means that the SQL statements they issue were coded, precompiled, compiled, and bound before execution time. With static SQL, the tables your SQL statements access and the functions your statements perform are fixed before the program that contains them runs.

Although a static SQL statement performs predetermined functions, that doesn't mean its operations are limited. Because you can use host variables in a static SQL statement, its operation can vary. As a result, you can code application programs that issue static SQL statements to meet a wide variety of application requirements. In fact, static SQL lets you accomplish nearly all of the tasks you need to perform in application programs.

In contrast, *dynamic SQL* lets you build and issue statements that can vary completely from one execution to another. Your program constructs a text string that contains the specifications for the statement and stores it in a host variable. Then, when you invoke the statement dynamically at run time, DB2 interprets the string, translates it into an executable SQL statement, binds it, and runs it.

Figure 3-1 compares the preparation and execution of programs that use only static SQL with programs that use dynamic SQL as well as static SQL. As you can see, the execution of a program that uses only static SQL is straight-forward. Because the static SQL statements it contains are "pre-packaged" for execution, they operate relatively efficiently.

Although the steps that are required to prepare a program that contains dynamic SQL for execution are the same as for one that contains only static SQL, additional processing is required when the program is run. First, the program has to format a text string, called a *statement string*, that contains the SQL statement to be executed. Usually, formatting the statement string requires capturing processing specifications from a user. Second, the statement string must be translated so DB2 can run it. This requires the same sort of processing that's done for static SQL statements during the precompile step of the program preparation process. Third, the statement must be bound.

Because this dynamic program preparation takes place in the production environment, it can have a significant effect on the efficiency of the program. So you should use dynamic SQL only when a program must perform a function that you can't anticipate before execution time.

Static and dynamic SQL

Developing and executing a
program that uses static SQL

Developing and executing a
program that uses dynamic SQL

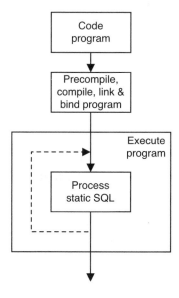

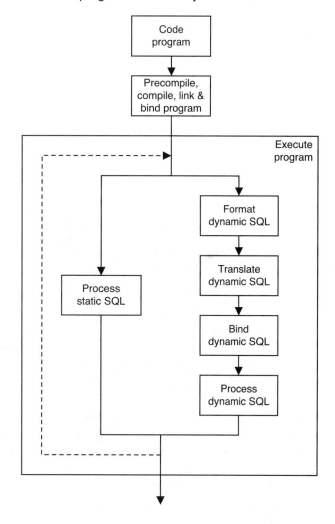

Description

- *Static SQL statements* are created during the coding phase of program development. Because they are precompiled, compiled, and bound before the program is executed, they can't be changed during the execution of the program.

- *Dynamic SQL statements* are created, translated, and bound during program execution. That way, the program can issue different statements from one execution to another.

- A single program can use both static and dynamic SQL.

Figure 3-1   Static versus dynamic SQL

Statements you can and can't issue dynamically

Figure 3-2 lists the SQL statements you can and can't issue dynamically. If you need to develop a program that uses dynamic SQL, it will probably involve the basic data manipulation statements: SELECT, INSERT, UPDATE, and DELETE. But you can also issue Data Definition Language (DDL) statements like CREATE and ALTER dynamically.

The statements you can't issue dynamically fall into three groups. First, you can't issue cursor-processing statements dynamically. As you'll see in a moment, though, you must use cursor-processing statements to work with data you retrieve using a SELECT statement that you issue dynamically. Second, you can't issue precompiler directives dynamically. That's because your program will already have been precompiled and compiled when it processes a statement dynamically. And third, you can't issue statements for dynamic SQL processing dynamically. Their purpose is to invoke *other* statements dynamically.

Performance features for dynamic SQL

Experts differ on the performance implications of dynamic SQL. Some argue that because dynamic binds occur on an ad hoc basis, they can't be tuned to optimize overall system performance. Others argue that because a dynamic bind occurs at the last minute, it lets the DB2 optimizer choose the best way to process tables based on current information.

Both sides agree, however, that dynamic SQL can use an unpredictable amount of system resources. To help limit the resources dynamic SQL can use, release 2.1 of DB2 introduced a *governor* feature, called the *Resource Limit Facility (RLF)*. This facility can interrupt the execution of a dynamic SQL statement if it uses system resources that exceed a threshold value. When the RLF cancels a dynamic SQL statement, DB2 returns an SQLCODE of -905. Note, however, that even if the governor interrupts the processing of one dynamic statement, the program that issued it continues to run and can issue other statements.

DB2 version 5 introduced another performance enhancement for dynamic SQL: the KEEPDYNAMIC bind option. When a plan or package is bound with KEEPDYNAMIC(YES), dynamic statements that are prepared and stored in an executable form are maintained even after a COMMIT or ROLLBACK statement is issued. Prior to version 5, only cursors using the WITH HOLD option kept the prepared statement after a COMMIT or ROLLBACK. You'll learn more about prepared statements in a moment.

Statements you can issue dynamically

Statements you're most likely to use	Statements you're not likely to use
DELETE	ALTER
INSERT	COMMENT
SELECT	COMMIT
UPDATE	CREATE
	DROP
	EXPLAIN
	GRANT
	LABEL
	LOCK TABLE
	REVOKE
	ROLLBACK
	SET CURRENT DEGREE
	SET CURRENT RULES
	SET CURRENT SQLID

Statements you can't issue dynamically

Cursor processing	Precompiler directives	Dynamic SQL
OPEN	DECLARE	EXECUTE IMMEDIATE
FETCH	INCLUDE	PREPARE
CLOSE	WHENEVER	EXECUTE
		DECLARE

Notes

* Although you can't issue the cursor processing statements dynamically, you can use them to work with data that you retrieve from a SELECT statement that's issued dynamically.

* You can't issue precompiler directives dynamically because the program must be precompiled before it's executed.

* You can't issue statements that are used to process dynamic SQL dynamically. These statements are used to invoke other statements dynamically, and they must be precompiled, compiled, and bound before the program is executed.

Figure 3-2   Statements you can and can't issue dynamically

How to issue SQL statements dynamically

Figure 3-3 presents the four approaches you can use to issue SQL statements dynamically. You use the first approach to process a dynamic statement other than SELECT that's only executed once. To do that, you use the EXECUTE IMMEDIATE statement. It's appropriate when your program needs to issue a statement like INSERT, UPDATE, or DELETE dynamically.

You use the second approach to process a dynamic non-SELECT statement that's executed more than once. To do that, you use the PREPARE statement to translate and bind the statement string into an executable form called a *prepared statement*. Then, you can use the EXECUTE statement to execute the prepared statement as many times as needed.

You use the third approach to process a dynamic SELECT statement that produces a known result table, called a *fixed-list SELECT*. Notice that when you issue a SELECT statement dynamically, you must process the result table it creates through a cursor. That's true even if you know the statement will return a single-row result table. So, instead of using the EXECUTE statement to invoke a prepared SELECT statement, you use special forms of the DECLARE CURSOR, OPEN, FETCH, and CLOSE statements.

You use the fourth approach to process a dynamic SELECT statement that produces an unknown result table, called a *variable-list SELECT*. To implement a variable-list SELECT statement, you use the same features you use to implement a fixed-list SELECT. In addition, your program must include a DESCRIBE statement that contains information about the structure of the result table the SELECT statement will create. And, it must prepare main storage to provide a place for the retrieved data.

Later in this chapter, you'll learn how to use the first three approaches shown in this figure in COBOL programs. Because the fourth approach (the variable-list SELECT) is so seldom used, however, it won't be described further in this book. If you need to learn more about this approach, you can refer to the IBM manual *DB2 Application Programming and SQL Guide*.

Processing requirements for dynamic SQL statements

A non-SELECT statement executed once	A non-SELECT statement executed more than once	A SELECT statement that produces a known result table	A SELECT statement that produces an unknown result table
EXECUTE IMMEDIATE	PREPARE EXECUTE	DECLARE CURSOR PREPARE OPEN FETCH CLOSE	DECLARE CURSOR PREPARE DESCRIBE Allocate storage for host variables OPEN FETCH CLOSE

Description

- Before you can use the statements shown above, you must format the SQL statement you want to execute and store it in a variable-length string host variable. Then, you can refer to that host variable from the appropriate statements.

- The EXECUTE IMMEDIATE statement causes the SQL statement in the specified host variable to be translated, bound, and executed.

- The PREPARE statement translates and binds an SQL statement into an executable form called a *prepared statement*. If the SQL statement is a non-SELECT statement, you can then issue the EXECUTE statement to execute the prepared statement.

- You can also use the PREPARE statement to create a prepared statement from a statement string that contains a SELECT statement. Then, you use special forms of the DECLARE CURSOR, OPEN, FETCH, and CLOSE statements to retrieve and process the result table the SELECT statement specifies.

- If you know in advance what columns a SELECT statement will return, you can use a *fixed-list SELECT*. Otherwise, you can use a *variable-list SELECT*.

- For a variable-list SELECT, you use the DESCRIBE statement to collect information about the structure of the result table. In addition, the program must provide a place for the retrieved data in main storage.

Figure 3-3   How to issue SQL statements dynamically

How to construct a statement string

To issue an SQL statement dynamically using any of the four approaches just described, a program must first construct a statement string that contains the SQL statement to be executed. How you do that depends on the requirements of the application. In the simplest case, a program can prompt the user to key in an entire SQL statement, then use it directly in a PREPARE or EXECUTE IMMEDIATE statement. However, it's more likely that a program will prompt the user for one or more specific elements of the statement, like a table name or a selection condition. Then, the program can use COBOL's string-handling features to combine that data with literals to build a complete statement string as illustrated in the first example in figure 3-4.

In addition to literal values and data entered by the user, you can include parameter markers in a statement string as shown in the second example in this figure. A *parameter marker* is coded as a question mark within a statement string. Then, when the prepared statement is executed, you supply a value for each parameter marker in the statement string. You'll see a COBOL program that uses parameter markers later in this chapter.

This figure also presents the data area for a sample statement string. This area must be compatible with DB2's VARCHAR data type. That means it must be coded as a group item with two subordinate fields. The first field must be defined as a binary halfword (PIC S9(4) COMP), and its value must specify the length of the second field. The second field must be defined as a character string that will contain the text of the SQL statement. When you use this structure for a dynamic SQL statement string, you can set the value of the length field to the maximum size of the text field as shown in this figure.

Note that the size that's specified for the length of the text component in this figure (320) is arbitrary. It's used because it's the amount of data that fits into four 80-byte character lines. Although that's enough for most dynamic SQL statements, the upper limit for the length of an SQL statement is over 32K.

When you code a statement string for a dynamic SQL statement, you should note that unlike static SQL statements, you don't bracket the statement with EXEC SQL and END-EXEC. They're necessary only for SQL statements that are processed by the precompiler, and dynamic SQL statements aren't. Also note that you can't include host variables in a statement string. If you need to include a variable value in a string, you can use parameter markers.

A statement string created using a COBOL STRING statement

```
STRING 'DELETE FROM MM01.CUSTOMER '
       'WHERE CUSTNO = ''' CUSTOMER-NUMBER ''''
       DELIMITED BY SIZE
       INTO SQL-STATEMENT-TEXT
```

A statement string that contains parameter markers

```
MOVE 'DELETE FROM ? WHERE CUSTNO = ?' TO SQL-STATEMENT-TEXT
```

The data area for a statement string

```
01  SQL-STATEMENT.
*
    49  SQL-STATEMENT-LEN         PIC  S9(4) COMP VALUE +320.
    49  SQL-STATEMENT-TEXT        PIC  X(320).
```

Description

*   You can construct a statement string by accepting an entire statement from the user or by prompting the user for one or more elements of the string. If you prompt for string elements, you can use COBOL's string-handling features to combine that data with literals to construct a complete statement string.

*   A statement string that's used to create a prepared statement can contain *parameter markers*, which are coded as question marks. When the statement is executed, you supply values that DB2 substitutes for the parameter markers. You can't use parameter markers when you execute a statement using EXECUTE IMMEDIATE.

*   The data area that will contain a statement string for dynamic processing must be compatible with DB2's VARCHAR data type. That means it must contain a binary halfword field that indicates the number of characters in the statement string along with a field that contains the actual statement string.

*   A statement string cannot contain host variables and should not be bracketed with EXEC SQL and END-EXEC.

Figure 3-4   How to construct a statement string

How to use EXECUTE IMMEDIATE to issue non-SELECT statements dynamically

The easiest way to work with dynamic SQL is to use the EXECUTE IMMEDIATE statement. You can use the EXECUTE IMMEDIATE statement to run any of the dynamic-eligible statements listed in figure 3-2 except the SELECT statement. But you should use it only for statements you intend to execute only once.

How to code the EXECUTE IMMEDIATE statement

Figure 3-5 presents the syntax of the EXECUTE IMMEDIATE statement and shows you how to use it in a COBOL program. On this statement, you simply code the name of a host variable that contains the statement string you want to execute. Notice that the host variable in this example is compatible with DB2's VARCHAR data type. When DB2 processes the EXECUTE IMMEDI-ATE statement, it translates, binds, and executes the statement contained in the host variable. Then, DB2 disposes of the statement.

The sample code in this figure issues a DELETE statement that deletes a row from the CUSTOMER table. To create that statement, it first accepts the customer number that identifies the row to be deleted from the user. Then, it uses a STRING statement to combine the customer number with the rest of the DELETE statement and stores the result in the text portion of the host variable. Finally, it uses the EXECUTE IMMEDIATE statement to execute the statement.

If there's a problem with a statement that you try to issue with EXECUTE IMMEDIATE, DB2 reports it through the SQLCODE field. In addition to the operational errors that can occur when you execute a static SQL statement, though, you can also receive syntax errors when you issue a dynamic SQL statement. That's because syntax errors can't be detected until the statement is translated, and a dynamic statement isn't translated until the EXECUTE IMME-DIATE statement is issued. Errors can also occur when the translated statement is bound.

Although you can use dynamic SQL to implement the delete operation in this figure, you should realize that this operation can also be done using static SQL. To do that, you would simply use a host variable for the customer number in the WHERE clause. In the program that's presented next, though, you'll see an operation that can only be implemented using dynamic SQL.

You should also realize that, although the sample code in this figure issues a single SQL statement, you can use a single EXECUTE IMMEDIATE statement to issue any number of SQL statements. To do that, you simply change the contents of the statement string so it contains the text for the statement you want to execute. Before you delete a row from the CUSTOMER table as shown in this figure, for example, you might want to issue an INSERT statement to add the row to another table.

The syntax of the EXECUTE IMMEDIATE statement

```
EXEC SQL
    EXECUTE IMMEDIATE :host-var
END-EXEC.
```

Explanation

host-var	The name of the COBOL host variable that contains the statement string to be translated, bound, and executed. Must contain data compatible with the DB2 VARCHAR data type.

Example

```
WORKING-STORAGE SECTION.
*
01  WORK-FIELDS.
*
    05  CUSTOMER-NUMBER            PIC X(6).
    05  DELETE-STATEMENT.
        49  DELETE-STATEMENT-LEN   PIC S9(4) COMP VALUE +320.
        49  DELETE-STATEMENT-TEXT  PIC X(320).
    .
    .
    .
PROCEDURE DIVISION.
    .
    .
    ACCEPT CUSTOMER-NUMBER.
    .
    .

500-DELETE-CUSTOMER-ROW.
*
    MOVE SPACES TO DELETE-STATEMENT-TEXT.
    STRING 'DELETE FROM MM01.CUSTOMER '
           'WHERE CUSTNO = ''' CUSTOMER-NUMBER ''''
           DELIMITED BY SIZE
           INTO DELETE-STATEMENT-TEXT.
*
    EXEC SQL
        EXECUTE IMMEDIATE :DELETE-STATEMENT
    END-EXEC.
    .
    .
```

Note

- Two types of errors can occur when you issue an SQL statement using EXECUTE IMMEDIATE: syntax errors and operational errors. Both of these types of errors are reported through the SQLCODE field.

Figure 3-5   How to code the EXECUTE IMMEDIATE statement

A COBOL program that uses EXECUTE IMMEDIATE

The COBOL program presented here is based on a hypothetical application that uses the CUSTOMER table as a master table and as the source of data for a number of temporary work tables. All of the temporary tables have the same structure as the CUSTOMER table. In other words, they contain the same number of columns with the same lengths, data types, and names. The temporary tables are extracted from the CUSTOMER table so users can manipulate them without worrying about damaging the CUSTOMER table or causing processing bottlenecks. The purpose of the program presented here is to let users delete specified rows from any of the temporary work tables.

The interactive screens

Figure 3-6 shows the screens from two sample sessions of this dynamic delete program. This program starts by prompting the user to enter the name of a table and the customer number that identifies the row to be deleted. Then, the program uses those values to create a statement string that's used in an EXECUTE IMMEDIATE statement to delete the specified row. After this statement is issued, the result is displayed on the screen. Note that in addition to entering a table name or customer number, the user can also enter 999999 to end the program.

In the first session, the user attempted to delete customer number 400002 from a table named CUST1026. Because that table doesn't contain a customer with this number, however, an SQLCODE of 100 is displayed. Then, the user attempts to delete customer number 400003 from the same table. This time, the record is found and deleted. Finally, the user enters 999999 for the table name to end the program.

In the second session, the user starts by deleting customer number 400004 from a table named CUST1027. Next, the user attempts to delete the same customer from a table named CUST1028. Because that table doesn't exist, an SQLCODE of –204 is displayed. Then, the user enters 999999 to end the program.

Delete session 1

In the first delete session, the user starts by entering CUST1026 for the table name and 400002 for the customer number. Because that customer isn't in the specified table, an SQLCODE of 100 is returned. Next, the user enters the same table name and customer number 400003. Then, the row for that customer is retrieved and deleted. Finally, the user enters 999999 to end the program.

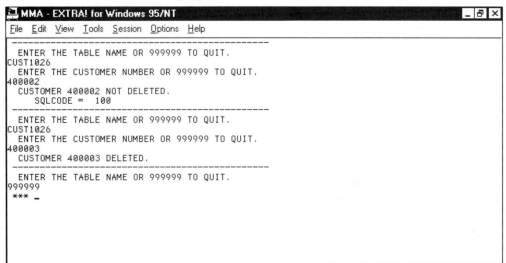

Delete session 2

In the second delete session, the user starts by deleting customer number 400004 from the CUST1027 table. Next, the user tries to delete customer number 400004 from the table named CUST1028. Because that table doesn't exist, an SQLCODE of –204 is returned. Then, the user ends the program.

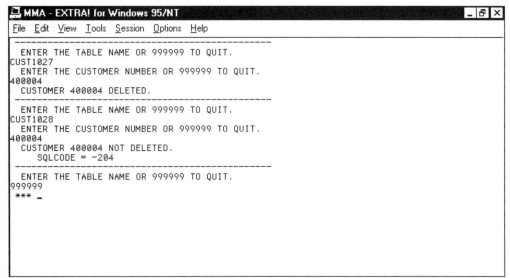

Figure 3-6   The interactive screens of the dynamic delete program

The structure chart

Figure 3-7 presents a *structure chart* for this program. This is the design document that we presented in *Part 1* of this DB2 series and that we recommend using to develop structured COBOL programs. In case you didn't read *Part 1*, the technique for creating a structure chart is summarized in this figure. When you design a program with a structure chart, the process can be referred to as *structured design*, or *top-down design*. If you want to learn more about structured design and structured coding methods, I recommend our book, *Structured COBOL Methods*.

The top module (000) in the structure chart in this figure represents the entire program. This module performs module 100 to process the customer rows until the user ends the program. Module 100, in turn, performs module 110 to get the table name from the user. If the user doesn't enter 999999 to end the program, module 100 then performs module 120 to get the next customer number from the user. Then, if the user doesn't enter 999999 to end the program, module 100 performs module 130 to delete the customer row that corresponds to the customer number entered by the user. Finally, module 100 performs module 140 to display a message that indicates whether or not the delete operation was successful.

The structure chart

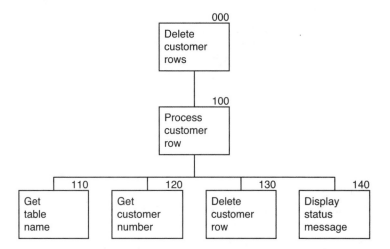

Description

- Module 000 in this structure chart performs module 100 once for each table name and customer number entered by the user. To end the program, the user can enter 999999 for either the table name or customer number.

- Module 100 performs modules 110 and 120 to get a table name and customer number from the user. Then, it performs module 130 to delete the customer row and module 140 to display a message indicating if the customer was deleted.

How to create a structure chart

- Each box on a structure chart represents one module of the program, and each module represents a single function.

- You design a structure chart from the top down by dividing each module into its component functions. This process continues until each of the modules represents an independent function that can be coded in a single COBOL paragraph…without the use of in-line PERFORM statements.

- The name for each COBOL paragraph is derived from the module number and module name as in 000-DELETE-CUSTOMER-ROWS.

Figure 3-7   The structure chart for the dynamic delete program

The COBOL listing

Figure 3-8 presents the COBOL source code for the dynamic delete program (DYNAM1). In the Working-Storage Section, the field definitions that you should notice are shaded. The first two, TABLE-NAME and CUSTOMER-NUMBER, are text fields that will contain the values that are accepted from the user in modules 110 and 120 using these statements:

```
ACCEPT TABLE-NAME.
```

and

```
ACCEPT CUSTOMER-NUMBER.
```

So, when the statement string for the dynamic DELETE statement is formatted in module 130, these fields already contain the right values.

The next item in the shaded block, DELETE-STATEMENT, is the data area that will contain the statement string the EXECUTE IMMEDIATE statement will process. Finally, the EDITED-SQLCODE field is simply a numeric-edited field that the program uses if it needs to display a non-zero SQLCODE value. The PIC clause for this field may look strange to you, but it simply specifies that the value moved into the field should be displayed with a leading minus sign if it's negative. Four minus signs are used because no SQLCODE value has more than three digits.

The dynamic delete program   **Page 1**

```
 IDENTIFICATION DIVISION.
*
 PROGRAM-ID.    DYNAM1.
*
 ENVIRONMENT DIVISION.
*
 INPUT-OUTPUT SECTION.
*
 FILE-CONTROL.
*
 DATA DIVISION.
*
 FILE SECTION.
*
 WORKING-STORAGE SECTION.
*
 01  SWITCHES.
*
     05   END-OF-DELETES-SW            PIC X     VALUE 'N'.
          88   END-OF-DELETES                    VALUE 'Y'.
*
 01  WORK-FIELDS.
*
     05   TABLE-NAME                   PIC X(18).
     05   CUSTOMER-NUMBER              PIC X(6).
     05   DELETE-STATEMENT.
          49   DELETE-STATEMENT-LEN    PIC S9(4) COMP VALUE +320.
          49   DELETE-STATEMENT-TEXT   PIC X(320).
     05   EDITED-SQLCODE               PIC -(4).
*
     EXEC SQL
         INCLUDE SQLCA
     END-EXEC.
*
 PROCEDURE DIVISION.
*
 000-DELETE-CUSTOMER-ROWS.
*
     PERFORM 100-PROCESS-CUSTOMER-ROW
         UNTIL END-OF-DELETES.
     STOP RUN.
*
 100-PROCESS-CUSTOMER-ROW.
*
     PERFORM 110-GET-TABLE-NAME.
     IF NOT END-OF-DELETES
         PERFORM 120-GET-CUSTOMER-NUMBER.
     IF NOT END-OF-DELETES
         PERFORM 130-DELETE-CUSTOMER-ROW
         PERFORM 140-DISPLAY-STATUS-MESSAGE.
*
```

Figure 3-8   The COBOL listing for the dynamic delete program (part 1 of 2)

After the table name and customer number are accepted in modules 110 and 120, module 130 constructs and executes the statement string for the dynamic DELETE statement. This module starts by moving spaces to DELETE-STATEMENT-TEXT, the text component of the variable-length item DELETE-STATEMENT. Then, it uses a COBOL STRING statement to combine the values the user entered for the table name and customer number with literals to construct the statement string. So, for example, if the user enters CUST1026 for the table name and 400002 for the customer number, the result of this STRING statement is

```
DELETE FROM MM01.CUST1026 WHERE CUSTNO = '400002'
```

The resulting string is stored in the DELETE-STATEMENT-TEXT field.

Notice in this example that the statement string doesn't include EXEC SQL and END-EXEC as delimiters for the statement. Also, notice that the customer number value is supplied as a literal value and not as a host variable. That's because you can't use host variables in dynamic SQL statements.

Module 130 also contains the EXECUTE IMMEDIATE statement that processes the statement string. This statement simply names the program host variable that contains the statement string that is to be executed dynamically. Here, the EXECUTE IMMEDIATE statement is bracketed by EXEC SQL and END-EXEC and contains a host variable. Note that this is not a violation of the coding rules for dynamic statements because EXECUTE IMMEDIATE isn't the dynamic statement; it invokes the dynamic statement.

The dynamic delete program   **Page 2**

```
110-GET-TABLE-NAME.
*
    DISPLAY '----------------------------------------------'.
    DISPLAY ' ENTER THE TABLE NAME OR 999999 TO QUIT.'.
    ACCEPT TABLE-NAME.
    IF TABLE-NAME = '999999'
        MOVE 'Y' TO END-OF-DELETES-SW.
*
120-GET-CUSTOMER-NUMBER.
*
    DISPLAY ' ENTER THE CUSTOMER NUMBER OR 999999 TO QUIT.'.
    ACCEPT CUSTOMER-NUMBER.
    IF CUSTOMER-NUMBER = '999999'
        MOVE 'Y' TO END-OF-DELETES-SW.
*
130-DELETE-CUSTOMER-ROW.
*
    MOVE SPACES TO DELETE-STATEMENT-TEXT.
    STRING 'DELETE FROM MM01.' TABLE-NAME
           ' WHERE CUSTNO = '''' CUSTOMER-NUMBER ''''
           DELIMITED BY SIZE
           INTO DELETE-STATEMENT-TEXT.
*
    EXEC SQL
        EXECUTE IMMEDIATE :DELETE-STATEMENT
    END-EXEC.
*
140-DISPLAY-STATUS-MESSAGE.
*
    IF SQLCODE = 0
        DISPLAY ' CUSTOMER ' CUSTOMER-NUMBER ' DELETED.'
    ELSE
        DISPLAY ' CUSTOMER ' CUSTOMER-NUMBER ' NOT DELETED.'
        MOVE SQLCODE TO EDITED-SQLCODE
        DISPLAY '    SQLCODE = ' EDITED-SQLCODE.
*
```

Figure 3-8   The COBOL listing for the dynamic delete program (part 2 of 2)

How to use PREPARE and EXECUTE to issue non-SELECT statements dynamically

The two statements presented next, PREPARE and EXECUTE, separate the functions of the EXECUTE IMMEDIATE statement. PREPARE causes a statement string to be translated and bound, and it produces a *prepared statement*. Then, you can use EXECUTE to invoke that prepared statement again and again.

How to code the PREPARE statement

Figure 3-9 presents the syntax of the PREPARE statement. You can use this statement with any of the dynamic-eligible statements, including SELECT. Here, you'll see examples that use PREPARE with non-SELECT statements. Later in this chapter, you'll see examples of PREPARE with SELECT statements.

Two items are required when you code the PREPARE statement. The first, *prepared-statement-name*, is a symbolic name that identifies the prepared statement. You'll specify this name on the EXECUTE statement that invokes the prepared statement. Note that if the statement name you specify is already in use, the newly prepared statement will replace the old one. So be sure you code a unique name if that's not what you want.

The second required item for the PREPARE statement is the FROM clause. On it, you specify the name of the host variable that contains the statement string you want to process. As with EXECUTE IMMEDIATE, this host variable must be defined so it's compatible with DB2's VARCHAR data type.

The optional clause of the PREPARE statement, INTO, lets you specify a storage area that will receive information about the prepared statement. Although receiving this kind of information is necessary when you work with variable-list SELECT statements, it's not important for fixed-list SELECT statements or non-SELECT statements. So we won't cover it here.

As indicated earlier in this chapter, you can include parameter markers in statement strings that are used to create prepared statements. That way, you can change the SQL statement that's issued each time the prepared statement is executed. You'll see an example of a parameter marker when I present the COBOL program that uses PREPARE and EXECUTE. For now, you should know that DB2 imposes some restrictions on how you can use parameter markers. These restrictions are listed in this figure.

The syntax of the PREPARE statement

```
EXEC SQL
    PREPARE prepared-statement-name
        [INTO sqlda-name]
         FROM :host-var
END-EXEC.
```

Explanation

prepared-statement-name	The name to be used for the prepared statement. It should be 18 or fewer characters long and should not refer to a prepared statement currently associated with an open cursor.
sqlda-name	The name of an SQL Descriptor Area where information about the prepared statement will be stored.
host-var	The name of the COBOL host variable that contains the statement string that will be translated and bound to create the prepared statement. The statement string can contain parameter markers except as indicated below.

Example

```
EXEC SQL
    PREPARE DELSTMT FROM :DELETE-STATEMENT
END-EXEC.
```

Parameter markers may not be used:

*   Where a host variable would not be allowed in a static statement
    (as in FROM ?)
*   As column specifications
    (as in SELECT ?, ?, ?)
*   As both elements in a comparison
    (as in WHERE ? = ?)
*   As both elements of an arithmetic operation
    (as in WHERE INVTOTAL = ? + ?)

Note

*   Because the PREPARE statement translates the statement string, syntax errors can occur when you issue this statement. Similarly, errors can occur when the statement is bound. These errors are returned in the SQLCODE field.

Figure 3-9   How to code the PREPARE statement

How to code the EXECUTE statement

Figure 3-10 presents the syntax of the SQL EXECUTE statement. After you've prepared a non-SELECT statement, you use the EXECUTE statement to invoke it. As you can see in this figure, you can code two items on the EXECUTE statement. First, you have to code the symbolic name you assigned to the dynamic SQL statement on the PREPARE statement. Second, if the statement includes parameter markers, you have to code a USING clause that specifies the values for those markers.

To specify the value for a parameter marker, you code the name of the host variable that contains the value. Then, DB2 will substitute the value of that variable for the parameter marker. Note that if a statement contains two or more parameter markers, the host variables you code on the USING clause must be in the same order as the parameter markers they replace.

You can also supply values for parameter markers using an SQL Descriptor Area as indicated in the syntax for the EXECUTE statement. Because this is an advanced feature that you're not likely to use with the EXECUTE statement, however, we won't present it here.

The sample code in this figure shows how you might use the PREPARE and EXECUTE statements to delete a record for a customer and table specified by the user. The code in module 400 starts by moving spaces to the field that will contain the SQL statement processed by the PREPARE statement (DELETE-STATEMENT-TEXT). Then, a STRING statement is used to construct the DELETE statement in this field. Notice that a variable is used in the FROM clause to indicate the table that the record will be deleted from. If you look back to figure 3-9, you'll see that you can't use a parameter marker in the FROM clause. That means that the table name must be accepted from the user before the statement is prepared. Then, to process a different table, the statement will have to be prepared again. In contrast, a parameter marker is included for the customer number. That means that its value can be specified when the prepared statement is executed.

The STRING statement is followed by a PREPARE statement. This statement creates a prepared statement using the data in the DELETE-STATEMENT group item, and it assigns the name DELSTMT to the prepared statement. Then, the EXECUTE statement in module 500 executes the prepared statement, substituting the value of the host variable named CUS-TOMER-NUMBER for the parameter marker in the statement string.

After you prepare a statement, you can execute it many times within the same unit of work. If the program issues a COMMIT or ROLLBACK statement, however, the prepared statement is destroyed. Then, you must prepare the statement again before you can re-execute it. The exception is if you bind the package or plan that contains the program with the KEEPDYNAMIC(YES) option. Then, the statement is maintained across commit points. This option became available with version 5 of DB2.

The syntax of the EXECUTE statement

```
EXEC SQL
    EXECUTE prepared-statement-name
        [USING {:host-var[ ,:host-var]… | DESCRIPTOR sqlda-name}]
END-EXEC.
```

Explanation

prepared-statement-name	The name of the prepared statement you want to execute. The prepared statement may not be a SELECT statement.
host-var	The name of the COBOL host variable that will be substituted for a parameter marker in the prepared statement.
sqlda-name	The name of an SQL Descriptor Area that contains descriptions of the host variables whose values will be substituted for parameter markers in the prepared statement.

Example

```
    .
    .
 400-PREPARE-DELETE-STATEMENT.
*
     MOVE SPACES TO DELETE-STATEMENT-TEXT.
     STRING 'DELETE FROM MM01.' TABLE-NAME
            'WHERE CUSTNO = ?'
            DELIMITED BY SIZE
            INTO DELETE-STATEMENT-TEXT.
     EXEC SQL
         PREPARE DELSTMT FROM :DELETE-STATEMENT
     END-EXEC.
    .
    .
 500-DELETE-CUSTOMER-ROW.
*
     EXEC SQL
         EXECUTE DELSTMT USING :CUSTOMER-NUMBER
     END-EXEC.
```

Description

- If host variables are included on the EXECUTE statement, their values are substituted for the parameter markers in the prepared statement.

- If the program issues a COMMIT or ROLLBACK statement, any prepared statements are destroyed unless the plan or package was bound with the KEEPDYNAMIC(YES) option. Once a prepared statement is destroyed, it must be prepared again before it can be executed.

Figure 3-10   How to code the EXECUTE statement

A COBOL program that uses PREPARE and EXECUTE

Now that you understand how to use the PREPARE and EXECUTE statements to process a non-SELECT statement dynamically, I'll present an enhanced version of the dynamic delete program that uses these statements. Like the dynamic delete program presented earlier in this chapter (DYNAM1), this program lets a user specify a table and a customer number to delete a row from a temporary customer table. However, this program is designed and coded so it uses system resources more efficiently.

The interactive screen

Figure 3-11 presents a short session of the enhanced dynamic delete program. This program starts by prompting the user for the name of the table to be processed. In this example, the user entered the name CUST1026.

Although it's not obvious in this figure, after the program accepts a table name from the user, it prepares a DELETE statement for that table. This statement uses a parameter marker for the customer number in the statement's WHERE clause instead of including the customer number as a literal as in the first dynamic delete program. That way, the program can execute the prepared statement multiple times to delete rows from the specified table without having to prepare the statement each time. The statement will only need to be prepared again if the user specifies a different table.

After the statement is prepared, this program prompts the user for the customer number of the row to be deleted. In this example, the user entered customer number 400001. Then, the program executed the prepared DELETE statement using the customer number as the value for the parameter marker and displayed a message indicating that the customer was deleted.

Next, the user attempted to delete customer number 400002 from the same table. This time, an SQLCODE of 100 is displayed because a customer with that number couldn't be found. Then, the user entered 999999 to specify a different table and entered a table named CUST1028. When the PREPARE statement was executed for that table, however, an SQLCODE of −204 was returned because the table couldn't be found. Then, the user entered 999999 to end the program.

A delete session for the enhanced program

```
🖳 MMA - EXTRA! for Windows 95/NT                                    _ 🗗 ✕

 File  Edit  View  Tools  Session  Options  Help
 ─────────────────────────────────────────────────────────────
  ENTER THE TABLE NAME OR 999999 TO QUIT.
CUST1026
  ENTER THE CUSTOMER NUMBER OR 999999 TO SPECIFY ANOTHER TABLE.
400001
  CUSTOMER 400001 DELETED.
  ENTER THE CUSTOMER NUMBER OR 999999 TO SPECIFY ANOTHER TABLE.
400002
  CUSTOMER 400002 NOT DELETED.
     SQLCODE =   100
  ENTER THE CUSTOMER NUMBER OR 999999 TO SPECIFY ANOTHER TABLE.
999999
 ─────────────────────────────────────────────────────────────
  ENTER THE TABLE NAME OR 999999 TO QUIT.
CUST1028
  DELETE STATEMENT COULD NOT BE PREPARED FOR CUST1028
     SQLCODE = -204
 ─────────────────────────────────────────────────────────────
  ENTER THE TABLE NAME OR 999999 TO QUIT.
999999
  *** _
```

Description

- During this session, the user starts by deleting customer number 400001 from the table named CUST1026. Then, the user tries to delete customer number 400002 from the same table. Because this customer doesn't exist, an SQLCODE of 100 is returned.

- Next, the user enters 999999 for the customer number to specify another table and enters the table named CUST1028. Because this table doesn't exist, an SQLCODE of −204 is returned.

- Finally, the user enters 999999 for the table name to end the program.

Figure 3-11   The interactive screen of the enhanced dynamic delete program

The structure chart

Figure 3-12 presents the structure chart for this enhanced dynamic delete program. Module 100 first performs module 110 to get the name of the table to be processed. Next, it invokes module 120 to prepare the statement that will delete rows from the table. After it has prepared the dynamic DELETE statement, the program can repeatedly perform module 130 to delete rows from the specified table as you saw in the example in the previous figure.

Module 130 has three subordinates. The first, 140-GET-CUSTOMER-NUMBER, prompts the user for the customer number for the row to be deleted. Module 150 issues an EXECUTE statement to run the dynamic DELETE statement using the customer number entered in module 140. Finally, module 160 displays a message indicating the success or failure of the prepared statement.

The structure chart

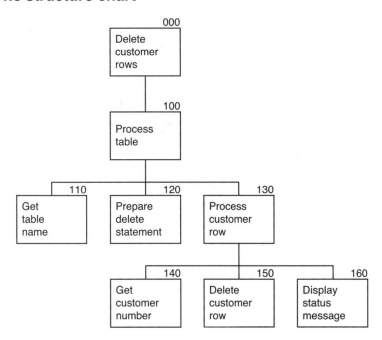

Description

- Module 000 in this structure chart performs module 100 until the user enters 999999 to end the program.

- Module 100 first performs module 110 to get the name of the table to be processed. Next, it invokes module 120 to prepare the statement that will delete rows from this table. Then, it performs module 130 repeatedly to delete rows from the specified table.

- For each row to be deleted, module 130 performs module 140 to get the customer number for the row. Then, module 150 executes the prepared statement to delete the specified row. Finally, module 160 reports the success or failure of the delete operation.

Figure 3-12   The structure chart for the enhanced dynamic delete program

The COBOL listing

Figure 3-13 presents the COBOL listing for the enhanced dynamic delete program (DYNAM2). If you look at the Working-Storage Section of this program, you'll notice that it's almost identical to the Working-Storage Section of the DYNAM1 program. In fact, the only difference is that another switch has been added to this program. This switch (END-OF-CUSTOMERS-SW) is used in module 100 to determine when no more customers are to be deleted from the current table. The other switch (END-OF-DELETES-SW) is used in module 000 to determine when no more tables are to be processed and the program should end. In the first dynamic delete program, the user could end the program by entering 999999 for either the table name or the customer number, so it required a single switch (END-OF-DELETES-SW).

The enhanced dynamic delete program   **Page 1**

```
IDENTIFICATION DIVISION.
*
PROGRAM-ID.    DYNAM2.
*
ENVIRONMENT DIVISION.
*
INPUT-OUTPUT SECTION.
*
FILE-CONTROL.
*
DATA DIVISION.
*
FILE SECTION.
*
WORKING-STORAGE SECTION.
*
01  SWITCHES.
*
    05  END-OF-DELETES-SW           PIC X     VALUE 'N'.
        88  END-OF-DELETES                    VALUE 'Y'.
    05  END-OF-CUSTOMERS-SW         PIC X     VALUE 'N'.
        88  END-OF-CUSTOMERS                  VALUE 'Y'.
*
01  WORK-FIELDS.
*
    05  TABLE-NAME                  PIC X(18).
    05  CUSTOMER-NUMBER             PIC X(6).
    05  DELETE-STATEMENT.
        49  DELETE-STATEMENT-LEN    PIC S9(4) COMP VALUE +320.
        49  DELETE-STATEMENT-TEXT   PIC X(320).
    05  EDITED-SQLCODE              PIC -(4).
*
    EXEC SQL
        INCLUDE SQLCA
    END-EXEC.
*
PROCEDURE DIVISION.
*
000-DELETE-CUSTOMER-ROWS.
*
    PERFORM 100-PROCESS-TABLE
        UNTIL END-OF-DELETES.
    STOP RUN.
*
100-PROCESS-TABLE.
*
    PERFORM 110-GET-TABLE-NAME.
    IF NOT END-OF-DELETES
        MOVE 'N' TO END-OF-CUSTOMERS-SW
        PERFORM 120-PREPARE-DELETE-STATEMENT
        PERFORM 130-PROCESS-CUSTOMER-ROW
            UNTIL END-OF-CUSTOMERS.
*
```

Figure 3-13   The COBOL listing for the enhanced dynamic delete program (part 1 of 2)

In the Procedure Division, notice the code that's shaded in module 120. It formats the statement string for the dynamic DELETE statement and then prepares it using a PREPARE statement. As in DYNAM1, this program uses the COBOL STRING statement to combine the literal text for the statement with data entered by the user. Unlike the STRING statement in DYNAM1, though, only the table name is coded as a variable. The customer number is coded as a parameter marker so it can be changed for each execution of the statement.

Module 120 also includes error-checking code to verify the success of the PREPARE statement. If the PREPARE statement results in a non-zero SQLCODE value, it indicates that an error occurred and the statement wasn't prepared. Then, module 120 turns the END-OF-CUSTOMERS-SW on, and it displays an error message along with the value of SQLCODE. If this error-checking code hadn't been included, an error would have occurred when the program tried to execute the prepared statement since the prepared statement wouldn't exist. Because of that, it's more efficient to check the result of the PREPARE statement before proceeding.

If the PREPARE statement in module 120 is successful, module 130 is executed for each customer to be deleted from the specified table. Module 130 starts by performing module 140 to prompt the user for a customer number. The value that's entered by the user is stored in the program variable named CUSTOMER-NUMBER. Then, if the user didn't enter 999999 to signal that there are no more rows to be deleted, module 130 continues by performing module 150.

Module 150 contains an EXECUTE statement that names the prepared statement created in module 120: DELSTMT. This EXECUTE statement also names the program host variable whose value will be substituted for the parameter marker in the prepared statement. So, for example, when the user entered CUST1026 for the table name and 400001 for the customer number as shown in the sample session in figure 3-11, the actual statement that was executed looked like this:

```
DELETE FROM MM01.CUST1026
    WHERE CUSTNO = '400001'
```

Notice that quotes are included around the customer number. DB2 adds these quotes automatically for fields that contain character data. If a field contains numeric data, however, the quotes are omitted.

After the prepared statement is executed, module 160 is performed to display the status of the operation. This module checks the SQLCODE and displays a message indicating if the selected customer was deleted. If not, the SQLCODE is also displayed.

The enhanced dynamic delete program   **Page 2**

```
 110-GET-TABLE-NAME.
*
     DISPLAY '---------------------------------------'
             '-------------------------'.
     DISPLAY ' ENTER THE TABLE NAME OR 999999 TO QUIT.'.
     ACCEPT TABLE-NAME.
     IF TABLE-NAME = '999999'
         MOVE 'Y' TO END-OF-DELETES-SW.
*
 120-PREPARE-DELETE-STATEMENT.
*
     MOVE SPACES TO DELETE-STATEMENT-TEXT.
     STRING 'DELETE FROM MM01.' TABLE-NAME
            ' WHERE CUSTNO = ?'
            DELIMITED BY SIZE
            INTO DELETE-STATEMENT-TEXT.
     EXEC SQL
         PREPARE DELSTMT FROM :DELETE-STATEMENT
     END-EXEC.
     IF SQLCODE NOT = 0
         MOVE 'Y' TO END-OF-CUSTOMERS-SW
         DISPLAY ' DELETE STATEMENT COULD NOT BE PREPARED FOR '
                   TABLE-NAME
         MOVE SQLCODE TO EDITED-SQLCODE
         DISPLAY '   SQLCODE = ' EDITED-SQLCODE.
*
 130-PROCESS-CUSTOMER-ROW.
*
     PERFORM 140-GET-CUSTOMER-NUMBER.
     IF NOT END-OF-CUSTOMERS
         PERFORM 150-DELETE-CUSTOMER-ROW
         PERFORM 160-DISPLAY-STATUS-MESSAGE.
*
 140-GET-CUSTOMER-NUMBER.
*
     DISPLAY ' ENTER THE CUSTOMER NUMBER OR 999999 '
             'TO SPECIFY ANOTHER TABLE.'.
     ACCEPT CUSTOMER-NUMBER.
     IF CUSTOMER-NUMBER = '999999'
         MOVE 'Y' TO END-OF-CUSTOMERS-SW.
*
 150-DELETE-CUSTOMER-ROW.
*
     EXEC SQL
         EXECUTE DELSTMT USING :CUSTOMER-NUMBER
     END-EXEC.
*
 160-DISPLAY-STATUS-MESSAGE.
*
     IF SQLCODE = 0
         DISPLAY ' CUSTOMER ' CUSTOMER-NUMBER ' DELETED.'
     ELSE
         DISPLAY ' CUSTOMER ' CUSTOMER-NUMBER ' NOT DELETED.'
         MOVE SQLCODE TO EDITED-SQLCODE
         DISPLAY '    SQLCODE = ' EDITED-SQLCODE.
*
```

Figure 3-13   The COBOL listing for the enhanced dynamic delete program (part 2 of 2)

How to use dynamic SQL in fixed-list SELECT statements

To process a SELECT statement dynamically, you create a prepared statement using the PREPARE statement just as you do for other SQL statements. Because a SELECT statement returns a result table, though, you can't use the EXECUTE statement to invoke the prepared statement. Instead, you use the cursor processing statements just as you do for static SELECT statements. However, the format of these statements is somewhat different when you work with prepared statements as you'll see in a minute. First, I want you to see how using these statements compares to using PREPARE and EXECUTE.

How fixed-list dynamic SELECT statements compare to dynamic non-SELECT statements

Figure 3-14 illustrates the operation of the statements you use to process a fixed-list dynamic SELECT statement and compares them with the operation of the PREPARE and EXECUTE statements with non-SELECT statements. (Remember, you use a fixed-list SELECT statement when you know the structure of the result table it will produce. If you don't know what the structure of the result table will be, you have to use a variable-list SELECT, which isn't presented in this book.) With a non-SELECT statement, you simply prepare the statement and then execute it as many times as you need to. With a fixed-list SELECT statement, you start by declaring a cursor using the DECLARE CURSOR statement. Then, you prepare the statement just as you do for a non-SELECT statement. (Actually, you can prepare the statement before you declare the cursor, but since the DECLARE CURSOR statement is non-procedural, you'll normally code it in the Working-Storage Section.)

After you declare the cursor and create the prepared statement, you generate the result table using the OPEN statement. Then, you use the FETCH statement to retrieve each row from the result table. When you're done, you close the cursor using the CLOSE statement. If you've used the cursor processing commands to process static SELECT statements, you shouldn't have any trouble using them to process dynamic SELECT statements.

Non-SELECT statement

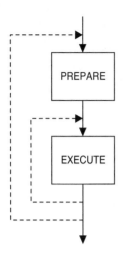

Fixed-list SELECT statement

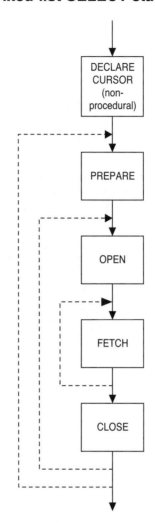

Description

- To issue a non-SELECT statement dynamically, you simply prepare the statement and then execute it repeatedly using the EXECUTE statement. To issue a fixed-list SELECT statement dynamically, you have to use cursors and the four SQL statements for cursor processing.

- You use the DECLARE CURSOR statement to name the cursor that will be used with the prepared statement. Next, you use the PREPARE statement to create a prepared statement for the SELECT statement that defines the result table. Then, you use the OPEN statement to generate the result table, and you use the FETCH statement to retrieve rows from the result table. When you're done with the cursor, you use the CLOSE statement to close it.

Figure 3-14   How fixed-list dynamic SELECT statements compare to dynamic non-SELECT statements

How to code the DECLARE CURSOR and OPEN statements

Figure 3-15 shows the syntax of the DECLARE CURSOR statement for dynamic SQL. Notice that this syntax doesn't include a SELECT statement as it does when you work with static SQL. Instead, it simply specifies the name of a prepared statement that contains the SELECT statement.

The first example in this figure declares a cursor with the name SELCURS. When this cursor is opened, it will invoke the SELECT statement that's stored in the prepared statement named DYNAMSELECT. This is the name that's coded on the PREPARE statement that's used to create the prepared statement.

This figure also presents the syntax of the OPEN statement for dynamic processing. Notice that this version of the OPEN statement includes a USING clause. You can use this clause to specify the host variables that contain substitute values for any parameter markers included in the prepared SELECT statement just as you do for the EXECUTE statement. You can also supply these values using an SQLDA, but you'll only do that with variable-list SELECT statements.

The second example in this figure shows an OPEN statement that opens the cursor defined in the first example. Here, two host variables are included on the USING clause, which indicates that the prepared statement contains two parameter markers. DB2 substitutes the values of those host variables for the parameter markers and creates the result table based on the resulting statement.

The syntax of the DECLARE CURSOR statement for working with a dynamic SELECT statement

```
EXEC SQL
    DECLARE cursor-name CURSOR [WITH HOLD] FOR prepared-select-name
END-EXEC.
```

Explanation

cursor-name	The name to be used for the cursor.
WITH HOLD	Prevents the cursor from being closed as a result of a commit operation.
prepared-select-name	The name of a prepared SELECT statement (specified on a PREPARE statement) that will be processed when the cursor is opened.

Example

```
EXEC SQL
    DECLARE SELCURS CURSOR FOR DYNAMSELECT
END-EXEC.
```

The syntax of the SQL OPEN statement for working with a dynamic SELECT statement

```
EXEC SQL
    OPEN cursor-name USING {:host-var[ ,:host-var]… |
                            DESCRIPTOR sqlda-name}
END-EXEC.
```

Explanation

cursor-name	The name of a cursor to be opened.
host-var	The name of the COBOL host variable that will be substituted for a parameter marker in the prepared statement.
sqlda-name	The name of an SQLDA that describes the host variables whose values will be substituted for parameter markers in the prepared SELECT statement. Used only with variable-list SELECT statements.

Example

```
EXEC SQL
    OPEN SELCURS USING :CUSTOMER-CITY, :CUSTOMER-STATE
END-EXEC.
```

Note

- If you don't include the WITH HOLD clause on the DECLARE CURSOR statement, the cursor associated with the prepared statement is closed and the prepared statement is destroyed when you commit or rollback the unit of work. In that case, you need to prepare the statement again before you can execute it. The exception is if the plan or package is bound with the KEEPDYNAMIC(YES) option.

Figure 3-15 How to code the DECLARE CURSOR and OPEN statements

How to code the FETCH and CLOSE statements

Figure 3-16 presents the syntax of the FETCH statement for working with dynamic SELECT statements. As you can see, this statement retrieves data from the cursor-controlled result table and stores it in host variables or a host structure just as it does with static SQL. As with many of the other dynamic SQL statements, you can also code the name of an SQLDA on the USING clause of the FETCH statement, but it's relevant only for variable-list SELECT statements.

In the first example in this figure, the FETCH statement retrieves data from the cursor-controlled result table defined by a cursor named SELCURS. Then, it places the fetched row into the host structure named CUSTOMER-ROW.

This figure also presents the syntax of the CLOSE statement for working with dynamic SELECT statements. It's the same as the syntax you use for static SELECT statements. On this statement, you simply code the name of the cursor you want to close.

As with static SQL, you close a cursor to release a cursor-controlled result table when you've finished working with it. In addition, you must close a cursor if you want to prepare another SELECT statement that will be processed using that cursor. If you issue a PREPARE statement that specifies a statement name that's already associated with an open cursor, the prepare operation will fail with an SQLCODE of -519.

The syntax of the FETCH statement for working with a dynamic SELECT statement

```
EXEC SQL
    FETCH cursor-name
        INTO {:host-var[ ,:host-var]… | :host-structure}
        [USING DESCRIPTOR sqlda-name]
END-EXEC.
```

Explanation

cursor-name	The name of an open cursor.
host-var	The COBOL name of the host variable where DB2 will place the data it fetches from the corresponding column in the result table produced by the prepared SELECT statement.
host-structure	The COBOL name of the group item where DB2 will place the data it fetches from the result table.
sqlda-name	The name of an SQLDA that describes the host variables to be used to receive the result of the prepared SELECT statement. Used only with variable-list SELECT statements.

Example

```
EXEC SQL
    FETCH SELCURS INTO :CUSTOMER-ROW
END-EXEC.
```

The syntax of the SQL CLOSE statement for working with a dynamic SELECT statement

```
EXEC SQL
    CLOSE cursor-name
END-EXEC.
```

Explanation

cursor-name	The name of an open cursor whose resources you want to release.

Example

```
EXEC SQL
    CLOSE SELCURS
END-EXEC.
```

Figure 3-16   How to code the FETCH and CLOSE statements

A COBOL program that uses a fixed-list SELECT statement

Now that you understand the statements for working with fixed-list SELECT statements, you'll see how to use a fixed-list SELECT in a COBOL program. This program (DYNAM3) operates with the same customer tables as the dynamic delete programs. But instead of deleting rows, this program lets the user display data from a range of rows in the current table. To do that, it generates a SELECT statement whose WHERE clause uses the BETWEEN keyword. The WHERE clause contains two parameter markers: one for the starting customer number and one for the ending customer number.

The interactive screens

The screens in figure 3-17 illustrate a session with the dynamic inquiry program. When this program starts, it prompts the user for the name of the table to be accessed. In this case, the user entered the name CUSTOMER. At that point, the program can generate the prepared SELECT statement to retrieve rows from that table. Then, the program can use that statement over and over to retrieve ranges of customer rows from the table.

After the SELECT statement is prepared, the program prompts the user for the starting and ending values for the range of customers to be displayed. In this example, the user entered customer number 400006 as the starting value and 400008 as the ending value. Then, the program opened the cursor-controlled result table using these values for the parameter markers in the prepared SELECT statement. The result is a table with the three rows in the specified range. These rows are then retrieved and displayed on the screen as you can see in this figure. The program also displayed a message indicating it had reached the end of the result table, and it closed the cursor.

After it displays the rows in the result table, the program prompts the user for the starting and ending values for another range in the same table. Here, the use entered 400010 and 400011. Because these records are to be retrieved from the same table as the previous records, the program doesn't need to prepare the statement again. Instead, it just opens the cursor and retrieves and displays the records in the specified range.

The next time the program prompted the user for a range, the user entered 999999 to indicate that another table is to be browsed. You can see this entry in part 2 of the session. Then, the user entered CUST1026 to display records from this temporary table. At this point, the program must rebuild the statement string for the SELECT statement to use the new table and create a new prepared statement for that table.

Next, the user entered the range 400002 to 400004. Because the CUST1026 table didn't contain rows 400002 and 400003, only row 400004 was displayed. Then, the user entered 999999 to end the processing of this table, and 999999 again to end the program.

Query session part 1

During this query session, the user displays the three customers in the CUSTOMER table with numbers from 400006 to 400008. Then, the user displays customer 400010 and 400011.

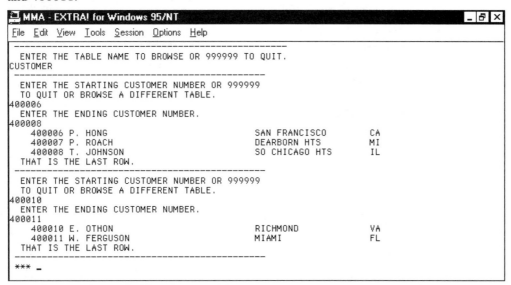

Query session part 2

Next, the user enters 999999 to display customers from another table and enters the table named CUST1026. Then, the user requests customers 400002 through 400004. Because customers 400002 and 400003 don't exist, only customer 400004 is displayed. To end the program, the user enters 999999 twice.

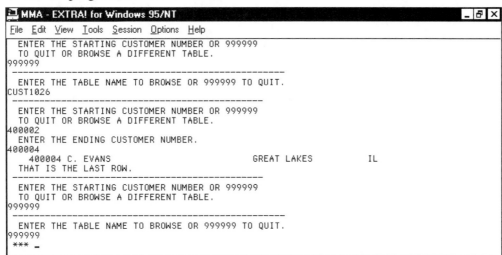

Figure 3-17   The interactive screens of the dynamic inquiry program

The structure chart

Figure 3-18 presents the structure chart for the dynamic inquiry program. If you compare this chart with the one in figure 3-12 for the enhanced dynamic delete program, you'll see that the dynamic inquiry program adds one more level of complexity. That's because it must be able to process a range of records instead of just a single record as in the delete program.

Module 100 of this program is performed for each table the user wants to browse. This module starts by performing module 200 to accept the name of the table to be processed. If the user doesn't enter 999999 to signal the end of the program, module 100 invokes module 300 to prepare the SELECT statement for the table. Then, module 100 performs module 400 for each browse of that table.

Each time it runs, module 400 accepts the range limits for the browse by performing module 410. If the user doesn't enter 999999 to indicate that no more browses should be done for the current table, module 400 proceeds by performing module 420 to open the cursor-controlled result table. Then, module 400 executes module 430 for each row in the cursor-controlled result table. Module 430, in turn, invokes modules 440 and 450 to retrieve and display each row. Finally, after it has displayed the last row in the result table, module 400 performs module 460 to close and release the cursor-controlled result table.

The structure chart

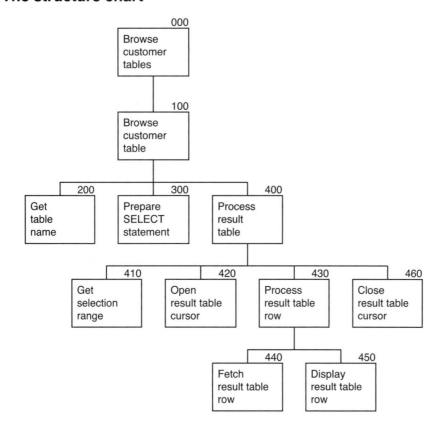

Description

- Module 000 in this structure chart performs module 100 for each table the user specifies.

- Module 100 invokes module 200 to accept the name of the table to be processed. If the user doesn't enter 999999 to signal the end of the program, module 100 invokes module 300 to prepare the SELECT statement. Then, module 100 performs module 400 for each browse of the current table.

- Module 400 starts by performing module 410 to accept the range of customer numbers to be displayed. If the user doesn't enter 999999 for the starting number, module 400 performs module 420 to open the cursor-controlled result table. Then, module 400 executes module 430 to process each row in the result table. When all the rows have been processed, module 400 performs module 460 to close the cursor.

- Module 430 performs two subordinate modules. Module 440 retrieves the next row from the result table, and module 450 displays the information in that row on the screen.

Figure 3-18   The structure chart for the dynamic inquiry program

The DCLGEN output

When you develop a COBOL program that gets data from a DB2 table, you include a description of the rows in the table called a *host structure*. In *Part 1* of this DB2 series, you learned how to use a DB2 utility called DCLGEN to generate the host structure from the data definitions for the table. Normally, DCLGEN output is stored as a member of a partitioned data set so it can be included in the Working-Storage Section of a COBOL program.

Figure 3-19 presents the DCLGEN output for the customer table used in this program. Here, you can see the SQL DECLARE TABLE statement that names the table and defines each of its columns. You can also see the *host structure* for the rows in the table, which contains the COBOL definitions of the *host variables* you can use for the columns of the table. These are the fields that receive the data that's returned for a row when an SQL statement is executed. These fields can also hold the data that's used to update a row or to add a row to a table. In the host variable declarations in this example, all of the fields contain character data. However, DB2 supports all of the data types summarized in this figure.

The DCLGEN output for the customer table

```
******************************************************************
* DCLGEN TABLE(MM01.CUSTOMER)                                    *
*         LIBRARY(MM01.DB2.DCLGENS(CUSTOMER))                    *
*         ACTION(REPLACE)                                        *
*         LANGUAGE(COBOL)                                        *
*         STRUCTURE(CUSTOMER-ROW)                                *
*         QUOTE                                                  *
* ... IS THE DCLGEN COMMAND THAT MADE THE FOLLOWING STATEMENTS   *
******************************************************************
      EXEC SQL DECLARE MM01.CUSTOMER TABLE
      ( CUSTNO                      CHAR(6) NOT NULL,
        FNAME                       CHAR(20) NOT NULL,
        LNAME                       CHAR(30) NOT NULL,
        ADDR                        CHAR(30) NOT NULL,
        CITY                        CHAR(20) NOT NULL,
        STATE                       CHAR(2) NOT NULL,
        ZIPCODE                     CHAR(10) NOT NULL
      ) END-EXEC.
******************************************************************
* COBOL DECLARATION FOR TABLE MM01.CUSTOMER                      *
******************************************************************
  01   CUSTOMER-ROW.
       10 CUSTNO            PIC X(6).
       10 FNAME             PIC X(20).
       10 LNAME             PIC X(30).
       10 ADDR              PIC X(30).
       10 CITY              PIC X(20).
       10 STATE             PIC X(2).
       10 ZIPCODE           PIC X(10).
******************************************************************
* THE NUMBER OF COLUMNS DESCRIBED BY THIS DECLARATION IS 7       *
******************************************************************
```

The DB2 data types

Data Type	COBOL Picture	COBOL Usage	Description
CHAR	PIC X(n)	DISPLAY	Fixed-length character (EBCDIC) data
VARCHAR	PIC X(n)	DISPLAY	Variable-length character data
SMALLINT	PIC S9(4)	COMP or COMP-4	Halfword integer data
INTEGER	PIC S9(9)	COMP or COMP-4	Fullword integer data
DECIMAL	PIC S9(n)V9(n)	COMP-3	Packed-decimal data
DATE	PIC X(10)	DISPLAY	Date data (yyyy-mm-dd)
TIME	PIC X(8)	DISPLAY	Time data (hh.mm.ss)
TIMESTAMP	PIC X(26)	DISPLAY	Date and time data with microseconds (yyyy-mm-dd-hh.mm.ss.mmmmmm)
GRAPHIC	PIC G(n)	DISPLAY-1	Double-byte character set (DBCS) data
VARGRAPHIC	PIC G(n)	DISPLAY-1	Variable-length DBCS data
FLOAT	None	COMP-1 or COMP-2	Floating-point data in single- or double-precision format

Figure 3-19   The DCLGEN output for the customer table

The COBOL listing

Figure 3-20 presents the code for the dynamic inquiry program. As you review this code, you'll notice that it's similar to the two dynamic delete programs presented earlier in this chapter. The biggest difference is that this program must use a cursor to process the records retrieved by the SELECT statement. If you understand the operation of this program as described in figures 1-18 and 1-19, then, you should find its source code easy to follow.

The Working-Storage Section of this program includes three switches. These switches serve purposes similar to the switches in the dynamic delete programs. The first one (END-OF-SELECTS-SW) is used to determine when no more tables are to be processed and the program should end. The second one (END-OF-BROWSES-SW) is used to determine when no more records are to be displayed for the current table. And the third one (END-OF-CUSTOM-ERS-SW) is used to determine when the end of the cursor-controlled result table has been reached.

The work fields used in this program are also similar to those used in the dynamic delete programs. Instead of a single field to hold the customer number, though, this program includes two fields to hold the high and low customer numbers for a range. It also includes a work field called FNAME-STRING that it uses to format the customer name for display.

The Working-Storage Section also contains an INCLUDE statement for the CUSTOMER table and a DECLARE CURSOR statement that defines the cursor that will be used with the dynamic SELECT statement. In this case, the cursor is named SELCURS, and it will be used with a prepared statement named DYNAMSELECT. This prepared statement is created in module 300.

The dynamic inquiry program   **Page 1**

```
IDENTIFICATION DIVISION.
*
PROGRAM-ID.     DYNAM3.
*
ENVIRONMENT DIVISION.
*
INPUT-OUTPUT SECTION.
*
FILE-CONTROL.
*
DATA DIVISION.
*
FILE SECTION.
*
WORKING-STORAGE SECTION.
*
01  SWITCHES.
*
    05  END-OF-SELECTS-SW          PIC X    VALUE 'N'.
        88  END-OF-SELECTS                  VALUE 'Y'.
    05  END-OF-BROWSES-SW          PIC X    VALUE 'N'.
        88  END-OF-BROWSES                  VALUE 'Y'.
    05  END-OF-CUSTOMERS-SW        PIC X    VALUE 'N'.
        88  END-OF-CUSTOMERS                VALUE 'Y'.
*
01  WORK-FIELDS.
*
    05  TABLE-NAME                 PIC X(18).
    05  HIGH-CUSTOMER-NUMBER       PIC X(6).
    05  LOW-CUSTOMER-NUMBER        PIC X(6).
    05  SELECT-STATEMENT.
        49  SELECT-STATEMENT-LEN   PIC S9(4) COMP VALUE +320.
        49  SELECT-STATEMENT-TEXT  PIC X(320).
    05  EDITED-SQLCODE             PIC -(4).
    05  FNAME-STRING.
        10  FNAME-INITIAL          PIC X.
        10  FILLER                 PIC X(19).
*
    EXEC SQL
        INCLUDE CUSTOMER
    END-EXEC.
*
    EXEC SQL
        INCLUDE SQLCA
    END-EXEC.
*
    EXEC SQL
        DECLARE SELCURS CURSOR FOR DYNAMSELECT
    END-EXEC.
*
```

Figure 3-20   The COBOL listing for the dynamic inquiry program (part 1 of 3)

Module 300 starts by moving spaces to the field that will contain the statement string for the SELECT statement (SELECT-STATEMENT-TEXT). This field is part of a group item named SELECT-STATEMENT that's defined to be compatible with DB2's VARCHAR data type. Then, it uses a COBOL STRING statement to format the statement string. This string includes the table name entered by the user and two parameter markers for the range of customer numbers to be displayed. If the user enters the table name CUSTOMER, for example, the result of this STRING statement is:

```
SELECT * FROM MM01.CUSTOMER WHERE CUSTNO BETWEEN ? AND ?
```

After it formats the statement string, module 300 issues a PREPARE statement to create a prepared statement using that string. In this case, the prepared statement is given the name DYNAMSELECT, which is the same name that was used in the DECLARE CURSOR statement. Then, the prepared statement can be used by module 400 to display a range of records entered by the user.

The dynamic inquiry program   **Page 2**

```
PROCEDURE DIVISION.
*
 000-BROWSE-CUSTOMER-TABLES.
*
     PERFORM 100-BROWSE-CUSTOMER-TABLE
         UNTIL END-OF-SELECTS.
     STOP RUN.
*
 100-BROWSE-CUSTOMER-TABLE.
*
     PERFORM 200-GET-TABLE-NAME.
     IF NOT END-OF-SELECTS
         MOVE 'N' TO END-OF-BROWSES-SW
         PERFORM 300-PREPARE-SELECT-STATEMENT
         PERFORM 400-PROCESS-RESULT-TABLE
             UNTIL END-OF-BROWSES.
*
 200-GET-TABLE-NAME.
*
     DISPLAY '------------------------------------------------------'.
     DISPLAY ' ENTER THE TABLE NAME TO BROWSE OR 999999 TO QUIT.'.
     ACCEPT TABLE-NAME.
     IF TABLE-NAME = '999999'
         MOVE 'Y' TO END-OF-SELECTS-SW.
*
 300-PREPARE-SELECT-STATEMENT.
*
     MOVE SPACES TO SELECT-STATEMENT-TEXT.
     STRING 'SELECT * FROM MM01.' TABLE-NAME
             ' WHERE CUSTNO BETWEEN ? AND ?'
             DELIMITED BY SIZE
             INTO SELECT-STATEMENT-TEXT.
     EXEC SQL
         PREPARE DYNAMSELECT FROM :SELECT-STATEMENT
     END-EXEC.
*
 400-PROCESS-RESULT-TABLE.
*
     PERFORM 410-GET-SELECTION-RANGE.
     IF NOT END-OF-BROWSES
         MOVE 'N' TO END-OF-CUSTOMERS-SW
         PERFORM 420-OPEN-RESULT-TABLE-CURSOR
         PERFORM 430-PROCESS-RESULT-TABLE-ROW
             UNTIL END-OF-CUSTOMERS
         PERFORM 460-CLOSE-RESULT-TABLE-CURSOR.
*
```

Figure 3-20   The COBOL listing for the dynamic inquiry program (part 2 of 3)

After module 410 accepts a range of customers from the user, module 420 issues an OPEN statement to create a cursor-controlled result table. Notice that this statement includes a USING clause that refers to the two host variables that contain the high and low customer numbers in the range. The values of these variables are substituted for the parameter markers in the DYNAMSELECT prepared statement before the statement is issued. DB2 knows to use the DYNAMSELECT prepared statement because it was associated with the SELCURS cursor in the DECLARE CURSOR statement. So, if the user enters a customer range from 400006 to 400008, this statement is issued:

```
SELECT * FROM MM01.CUSTOMER
    WHERE CUSTNO BETWEEN '400006' AND '400008'
```

Notice again that DB2 includes quotes around the customer numbers since they contain character, and not numeric, data. The result of this statement is a table that includes only the customers in the specified range.

Module 420 also includes error-checking code that checks the results of the OPEN statement. If an error occurs during the processing of this statement, the END-OF-CUSTOMERS-SW is turned on and an error message is displayed. Then, the user can enter another range of customers and try the open operation again.

If the open operation is successful, the program uses the FETCH statement in module 440 to retrieve each of the rows in this table. This statement is just like one you might code in a static SQL program. It simply identifies the cursor and the host structure that will hold the retrieved row.

Module 440 also includes code that detects the end of the cursor-controlled result table and checks for errors. To do that, it tests the value of SQLCODE. If its value is 100, indicating that the last row of the table has been retrieved, the program moves 'Y' to the END-OF-CUSTOMERS-SW to end the browse. The browse also ends if the value of SQLCODE is equal to any other value other than zero. In either case, control returns to module 400, which then performs module 460 to close the cursor.

At this point, the cursor has been closed, but the prepared statement is still available (closing a cursor doesn't affect the prepared statement). Because of that, another range of customers can be accepted from the user and another cursor-controlled results table can be generated using these values. To generate a result table from a different table, though, the statement string must be modified and the SELECT statement must be prepared again.

The dynamic inquiry program   **Page 3**

```
 410-GET-SELECTION-RANGE.
*
     DISPLAY '----------------------------------------------------'.
     DISPLAY ' ENTER THE STARTING CUSTOMER NUMBER OR 999999 '.
     DISPLAY ' TO QUIT OR BROWSE A DIFFERENT TABLE.'.
     ACCEPT LOW-CUSTOMER-NUMBER.
     IF LOW-CUSTOMER-NUMBER = '999999'
         MOVE 'Y' TO END-OF-BROWSES-SW
     ELSE
         DISPLAY ' ENTER THE ENDING CUSTOMER NUMBER.'
         ACCEPT HIGH-CUSTOMER-NUMBER.
*
 420-OPEN-RESULT-TABLE-CURSOR.
*
     EXEC SQL
         OPEN SELCURS USING :LOW-CUSTOMER-NUMBER,
                            :HIGH-CUSTOMER-NUMBER
     END-EXEC.
     IF SQLCODE NOT = 0
         MOVE 'Y' TO END-OF-CUSTOMERS-SW
         MOVE SQLCODE TO EDITED-SQLCODE
         DISPLAY ' PROCESSING ERROR - SQLCODE = ' EDITED-SQLCODE.
*
 430-PROCESS-RESULT-TABLE-ROW.
*
     PERFORM 440-FETCH-RESULT-TABLE-ROW.
     IF NOT END-OF-CUSTOMERS
         PERFORM 450-DISPLAY-RESULT-TABLE-ROW.
*
 440-FETCH-RESULT-TABLE-ROW.
*
     EXEC SQL
         FETCH SELCURS INTO :CUSTOMER-ROW
     END-EXEC.
     IF SQLCODE = 100
         MOVE 'Y' TO END-OF-CUSTOMERS-SW
         DISPLAY ' THAT IS THE LAST ROW.'
     ELSE
         IF SQLCODE NOT = 0
             MOVE 'Y' TO END-OF-CUSTOMERS-SW
             MOVE SQLCODE TO EDITED-SQLCODE
             DISPLAY ' PROCESSING ERROR - SQLCODE = '
                     EDITED-SQLCODE.
*
 450-DISPLAY-RESULT-TABLE-ROW.
*
     MOVE FNAME TO FNAME-STRING.
     DISPLAY '   ' CUSTNO ' ' FNAME-INITIAL '. ' LNAME
             ' ' CITY ' ' STATE.
*
 460-CLOSE-RESULT-TABLE-CURSOR.
*
     EXEC SQL
         CLOSE SELCURS
     END-EXEC.
```

Figure 3-20   The COBOL listing for the dynamic inquiry program (part 3 of 3)

Perspective

Now that you've finished this chapter, you should be able to see some of the advantages of using dynamic SQL. In particular, it lets you determine the tables and columns that will be processed by a program at run-time. Keep in mind, however, that dynamic SQL is more costly in terms of system resources than static SQL. That's because dynamic SQL must be translated and bound at run-time using production resources. As a result, you should use dynamic SQL only when static SQL doesn't provide the flexibility you need.

4

How to work with distributed data

In chapter 1, you learned how to share data that's managed by a DB2 subsystem in a parallel sysplex configuration. But what if the data is managed by a DBMS on a system that's connected over a network? To access this type of data, called *distributed data*, you need to use special system software, access methods, and coding techniques. That's what you'll learn about in this chapter.

An introduction to distributed processing

Distributed processing implies that the data needed to perform business operations is distributed over two or more DB2 subsystems. Although those subsystems can be running on the same machine, it's more likely that they're running on separate machines connected over a network. Before you learn how to access this type of data, you need to understand how DB2 implements distributed processing.

How distributed processing works in a DB2 environment

Figure 4-1 illustrates how DB2 processes data in a distributed environment. As this figure indicates, an application program interacts with DB2 through your *local subsystem*, just as if you weren't going to do distributed processing. If the program issues an SQL statement that identifies a remote object rather than a local one, however, DB2 routes the statement to the *remote subsystem* that manages that object. Then, the remote subsystem processes the request and returns the results to the local subsystem.

To communicate with each other, the local and remote subsystems use a DB2 facility called the *distributed data facility*, or *DDF*. Notice that DDF must be present on both the local and the remote subsystem. You'll learn more about how DDF coordinates the communication between subsystems in the next topic.

DB2 currently supports two methods for accessing distributed data. If you're using version 4 of DB2, these access methods are called *application-directed access* and *system-directed access*. With version 5, these access methods are called *DRDA (Distributed Relational Database Architecture) access* and *private protocol access*. In this chapter, we'll use the version 5 names to refer to these access methods since they're the most current.

Although you can use either access method to access distributed data, you should know that IBM is phasing out DB2 private protocol access. For new program development, then, you should use DRDA access. Since you may need to maintain programs that are written using DB2 private protocol access, however, you'll learn how to use both methods in this chapter.

DB2 in a distributed environment

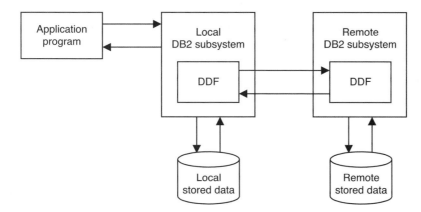

Description

- *Distributed processing* provides for a DB2 application program running in a local DB2 subsystem to access data in a remote DB2 subsystem. The remote subsystem can reside on the same machine as the local subsystem, or it can reside on another machine connected over a network.

- Under DB2, the facility that provides for distributed processing is called the *distributed data facility*, or *DDF*. DDF coordinates the communication of the subsystems.

- When an application program issues an SQL statement that refers to a remote object, the local DB2 subsystem routes the statement to the remote DB2 subsystem where that object resides. When the processing is complete, the remote subsystem sends a reply back to the local subsystem, which in turn passes it to the application program.

- DB2 supports two methods for accessing remote data: *DRDA* (*Distributed Relational Database Architecture*) *access* and *private protocol access*. With DB2 version 4, DRDA access was called *application-directed access* and private protocol access was called *system-directed access*.

- Private protocol access is specific to DB2 and can be used only to access DB2 subsystems. DRDA access is based on a set of protocols that allow any DRDA-compliant RDBMS to communicate with any other DRDA-compliant RDBMS.

Figure 4-1   How distributed processing works in a DB2 environment

How DDF implements data distribution

DDF is the DB2 facility that carries out the distributed data requests. It consists of several components as illustrated in figure 4-2. As you can see, the same components are present on the *local server* and the *remote server*. In some cases, though, these components perform different functions depending on where they're located and what access method is used. By the way, the local server can also be referred to as the *requester* since it initiates the data access request, and the remote server can be referred to as just the *server* since it receives and processes the request.

Although it's not essential that you understand how each of the DDF components work, it helps to have a general understanding of how a local and remote server communicate with each other. This communication between two servers is called a *conversation*, and the two most common software products used for this communication are VTAM and TCP/IP.

Both *Virtual Telecommunications Access Method* (*VTAM*), an IBM licensed product, and *Transmission Control Protocol/Internet Protocol* (*TCP/IP*), a standard protocol, have been integrated into IBM's *eNetwork Communications Server* for OS/390. Within eNetwork Communications Server, VTAM is now known as *SNA Services* and TCP/IP is known as *IP Services*. The integration of these two products means that local and remote servers can communicate with each other whether connected over TCP/IP, SNA, or a mixture of these network protocols.

The distributed data facility components

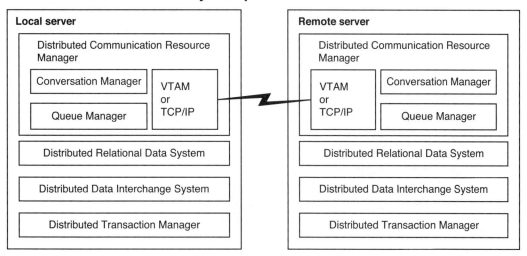

Description

- DB2 implements data distribution using a product called the *distributed data facility*, or *DDF*. To do that, DDF must reside on the local server where the application will run and on the remote servers that contain the data the application needs to access.

- The *Distributed Communication Resource Manager* (*DCRM*) manages the interfaces to other resources. The DCRM on the local server creates the conversations that are sent to the remote server. The DCRM on the remote server accepts the requests and creates a *database access thread* to handle distributed requests.

- The *Conversation Manager* manages the connections to the server. It receives messages from remote clients and sends messages from the server back to the requester. It also manages the creation and termination of the connections used to support data access requests.

- The *Queue Manager* creates and routes work requests for *allied threads*. These requests are queued by the Queue Manager and then routed for further processing.

- The Conversation Manager uses *VTAM* or *TCP/IP* to communicate with other DBMSs in the network. It reads the communication database (version 4) or DB2 catalogs (version 5) to determine how communication resources are to be used by DDF.

- The function of the *Distributed Relational Data System* (*DRDS*) depends on whether a private protocol or DRDA request is received. For a private protocol request, the DRDS invokes the DCRM to communicate with DCRM on the remote server. For a DRDA request, the DRDS enables the requester to perform remote binds (see figure 4-8).

- The *Distributed Data Interchange System* (*DDIS*) performs object mapping for remote objects accessed by DRDA requests.

- The *Distributed Transaction Manager* (*DTM*) manages transactions by monitoring for errors, managing recovery, and controlling commits and aborts.

Figure 4-2   How DDF implements data distribution

An introduction to DRDA

Prior to DB2 version 2.2, a program accessing DB2 through one subsystem could not process data managed by another subsystem even if the subsystems ran on the same machine. Then, with version 2.2, IBM added support for distributed data management, which allowed access of DB2 data across multiple subsystems. The access method used to work with distributed data in this version of DB2 is the method that would later be called DB2 private protocol access. This access method can be used only to access DB2 subsystems.

Because IBM realized the need to communicate with RDBMSs other than DB2, they developed DRDA. DRDA is a set of protocols, or rules, that allow access to distributed data, regardless of where it resides. Any product that follows these rules can communicate with any other DRDA-compliant product. DB2 became DRDA-compliant with version 2.3, and more recent releases have expanded on its capabilities.

To understand how DRDA works, you need to understand its three functions. These functions are presented in figure 4-3. As you can see, when a local DBMS receives a remote request, it sends the request to the *application requester*. Then, the application requester sends the request to the *application server* on a remote server. The application server than passes the request to the DMBS on that server, which processes the request and sends the results back to the application server. Finally, the application server passes the results back to the application requester.

Before I go on, I want to reiterate that DRDA defines a standard that can be implemented by any RDBMS. Under DB2, for example, the application requester and application server functions are implemented by DDF as described in the previous topic. Under other database management systems, other facilities are used to implement these functions. Regardless of the DBMS, though, the application requester and application server must provide the functions defined by DRDA.

The third function defined by DRDA is the *database server* function. Because this function has not yet been implemented by DB2, it's difficult to tell how it will work. In general, though, it will process requests sent to it from the application server. This might happen, for example, if the application server receives a request for data that resides on two or more servers. As you'll see in the next topic, however, this capability is not yet available with DB2.

The three DRDA functions

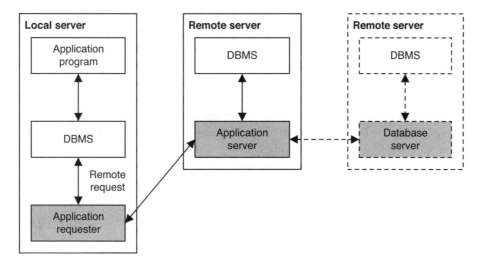

Concepts

- The *Distributed Relational Database Architecture*, or *DRDA*, is a standard developed by IBM that defines how two database management systems communicate. This standard defines three functional components: the application requester, the application server, and the database server.

- When an application program requests access to remote data, the request is sent from the RDBMS to the *application requester* on the same server. The application requester then sends the request to the *application server* on a remote server.

- If the requested data resides on the same server as the application server, the request is processed by the RDBMS on that server. Then, the application server sends the results back to the application requester.

- If all or part of the requested data resides on other remote servers, the application server sends the appropriate requests to the *database servers* on the remote servers where the data resides. Then, the results are returned to the application server where the request is completed, and the results are returned to the application requester.

- The protocol that the application requester and application server use to communicate is call the *Application Support Protocol*. The application server and the database server communicate using the *Database Support Protocol.*

- Under DB2 versions 4 and 5, the application requester and application server functions are implemented by DDF. The database server function has not yet been implemented.

- The software that implements the application requester and server functions can be part of the DBMS as is the case with DDF, or it can be a separate product.

Figure 4-3   The functions defined by DRDA

The four levels of DRDA

DRDA can be implemented at four different levels as described in figure 4-4. As this figure indicates, each level is based on the number of SQL statements that can be executed within each unit of work; the number of DBMSs that can be accessed within each unit of work; and the number of DBMSs that can be accessed within each SQL statement. At the remote request level, for example, only one SQL statement can be executed within a unit of work, and only one DBMS can be accessed within each SQL statement and each unit of work.

Currently, DB2 implements the third level of DRDA, called the distributed unit of work level. At this level, multiple statements can be issued within each unit of work, and multiple DBMSs can be accessed within each unit of work. However, only one DBMS can be accessed by each statement. Only the fourth level of DRDA provides for accessing two or more DBMSs in a single statement, and that level has not yet been implemented by DB2.

If two or more DBMSs are accessed and updated during a single unit of work, a *two-phase commit protocol* is required. This protocol ensures that the changes that are made to each DBMS within a unit of work are synchronized. In other words, either the changes are committed to both databases or neither database. Later in this chapter, you'll see how a two-phase commit is implemented in a COBOL program that accesses data in two DB2 databases.

The four DRDA levels in order of increasing complexity

DRDA level	SQL statements per unit of work	DBMSs per unit of work	DBMSs per SQL statement
Remote request	1	1	1
Remote unit of work	1 or more	1	1
Distributed unit of work	1 or more	1 or more	1
Distributed request	1 or more	1 or more	1 or more

Concepts

- The four levels of DRDA are defined by the number of SQL statements that can be processed within a unit of work, the number of RDBMSs that can be accessed within a unit of work, and the number of DBMSs that can be accessed within a single SQL statement.

- DB2 versions 4 and 5 support the first three levels of DRDA: remote request, remote unit of work, and distributed unit of work. Out of these levels, distributed unit of work is the only level that lets you access two or more DBMSs within a single unit of work.

- To process data in two or more DBMSs within a single unit of work, a *two-phase commit protocol* must be established. This protocol synchronizes the commit across the affected DBMSs.

- To access two or more DBMSs with a single SQL statement, you must have distributed request capabilities. Currently, DB2 doesn't support this level of DRDA.

Figure 4-4   The four levels of DRDA

How to access distributed data

Now that you understand how DB2 implements distributed processing, you're ready to learn how to access distributed data from a COBOL program. To start, I'll compare the features of the two access methods so you'll know what's required when you use them and what you can and can't do with each. Then, I'll present the specific techniques you need to use with each method.

A comparison of DRDA and DB2 private protocol access

Figure 4-5 presents the requirements for using DRDA and DB2 private protocol access and the features that are available with each. If you review this information, you'll see that the DRDA access method has several advantages over the private protocol access method. To start, the DRDA access method is DRDA compliant. That means that you can use it to access data in any DRDA-compliant database. With the DB2 private protocol access method, you can access only DB2 data.

Another advantage of DRDA access is that you can use it to execute any SQL statement that the DBMS supports. In contrast, private protocol access lets you execute only INSERT, UPDATE, and DELETE statements along with the statements for working with cursors: OPEN, FETCH, and CLOSE. You can also call stored procedures using DRDA access as described in chapter 5, and you can execute dynamic SQL as described chapter 3.

Before a program can execute an SQL statement on a remote server using DRDA access, it has to explicitly connect to that server. Then, any SQL statements it executes are sent to that server. In contrast, when you use private protocol access, you don't have to explicitly connect to the server. Instead, you identify the server in each SQL statement that's executed. You'll see the coding that's required for both of these access methods in just a moment.

DRDA access and private protocol access also differ in the binding they require. DRDA programs must be bound to a package on both the remote and the local server before they're executed. In contrast, private protocol programs have to be bound only at the local server, and they can be bound directly to a plan. Then, any SQL statement that's sent to the server is bound at the server the first time it's executed. Although this eliminates additional binding up front, it can reduce the efficiency of the program since the binding takes place as the program executes.

Requirements and features of DRDA and DB2 private protocol access

Requirement/feature	DRDA	DB2 private protocol
Must connect explicitly to a server	Yes	No
Locates data using a three-part object name	No	Yes
Can use any SQL statement that's supported by the DBMS that will execute it	Yes	INSERT, UPDATE, DELETE, OPEN, FETCH, and CLOSE only
Can call stored procedures	Yes	No
Requires that static SQL statements be bound to a package on the remote server before execution	Yes	No
DBRM can be bound directly to a plan	No (must be bound to a package)	Yes
Can execute dynamic SQL at the server	Yes	No
Can connect from DB2 to any DBMS	Yes	DB2 only
Supports block fetch	Limited only	Continuous
Can perform read and update operations at remote locations using CAF, TSO, CICS, or IMS/TM	Yes	Yes (unless using CICS or IMS to access a DB2 version 2 release 3 subsystem)
Can access DBMSs in multiple locations from a single SQL statement	No	No

Notes

- An SQL statement that's sent to a remote server using private protocol access is bound at the server the first time it's executed in a unit of work. An SQL statement that's sent to a remote server using DRDA access must be bound at the server before the program that contains it is executed. See figure 4-8 for details on binding.
- DRDA also uses a more compact format for sending data over the network, which can improve performance.

Figure 4-5   A comparison of DRDA and DB2 private protocol access

How to use DB2 private protocol access

Figure 4-6 presents the coding that's required to access data using the DB2 private protocol access method. In general, you simply identify the location of the server that contains the table you want to access in each SQL statement. To do that, you use a three-part table name as shown in the first example in this figure. Here, the first part of the table name specifies the location name of the server as FRESNO.

When you specify a location name, DB2 looks for it in one of the system tables. Under DB2 version 4, that table is SYSIBM.SYSLOCATIONS. Under DB2 version 5, the table is SYSIBM.LOCATIONS. The location names in this table are mapped to other tables that contain information about how to connect to the remote server. DB2 uses this information to make implicit connections.

Another way to refer to a table on a remote server is to create an alias for the table. This is illustrated in the second coding example in this figure. Here, the CREATE ALIAS statement is used to create an alias named CUST that refers to the MM01.CUSTOMER table on the remote server named FRESNO. Once the alias is created, you can use it in any SQL statement in place of a three-part table name as illustrated in the third coding example. That makes it possible to access a remote table without knowing its location.

A SELECT statement that refers to a remote table using a three-part table name

```
EXEC SQL
    SELECT CUSTNO, LNAME, FNAME
        INTO CUSTOMER-ROW
        FROM FRESNO.MM01.CUSTOMER
            WHERE CUSTNO = :CUSTNO
END-EXEC.
```

A CREATE ALIAS statement that creates an alias for a remote table

```
CREATE ALIAS CUST
    FOR FRESNO.MM01.CUSTOMER;
```

A SELECT statement that refers to a remote table using an alias

```
EXEC SQL
    SELECT CUSTNO, LNAME, FNAME
        INTO CUSTOMER-ROW
        FROM CUST
            WHERE CUSTNO = :CUSTNO
END-EXEC.
```

Description

* To access a table using private protocol access, you specify a three-part table name. The first part of the name specifies the location name of the remote server where the data resides.

* The location name for a remote server is recorded in the SYSIBM.SYS-LOCATIONS (DB2 version 4) or SYSIBM.LOCATIONS (DB2 version 5) table of the system. These names are mapped to information in other tables that tell DB2 how to connect to the remote server. DB2 manages the connection implicitly.

* You can also create an alias for a remote table and then use the alias in place of the three part table name. To create an alias, you can issue the CREATE ALIAS statement using SPUFI or QMF.

Figure 4-6   How to use DB2 private protocol access

How to use DRDA access

Figure 4-7 illustrates how to access distributed DB2 data using the DRDA access method. To start, you have to establish a connection, or *conversation*, to the remote locations you want to access using the CONNECT statement as shown in the first set of examples. On the CONNECT statement, you can specify the location name or a host variable that contains the location name. You can also use the keyword RESET to connect to the local server.

By default, the last server you connect to is the *current server*. This is the server where any SQL statements the program issues are executed. To change the current server, you use the SET CONNECTION statement as shown in the second set of examples in this figure. As with the CONNECT statement, you can specify the name of the server by coding a location name or a host variable that contains the location name.

After a connection is established, it's available for the duration of the program unless it's released. To release one or more connections explicitly, you use the RELEASE statement as shown in the third set of examples. To release a single connection, you specify the location name or a host variable that contains the location name. You can also release the connection to the current server by specifying the CURRENT keyword. You can release all connections by specifying the ALL keyword. And you can release connections that are established implicitly using the private protocol access method by specifying the ALL PRIVATE keywords.

Statements that connect to a server

`CONNECT TO FRESNO`	Establishes a connection to the server named FRESNO.
`CONNECT TO :LOCNAME`	Establishes a connection to the server specified in the LOCNAME host variable.
`CONNECT RESET`	Establishes a connection to the local server.

Statements that change the current server

`SET CONNECTION FRESNO`	Makes the server named FRESNO the current server.
`SET CONNECTION :LOCNAME`	Makes the server specified in the LOCNAME host variable the current server.

Statements that release connections

`RELEASE FRESNO`	Releases the connection to the server named FRESNO.
`RELEASE :LOCNAME`	Releases the connection to the server specified in the LOCNAME host variable.
`RELEASE CURRENT`	Releases the connection to the current server.
`RELEASE ALL`	Releases all connections.
`RELEASE ALL PRIVATE`	Releases all private connections.

Description

- The CONNECT statement establishes a connection with the server at the specified location. The location name must be defined in the SYSIBM.SYSLOCATIONS (DB2 version 4) or SYSIBM.LOCATIONS (DB2 version 5) table.
- The last connection that's established identifies the *current server*. The location name of the current server is stored in the CURRENT SERVER special variable.
- Any SQL statements issued by the program are executed on the current server. To change the current server, you use the SET CONNECTION statement.
- You can release one or more connections using the RELEASE statement. This statement places the connections in a release-pending state so they're released at the next commit point.

Notes

- If you try to connect to a location that's not defined, you'll get an SQLCODE of –904. If you try to activate a server whose connection hasn't been defined, you'll get an SQLCODE of –843.
- A connection can also be released at a commit point if the DISCONNECT(AUTOMATIC) or DISCONNECT(CONDITIONAL) option is specified when the plan is bound (see figure 4-8).

Figure 4-7   How to use DRDA access

How to prepare a DRDA program

Before you can execute a program that uses DRDA access, you have to precompile it just as you do any other DB2 program. When you precompile a program that uses DRDA access, though, you'll want to be sure that the CONNECT and SQL options are set properly. These two options are described at the top of figure 4-8.

The CONNECT option determines how many DBMSs you can connect to during a single unit of work. The default for this option is CONNECT(2), which lets you connect to as many DBMSs as you need. If you're using version 2.3 of DB2, you'll need to change the default to CONNECT(1) since that release doesn't support accessing more than one DBMS within a unit of work.

The SQL option determines the SQL statements you can issue. The default for this option is SQL (DB2), which only lets you issue SQL statements that are recognized by DB2 for MVS/ESA or OS/390. If you want to issue SQL statements that are recognized by another DBMS, you can change this option to SQL(ALL). Then, you can issue any statement that obeys DRDA rules.

A program that uses DRDA access must be bound to a package on the server before it can be executed. When you bind the package, you need to be aware of the two options shown in this figure. The first option specifies the location name of the server where the package is bound. If you omit this name, the package will be bound at the local server.

If you specify the SQL(ALL) option when you precompile a program, errors will occur during the bind process if the program issues SQL statements that aren't recognized by DB2. In that case, you need to code the SQLERROR(CONTINUE) option when you bind the package so the package is created anyway. If you specify the SQL(DB2) option when you precompile the program, you can leave the SQLERROR option at its default of SQLERROR(NOPACKAGE). Then, a package isn't created if the bind process finds SQL errors.

This figure also presents the BIND PLAN options that can affect programs that use DRDA access. The first option, DISCONNECT, determines whether all remote connections are released automatically at a commit point (AUTO-MATIC), or whether they must be released explicitly using a RELEASE statement (EXPLICIT). You can also release all connections except those that are associated with a cursor that's opened with the WITH HOLD option by specifying DISCONNECT(CONDITIONAL).

The SQLRULES option determines if a CONNECT statement causes an error if the program is already connected to the location it specifies. The default is SQLRULES(DB2), which doesn't cause an error to be returned. If you want an error to be returned in this situation, use SQLRULES(STD).

This figure also shows sample statements for binding a package at a remote location and then binding that package, along with a package for the same program bound at the local server, to a plan on the local server. Notice that no special BIND PACKAGE or BIND PLAN options are specified. In most cases, the defaults are what you want.

Precompiler options

CONNECT	Determines whether type 1 or type 2 CONNECT statement rules apply. CONNECT(1) lets you connect to a single DBMS within a unit of work, and CONNECT(2) lets you connect to more than one DBMS within a unit of work. CONNECT(2) is the default.
SQL	Indicates whether the application contains SQL statements other than those recognized by DB2 for MVS/ESA (version 4) or DB2 for OS/390 (version 5). SQL(ALL) lets you include any SQL statement that obeys DRDA rules. SQL (DB2) lets you include only DB2 for MVS/ESA or OS/390. SQL (DB2) is the default.

BIND PACKAGE options

location-name	The location name of the server where the package will run. The owner of the package must be granted the privileges needed to run the package at the server.
SQLERROR	Determines whether or not a package is created if SQL errors are encountered when the program is precompiled. SQLERROR(CONTINUE) causes the package to be created and should be used if the SQL(ALL) precompiler option is specified. SQL(NOPACKAGE) is the default, and should be used when the SQL(DB2) precompiler option is specified.

BIND PLAN options

DISCONNECT	Determines whether the RELEASE statement must be used to release connections. DISCONNECT(EXPLICIT) requires the use of RELEASE statements and is the default. DISCONNECT(AUTOMATIC) causes all remote connections to be released automatically during a commit operation. DISCONNECT(CONDITIONAL) causes all remote connections to be released automatically during a commit operation unless a cursor opened as WITH HOLD is associated with the connection.
SQLRULES	Determines whether an error is returned if you issue a CONNECT statement and the application is already connected to the specified location. SQLRULES(STD) causes an error to be returned, and SQLRULES(DB2) does not. SQLRULES(DB2) is the default.

A statement that binds the DBRM for the EMPLTRANS program to the PYRLCOL collection on the FRESNO server

```
BIND PACKAGE(FRESNO.PYRLCOL) MEMBER(EMPLTRNS)
```

A statement that binds all the packages in the PYRLCOL collection on the local and FRESNO servers into the PRSNLPLN plan on the local server

```
BIND PLAN(PRSNLPLN) PKLIST(PYRLCOL.*, FRESNO.PYRLCOL.*)
```

Description

- The DBRM for a program that contains statements to be executed at a remote server must be bound to a package on that server as well as to a package on the local server. Then, both the local and remote packages must be bound to a plan on the local server.
- You can also specify the CURRENTDATA(NO) option when binding a package or plan to force block fetching for ambiguous cursors. See figure 4-10 for details.

Figure 4-8   How to prepare a DRDA program

How to use block fetching

Because the network communication between a local and remote server in a distributed application can cause bottlenecks, it's important that data be transmitted as efficiently as possible. One way to do that is to retrieve data by blocks rather than one row at a time using a process called *block fetching*. In the following topics, you'll learn how block fetching works and how you can ensure that your applications use it whenever possible.

How block fetching works

Figure 4-9 illustrates the difference between a *blocked fetch* and an *unblocked fetch*. As you can see, each unblocked fetch results in the transmission of one row of data across the network. When you use block fetching, though, the retrieved rows are grouped into a large block of data that's stored in the *message buffer* on the remote server. Then, when the message buffer becomes full, its contents are transmitted over the network as a single message.

When you use DB2 private protocol access to retrieve distributed data, DB2 uses a type of block fetch called *continuous block fetch*. With a continuous block fetch, a separate conversation is established for each open cursor, which means that data requests can be processed asynchronously. In contrast, when you use DRDA access, DB2 uses *limited block fetch*. With this type of block fetch, a single conversation is used for all communications between the local and remote server for multiple cursors. Because of that, each transmission must be processed synchronously, which means that one request for data must complete before the next one can begin.

Although block fetching reduces network traffic, you may not always want to use it. In particular, you won't want to use block fetching if the data you're retrieving changes frequently and your program relies on current data. That's because data that's stored in the message buffer during a block fetch isn't updated if the data in the base tables that the data was retrieved from changes. And that means that your program may receive data that's out of date. The easiest way to avoid this situation is to code the FOR UPDATE OF clause on the DECLARE CURSOR statement, since block fetching isn't used with updateable cursors.

An unblocked fetch

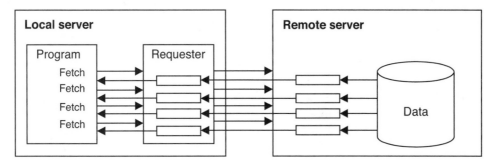

A blocked fetch

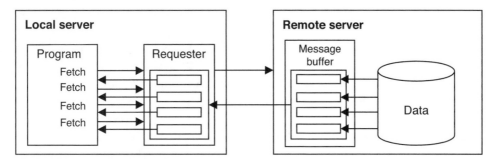

Description

- An *unblocked fetch* causes each row of data retrieved by an application to be passed over the network as a single message.

- A *blocked fetch* causes the rows of data retrieved by an application to be grouped into blocks that are stored in the *message buffer* on the remote server. When the message buffer is full, the entire block is passed over the network as a single message.

- A block fetch can be used with read-only cursors. If data can be updated through the cursor, DB2 must send the data over the network one row at a time.

- Two types of block fetch are available with DB2: limited and continuous. *Limited block fetch* can be used with DRDA access and *continuous block fetch* can be used with DB2 private protocol access.

- A limited block fetch uses a single conversation to pass data between the requester and the server. When limited block fetch is used, synchronous processing occurs between the requester and the server.

- A continuous block fetch uses one conversation for each open cursor. When continuous block fetch is used, asynchronous processing occurs between the requester and the server.

Figure 4-9   How block fetching works

How to ensure block fetching

To use block fetching, DB2 must be able to determine that the cursor cannot be used to update or delete the data that it contains. In other words, the cursor must be read-only. The best way to ensure that DB2 recognizes a cursor as read-only is to code the FOR READ ONLY or FOR FETCH ONLY clause on the DECLARE CURSOR statement. The FOR READ ONLY clause is illustrated in the code at the top of figure 4-10.

Even if you don't include the FOR READ ONLY or FOR FETCH ONLY clause on the DECLARE CURSOR statement, a cursor is considered read-only if it meets one of the conditions listed in this figure. If a cursor joins data from two or more tables, for example, or if the SELECT statement that defines the cursor contains an ORDER BY clause, a read-only cursor is created and block fetching can be used.

Block fetching can also be used if the cursor is ambiguous and the CURRENTDATA(NO) option was specified on the BIND PACKAGE or BIND PLAN statement that was used to bind the program. A cursor is ambiguous if DB2 can't determine if it's updateable. That happens if the FOR READ ONLY, FOR FETCH ONLY, or FOR UPDATE OF clause isn't included on the DE-CLARE CURSOR statement; if the SELECT statement that defines the cursor doesn't result in a read-only table; if a DELETE WHERE CURRENT OF or UPDATE WHERE CURRENT OF statements isn't associated with the cursor; and if the plan or package executes dynamic SQL statements. In that case, the CURRENTDATA(NO) option indicates that data currency is not required and, therefore, block fetching can be used.

If it isn't your shop's standard to code the FOR clause on all DECLARE CURSOR statements, it should be your standard. By coding this clause, you can eliminate all ambiguous cursors and ensure that block fetching is used for all cursors that are not used for updating.

How to code a cursor to ensure a block fetch

```
EXEC SQL
    DECLARE CUSTCURS CURSOR FOR
        SELECT FNAME, LNAME
            FROM MM01.CUSTOMER
            WHERE STATE = 'CA'
        FOR READ ONLY
END-EXEC.
```

Conditions that cause a read-only cursor

- Joining tables
- Specifying the DISTINCT keyword in the first SELECT clause
- Using either UNION or UNION ALL
- Specifying a subquery where the same table is specified in the FROM clauses of both the subquery and the outer query
- Using a scalar function in the first SELECT clause
- Using either a GROUP BY or HAVING clause in the outer SELECT clause
- Specifying an ORDER BY clause

Description

- To ensure a block fetch, specify the FOR READ ONLY or FOR FETCH ONLY clause on cursors that will not be used to update data. FOR READ ONLY became available with DB2 version 4 and is preferable to FOR FETCH ONLY because it is ODBC-compliant.

- If you do not specify FOR READ ONLY or FOR FETCH ONLY, a block fetch is used if the SELECT statement results in a read-only cursor as indicated above. Even if a SELECT statement does not result in a read-only cursor, a block fetch may be used if the program doesn't include a DELETE or UPDATE statement with the WHERE CURRENT OF clause and doesn't include any dynamic statements.

- A cursor is considered updateable if it is declared with the FOR UPDATE OF clause or a DELETE WHERE CURRENT OF or UPDATE WHERE CURRENT OF statement is associated with the cursor. If the cursor is not updateable but the program contains a PREPARE or EXECUTE IMMEDIATE statement, the cursor is considered ambiguous.

- To use a block fetch with an *ambiguous cursor*, specify the CURRENTDATA(NO) option on either the BIND PACKAGE or BIND PLAN statement. The default is CURRENTDATA(YES). Prior to DB2 version 4.1 the default was (NO).

Figure 4-10   How to ensure block fetching

A COBOL program that uses distributed DB2 data

This chapter closes by presenting a COBOL program that accesses distributed data using the DRDA access method. The purpose of this program is to transfer employees from one site to another. To keep this program simple, the location names of the sites where the employees are transferred to and from are hardcoded into the program. In a production application, though, the user would probably be allowed to enter the names of the two sites.

The interactive screen

This employee transfer program runs at a TSO terminal and accepts employee numbers from the user. For each employee number, the program gets employee information from an employee table at one site, in this case, a site named FRSN (Fresno). Then, the employee is deleted from that site, and the division code column for the employee is changed to the new site, in this case, a site named SCTO (Sacramento). Finally, the employee is added to the employee table at the second site.

Figure 4-11 presents an interactive terminal session for this program. To start, the user entered the employee number 4001. As you can see, this employee number was not found at the Fresno site so an error message was displayed.

Next, the user entered the employee number 3001. This employee was found at the Fresno site, and the message that's displayed indicates that the employee was successfully transferred to the Sacramento site. Then, to end the program, the user entered 9999 for the employee number.

You'll notice in this interactive session that employees are transferred from one site to another without any verification. In a production application, though, you'd probably want to display some of the information for an employee before it's transferred so the user can verify that they've entered the correct employee number. The code for doing that has been excluded from this sample application so you can focus on the code for working with distributed data. But you shouldn't have any trouble adding the necessary code if you need to do that.

An interactive session

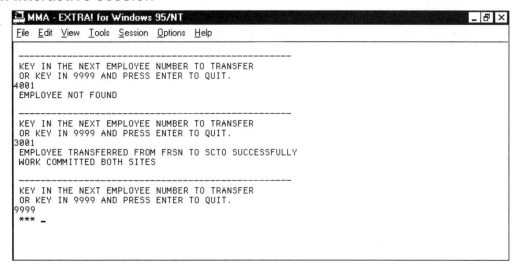

Description

- At the first prompt, the user entered an employee number that wasn't found in the employee table and an error message was displayed.
- At the second prompt, the user entered an employee number that was found in the employee table. Then, the program displayed messages indicating that the employee was successfully transferred from site FRSN to site SCTO and that the unit of work was committed on both sites.
- At the third prompt, the user entered 9999 to end the program.

Figure 4-11   The interactive screen for the employee transfer program

The structure chart

Figure 4-12 presents the structure chart for the employee transfer program. Here, module 0000 starts by performing module 1000 to establish connections to the two sites. Then, module 0000 performs module 2000 repeatedly to transfer each employee entered by the user. Finally, module 0000 performs module 3000 to release the connections established in module 1000.

Module 2000 starts by performing module 2100 to get an employee number from the user. Then, it performs module 2200 to process the employee at the first site. This module starts by performing module 2210 to establish that site as the current server. Then, it performs module 2220 to open a cursor at that site that contains the row for the employee number entered by the user, and it performs module 2230 to fetch that row. Finally, it performs module 2240 to delete the row from that site, and it performs module 2250 to close the cursor.

If the data on the first site is processed successfully, module 2000 performs module 2300 to update the employee row so it indicates the location name of the site where the employee is being transferred. Then, it performs module 2400 to process the employee at that site, and that module performs two additional modules. Module 2410 changes the current server to the second site, and module 2420 adds the employee row to the employee table at that site.

If the data on both sites is processed successfully, module 2000 performs module 2500 to commit the work at both sites. Otherwise, it performs module 2600 to rollback the work. This two-phase commit ensures that the data at the two sites is always synchronized.

The structure chart

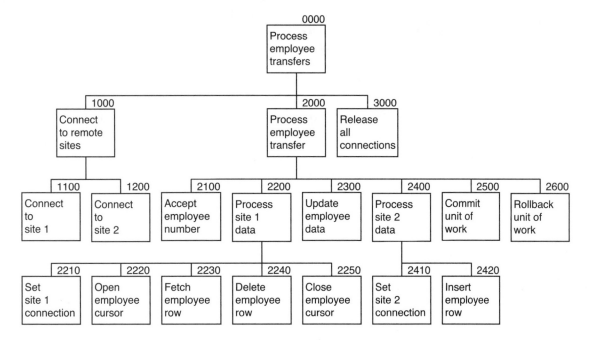

Description

- Module 0000 performs module 1000 to connect to the two sites. Then, it performs module 2000 repeatedly until the user keys in 9999 to end the program. Finally, it performs module 3000 to release the connections.

- Module 2000 performs module 2100 to accept the employee number. If the user doesn't enter 9999, module 2200 is performed to process the data for site 1.

- Each time module 2200 is performed, it performs module 2210 to set the current connection to site 1, module 2220 to open the employee cursor, module 2230 to fetch the employee row, module 2240 to delete the employee from site 1, and module 2250 to close the employee cursor.

- If the processing on site 1 completes successfully, module 2300 is performed to update the employee row so it indicates its new location. Then, module 2400 is performed to process the data for site 2. Module 2400 performs module 2410 to set the current connection to site 2 and module 2420 to insert the row into the employee table at site 2.

- If the insertion is successful, module 2000 performs module 2500 to commit the work on both sites. If the insertion fails, the unit of work is rolled back by module 2600. This *two-phase commit* process ensures that the data on both sites is synchronized.

Figure 4-12   The structure chart for the employee transfer program

The DCLGEN output

Figure 4-13 presents the DCLGEN output for the employee table that the employee update program uses. Note that for this program to work successfully, this employee table must reside at both locations. Also note that the column named DIVCD contains the location name of the site where a row resides. In the test data for this table at the Fresno site that's shown at the bottom of this figure, for example, you can see that the value of this field is FRSN. When a row is transferred to the employee table at the Sacramento site, the value of this field is changed to SCTO.

The DCLGEN output for the employee table

```
**********************************************************************
* DCLGEN TABLE(MM01.EMPLOYEE)                                        *
*        LIBRARY(MM01.DB2.DCLGENS(EMPLOYEE))                         *
*        ACTION(REPLACE)                                             *
*        LANGUAGE(COBOL)                                             *
*        STRUCTURE(EMPLOYEE-ROW)                                     *
*        QUOTE                                                       *
* ... IS THE DCLGEN COMMAND THAT MADE THE FOLLOWING STATEMENTS      *
**********************************************************************
      EXEC SQL DECLARE MM01.EMPLOYEE TABLE
      ( EMPNO                     CHAR(4) NOT NULL,
        LNAME                     CHAR(15) NOT NULL,
        FNAME                     CHAR(10) NOT NULL,
        DIVCD                     CHAR(4) NOT NULL,
        ADDR                      CHAR(20) NOT NULL,
        CITY                      CHAR(20) NOT NULL,
        STATE                     CHAR(2) NOT NULL,
        ZIPCODE                   CHAR(10) NOT NULL
      ) END-EXEC.
**********************************************************************
* COBOL DECLARATION FOR TABLE MM01.EMPLOYEE                         *
**********************************************************************
  01   EMPLOYEE-ROW.
       10 EMPNO              PIC X(4).
       10 LNAME              PIC X(15).
       10 FNAME              PIC X(10).
       10 DIVCD              PIC X(4).
       10 ADDR               PIC X(20).
       10 CITY               PIC X(20).
       10 STATE              PIC X(2).
       10 ZIPCODE            PIC X(10).
**********************************************************************
* THE NUMBER OF COLUMNS DESCRIBED BY THIS DECLARATION IS 8          *
**********************************************************************
```

Test data for an employee table at the FRSN site

EMPNO	LNAME	FNAME	DIVCD	ADDR	CITY	STATE	ZIPCODE
3001	VASQUEZ	DEBBIE	FRSN	211 MAIN ST	FRESNO	CA	93712-1226
3002	HOWARTH	JOHN	FRSN	2112 FIRST AVE	FRESNO	CA	93705-1228
3003	ALLEN	JEANETTE	FRSN	2323 LINCOLN AVE	FRESNO	CA	93705-1226
3004	JONES	EILEEN	FRSN	12542 THIRD ST	FRESNO	CA	93707-1228
3005	HOOD	CHESTER	FRSN	12123 PRIMROSE LN	SELMA	CA	93775-1446
3007	BUSKER	SHIRLEY	FRSN	312 BROADWAY AVE	FRESNO	CA	93705-1226
3011	DESANTIS	LOUIS	FRSN	312 SECOND AVE	SELMA	CA	93775-1446
3015	JOLLIFF	LEFF	FRSN	2534 CENTRAL AVE	MADERA	CA	93788-1212
3024	MOUNTAIN	MIKE	FRSN	2943 TULARE ST	VISALIA	CA	93123-2424
3025	FOULKS	MICHAEL	FRSN	3569 YOSEMITE PL	SELMA	CA	93755-1446

Figure 4-13   The DCLGEN output and the contents of an employee table

The COBOL listing

Figure 4-14 presents the COBOL listing for this program. Since this program works much like the programs you've already seen, you shouldn't have any trouble understanding its logic. To help you focus on the code related to distributed processing, that code has been shaded.

The two lines in the first shaded block on page one of this listing define the working-storage host variables that contain the location names for the two sites. Here, you can see that the host variable for site 1 contains the value "FRSN" and the site 2 variable contains the value "SCTO". You'll see how these variables are used later in this program.

The second shaded block on page one is the DECLARE CURSOR statement that's used to get the employee row for the employee number entered by the user. Notice that the FROM clause doesn't indicate the location of the employee table. Because DRDA access is being used, this cursor will retrieve data from the current server. Also notice that the FOR UPDATE OF clause is included on this statement to prevent the cursor from being ambiguous. Because this cursor is used for updating, block fetching will not be used.

The employee transfer program   Page 1

```
IDENTIFICATION DIVISION.
*
PROGRAM-ID.      EMPLTRNS.
*
ENVIRONMENT DIVISION.
*
INPUT-OUTPUT SECTION.
*
FILE-CONTROL.
*
DATA DIVISION.
*
FILE SECTION.
*
WORKING-STORAGE SECTION.
*
 01 SWITCHES.
*
     05 VALID-CONNECTIONS-SW        PIC X    VALUE 'N'.
        88 VALID-CONNECTIONS                 VALUE 'Y'.
     05 VALID-TRANSFERS-SW          PIC X    VALUE 'N'.
        88 VALID-TRANSFERS                   VALUE 'Y'.
     05 END-OF-TRANSFERS-SW         PIC X    VALUE 'N'.
        88 END-OF-TRANSFERS                  VALUE 'Y'.
*
 01 WORK-AREA.
*
     05 SITE-1                      PIC X(4) VALUE 'FRSN'.
     05 SITE-2                      PIC X(4) VALUE 'SCTO'.
     05 EDITED-SQLCODE              PIC -(4).
*
     EXEC SQL
         INCLUDE EMPLOYEE
     END-EXEC.
*
     EXEC SQL
         INCLUDE SQLCA
     END-EXEC.
*
     EXEC SQL DECLARE EMPLCURS CURSOR FOR
         SELECT EMPNO, LNAME, FNAME, DIVCD, ADDR, CITY,
                STATE, ZIPCODE
            FROM MM01.EMPLOYEE
            WHERE EMPNO = :EMPNO
         FOR UPDATE OF DIVCD
     END-EXEC.
*
```

Figure 4-14   The COBOL listing for the employee transfer program (part 1 of 5)

On page two of the COBOL listing, you can see the beginning of the Procedure Division. This program starts by performing module 1000 to connect to the two sites that contain the employee tables used by this application. The two CONNECT statements are shaded in this example. Notice that both statements refer to a host variable. Since those variables contain the values of the location names, these statements connect to the sites identified by those location names, in this case, FRSN and SCTO.

After each CONNECT statement is executed, the SQLCODE is checked to be sure that the connection was successful. If not, an error message is displayed and the valid-connections switch is turned off. This switch is set at the beginning of module 0000 and is then tested after the first CONNECT statement is executed from module 1000 to determine if the second CONNECT statement should be executed. It's also tested in module 0000 after both CONNECT statements are executed to determine if processing should continue.

If the connections are successful, module 2000 is performed to process each employee entered by the user. If you study the code for module 2000, you'll see the logic that's required for a two-phase commit. Notice here that the processing that's done at the first site isn't committed unless the processing at the second site completes successfully. Then, the work is committed on both sites at the same time. On the other hand, if the processing at the second site is not successful, the processing at the first site is rolled back.

The employee transfer program

```
PROCEDURE DIVISION.
*
0000-PROCESS-EMPL-TRANSFERS.
*
    MOVE 'Y' TO VALID-CONNECTIONS-SW.
    PERFORM 1000-CONNECT-TO-REMOTE-SITES.
    IF VALID-CONNECTIONS
        PERFORM 2000-PROCESS-EMPL-TRANSFER
            UNTIL END-OF-TRANSFERS
        PERFORM 3000-RELEASE-ALL-CONNECTIONS.
    STOP RUN.
*
1000-CONNECT-TO-REMOTE-SITES.
*
    PERFORM 1100-CONNECT-TO-SITE-1.
    IF VALID-CONNECTIONS
        PERFORM 1200-CONNECT-TO-SITE-2.
*
1100-CONNECT-TO-SITE-1.
*
    EXEC SQL
        CONNECT TO :SITE-1
    END-EXEC.
    IF SQLCODE NOT = 0
        MOVE 'N' TO VALID-CONNECTIONS-SW
        MOVE SQLCODE TO EDITED-SQLCODE
        DISPLAY 'INITIAL CONNECTION TO SITE ' SITE-1 ' FAILED'
        DISPLAY 'SQLCODE = ' EDITED-SQLCODE.
*
1200-CONNECT-TO-SITE-2.
*
    EXEC SQL
        CONNECT TO :SITE-2
    END-EXEC.
    IF SQLCODE NOT = 0
        MOVE 'N' TO VALID-CONNECTIONS-SW
        MOVE SQLCODE TO EDITED-SQLCODE
        DISPLAY 'INITIAL CONNECTION TO SITE ' SITE-2 ' FAILED'
        DISPLAY 'SQLCODE = ' EDITED-SQLCODE.
*
2000-PROCESS-EMPL-TRANSFER.
*
    MOVE 'Y' TO VALID-TRANSFERS-SW.
    PERFORM 2100-ACCEPT-EMPLOYEE-NUMBER.
    IF NOT END-OF-TRANSFERS
        PERFORM 2200-PROCESS-SITE-1-DATA
        IF VALID-TRANSFERS
            PERFORM 2300-UPDATE-EMPLOYEE-DATA
            PERFORM 2400-PROCESS-SITE-2-DATA
            IF VALID-TRANSFERS
                PERFORM 2500-COMMIT-UNIT-OF-WORK
            ELSE
                PERFORM 2600-ROLLBACK-UNIT-OF-WORK.
*
```

Figure 4-14   The COBOL listing for the employee transfer program (part 2 of 5)

Module 2200 controls the processing of the data at the first site. This module starts by executing module 2210 to change the current server to the first site. The SET CONNECTION statement in that module is shaded on page three of the COBOL listing. Notice that, like the CONNECT statements, this statement refers to a host variable that contains the location name of the site.

If the SET CONNECTION statement is successful, module 2220 is performed to open the employee cursor using the employee number entered by the user. Since the DECLARE CURSOR statement for this cursor doesn't specify the location of the employee table, the table on the current server is used to create the cursor. Then, module 2230 is performed to fetch the employee row from that cursor.

After the employee row is fetched, module 2240 deletes it from the table and module 2250 closes the cursor since it's no longer needed. At that point, the processing at the first site is complete, but the changes have not been committed.

Before the employee row is added to the second site, module 2300 is performed to change the DIVCD column of the employee row to the location name of that site. Then, module 2400 performs module 2410 to change the current server to the second site. The SET CONNECTION statement in that module is shaded on page four of the COBOL listing. If this statement is successful, module 2420 is performed to insert the employee row at the second site.

The code for module 2420 is presented on page five of the COBOL listing. Notice that the name of the employee table in the INSERT statement is not qualified with a location name. Because of that, the row is inserted into the employee table on the current server.

If all of the processing completes successfully, module 2500 is performed to commit the work on both servers. If an error occurs during the processing on the second site, however, module 2600 is performed to rollback the work done on the first site. If that work wasn't rolled back, the employee would no longer exist because it would have been deleted from the table on the first site but not added to the table on the second site. That's why a two-phase commit is required.

When the user enters 9999 to end the program, module 3000 is performed to release the connections that were established by the program. In this case, the ALL keyword is used on the RELEASE statement so that both connections are released. Another way to do this would be to issue a separate RELEASE statement for each server.

The employee transfer program   **Page 3**

```
 2100-ACCEPT-EMPLOYEE-NUMBER.
*
     MOVE SPACE TO EMPNO.
     DISPLAY ' '.
     DISPLAY '----------------------------------------------------'.
     DISPLAY 'KEY IN THE NEXT EMPLOYEE NUMBER TO TRANSFER'.
     DISPLAY 'OR KEY IN 9999 AND PRESS ENTER TO QUIT.'.
     ACCEPT EMPNO.
     IF EMPNO = '9999'
         MOVE 'Y' TO END-OF-TRANSFERS-SW.
*
 2200-PROCESS-SITE-1-DATA.
*
     MOVE 'Y' TO VALID-CONNECTIONS-SW.
     PERFORM 2210-SET-SITE-1-CONNECTION.
     IF VALID-CONNECTIONS
         MOVE 'Y' TO VALID-TRANSFERS-SW
         PERFORM 2220-OPEN-EMPLOYEE-CURSOR
         IF VALID-TRANSFERS
             PERFORM 2230-FETCH-EMPLOYEE-ROW
             IF VALID-TRANSFERS
                 PERFORM 2240-DELETE-EMPLOYEE-ROW
                 PERFORM 2250-CLOSE-EMPLOYEE-CURSOR
             ELSE
                 PERFORM 2250-CLOSE-EMPLOYEE-CURSOR.
*
 2210-SET-SITE-1-CONNECTION.
*
     EXEC SQL
         SET CONNECTION :SITE-1
     END-EXEC.
     IF SQLCODE NOT = 0
         MOVE 'N' TO VALID-CONNECTIONS-SW
         MOVE 'Y' TO END-OF-TRANSFERS-SW
         MOVE SQLCODE TO EDITED-SQLCODE
         DISPLAY 'CONNECTION TO SITE ' SITE-1 ' FAILED'
         DISPLAY 'SQLCODE = ' EDITED-SQLCODE.
*
 2220-OPEN-EMPLOYEE-CURSOR.
*
     EXEC SQL
         OPEN EMPLCURS
     END-EXEC.
     IF SQLCODE NOT = 0
         MOVE 'N' TO VALID-TRANSFERS-SW
         MOVE SQLCODE TO EDITED-SQLCODE
         DISPLAY 'OPEN CURSOR FAILED'
         DISPLAY 'SQLCODE = ' EDITED-SQLCODE.
*
 2230-FETCH-EMPLOYEE-ROW.
*
     EXEC SQL
         FETCH EMPLCURS
             INTO :EMPNO, :LNAME, :FNAME, :DIVCD, :ADDR, :CITY,
                  :STATE, :ZIPCODE
     END-EXEC.
```

Figure 4-14   The COBOL listing for the employee transfer program (part 3 of 5)

The employee transfer program

```
    IF SQLCODE NOT = 0
        MOVE 'N' TO VALID-TRANSFERS-SW
        IF SQLCODE = +100
            DISPLAY 'EMPLOYEE NOT FOUND'
        ELSE
            MOVE SQLCODE TO EDITED-SQLCODE
            DISPLAY 'FETCH CURSOR FAILED'
            DISPLAY 'SQLCODE = ' EDITED-SQLCODE.
*
 2240-DELETE-EMPLOYEE-ROW.
*
    EXEC SQL
        DELETE FROM MM01.EMPLOYEE
            WHERE EMPNO = :EMPNO
    END-EXEC.
    IF SQLCODE NOT = 0
        MOVE 'N' TO VALID-TRANSFERS-SW
        MOVE SQLCODE TO EDITED-SQLCODE
        DISPLAY 'DELETE FAILED'
        DISPLAY 'SQLCODE = ' EDITED-SQLCODE.
*
 2250-CLOSE-EMPLOYEE-CURSOR.
*
    EXEC SQL
        CLOSE EMPLCURS
    END-EXEC.
    IF SQLCODE NOT = 0
        MOVE 'N' TO VALID-TRANSFERS-SW
        MOVE SQLCODE TO EDITED-SQLCODE
        DISPLAY 'CLOSE CURSOR FAILED'
        DISPLAY 'SQLCODE = ' EDITED-SQLCODE.
*
 2300-UPDATE-EMPLOYEE-DATA.
*
    MOVE SITE-2 TO DIVCD.
*
 2400-PROCESS-SITE-2-DATA.
*
    MOVE 'Y' TO VALID-CONNECTIONS-SW.
    PERFORM 2410-SET-SITE-2-CONNECTION.
    IF VALID-CONNECTIONS
        PERFORM 2420-INSERT-EMPLOYEE-ROW.
*
 2410-SET-SITE-2-CONNECTION.
*
    EXEC SQL
        SET CONNECTION :SITE-2
    END-EXEC.
    IF SQLCODE NOT = 0
        MOVE 'N' TO VALID-CONNECTIONS-SW
        MOVE 'Y' TO END-OF-TRANSFERS-SW
        MOVE SQLCODE TO EDITED-SQLCODE
        DISPLAY 'CONNECTION TO SITE ' SITE-2 ' FAILED'
        DISPLAY 'SQLCODE = ' EDITED-SQLCODE.
*
```

Figure 4-14   The COBOL listing for the employee transfer program (part 4 of 5)

The employee transfer program   **Page 5**

```
 2420-INSERT-EMPLOYEE-ROW.
*
     EXEC SQL
         INSERT INTO MM01.EMPLOYEE VALUES
         ( :EMPNO,
           :LNAME,
           :FNAME,
           :DIVCD,
           :ADDR,
           :CITY,
           :STATE,
           :ZIPCODE )
     END-EXEC.
     IF SQLCODE = 0
         DISPLAY 'EMPLOYEE TRANSFERRED FROM ' SITE-1
                 ' TO ' SITE-2 ' SUCCESSFULLY'
     ELSE
         MOVE 'N' TO VALID-TRANSFERS-SW
         IF SQLCODE = -803
             DISPLAY 'EMPLOYEE NUMBER ' EMPNO
                     ' ALREADY AT SITE ' SITE-2
         ELSE
             MOVE SQLCODE TO EDITED-SQLCODE
             DISPLAY 'INSERT FAILED'
             DISPLAY 'SQLCODE = ' EDITED-SQLCODE.
*
 2500-COMMIT-UNIT-OF-WORK.
*
     EXEC SQL
         COMMIT
     END-EXEC.
     IF SQLCODE = 0
         DISPLAY 'WORK COMMITTED BOTH SITES'
     ELSE
         MOVE 'Y' TO END-OF-TRANSFERS-SW
         MOVE SQLCODE TO EDITED-SQLCODE
         DISPLAY 'COMMIT FAILED'
         DISPLAY 'SQLCODE = ' EDITED-SQLCODE.
*
 2600-ROLLBACK-UNIT-OF-WORK.
*
     EXEC SQL
         ROLLBACK
     END-EXEC.
     IF SQLCODE = 0
         DISPLAY 'ROLLBACK SUCCESSFUL'
     ELSE
         MOVE 'Y' TO END-OF-TRANSFERS-SW
         MOVE SQLCODE TO EDITED-SQLCODE
         DISPLAY 'ROLLBACK FAILED'
         DISPLAY 'SQLCODE = ' EDITED-SQLCODE.
*
 3000-RELEASE-ALL-CONNECTIONS.
*
     EXEC SQL
         RELEASE ALL
     END-EXEC.
*
```

Figure 4-14   The COBOL listing for the employee transfer program (part 5 of 5)

Perspective

Today, more and more companies are using distributed processing to access data at remote sites. Fortunately, the programming required to implement distributed processing is straightforward. So if you understand the material presented in this chapter, you shouldn't have any trouble developing programs that access distributed data.

In October of 1998, The Open Group, an IT industry consortium for promoting open technologies, adopted the DRDA protocol. Already, many major international companies such as Allstate Insurance, Chrysler, CIGNA Insurance, Ford, Lockhead Martin, McDonald's, Spiegel, Swiss Bank, and Wilmington Trust use products that support DRDA. So it appears that DRDA is the standard of the future for accessing distributed data. To find out more about The Open Group, you can go to their web site at www.opengroup.org. You'll also find the latest publications that describe the DRDA standard at this site.

5

How to create and execute stored procedures

DB2 version 4 introduced *stored procedures*. Simply put, a stored procedure is a compiled program that executes one or more SQL statements and that's stored in the DBMS rather than in an external code library. Although a stored procedure can be written in many different languages, this chapter teaches you how to develop stored procedures in COBOL. It also teaches you how to execute a stored procedure regardless of the language it's written in. But first, it presents the benefits of using stored procedures and describes how they're processed.

An introduction to stored procedures

If you've ever worked with subprograms, you won't have any trouble working with stored procedures. In fact, the techniques you use to create and execute stored procedures are almost identical to the techniques you use with subprograms. The main difference is that a stored procedure is stored by DB2 rather than in an external code library. Because of that, you have to use the SQL CALL statement to execute a stored procedure.

Benefits of using stored procedures

Figure 5-1 compares the processing of a program that uses a stored procedure with one that doesn't. As you can see, one of the benefits of using stored procedures is that they reduce the amount of traffic that goes across the network between the client and the server. Because stored procedures are stored on the server, only the requests to execute them are sent from the client. Then, the stored procedures and any data requests they contain are processed on the server. In contrast, each individual data request must be sent from the client to the server when stored procedures aren't used, which can result in poor performance.

Another benefit of using stored procedures is that they can access data that can't be accessed from a DB2 program. For example, they can access data that's stored in IMS or IDMS databases. They can also access flat files and CICS transactions.

This figure also illustrates that when DB2 receives a request to execute a stored procedure, it schedules that procedure for execution in a separate DB2 *address space* called the *stored procedures address space* (*SPAS*). You can think of an address space as a reserved portion of the CPU. As the procedure executes, its data requests are sent from the SPAS to DB2 for processing. Then, when the procedure finishes, DB2 sends its results back to the client program.

The advantage of stored procedures executing in a separate address space is that the address space is isolated from DB2. That means that if an error occurs in a stored procedure, it doesn't affect DB2. If necessary, you can even stop and start the stored procedure address space without affecting DB2.

Client and server processing without stored procedures

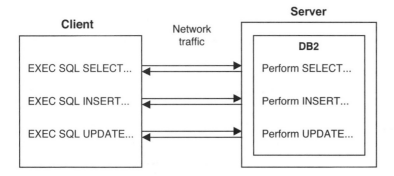

Client and server processing with stored procedures

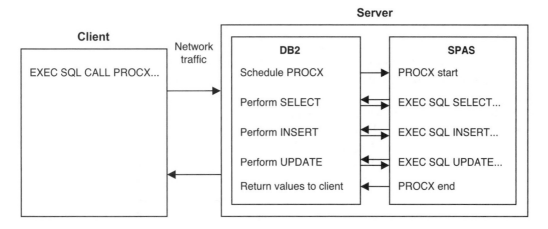

Description

- Without stored procedures, each individual data request is passed from the client to the server over the network. The server then processes the data request and passes the results back to the client.

- When you use stored procedures, only the requests to execute the stored procedures are sent to the server, and only the results of the stored procedures are returned to the client. The data requests and data processing are handled by the server.

- You can use stored procedures to encapsulate many of your application's SQL statements into a single program that's stored on the DB2 server. You can also use stored procedures to access data that you can't access from a DB2 program, such as data stored in IMS or IDMS databases.

- Stored procedures execute in a separate DB2 address space called a *stored procedures address space* (SPAS). When the stored procedure issues an SQL statement, it passes it to DB2. Then, DB2 processes the statement and returns the results to the stored procedure.

Figure 5-1   Processing with and without stored procedures

How stored procedures are processed

Although figure 5-1 shows the general processing of a stored procedure, the actual processing is much more complicated. This processing is shown in more detail in figure 5-2.

To start, a thread must be established between the application that calls the stored procedure and DB2. A *thread* is a control structure used by DB2 to communicate with an application program. If the application is running on a local machine, the thread is established when the application issues its first SQL statement. If the application is running on a remote machine, it must issue a CONNECT statement to establish the thread. Note that a thread is established for any program that contains embedded SQL, not just for programs that call stored procedures.

To execute a stored procedure, the program must issue an SQL CALL statement that identifies the stored procedure and lists the parameters that will be passed to the stored procedure. Then, DB2 locates the stored procedure in its SYSIBM.SYSPROCEDURES catalog table. Later in this chapter, you'll learn how to add entries to this table for the stored procedures you create. For now, just realize that this table contains information about all of the stored procedures available to DB2. In particular, it contains the name of the load module for each stored procedure, which DB2 uses to execute the stored procedure. In addition, this table contains the definitions of the parameters that are used by each stored procedure. These definitions identify the type and size of data that can be stored by each parameter and whether the parameter will be used for input, output, or both input and output. DB2 uses these definitions to store the parameter values that are passed from the calling program before they are passed on to the stored procedure and to store the parameter values that are returned from the stored procedure before they're returned to the calling program.

If DB2 finds the stored procedure in the SYSPROCEDURES table, it schedules it for execution in the SPAS. Note that under DB2 version 4, a single address space, called the *DB2-established address space*, is available. Under DB2 version 5, however, you can use the MVS workload manager (WLM) to establish additional address spaces, called *WLM-established address spaces*.

When the stored procedure is ready to execute, DB2 passes control to it. It also passes the values of any parameters that were passed to it from the calling program. Then, the stored procedure can use those parameters in its processing. When it's done, the stored procedure passes the parameters back to DB2, and DB2, in turn, passes them back to the calling program.

When control returns to the calling program, it can then commit the work done by the stored procedure by issuing a COMMIT statement, or it can continue with the current unit of work. In most cases, if the program has additional processing to do after the stored procedure completes, it should commit the work to free up the locks acquired by the stored procedure. With DB2 version 5, you can also define a stored procedure so its work is committed automatically if it completes successfully.

DB2 stored procedure flow

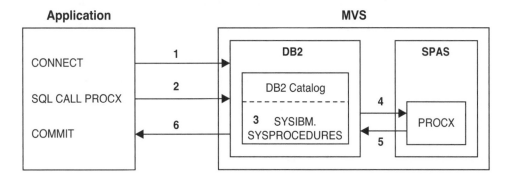

Description

1. When an application issues its first SQL statement, a *thread* is created to provide a connection to DB2.

2. When an application issues an SQL CALL statement to execute a stored procedure, the name of the stored procedure and the parameters coded on the CALL statement are passed to DB2.

3. When DB2 receives the CALL statement, it looks for a procedure with the specified name in the SYSIBM.SYSPROCEDURES catalog table. This table contains information about the stored procedure, including the name of its load module and a description of its parameters. The parameters are stored by DB2 in an intermediate area according to those descriptions.

4. DB2 schedules the stored procedure for execution in a stored procedures address space. Then, DB2 passes control to the stored procedure along with any parameters that were passed from the client application.

5. When it's done executing, the stored procedure passes its parameters back to DB2 where they're stored in an intermediate area, and then returns control to DB2.

6. DB2 in turn passes the parameters back to the client application and then returns control to the application. The application can then commit the work done by the stored procedure or continue with the current unit of work.

Notes

- Under DB2 version 4, stored procedures execute in a single address space, called the *DB2-established address space*. Under DB2 version 5, additional address spaces can be established by the workload manager (WLM), called *WLM-established address spaces*.

- By default, a stored procedure is included in the current unit of work of the calling program. With DB2 version 5, however, you can define the stored procedure so its work is committed automatically if it completes successfully (see figure 5-6).

Figure 5-2   How stored procedures are processed

How to develop stored procedures

In this topic, you'll learn how to develop stored procedures that are written in COBOL. As you'll see in a minute, the techniques you use to code a stored procedure are almost identical to the techniques you use to code a subprogram. However, you use some special code to prepare a stored procedure for execution. And you have to use the SQL INSERT statement to define the stored procedure to DB2 before you can use it.

Basic requirements for coding stored procedures

Figure 5-3 presents a simple stored procedure. This procedure issues a SELECT statement that retrieves data from a single row in the customer table. The row that's retrieved depends on the value of the CUSTNO column that's passed to the stored procedure as an input parameter.

To define the parameters that are used by a stored procedure, you code a field definition for each parameter in the Linkage Section of the program. Then, you include the field names on the USING clause of the PROCEDURE DIVISION statement just as you do for a subprogram. Note that these fields must be in the same order as the parameters on the CALL statement that executes the stored procedure.

Now, take a look at the SELECT statement in module 000 of this stored procedure. When this statement executes, it retrieves data from the row in the customer table with the customer number that was passed to the procedure as an input parameter. Then, it stores the values of several columns of that row in host variables just like any other SELECT statement. The difference is that these host variables are defined in the LINKAGE SECTION and are passed back to the calling program as output parameters when the stored procedure ends. That happens when the GOBACK statement in module 100 is executed.

The last statement in module 000 sets the value of an output parameter named OUT-CODE to the value of the SQLCODE field. This value is then passed back to the calling program, and the program can use it to be sure that the SELECT statement executed without error. It's common practice to include a parameter like this in a stored procedure. Note, however, that it doesn't have to contain the value of SQLCODE. Instead, you may want to use your own set of values to indicate various conditions. That's particularly true if a stored procedure issues two or more SQL statements. Then, OUT-CODE can represent the success or failure of the entire procedure, not just a single statement.

At this point, you may be wondering why you would use a stored procedure like the one shown in this figure instead of just coding the SELECT statement in the calling program. The answer is, you probably wouldn't. Instead, you're more likely to code stored procedures that perform a series of SQL statements or that access data that can't be retrieved by DB2. This procedure is presented here simply to illustrate the basic coding requirements for stored procedures.

The get-customer stored procedure

```
IDENTIFICATION DIVISION.
*
PROGRAM-ID.     GETCUST.
*
ENVIRONMENT DIVISION.
*
INPUT-OUTPUT SECTION.
*
FILE-CONTROL.
*
DATA DIVISION.
*
FILE SECTION.
*
WORKING-STORAGE SECTION.
*
    EXEC SQL
        INCLUDE SQLCA
    END-EXEC.
*
LINKAGE SECTION.
*
01  CUSTNO                  PIC X(6).
01  FNAME                   PIC X(20).
01  LNAME                   PIC X(30).
01  ADDR                    PIC X(30).
01  CITY                    PIC X(20).
01  STATE                   PIC X(2).
01  ZIPCODE                 PIC X(10).
01  OUT-CODE                PIC S9(9) USAGE BINARY.
*
PROCEDURE DIVISION USING CUSTNO, FNAME, LNAME, ADDR, CITY,
         STATE, ZIPCODE, OUT-CODE.
*
000-GET-CUSTOMER-ROW.
*
    EXEC SQL
        SELECT CUSTNO,      FNAME,          LNAME,
               ADDR,        CITY,           STATE,
               ZIPCODE
        INTO  :CUSTNO,     :FNAME,         :LNAME,
              :ADDR,       :CITY,          :STATE,
              :ZIPCODE
        FROM   MM01.CUSTOMER
            WHERE  CUSTNO = :CUSTNO
    END-EXEC.
*
    MOVE SQLCODE TO OUT-CODE.
*
100-RETURN.
*
    GOBACK.
*
```

Figure 5-3   The COBOL listing for the get-customer stored procedure

Rules for coding stored procedures

Figure 5-4 presents the languages you can use to code stored procedures. Notice that you can use only *LE/370 languages*, which means that you can't use VS COBOL II. Keep in mind, however, that although you can't use COBOL II to code stored procedures, you can still call a stored procedure from a COBOL II program.

LE/370, which stands for *Language Environment/370*, provides a common runtime environment for different languages. That means that only one runtime library is required regardless of the languages that are used and the number of stored procedures that are executing in the SPAS. The runtime services provided by this library include storage management (including the ability to make stored procedures resident in the SPAS), error handling, and debugging.

Along with LE/370, IBM offers an integrated tool set called *CoOperative Development Environment/370,* or *CODE/370*. This tool set consists of editing, compilation, and debugging tools. If you're responsible for developing stored procedures or other programs written in an LE/370 language, you'll want to find out about the CODE/370 tools.

Figure 5-4 also lists the SQL statements you can't code in a stored procedure. In particular, you can't use the CALL statement to call another stored procedure. In other words, you can't nest stored procedure calls. Keep in mind, however, that you can use the COBOL CALL statement to call a subprogram from a stored procedure.

The LE/370 languages for stored procedures

C

C++ (requires LE/370 Version 1 Release 4)

COBOL/370

FORTRAN

OO COBOL (requires LE/370 Version 1 Release 5)

PL/1

Assembler

FORTRAN

The SQL statements that can't be used in stored procedures

CALL	ROLLBACK
COMMIT	SET CONNECTION
CONNECT	SET CURRENT SQLID
RELEASE	

Description

- Stored procedures can only be developed using one of the LE/370 languages. *LE/370* establishes a common runtime environment for different programming languages. Its services include storage management, error handling, and debugging.
- Although you can't issue an SQL CALL statement in your stored procedure, you can call other programs or routines from a stored procedure by using statements of the programming language.
- If you try to use any of the unsupported SQL statements, SQLCODE will be set to -751.
- Future versions of DB2 may support the CALL, CONNECT, SET CONNECTION, and RELEASE SQL statements.

Figure 5-4   Rules for coding stored procedures

How to prepare a stored procedure for execution

The steps for preparing a stored procedure for execution are essentially the same as for any other program that accesses DB2: you precompile, compile, link-edit, and bind it. Figure 5-5 presents JCL you can use to do that. If you've used JCL to prepare other DB2 programs, the JCL in this figure should look familiar. However, you should notice a few items specific to stored procedures.

When you prepare a stored procedure, you should make it reentrant so that a single copy can be used for multiple calls to the stored procedure. By doing that, you reduce the amount of virtual storage that's required for the SPAS, and you eliminate the need to load a separate copy of the stored procedure for each program that calls it. To make a stored procedure reentrant, you specify the RENT option as input to the compile (COB) step of the DB2 procedure, and you specify the RENT and REUS options as input to the link-edit (LKED) step.

In addition to making a stored procedure reentrant, you may also want to make it resident. That way, it will remain in memory after the stored procedure finishes executing and won't need to be loaded the next time it's called. To make a stored procedure resident, you code the RES option as input to the COB step. This option works in conjunction with the STAYRESIDENT column of SYSIBM.SYSPROCEDURES, which you'll learn about in the next topic.

One final compiler option you'll need to specify is NODYNAM. This option is required when you prepare a stored procedure coded in COBOL.

To use the LE/370 runtime library, you must include it in the link-edit step. To do that, you code a DD statement for SYSLIB as shown in this figure. Here, Version 1 Release 5 of LE/370 is included. You must also link-edit the stored procedure into a load library that's available to the stored procedures address space. You may need to check with your DBA or systems programmer to find out what library to use.

For a stored procedure to communicate with DB2 and use its services, it must be link-edited with an attachment facility. Under DB2 version 4.1, the attachment facility is *CAF (Call Attachment Facility)*, and the module for that facility is DSNALI. You include this module for SYSIN in the link-edit step as shown in this figure. You can also use CAF under DB2 version 5. If the procedure will run in a WLM-established address space, however, you can use a newer facility called *RRSAF (Recoverable Resource Manager Services Attachment Facility)*. The module for that facility is DSNRLI.

To reduce the storage that's required below the 16 MB line, you'll also want to link-edit your stored procedures with the AMODE(31) and RMODE(ANY) options as shown in the figure. Note that the AMODE(31) option is required for WLM-established address spaces.

Sample JCL to prepare a stored procedure

```
//MM01S    JOB  (99999),CURTIS.GARVIN,CLASS=C,MSGCLASS=X,
//              REGION=4M,NOTIFY=&SYSUID
//JOBLIB   DD  DSN=DSN410.SDSNEXIT,DISP=SHR
//         DD  DSN=DSN410.SDSNLOAD,DISP=SHR
//*----------------------------------------------------------------*
//STEP010 EXEC DSNHCOB2,MEM=TEMPNAME,USER='MM01',                    1
//    PARM.PC='HOST(COB2),APOST,APOSTSQL,SOURCE,XREF',
//    PARM.COB=('OBJECT,APOST,MAP,XREF,NONUM,OFF,FLAG(I,E),TRUNC(BIN)', X
//             'RENT,RES,LIB,NODYNAM'),                              2
//    PARM.LKED='RENT,REUS,LIST,XREF,LET,AMODE=24'
//PC.DBRMLIB DD DSN=MM01.DB2.DBRMLIB(GETCUST),DISP=SHR
//PC.SYSLIB  DD DSN=MM01.DB2.DCLGENS,DISP=SHR
//PC.SYSIN   DD DSN=MM01.DB2.STORED.PROCS(GETCUST),DISP=SHR
//*----------------------------------------------------------------*
//COB.SYSLIB DD DSN=MM01.DB2.COPYLIB,DISP=SHR
//*----------------------------------------------------------------*
//LKED.SYSLIB  DD DSN=CEE.V1R5M0.SCEELKED,DISP=SHR                   3
//             DD DSN=DSN410.SDSNLOAD,DISP=SHR
//LKED.SYSLMOD DD DSN=MM01.DB2.LOADLIB(GETCUST),DISP=SHR             4
//LKED.SYSIN   DD *
    INCLUDE SYSLIB(DSNALI)                                           5
    MODE AMODE(31) RMODE(ANY)                                        6
//*----------------------------------------------------------------*
//STEP020  EXEC PGM=IKJEFT01,DYNAMNBR=20,COND=(4,LT)
//DBRMLIB    DD DSN=MM01.DB2.DBRMLIB,DISP=SHR
//SYSTSPRT   DD SYSOUT=*
//SYSPRINT   DD SYSOUT=*
//SYSUDUMP   DD SYSOUT=*
//SYSOUT     DD SYSOUT=*
//REPORT     DD SYSOUT=*
//SYSTSIN    DD *
 DSN SYSTEM(DSN)
 BIND PACKAGE(PYRLCOL) MEMBER(GETCUST)  -                           7
   LIBRARY('MM01.DB2.DBRMLIB') -
   ACT(REP) ISOLATION(CS) VALIDATE(BIND)
 END
//
```

Description

1. Use the DB2 procedure for preparing COBOL programs.
2. Make your stored procedures reentrant, resident, and not loaded dynamically.
3. Include the LE/370 library in the link-edit step.
4. Save the load module for the stored procedure in a load library that's available to the stored procedure's address space.
5. Include a language interface module for an attachment facility in the link-edit step so the stored procedure can communicate with DB2. For DB2-established address spaces in DB2 version 4 or 5, include the DSNALI module to use the *Call Attachment Facility* (*CAF*). For WLM-established address spaces in DB2 version 5, include DSNALI to use CAF, or include DSNRLI to use the *Recoverable Resource Manager Services Attachment Facility* (*RRSAF*).
6. Code the AMODE(31) and RMODE(ANY) options on the link-edit step to reduce the storage required below 16 MB. If the procedure will use RRSAF, AMODE(31) is required.
7. Bind the package for the stored procedure.

Figure 5-5   JCL for the preparation of a stored procedure

How to define a stored procedure to DB2

Most DB2 database objects are defined using data definition language statements. To create a new DB2 table, for example, you use the CREATE TABLE statement. Then, DB2 automatically stores related data in the appropriate DB2 catalog tables. However, there is no DDL statement for defining stored procedures to DB2. (That will change with DB2 version 6, which includes the CREATE PROCEDURE statement.) Instead, you have to use the SQL INSERT statement as shown in figure 5-6. This statement adds a row that contains information about the stored procedure directly to the catalog table for stored procedures, named SYSIBM.SYSPROCEDURES.

To use the INSERT statement, you simply code the names of the columns you want to add information to on the INSERT clause, and you specify the values for those columns on the VALUES clause. The columns that are defined in the SYSPROCEDURES table are listed in the figure along with a brief description of each one.

Even if you're not responsible for defining the stored procedures you create to DB2, you'll want to understand how the values that are coded in the SYSPROCEDURES table affect the operation of the stored procedure. For example, if a stored procedure is used frequently, you may want it to remain in memory after it finishes executing. To do that, you set the value of the STAYRESIDENT column to Y. And if you want the work done by a stored procedure to be committed automatically if the procedure completes successfully, you set the value of the COMMIT_ON_RETURN column to Y. Note that this column only became available with DB2 version 5.

In the PARMLIST column, you include a definition of each parameter that will be used by the stored procedure. The definition includes the type of data that the parameter will hold, such as character or integer; the size of the parameter if it's required by the data type; and whether the parameter will be used as input, output, or both input and output. When you define these parameters, you'll want to be sure that they're consistent with the parameter definitions in the stored procedure.

You can also use the DB2I load utility to define a stored procedure, but we won't show you how to do that here. If you have access to DB2I, though, you'll want to find out how to use it to define stored procedures if you're responsible for doing that. By the way, if you call a stored procedure that hasn't been defined to DB2, you'll get an SQLCODE of –471.

An SQL INSERT statement that registers a stored procedure in a DB2 version 4.1 catalog

```
INSERT INTO SYSIBM.SYSPROCEDURES
      (PROCEDURE,  AUTHID,    LUNAME,   LOADMOD,      LINKAGE,
       COLLID,     LANGUAGE, ASUTIME, STAYRESIDENT, IBMREQD,
       RUNOPTS,    PARMLIST)
VALUES('GETCUST', ' ',       ' ',      'GETCUST',    ' ',
       'GETCUST', 'COBOL',   0,        'Y',          'N',
       ' ',               'CUSTNO CHAR(6) IN, FNAME CHAR(20) OUT,
      LNAME CHAR(30) OUT, ADDR CHAR(30) OUT, CITY CHAR(20) OUT,
      STATE CHAR(2) OUT, ZIPCODE CHAR(10) OUT, OUT-CODE INTEGER OUT);
```

SYSIBM.SYSPROCEDURES columns

Column name	Description
PROCEDURE	The name of the stored procedure.
AUTHID	The authid a user must have to run an application that calls the stored procedure. If blank, any user can run an application that calls the procedure.
LUNAME	The LUNAME a system must have to call the stored procedure. If blank, any system can call the procedure.
LOADMOD	The name of the load module for the stored procedure.
LINKAGE	The linkage convention that's used to pass parameters to the stored procedure. If blank, SIMPLE linkage is used. Code N to use SIMPLE WITH NULLS linkage.
COLLID	The collection ID of the package for this stored procedure.
LANGUAGE	The language used to code the stored procedure. Valid values are ASSEMBLE, PLI, COBOL, or C.
ASUTIME	The number of service units permitted before an execution of the stored procedure is canceled. A value of zero indicates no limit.
STAYRESIDENT	Indicates if the module is to remain in memory after the stored procedure finishes execution. If blank, the load module is removed from memory when the stored procedure ends. Code Y if you want the load module to remain resident.
IBMREQD	Indicates if the stored procedure was supplied by IBM (Y) or not (N).
RUNOPTS	The LE/370 runtime options to be used by the stored procedure.
PARMLIST	The parameters expected by the stored procedure.
RESULT_SETS	The maximum number of result sets that can be returned by the procedure.
WLM_ENV	The name of the WLM environment used to run the procedure. A blank indicates that the procedure is to run in the DB2-established address space.
PGM_TYPE	Indicates if stored procedure is a main program (M) or a subprogram (S).
EXTERNAL_SECURITY	Indicates if a special RACF environment is needed to control access to non-SQL resources. Code N (not required) or Y (required).
COMMIT_ON_RETURN	Indicates if work is committed upon successful completion of the stored procedure. Code Y to commit or N to continue the unit of work.

Note

- The RESULT_SETS, WLM_ENV, PGM_TYPE, EXTERNAL_SECURITY, and COMMIT_ON_RETURN columns are new to DB2 version 5.

Figure 5-6   How to define a stored procedure to DB2

How to code a COBOL program that calls a stored procedure

Now that you know how to develop a stored procedure, you'll learn how to call that procedure from a COBOL program. First, I'll show you how to use the features for working with stored procedures that are available with DB2 version 4. As you'll see, these features are limited because they don't let you work with stored procedures that return a result set with more than one row. Then, I'll present the new features of version 5 that let you work with multi-row result sets.

How to code the SQL CALL statement

Figure 5-7 presents the syntax of the SQL CALL statement. As you can see, this statement specifies the name of the stored procedure to be called, along with the parameters to be passed to the stored procedure. The sample statement in this figure, for example, calls the procedure named GETCUST that was presented in figure 5-3. If you look back to the code for that procedure, you'll see that it accepts the same eight parameters that are coded on this CALL statement.

When you code the name of a stored procedure on a CALL statement, you'll usually code it as shown in the example in this figure. Then, qualifiers are added to this name to identify the location of the stored procedure. However, you can also code these qualifiers along with the name of the stored procedure as described in the figure.

Each parameter that's included on a CALL statement can be coded as either the name of a host variable, a constant value, or the word NULL. In most cases, you'll use host variables. But you may want to use a constant when you know that the value of a parameter won't change. And you may want to use the NULL keyword when a parameter isn't required. You'll learn more about working with null values in a minute.

You can also code the USING DESCRIPTOR clause to specify the name of an SQLDA that contains the host variables to be used as parameters. However, you're not likely to use an SQLDA for this purpose.

When you define a host variable for a parameter, you'll want to be sure that its definition is consistent with the definition that's stored in the SYSPROCEDURES table. That's because when a stored procedure is called, its parameters are stored by DB2 according to the definition in that table. So if the definitions aren't consistent, errors can occur. In particular, an error will occur if a parameter contains a string value that's longer than its SYSPROCEDURES definition and the extra characters don't contain blanks. That conforms to the SQL ISO/ANSI rules for assigning values to variables. In contrast, when the parameter value is assigned to the variable defined in the stored procedure, the DB2 rules are used. With the DB2 rules, extra characters are truncated regardless of whether they contain blanks. If you define the parameters consistently, though, you won't have to worry about what rules are used.

The syntax of the SQL CALL statement

```
EXEC SQL
    CALL {procedure-name | :host-var}
        ({host-var | constant | NULL}
       [,{host-var | constant | NULL}]…)
         [USING DESCRIPTOR :sqlda-name]
END-EXEC.
```

Explanation

procedure-name	The name of the stored procedure to be executed. The name can be qualified or unqualified.
host-var	The name of a host variable that contains the name of the stored procedure to be executed or that defines a parameter to be passed to the stored procedure. If used for a parameter, the data type of the variable must be compatible with the data type of the corresponding parameter in the procedure. Can also include an indicator variable to be used with the parameter (see figure 5-8).
constant	A constant value to be used for the parameter. The data type of the constant must be compatible with the corresponding parameter of the procedure and that parameter must be defined as IN.
NULL	Indicates that a null value is to be used for the parameter. The corresponding parameter of the procedure must be defined as IN and the SIMPLE WITH NULLS linkage convention must be used.
sqlda-name	The name of an SQLDA that contains descriptions of the host variables to be used as parameters. If an SQLDA is specified and the stored procedure has no parameters, the SQLDA is not used.

An SQL CALL statement that calls a stored procedure

```
EXEC SQL
    CALL GETCUST(:CUSTNO, :FNAME, :LNAME,    :ADDR,
                 :CITY,    :STATE, :ZIPCODE, :OUT-CODE)
END-EXEC.
```

How to code qualified and unqualified procedure names

- A procedure name can be qualified to indicate its location and, like a table name, can consist of up to three qualifiers separated by periods.

- The first qualifier specifies the location name of the DBMS where the procedure is stored. If omitted, an implicit qualifier that identifies the location of the current server is added.

- The second qualifier depends on the application server. If the server is DB2 for OS/390 or MVS/ESA, for example, the qualifier is SYSPROC.

- The third qualifier is the name of the stored procedure.

Figure 5-7   How to code the SQL CALL statement

How to use nulls with stored procedure parameters

The technique you use to pass a null value to or from a stored procedure depends on the linkage convention that was specified when the procedure was defined to DB2. If you look back at figure 5-6, you'll see that you specify the linkage convention in the LINKAGE column of the SYSPROCEDURES table. If you leave this column blank, SIMPLE linkage is used. If you set this column to "N", SIMPLE WITH NULLS linkage is used.

Figure 5-8 presents the techniques you can use to work with null values when you use the SIMPLE or SIMPLE WITH NULLS linkage convention. In either case, you use an *indicator variable* to let DB2 know if a parameter contains a null value. The exception is if you code the NULL keyword for a parameter. In that case, no indicator variable is required. Note that you can use this keyword only to pass a null value to a stored procedure that's defined with SIMPLE WITH NULLS linkage, and you can use it only for input parameters.

In case you're not familiar with indicator variables, you define them as halfword binary fields (PIC S9(4) COMP). Then, you assign a value to each indicator variable depending on whether the related field contains a null value. If it does, you need to assign a negative value (usually –1) to the indicator variable for the field. If it doesn't, you can assign any non-negative value (usually zero) to the indicator variable. If you need more information on using indicator variables, see chapter 8 in *Part 1* of this series.

The first CALL statement in this figure calls a stored procedure named GETNOTES that's defined with SIMPLE linkage. The first two parameters of this procedure are defined as input, and the second two are defined as output. Notice that the first output parameter, NOTES, uses an indicator variable. That way, when this CALL statement is executed, only the indicator variable is sent to the stored procedure. This technique is particularly useful for working with output parameters that require a large amount of storage. By passing an indicator variable rather than the entire storage area to the stored procedure, network traffic is reduced and application efficiency is increased. Note that this technique can be used with stored procedures defined with either SIMPLE or SIMPLE WITH NULLS linkage.

The second CALL statement in this figure calls the same stored procedure, but this time it's defined with SIMPLE WITH NULLS linkage. Because of that, each parameter must have an associated indicator variable that indicates if it contains a null value. Then, the stored procedure can use those indicator variables as shown in the coding example in this figure. Notice that the USING clause of the PROCEDURE DIVISION statement includes a field that receives information about the indicator variables. This field is defined as a group item in the Linkage Section along with the other parameter definitions. As you can see, this group item includes an indicator variable for each of the parameters. Then, the Procedure Division code shows how you might use two of these indicator variables. Notice that when a value is moved to an output parameter like OUT-CODE, zero is moved to the related indicator variable so this value is passed back to the calling procedure.

A CALL statement that uses an indicator variable for an output parameter

```
EXEC SQL
    CALL GETNOTES (:CUSTNO, :STATE, :NOTES INDICATOR :IND-NOTE, :OUTCODE)
END-EXEC.
```

A CALL statement that uses indicator variables for all parameters

```
EXEC SQL
    CALL GETNOTES(:CUSTNO :IND-CUSTNO, :STATE :IND-STATE,
                  :NOTES :IND-NOTES,   :OUTCODE :IND-OUTCODE)
END-EXEC.
```

Stored procedure code that uses an indicator variable array

```
    LINKAGE SECTION.
*
    01  CUSTNO          PIC X(6).
    01  STATE           PIC X(2).
    01  NOTES           PIC X(250).
    01  OUT-CODE        PIC S9(9) USAGE BINARY.
    01  IND-PARM.
        05  IND-CUSTNO  PIC S9(4) USAGE BINARY.
        05  IND-STATE   PIC S9(4) USAGE BINARY.
        05  IND-NOTES   PIC S9(4) USAGE BINARY.
        05  IND-OUT-CODE PIC S9(4) USAGE BINARY.
*
    PROCEDURE DIVISION USING CUSTNO, STATE, NOTES, OUT-CODE, IND-PARM.
*
    000-GET-CUSTOMER-ROW.
*
    IF IND-CUSTNO < 0
        MOVE 9999 TO OUT-CODE
        MOVE 0    TO IND-OUT-CODE
    ELSE
        EXEC SQL
            SELECT CUSTNO, STATE, NOTES
                INTO :CUSTNO, :STATE, :NOTES
                FROM MM01.CUSTOMER
                WHERE CUSTNO = :CUSTNO
        END-EXEC
        MOVE SQLCODE TO OUT-CODE
        MOVE 0       TO IND-OUT-CODE.
```

Description

- When you use the SIMPLE linkage convention, an indicator variable can have a negative value (indicating a null) only if the parameter is defined as OUT.
- When you use the SIMPLE WITH NULLS linkage convention, you must use an indicator variable or the NULL keyword for each parameter. Then, the stored procedure must define an array of indicator variables to be used with the parameters.

Figure 5-8   How to use nulls with stored procedure parameters

How to receive and process known result sets

If you issue a SELECT statement that retrieves multiple rows from a stored procedure written using DB2 version 4, you'll get an error. That's because version 4 doesn't support the use of multi-row result sets with stored procedures. However, DB2 version 5 does. In addition, this version lets a stored procedure retrieve two or more result sets.

Figure 5-9 presents code you can use to retrieve and process multi-row result sets returned from a stored procedure when you know the number and contents of the result sets. Although you can also retrieve and process result sets when you don't know how many will be returned or what their contents will be, the techniques for doing that are beyond the scope of this book. For more information, see *DB2 for OS/390 V5 Application Programming and SQL Guide*.

To work with multi-row result sets, you need to perform several steps. First, you need to define *locator variables* that will be used to identify the result sets. To do that, you use the special form of the USAGE IS clause shown in the first coding example in this figure. In this example, two result sets will be returned by the stored procedure, so two locator variables are defined. The first result set will return information about the customers in the specified state. The second result set will return information about the customers in the specified zip code.

After you declare the result set locators, you issue the CALL statement that causes the stored procedure to be executed. Then, when control returns to the calling program, you check the SQLCODE to determine if result sets were returned. If so, the SQLCODE will have a value of +466. This code is shown in the second coding example in this figure.

If result sets were returned, you must then link the result set locators to the result sets. To do that, you use the ASSOCIATE LOCATORS statement as shown in the third coding example in this figure. Then, you use the ALLO-CATE CURSOR statement to allocate a cursor to each result set. Finally, you use the FETCH statement to retrieve rows from each result set using the cursors you just allocated as illustrated in the fourth coding example in this figure.

In addition to the code shown for the calling program in this figure, you also have to define the result sets in the stored procedure so that they can be processed once the procedure ends. To do that, you include the WITH RETURN clause on the DECLARE CURSOR statement for each result set that will be processed by the calling program. This clause tells DB2 that the result set will be returned to the calling program.

Code that declares locator variables for use with the result sets

```
WORKING-STORAGE SECTION.
*
01  CUSTLOC1    USAGE IS SQL TYPE IS RESULT-SET-LOCATOR VARYING.
*
01  CUSTLOC2    USAGE IS SQL TYPE IS RESULT-SET-LOCATOR VARYING.
```

Code that calls a procedure and processes the return codes

```
120-PROCESS-CUSTOMER-INQUIRY.
*
    EXEC SQL
        CALL CUSTDATA(:CUSTNO, :STATE, :ZIPCODE, :OUTCODE)
    END-EXEC.
    IF SQLCODE = +466
        IF OUT-CODE = 0
            PERFORM 130-SET-UP-CURSORS
            MOVE 'N' TO END-OF-CUSTOMERS-SW
            PERFORM 140-GET-RESULTS-SETS
                UNTIL END-OF-CUSTOMERS
        ELSE
            DISPLAY 'STORED PROCEDURE CUSTDATA ENDED UNSUCCESSFULLY'
    ELSE
        DISPLAY 'NO RESULT SETS RETURNED FROM STORED PROCEDURE CUSTDATA'.
```

Code that links result set locators and allocates cursors

```
130-SET-UP-CURSORS.
*
    EXEC SQL
        ASSOCIATE LOCATORS(:CUSTLOC1, :CUSTLOC2) WITH PROCEDURE CUSTDATA
    END-EXEC.
*
    EXEC SQL
        ALLOCATE CUSTCUR1 CURSOR FOR RESULT SET :CUSTLOC1
    END-EXEC.
    EXEC SQL
        ALLOCATE CUSTCUR2 CURSOR FOR RESULT SET :CUSTLOC2
    END-EXEC.
```

Code that fetches rows from the result sets

```
140-GET-RESULT-SETS.
*
    EXEC SQL
        FETCH CUSTCUR1 INTO :CUSTNO, :STATE
    END-EXEC.
.
.
    EXEC SQL
        FETCH CUSTCUR2 INTO :CUSTNO, :ZIPCODE
    END-EXEC.
.
.
```

Note

- To return a result set from a stored procedure, the DECLARE CURSOR statement for the result set must include the WITH RETURN clause.

Figure 5-9   How to receive and process known result sets

A COBOL program that calls a stored procedure

To give you a complete picture of how you work with stored procedures from a COBOL program, this topic presents a complete program. This program calls the GETCUST procedure you saw in figure 5-3 to retrieve a record from the customer table. If you read *Part 1* of this DB2 series, you'll note that this program is a modification of the customer inquiry program that was presented in chapter 1 of that book. So you may want to compare these two programs to see what changes were made to use a stored procedure.

The interactive screen

Figure 5-10 presents the opening screen for the call-customer program. In the first screen, you can see that the program prompts the user for a customer number. To end the program, the customer can enter 999999.

The second screen in this figure shows the display after the user entered two customer numbers. First, the user entered customer number 400001. The data for that customer was then retrieved using the GETCUST stored procedure and displayed on the screen. Next, the user entered customer number 400017. This time, an error occurred when the stored procedure tried to retrieve the data for the customer, so an error message was displayed. As indicated by that message, no row was found for the customer. Finally, the user entered 999999 to end the program.

The opening screen for the call-customer program

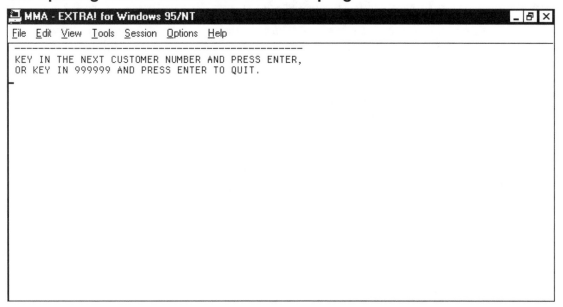

The interactive screen after the user has entered two customer numbers

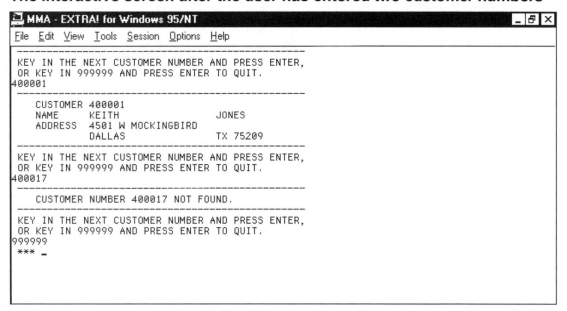

Figure 5-10   The interactive screen for the call-customer program

The structure chart

Figure 5-11 presents the structure chart for the call-customer program. As you can tell from this structure chart, the design of this program is simple. First, module 000 performs module 100 until the user signals the end of the program. Each time module 100 is performed, it performs module 110 to accept a customer number from the user and module 120 to call the stored procedure to get the customer row. If the customer row is found, module 100 calls module 130 to display the customer information. Otherwise, module 100 calls module 140 to display an error message.

If you compare this structure chart with the structure chart for the customer inquiry program in *Part 1* of this series, you'll see that they're identical. That makes sense because the two programs perform the same functions. The coding that's required to perform those functions, however, is different.

The structure chart

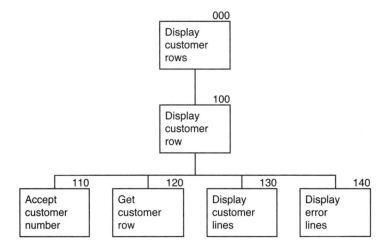

Description

- Module 000 in this structure chart performs module 100 once for each customer number that the user enters until the user ends the program by entering 999999 as the customer number.

- Module 100 performs module 110 to accept a customer number from the user. If the user doesn't end the program, module 100 performs module 120. Module 120 calls the GETCUST stored procedure, which retrieves the row for the specified customer.

- If the row for the customer is found, the customer information is returned to the call-customer program. Then, module 100 performs module 130 to display that information.

- If the customer row isn't found or if the call fails, module 100 performs module 140 to display an error message.

Figure 5-11   The structure chart for the call-customer program

The COBOL listing

Figure 5-12 presents the COBOL code for this program. Again, because this program is a modification of the customer inquiry program presented in *Part 1* of this series, you may want to compare these two programs to identify the differences. If you do, you'll see that the call-customer program uses an additional switch, CALL-FAILED-SW, that indicates when the call to the stored procedure was unsuccessful. This switch is used to determine the error message that's displayed.

This program also includes two new work fields. The field named OUT-CODE will be used to store the value of the SQLCODE that's returned by the stored procedure. And the field named EDITED-SQLCODE will be used to format the SQLCODE for display.

Even if you're not familiar with the customer inquiry program presented in *Part 1* of this series, you shouldn't have any trouble understanding the other fields in the Working-Storage Section of this program. The end-of-inquiries switch indicates when the program should end, and the customer-found switch indicates whether or not the requested row was retrieved from the customer table. The two INCLUDE statements include the DCLGEN output for the customer table and the definition of the SQL communication area.

The call-customer program   **Page 1**

```
IDENTIFICATION DIVISION.
*
PROGRAM-ID.     CALLCUST.
*
ENVIRONMENT DIVISION.
*
INPUT-OUTPUT SECTION.
*
FILE-CONTROL.
*
DATA DIVISION.
*
FILE SECTION.
*
WORKING-STORAGE SECTION.
*
01   SWITCHES.
*
     05   END-OF-INQUIRIES-SW      PIC X    VALUE 'N'.
          88   END-OF-INQUIRIES             VALUE 'Y'.
     05   CUSTOMER-FOUND-SW        PIC X.
          88   CUSTOMER-FOUND               VALUE 'Y'.
     05   CALL-FAILED-SW           PIC X.
          88   CALL-FAILED                  VALUE 'Y'.
*
01   WORK-AREA.
*
     05   OUT-CODE                 PIC S9(9) USAGE COMP.
     05   EDITED-SQLCODE           PIC -(4).
*
     EXEC SQL
         INCLUDE CUSTOMER
     END-EXEC.
*
     EXEC SQL
         INCLUDE SQLCA
     END-EXEC.
*
PROCEDURE DIVISION.
*
000-DISPLAY-CUSTOMER-ROWS.
*
     PERFORM 100-DISPLAY-CUSTOMER-ROW
         UNTIL END-OF-INQUIRIES.
     STOP RUN.
*
```

Figure 5-12   The COBOL listing for the call-customer program (part 1 of 2)

In part 2 of figure 5-12, you can see the code that's used to call the GETCUST stored procedure in module 120. This module is performed after module 110 accepts a customer number from the user. The CALL statement in this module passes the customer number that was entered by the user to the stored procedure as an input parameter. Then, the stored procedure issues a SELECT statement that retrieves the row for that customer and passes the information back to the calling program in the output parameters included on the CALL statement. It also returns the SQLCODE returned by the SELECT statement in the OUT-CODE parameter. That way, the calling program can determine whether or not the SELECT statement was successful.

After the CALL statement is executed, this program checks the SQLCODE to determine if the statement executed successfully. If the value of this field is anything other than zero, it indicates that an error occurred. Then, the call-failed switch is turned on and the customer-found switch is turned off. Note that these two switches are initialized in module 100 before it performs module 120.

If the CALL statement executes successfully, the program checks the value of the OUT-CODE field. If the value of this field is anything other than zero, it means that the customer row wasn't retrieved, and the customer-found switch is turned off.

If the customer row is retrieved, module 130 is performed to display the customer information. Otherwise, module 140 is performed to display an error message. This module starts by checking the call-failed switch to determine if the CALL statement in the calling program failed or if the SELECT statement in the stored procedure failed. If the CALL statement failed, the error code and error message (SQLERRMC) are displayed. If the SELECT statement failed, the OUT-CODE field is checked to determine if the customer row wasn't found (+100) or if another error occurred. Then, an appropriate error message is displayed.

The call-customer program

```
100-DISPLAY-CUSTOMER-ROW.
*
     PERFORM 110-ACCEPT-CUSTOMER-NUMBER.
     IF NOT END-OF-INQUIRIES
         MOVE 'Y' TO CUSTOMER-FOUND-SW
         MOVE 'N' TO CALL-FAILED-SW
         PERFORM 120-GET-CUSTOMER-ROW
         IF CUSTOMER-FOUND
             PERFORM 130-DISPLAY-CUSTOMER-LINES
         ELSE
             PERFORM 140-DISPLAY-ERROR-LINES.
*
 110-ACCEPT-CUSTOMER-NUMBER.
*
     DISPLAY '--------------------------------------------------'.
     DISPLAY 'KEY IN THE NEXT CUSTOMER NUMBER AND PRESS ENTER,'.
     DISPLAY 'OR KEY IN 999999 AND PRESS ENTER TO QUIT.'.
     ACCEPT CUSTNO.
     IF CUSTNO = '999999'
         MOVE 'Y' TO END-OF-INQUIRIES-SW.
*
 120-GET-CUSTOMER-ROW.
*
     EXEC SQL
         CALL GETCUST(:CUSTNO, :FNAME,    :LNAME,    :ADDR,
                      :CITY,    :STATE,    :ZIPCODE, :OUT-CODE)
     END-EXEC.
     IF SQLCODE NOT = 0
         MOVE 'Y' TO CALL-FAILED-SW
         MOVE 'N' TO CUSTOMER-FOUND-SW
     ELSE
         IF OUT-CODE NOT = 0
             MOVE 'N' TO CUSTOMER-FOUND-SW.
*
 130-DISPLAY-CUSTOMER-LINES.
*
     DISPLAY '--------------------------------------------------'.
     DISPLAY '    CUSTOMER ' CUSTNO.
     DISPLAY '    NAME     ' FNAME ' ' LNAME.
     DISPLAY '    ADDRESS  ' ADDR.
     DISPLAY '             ' CITY ' ' STATE ' ' ZIPCODE.
*
 140-DISPLAY-ERROR-LINES.
*
     DISPLAY '--------------------------------------------------'.
     IF CALL-FAILED
         MOVE SQLCODE TO EDITED-SQLCODE
         DISPLAY ' SQL CALL FAILED - SQLCODE = ' EDITED-SQLCODE
         DISPLAY ' SQLERRMC = ' SQLERRMC
     ELSE
         IF OUT-CODE = +100
             DISPLAY ' CUSTOMER NUMBER ' CUSTNO ' NOT FOUND'
         ELSE
             DISPLAY ' GETCUST FAILED DUE TO RC = ' OUT-CODE.
```

Figure 5-12   The COBOL listing for the call-customer program (part 2 of 2)

Perspective

Although stored procedures can reduce network traffic as illustrated in figure 5-1, they also require additional processing as illustrated in figure 5-2. Because of this additional processing, they're not as efficient as you might expect. In fact, while experimenting with stored procedures in DB2 version 4.1, a member of the Melbourne DB2 Users Group found that they took about 950% more processing time than the same code in a COBOL subprogram linked into the load module.

Even if you assume that this was an extraordinary case, and if you assume that DB2 version 5 processes stored procedures more efficiently than version 4.1, it's likely that using stored procedures is still less efficient than using linked subprograms. Because of that, your shop may have restrictions on the use of stored procedures. But even if it doesn't, you may want to restrict your own use of stored procedures to those situations where you know that their benefits will outweigh the reduction in processing efficiency. You may want to use them, for example, when you know that they will reduce network traffic dramatically or when you need to access data that you can't access from a DB2 program. In any case, you'll want to test each stored procedure you create thoroughly to be sure that the additional processing time it requires is acceptable.

Section 3

DB2 in CICS programs

Most interactive applications on S/390 systems run under CICS. Because new program development work is typically for interactive environments, the chances are good that you'll face the challenge of developing CICS/DB2 programs. As the chapters in this section will illustrate, once you understand the concepts and techniques for developing CICS programs, accessing DB2 data from those programs is easy.

Chapter 6 introduces CICS concepts and terminology for DB2 programmers. Even if you're an experienced CICS programmer, you should read this chapter. That's because it describes how using DB2 services from a CICS program changes the program development process. And it explains how the connection between CICS and DB2 is defined.

Chapters 7 and 8 illustrate design and programming techniques for developing CICS programs that process DB2 data. Chapter 7 covers basics you have to know to access DB2 data from any CICS program. And chapter 8 presents more advanced programming techniques you can use to develop CICS programs that process multi-row result tables.

Although this section will show you how to access DB2 data through CICS programs, it won't present all you need to know to develop CICS programs. For a complete CICS course, you can turn to Doug Lowe's *CICS for the COBOL Programmer*, a two-book set. You'll find ordering information at the end of this book.

6

CICS concepts and terminology for DB2 programmers

CICS (Customer Information Control System) is an IBM software product that lets computer systems support many terminal users who run a range of interactive application programs. CICS loads those programs, coordinates their execution, manages data transmissions between the programs and terminals, controls the programs' access to stored data (not just DB2 tables, but also IMS databases and VSAM data sets), and maintains the integrity of stored data. So, to develop application programs that access DB2 data under CICS, you have to understand not just DB2, but also CICS.

This chapter begins by describing how CICS works. If you're already an experienced CICS programmer, you can skim over most of this material. Then, this chapter describes how you prepare a CICS/DB2 program for execution and how you define a CICS/DB2 program to CICS. You should read this material even if you're experienced with CICS since it relates specifically to the CICS/DB2 interface.

How CICS works

Like DB2, CICS operates as an MVS subsystem. Simply put, the function of the CICS subsystem is to manage transactions. To do that, it provides a variety of services for processing application programs.

How CICS manages transactions and tasks

A *transaction* is a predefined unit of work, such as an inquiry or order-processing application, that can be invoked by a terminal user. A CICS transaction can be invoked in two ways. First, the user can enter a four-character code called a *transaction identifier* (or just *trans-id*) at a terminal. Then, CICS uses the trans-id to select the application to run. To run an inquiry program, for example, the user might enter a trans-id like INQ1. Then, CICS would retrieve the main load module for the application associated with that trans-id, load it into storage, and execute it.

The second way a user can invoke a transaction is to make a selection from a CICS menu program. Then, the menu program provides CICS with the trans-id for the selected program so it can retrieve, load, and execute the appropriate module. Menus make program access easier because the trans-ids are transparent to the user.

An interactive program that operates under CICS actually executes within CICS, and the storage it uses is CICS storage. This is illustrated in figure 6-1. Here, the CICS subsystem is running programs for four users. Because CICS provides the storage these programs occupy and services their requests, it insulates them from the operating system. In fact, as far as the operating system is concerned, CICS is the only program running in the CICS subsystem.

You should also notice in figure 6-1 that two of the CICS terminal users (1 and 4) are running the same transaction. When the user invokes a transaction, CICS starts a *task* for the user. The difference between a transaction and a task is that while several users may invoke the same transaction, CICS creates a separate task for each.

CICS provides distinct data areas for each task, even if they're associated with the same program. However, it loads only one copy of the program's executable code into storage, regardless of how many tasks are using the program. If CICS loaded the same program code into storage for each task, it would waste valuable virtual storage. Fortunately, the facility CICS uses so that only one copy of a program is loaded into storage is transparent to you as an application programmer.

If your shop is running in an S/390 parallel sysplex environment, you should be aware of a new systems management tool called *CICSPlex System Manager/ESA*, or *CICSPlex SM*. This tool can manage several CICS subsystems within the sysplex as if they were one. The workload can then be balanced dynamically across those subsystems.

CICS transactions and tasks

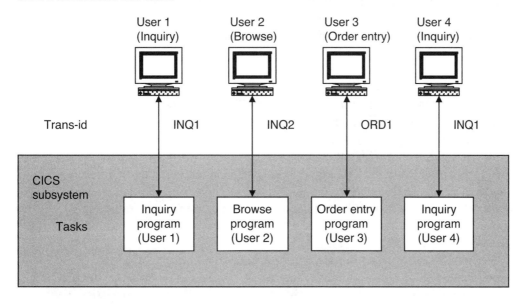

Concepts

- A *transaction* is a predefined unit of work that a terminal user can invoke by entering a *transaction identifier*, or *trans-id*.

- Each trans-id is associated with a program that CICS will load into storage and execute when the transaction is invoked.

- When a user invokes a transaction, CICS starts a *task* for that user. Although several users may invoke the same transaction, CICS creates a separate task for each.

- CICS keeps track of the programs that are already in storage so only one copy of a program is loaded. That copy can be used by one or more tasks at the same time.

Figure 6-1   CICS transactions and task initiation

How application programs use CICS services

To support the application program related to a task, CICS provides a variety of functional modules. Some of those modules are shown in figure 6-2. The terminal control and BMS modules, for example, control how CICS interacts with the display stations. Some of the other CICS modules that support application programs are task control, file control, transient data control, temporary storage control, journal control, program control, and interval control.

When DB2 is used with CICS, special DB2 interface modules are loaded into storage along with the CICS modules, and they're executed under the control of CICS. These interface modules make up the *CICS/DB2 attachment facility* shown in this figure. Although there are some systems programming considerations for controlling the CICS/DB2 interface, application programmers don't need to worry about them.

To access DB2 data, a program that runs under CICS issues SQL statements. Then, the attachment facility establishes a connection with DB2 called a *thread*. Once the connection is made, the attachment facility uses it to pass the SQL statement, and any subsequent SQL statements issued by the program, to DB2. Then, DB2 performs the requested function and passes the result back to the program through the attachment facility.

How DB2 uses Basic Mapping Support

It's possible for a CICS program to interact directly with the terminal control module. However, it's more likely that you'll use *Basic Mapping Support*, or *BMS*, as an interface between your program and terminal control. BMS provides a simplified way of formatting terminal displays. So, to receive data from or send data to a terminal, an application program requests BMS services.

When you use BMS, you can exercise a high degree of control over the format of data displayed on and retrieved from a terminal. To do that, you code a special kind of assembler language program called a *mapset*. When you assemble the mapset, the assembler creates both a physical map and a symbolic map. A *physical map* is a module BMS uses to determine the screen locations and attributes of data sent to and received from the terminal. A *symbolic map*, in COBOL, is a COPY library member that defines the format of data sent to or received from the terminal.

When a program requests that a map be sent to a terminal, BMS takes data from the symbolic map, formats (*maps*) it according to the physical map, and sends it to the terminal. Likewise, when a program requests that data be retrieved from a terminal, BMS uses the physical map to map the data from the screen into the symbolic map. In the next two chapters, you'll see the BMS mapsets and the related symbolic maps for two sample programs.

CICS services

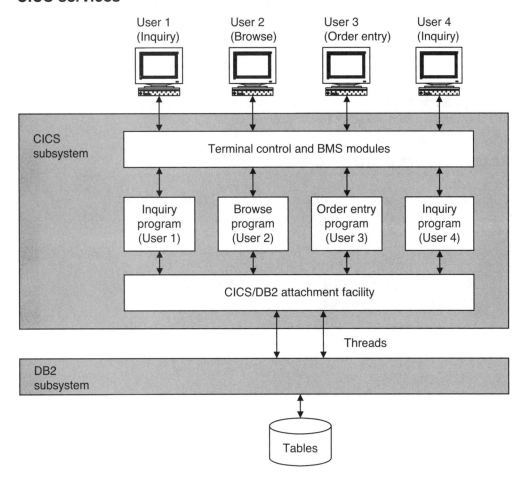

Concepts

- CICS provides functional modules that support application programs, including task control, terminal control, file control, transient data control, temporary storage control, journal control, program control, interval control, and *Basic Mapping Support* (*BMS*).

- The terminal control and BMS modules control interactions with display stations. These modules work together to provide an interface with the operating system's telecommunications access method, which provides support for the terminal devices.

- When DB2 is used with CICS, DB2 interface modules are loaded into storage along with the CICS modules. These modules make up the *CICS/DB2 attachment facility*.

- To access DB2 data, a CICS program issues SQL statements. Then, CICS sends a request to the attachment facility to establish a connection to DB2 called a *thread*.

- Once a connection is established with DB2, the attachment facility uses it to pass the SQL statement to DB2 and the results of the SQL statement back to the program.

Figure 6-2   How application programs use CICS services

How to prepare a CICS/DB2 program for execution

The process of preparing a CICS/DB2 program for execution is similar to the process you use to prepare any other DB2 program. After I present the basic steps for preparing a CICS/DB2 program, then, I'll summarize the special processing that's required for CICS.

The steps for preparing a CICS/DB2 program

Figure 6-3 presents the steps that are required to prepare a CICS/DB2 program for execution. As you can see, you still have to precompile, compile, link-edit, and bind the program. In addition, before you compile a program, you have to translate it using the *CICS command-level translator* (often called just the *CICS translator*). The CICS translator converts CICS commands to a form that's meaningful to the COBOL compiler. You'll see an example of translated code in the next chapter.

Program preparation for a CICS/DB2 COBOL program

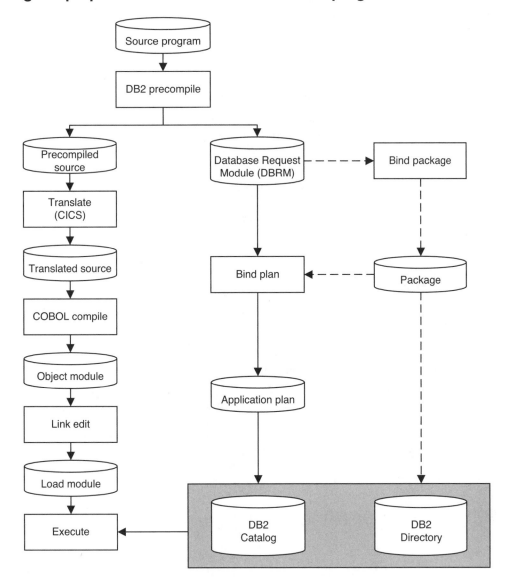

Notes

- Before you compile a CICS program, you must translate the CICS commands to a form that the compiler can interpret as described in figure 6-4.
- The module that provides the interface to the CICS/DB2 attachment facility must be included in the link-edit step.
- The bind options you use to specify the lock duration may be different from those you use with batch programs. See figure 6-5 for details.

Figure 6-3   The steps for preparing a CICS/DB2 program

How to translate a program

The easiest way to translate a program is to use DB2I. Figure 6-4 presents the DB2 Program Preparation panel that you can use to translate a CICS program. To do that, you simply set the Perform function? option for the CICS Command Translation function (function 9) to "Y". Then, the translation is performed automatically along with the other selected functions.

Note that before you translate a CICS/DB2 program, you need to precompile it. If you don't, the CICS translator will return a series of diagnostic messages because it doesn't recognize SQL statements. In contrast, the DB2 precompiler recognizes CICS commands and ignores them.

You can also translate a CICS/DB2 program using JCL. Since most shops have site-specific JCL for doing that, though, I won't present the JCL here. If you need to use your shop's JCL, you should check with your colleagues or DBA.

How to link-edit a program

The link-edit step of the CICS/DB2 program development process has a special requirement. To issue SQL statements from a CICS program, you must link-edit the program so it includes an interface to the CICS/DB2 attachment facility. The module that provides that interface is DSNCLI. If your shop uses a cataloged procedure for CICS/DB2 program development, it almost certainly contains the INCLUDE for this module. If you're using DB2I, this module is included automatically.

The DB2 Program Preparation panel

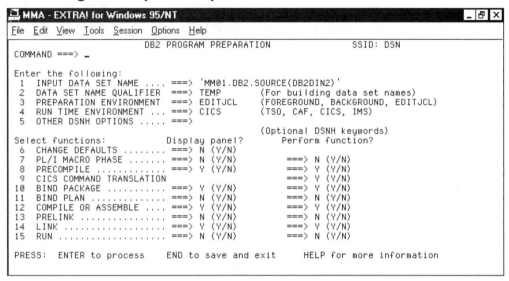

```
 MMA - EXTRA! for Windows 95/NT                                    _ 8 X
 File  Edit  View  Tools  Session  Options  Help

                    DB2 PROGRAM PREPARATION              SSID: DSN
 COMMAND ===> _

 Enter the following:
  1   INPUT DATA SET NAME .... ===> 'MM01.DB2.SOURCE(DB2DIN2)'
  2   DATA SET NAME QUALIFIER  ===> TEMP      (For building data set names)
  3   PREPARATION ENVIRONMENT  ===> EDITJCL   (FOREGROUND, BACKGROUND, EDITJCL)
  4   RUN TIME ENVIRONMENT ... ===> CICS      (TSO, CAF, CICS, IMS)
  5   OTHER DSNH OPTIONS ..... ===>
                                              (Optional DSNH keywords)
 Select functions:          Display panel?       Perform function?
  6   CHANGE DEFAULTS ........ ===> N (Y/N)
  7   PL/I MACRO PHASE ....... ===> N (Y/N)           ===> N (Y/N)
  8   PRECOMPILE ............. ===> Y (Y/N)           ===> Y (Y/N)
  9   CICS COMMAND TRANSLATION                        ===> Y (Y/N)
 10   BIND PACKAGE ........... ===> Y (Y/N)           ===> Y (Y/N)
 11   BIND PLAN .............. ===> N (Y/N)           ===> N (Y/N)
 12   COMPILE OR ASSEMBLE .... ===> Y (Y/N)           ===> Y (Y/N)
 13   PRELINK ................ ===> N (Y/N)           ===> N (Y/N)
 14   LINK ................... ===> Y (Y/N)           ===> Y (Y/N)
 15   RUN .................... ===> N (Y/N)           ===> N (Y/N)

 PRESS:   ENTER to process    END to save and exit    HELP for more information
```

Description

- To translate a program using DB2I, set the Perform function? option of the CICS Command Translation function to Y. Then, DB2I will translate the program automatically when the Precompile function is complete.

- You can also translate a program using JCL. For JCL that's specific to your site, check with your colleagues or your DBA.

Figure 6-4   How to translate a CICS/DB2 program

How to bind a program

It's common for a CICS program to be defined as a set of small, related programs. When that's the case, you'll want to bind each program into its own package and then group those packages into a collection. Then, you can bind all the packages in the collection into a plan.

When you bind the packages and plans, you'll want to be sure you specify the appropriate values for the RELEASE, ACQUIRE, and ISOLATION parameters of the bind statements. These values affect the duration of the locks that are used and may be different from the values you use for batch programs. The values you can specify for these parameters are described in figure 6-5. To change these values from DB2I, you use the Resource Release Time, Resource Acquisition Time, and Isolation Level options in the Defaults For Bind Plan and Defaults For Bind Package panels. The Defaults For Bind Plan panel is shown at the top of this figure.

For an interactive program, you'll typically set the ACQUIRE parameter to USE and the RELEASE parameter to COMMIT. Then, a table, partition, or table space lock is acquired when it's needed and released when a commit occurs. This maximizes concurrency with minimal effect on program performance. In addition, you'll want to set the ISOLATION parameter to CS (Cursor Stability). When this isolation level is used, read-only locks are released as soon as another page is accessed. This maximizes concurrency at the same time that it ensures data integrity.

The Defaults For Bind Plan panel

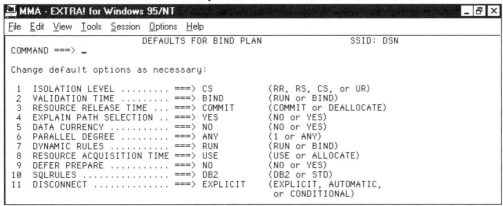

Bind parameters that affect table, partition, and table space locks

Parameter	Locks are acquired or released	Recommendation
ACQUIRE(ALLOCATE)	When the plan is allocated	Use for batch processing
ACQUIRE(USE)	As they are needed	Use for online processing
RELEASE(DEALLOCATE)	When the plan is terminated	Use for batch processing
RELEASE(COMMIT)	When a commit occurs	Use for online processing

Bind parameters that affect page and row locks

Isolation level	Description
RR (Repeatable Read)	Ensures that your program doesn't read a row that another program has changed until the other program releases the row and that other programs don't change a row that your program has read until your program commits the change or the program ends.
RS (Read Stability)	Ensures that your program doesn't read a row that another program has changed until the other program releases the row. Also ensures that other programs don't change qualifying rows (those that satisfy the search condition specified in your program) until your program commits the changes or ends. However, other programs can insert new rows or update non-qualifying rows.
CS (Cursor Stability)	Ensures that your program doesn't read a row that another program has changed until the other program releases the row, but doesn't prevent other programs from changing rows that your program reads before your program commits changes or ends. This option should be used for most packages and plans.
UR (Uncommitted Read)	Lets other programs change any row your application reads during the unit of work, and lets your program read any row that another program has changed even if the change hasn't been committed. This option can be used only with read-only operations and should be used for working with tables that are changed infrequently.

Figure 6-5   Bind parameters that affect lock duration

How to define a CICS/DB2 program to CICS

Even after you've prepared a CICS/DB2 program for execution, you still can't run it under CICS. For a program to access DB2 data from CICS, the connection between its CICS transaction and DB2 must be defined. That's done by making an entry in the CICS *Resource Control Table* (*RCT*).

The RCT contains the name of each CICS transaction that requests DB2 services along with the name of the DB2 application plan that's used with it, the threads that will be used to connect DB2 with CICS, and the DB2 authorization for the transaction. Although the systems programmer is usually responsible for updating the RCT, it's worth knowing what information related to threads and DB2 authorizations can be specified.

How DB2 uses threads

CICS programs request DB2 services through threads. The RCT specifies the total number of threads that will be available to connect CICS and DB2 and the type of thread that's used. Figure 6-6 lists the types of threads CICS can use.

An *entry thread* is dedicated to a specific transaction and can improve the overall performance of heavily used transactions. An entry thread can be either protected or unprotected. An *unprotected entry thread* is usually released when the program it was allocated to ends. The only exception is if another transaction bound with the same application plan is waiting to access DB2 data. Then, CICS uses the thread it allocated to the first transaction. In contrast, a *protected entry thread* is maintained for up to a minute after the program it was allocated to ends. If another transaction bound with the same application plan is initiated within that time, CICS assigns that thread to it. Otherwise, it releases the thread.

Transactions that aren't used heavily are usually defined so they use pool threads. A *pool thread* is one that's shared among transactions that may have different application plans. It's possible for many infrequently used transactions to operate effectively sharing a small number of pool threads. If CICS assigned entry threads to them instead, system resources would be wasted.

How DB2 authorizes CICS transactions

For a CICS program to access DB2 data, CICS must pass an appropriate authorization to DB2. DB2 uses that value to verify that the program has authority to perform the function it requests with SQL statements. The systems programmer is typically responsible for defining the functions a program can perform.

In the simplest case, the RCT entry for a transaction specifies an explicit authorization ID. But it can also specify that the CICS operator id, the id of the terminal where the transaction was initiated, the trans-id, or a USERID authorized by RACF (IBM's Resource Access Control Facility) be used for authorization.

Types of threads

Type	Description
Entry thread	A thread that's dedicated to a specific transaction.
Unprotected entry thread	A thread that's released when the program it was allocated to ends, unless another transaction bound with the same application plan is waiting to access DB2 data.
Protected entry thread	A thread that's maintained for up to a minute after the program it was allocated to ends. If another transaction bound with the same application plan is initiated within that time, CICS assigns the thread to it.
Pool thread	A thread that's shared among transactions that may have different application plans.

Concepts

- The *CICS Resource Control Table* (*RCT*) contains the names of all CICS transactions that request DB2 services and the application plan that's used with that transaction. The RCT also specifies the type of thread that will be used to connect the transaction to DB2 and the authorization for the transaction to access DB2 data.

- The number of threads that are available to connect CICS and DB2 is a limited resource. The default maximum number of threads is 12, but a larger number can be specified in the RCT.

- *Pool threads* are typically shared by transactions that are used infrequently. The performance of heavily used transactions can be improved by using *entry threads*.

- The authorization for a CICS transaction to use DB2 data can be specified as an authorization ID, an operator ID, the ID of the terminal where the transaction was initiated, the trans-id, or a USERID authorized by *RACF*, IBM's *Resource Access Control Facility*.

Figure 6-6   How to define a CICS/DB2 program to CICS

Perspective

Although this chapter presents the basic concepts for developing CICS programs that access DB2 data, there's more you need to know before you start developing your own programs. In particular, you need to know how to design your programs using a technique called pseudo-conversational program design; you need to know how to use CICS commands to request the functions your programs need; and you need to know how to code and prepare BMS mapsets. That's what you'll learn in the next chapter.

Keep in mind, though, that to work at a professional level as a CICS programmer, you need to know more than what's presented in this book. To learn more about using CICS in COBOL programs, we recommend our books *CICS for the COBOL Programmer, Part 1* and *Part 2* and *The CICS Programmer's Desk Reference*.

7

Basic CICS/DB2 programming techniques

In this chapter, you'll learn the programming techniques for developing CICS programs that access DB2 data. To illustrate those techniques, this chapter presents a CICS version of the customer inquiry program that was presented in *Part 1* of this series. But first, it presents some basic concepts and techniques related to CICS program development.

Program development concepts and techniques

Most CICS programs have to be written so that they don't tie up valuable virtual storage resources. Although a single CICS system can support hundreds of terminals, it can't operate efficiently if many programs remain in storage while they wait for user input. As a result, most CICS programs are written using pseudo-conversational programming.

Much of the difficulty in developing a CICS program is in implementing pseudo-conversational design. Before you can do that, though, you need to understand how pseudo-conversational programming works. In addition, you need to know how to code CICS programs, and you need to understand how the CICS translator modifies your source code. That's what you'll learn in the following topics.

How pseudo-conversational programming works

Figure 7-1 presents a flowchart that illustrates how *pseudo-conversational programming* works. As you can see, the program starts by sending its first map to the screen. Then, the program ends. That way, while the user is entering input, the program isn't taking up valuable virtual storage.

The program restarts when the user indicates that the entry is complete, usually by pressing an attention key. Then, if the user didn't indicate that the program should end, the program retrieves the input data, processes it, sends its output data, and ends. This continues until the user ends the program.

If you compare this processing with the processing required for a conversational program, you'll see why most CICS installations require that programs be written in pseudo-conversational style. When a *conversational program* starts, it sends its initial map just like a pseudo-conversational program. Instead of ending, though, the program remains in storage while it waits for input. Then, it retrieves the input data from the terminal, processes it, sends its output, and waits again. As you can imagine, much of the time the program is running it's waiting for input and wasting valuable CICS resources.

Pseudo-conversational programming can be confusing for CICS novices because the program must be coded so it can figure out what it should do each time it's restarted. This requires a different design and logic than conversational programs. If you're new to CICS, though, don't worry. The two programming examples in this chapter and the next chapter will help you understand how to implement pseudo-conversational programming.

Pseudo-conversational processing

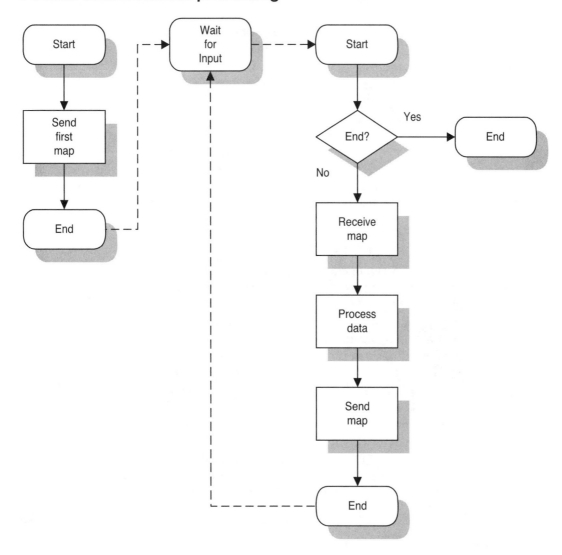

Description

- With *pseudo-conversational programming*, a program ends after it sends data to a terminal. Then, CICS restarts it when the user completes an entry.

- When you develop a pseudo-conversational program, the program must be able to figure out what to do each time it's restarted. To do that, it uses information stored in the program's *communication area*.

Figure 7-1   How pseudo-conversational programming works

How to code CICS programs

When you code a CICS program, you request CICS services by issuing CICS commands. To do that, you use an EXEC-level coding interface just like you do for DB2 SQL statements. For example, the command shown at the bottom of figure 7-2 directs CICS to receive data from the terminal formatted according to the specifications in a BMS map named DINMAP1 contained in a mapset named DINSET1. And, it directs CICS to return the terminal data to the program's Working-Storage group item named DINMAP1I.

This figure also lists some of the most commonly used CICS commands. As you can see, these commands let you request services from CICS modules. For example, the BMS-related commands RECEIVE MAP and SEND MAP let you accept and display formatted data. Although I won't present the syntax of the CICS commands in this book, I will use several of them in the program examples in this chapter and the next chapter. And, as I describe the source code for those programs, I'll describe how the CICS commands operate.

In addition to CICS commands, a CICS program can issue the full range of SQL DML statements to process data owned by the local DB2 subsystem. It can also retrieve data owned by remote DB2 subsystems, but it can't change that data. So, you can't code a CICS program that issues SQL statements like INSERT or UPDATE for data in remote tables.

Because online transaction processing programs need to be small and quick in their execution, it makes sense to minimize the number of different SQL statements you use, to code the simplest statements you can, and to minimize the number of different tables a program processes. That leads to more efficient program execution. You may also be able to improve performance by grouping SQL statements as closely as you can and deferring them to near the end of the execution of a program. Doing that can reduce the amount of time a program controls a thread, since the CICS/DB2 attachment facility doesn't create a thread for a transaction until the program makes its first DB2 request.

Just as with programs that process DB2 data in batch or under TSO, CICS/DB2 programs should commit their work often. Doing so reduces the amount of data DB2 has to maintain during a unit of work, and it makes the data available to other programs sooner. In addition, under CICS, committing a unit of work causes threads to be released and made available to other users.

Your programs won't use SQL COMMIT statements to commit work, though. And they won't use SQL ROLLBACK statements to reverse uncommitted table changes. Because CICS serves as the transaction manager for programs it controls, it coordinates recovery operations for the different subsystems it uses. So instead of COMMIT and ROLLBACK, you request recovery services through CICS with its SYNCPOINT command.

In CICS, a commit point is called a *synchronization point*, or *sync point*. A CICS sync point occurs when a transaction ends or when the program explicitly issues a SYNCPOINT command. The SYNCPOINT command with the ROLLBACK option achieves the same result as an SQL ROLLBACK statement: It causes CICS to direct DB2 to reverse uncommitted table changes.

CICS commands for doing BMS-controlled screen interactions	
RECEIVE MAP	Retrieves input data from the terminal.
SEND MAP	Sends information to the terminal for display.
CICS commands for passing control from one program to another	
LINK	Invokes a program at a lower level.
RETURN	Returns control to CICS.
XCTL	Transfers control to another program.
CICS commands for using temporary storage	
DELETEQ TS	Deletes a temporary storage queue.
READQ TS	Retrieves a record from a temporary storage queue.
WRITEQ TS	Adds a new record to a temporary storage queue, or updates an existing record.
CICS commands for processing VSAM data sets	
DELETE	Deletes a record from a VSAM file.
ENDBR	Terminates a browse operation.
READ	Retrieves a record from a VSAM keyed file.
READNEXT	Retrieves the next record during a browse operation.
READPREV	Retrieves the previous record during a browse operation.
RESETBR	Restarts a browse operation at a new position in the data set.
REWRITE	Updates a record in a file.
STARTBR	Initiates a browse operation, and identifies the location in the data set where the browse begins.
WRITE	Adds a record to a file.
CICS commands for handling exceptions	
HANDLE ABEND	Tells your program what to do if the program abends.
HANDLE AID	Tells your program what to do when the user presses an attention key.
HANDLE CONDITION	Tells your program what to do when an error is encountered.
CICS command for maintaining data integrity	
SYNCPOINT	Tells CICS that all updates made to protected resources to that point are final.

A CICS command that receives data from the terminal screen

```
EXEC CICS
    RECEIVE MAP('DINMAP1')
            MAPSET('DINSET1')
            INTO(DINMAP1I)
END-EXEC.
```

Description

- To request CICS services from a program, you use CICS commands. To do that, you use an EXEC-level coding interface just as you do for DB2 SQL statements.

- You can also issue SQL DML statements to process data on a local server, and you can issue DML statements to retrieve data from a remote server.

Figure 7-2   How to code CICS programs

How the CICS translator modifies your source program

Figure 7-3 illustrates how the CICS translator translates a program's CICS commands. As you can see, the CICS translator converts a CICS command into a series of COBOL MOVE statements followed by a CALL statement. The MOVE statements assign values to the program fields that are the arguments of the CALL statement's USING clause. The CALL statement activates the CICS command-level interface to invoke the required CICS services. The translator also includes the source code for the original command as comments in the translated version of the program. These comments can help you read the translated program.

Besides converting all CICS commands to MOVE and CALL statements, the translator inserts other code in your program's Working-Storage and Linkage Sections. Most of this code isn't directly relevant to you. However, one segment of code that the translator inserts contains definitions for a storage area called the *Execute Interface Block*, or *EIB*. CICS returns several pieces of useful information to programs through the EIB fields. You'll see examples of how to use EIB data in the sample programs in this chapter and the next chapter.

Source code for a CICS command

```
EXEC CICS
    RECEIVE MAP('INQMAP1')
            MAPSET('INQSET1')
            INTO(INQMAP1I)
END-EXEC.
```

Translated source code

```
*
*EXEC CICS
*    RECEIVE MAP('INQMAP1')
*            MAPSET('INQSET1')
*            INTO(INQMAP1I)
*END-EXEC.
    MOVE '..}............00061   ' TO DFHEIV0
    MOVE 'INQMAP1' TO DFHC0070
    MOVE 'INQSET1' TO DFHC0071
    CALL 'DFHEI1' USING DFHEIV0  DFHC0070 INQMAP1I DFHDUMMY
    DFHC0071.
```

Description

- The CICS translator converts each CICS command in a program into a series of COBOL MOVE statements followed by a CALL statement. The MOVE statements assign values to fields used by the CALL statement, and the CALL statement invokes the required CICS services.

- The CICS translator also inserts code into the Linkage Section of the program that contains definitions for the *Execute Interface Block* (*EIB*). You can use the fields in the EIB to get information about the current task.

Figure 7-3   How the CICS translator modifies your source program

A CICS/DB2 COBOL program

Now that you understand the basic logic and coding required for a CICS program, you're ready to see how an actual CICS/DB2 program works. In this section, then, I'll present a simple inquiry program that accepts a customer number from a terminal user, retrieves the corresponding row from the customer table, and displays the contents of the row. If you have *Part 1* of this series, you might want to compare this program with the inquiry program in chapter 1 of that book that runs under TSO. If you do, you'll see that although the two programs perform the same function, the requirements of CICS make the programming more complicated.

The interactive screen

Figure 7-4 presents two screen displays from a session of the CICS version of the customer inquiry program. This program uses screens that are more complicated than those the TSO version uses. These screen designs follow the rules of IBM's *Common User Access*, or *CUA*. CUA provides sets of standards that insure that programs interact with users in consistent ways. For more information about CUA, you can refer to the IBM manual *Common User Access Basic Interface Design Guide*.

When this program was started, CICS responded by retrieving the program's load module and executing it. During its first execution, the program issued a CICS command to display the first screen in this figure. This screen shows the name of the map from the BMS mapset, "DINMAP1," the name of the program, "Customer Inquiry," and directions for the user, "Type a customer number. Then press Enter." From this screen, the user can enter a customer number into the field that appears on the screen as a series of underscores following the label "Customer number."

Notice at the bottom of the screen that the user can press either of two PF (Program Function) keys to end the program: Exit (F3) or Cancel (F12). In other programs, these two keys may do different things. A more complicated program may also offer other PF key options as you'll see in the sample program in the next chapter.

The second part of this figure shows the screen after the user entered a customer number and pressed the Enter key. As you can see, the program responded by displaying information for the specified customer. At this point, the user can enter a different customer number to retrieve and display the data for that customer or press PF3 or PF12 to end the program.

Part 1

The inquiry program displays its initial screen and then ends.

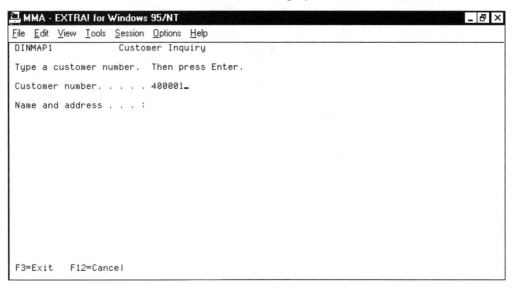

Part 2

The user enters a customer number and presses the Enter key. The program is restarted, and the data for the customer is retrieved and displayed.

Figure 7-4   The interactive screen for the CICS/DB2 inquiry program

The BMS mapset

CICS's Basic Mapping Support (BMS) manages formatted displays like the ones in figure 7-4. As you may remember from the last chapter, BMS is a CICS module that works with the terminal control module to support terminal interactions. BMS uses the specifications contained in an assembler language mapset to prepare and display formatted data on a terminal screen.

Figure 7-5 presents the BMS mapset for the displays in figure 7-4. Although this mapset specifies a number of options, I won't discuss all of them here. For a full treatment of BMS, you can refer to another of our books, *CICS for the COBOL Programmer, Part 1.*

The first thing you should notice in this mapset are the lines near the beginning that specify values for the macro called DFHMSD. They specify that the symbolic map that BMS generates from this mapset should be in COBOL (LANG=COBOL), that the symbolic map should include fields for both input and output (MODE=INOUT), that the mapset should work with a standard 3270-type display station (TERM=3270-2), and that it should support color (MAPPATTS=COLOR).

The next macro, DFHMDI, defines the map (that is, a screen display) within the mapset. It specifies that the size of the screen display is 24 lines of 80 characters each (SIZE=(24,80)). In this example, the mapset consists of just one map, so it contains just one DFHMDI macro. More complicated mapsets can include multiple maps.

The other macros in the mapset are DFHMDF macros. They define the fields on the display screen. For example, the DFHMDF macro highlighted in this figure defines the literal value that appears in the upper left corner of the screen. As you can see, several parameters are used to define this field.

The POS parameter determines the location of the field. Actually, POS determines the location of the attribute byte for the field. An *attribute byte* is a single-character value that takes up a screen position and specifies the characteristics of a field. In this example, since the attribute byte is in column 1, the field will appear starting at column 2.

The next parameter, LENGTH, specifies the maximum number of characters the field can contain. In this case, the field can hold up to seven characters. If you combine the information the POS and LENGTH options provide, you can figure out that this field will appear on the screen in columns 2 through 8 of line 1.

The ATTRB and COLOR parameters specify the attributes for the screen field. The NORM option of the ATTRB parameter means the field should be displayed in normal (rather than bright) intensity; PROT means that the field should be protected so the user can't change its contents. The COLOR parameter specifies that the field should be displayed in blue, the CUA standard for a screen title.

The code for the BMS mapset   Page 1

```
          PRINT NOGEN
DINSET1   DFHMSD TYPE=&SYSPARM,                                       X
                 LANG=COBOL,                                          X
                 MODE=INOUT,                                          X
                 TERM=3270-2,                                         X
                 CTRL=FREEKB,                                         X
                 MAPATTS=COLOR,                                       X
                 STORAGE=AUTO,                                        X
                 TIOAPFX=YES
***********************************************************************
DINMAP1   DFHMDI SIZE=(24,80),                                       X
                 LINE=1,                                              X
                 COLUMN=1
***********************************************************************
          DFHMDF POS=(1,1),                                          X
                 LENGTH=7,                                           X
                 ATTRB=(NORM,PROT),                                  X
                 COLOR=BLUE,                                         X
                 INITIAL='DINMAP1'
          DFHMDF POS=(1,20),                                         X
                 LENGTH=16,                                          X
                 ATTRB=(NORM,PROT),                                 X
                 COLOR=BLUE,                                         X
                 INITIAL='Customer Inquiry'
***********************************************************************
          DFHMDF POS=(3,1),                                          X
                 LENGTH=42,                                          X
                 ATTRB=(NORM,PROT),                                 X
                 COLOR=GREEN,                                        X
                 INITIAL='Type a customer number.  Then press Enter.'
          DFHMDF POS=(5,1),                                          X
                 LENGTH=24,                                          X
                 ATTRB=(NORM,PROT),                                 X
                 COLOR=GREEN,                                        X
                 INITIAL='Customer number. . . . .'
CUSTNO    DFHMDF POS=(5,26),                                         X
                 LENGTH=6,                                           X
                 ATTRB=(NORM,UNPROT,IC),                            X
                 COLOR=TURQUOISE,                                    X
                 INITIAL='_____'
          DFHMDF POS=(5,33),                                         X
                 LENGTH=1,                                           X
                 ATTRB=ASKIP
***********************************************************************
          DFHMDF POS=(7,1),                                          X
                 LENGTH=24,                                          X
                 ATTRB=(NORM,PROT),                                 X
                 COLOR=GREEN,                                        X
                 INITIAL='Name and address . . . :'
LNAME     DFHMDF POS=(7,26),                                         X
                 LENGTH=30,                                          X
                 COLOR=TURQUOISE,                                    X
                 ATTRB=(NORM,PROT)
```

Figure 7-5   The BMS mapset for the CICS/DB2 inquiry program (part 1 of 2)

Finally, the INITIAL parameter supplies the starting value for the field: DINMAP1. Because this is a protected field, the user can't change this value. That's appropriate for a screen's name. If you count the number of characters in the INITIAL value, you'll see that the number is the same as the value for LENGTH: 7.

Most of the fields the mapset in this figure defines have the same combination of options in the ATTRB parameter: normal display intensity and protected from change. However, the fields named CUSTNO and MESSAGE specify different options for this parameter. Also, many of the fields have different colors. All these fields follow the CUA standards.

CUSTNO is the field where the user will enter the number of the customer to be displayed. It's defined with the UNPROT attribute, which means the user can change its value. A third option, IC (Initial Cursor), is also included on the ATTRB parameter. This option specifies that the cursor should be positioned at this field when the screen is displayed. Its color, turquoise, is also different.

The MESSAGE field is where error messages will be displayed. It uses the BRT attribute instead of NORM. This insures that any error message values that appear in this field display in high intensity characters rather than normal intensity characters. Also, its color is yellow.

To indicate the end of a mapset, you code another DFHMSD macro as shown in this figure. This time, though, you code only the TYPE=FINAL parameter. Then, you code an END macro.

The code for the BMS mapset   Page 2

```
FNAME     DFHMDF POS=(8,26),                                       X
                 LENGTH=20,                                        X
                 COLOR=TURQUOISE,                                  X
                 ATTRB=(NORM,PROT)
ADDR      DFHMDF POS=(9,26),                                       X
                 LENGTH=30,                                        X
                 COLOR=TURQUOISE,                                  X
                 ATTRB=(NORM,PROT)
CITY      DFHMDF POS=(10,26),                                      X
                 LENGTH=20,                                        X
                 COLOR=TURQUOISE,                                  X
                 ATTRB=(NORM,PROT)
STATE     DFHMDF POS=(10,47),                                      X
                 LENGTH=2,                                         X
                 COLOR=TURQUOISE,                                  X
                 ATTRB=(NORM,PROT)
ZIPCODE   DFHMDF POS=(10,50),                                      X
                 LENGTH=10,                                        X
                 COLOR=TURQUOISE,                                  X
                 ATTRB=(NORM,PROT)
*********************************************************************
MESSAGE   DFHMDF POS=(23,1),                                       X
                 LENGTH=79,                                        X
                 ATTRB=(BRT,PROT),                                 X
                 COLOR=YELLOW
          DFHMDF POS=(24,1),                                       X
                 LENGTH=20,                                        X
                 ATTRB=(NORM,PROT),                                X
                 COLOR=BLUE,                                       X
                 INITIAL='F3=Exit    F12=Cancel'
DUMMY     DFHMDF POS=(24,79),                                      X
                 LENGTH=1,                                         X
                 ATTRB=(DRK,PROT,FSET),                            X
                 INITIAL=' '
*********************************************************************
          DFHMSD TYPE=FINAL
          END
```

Description

- A *mapset* is an assembler language program that defines the format of a BMS map. It consists of three types of BMS macros: DFHMSD, DFHMDI, and DFHMDF.

- DFHMSD macros mark the beginning and end of the mapset. The parameters on the beginning macro supply information such as the language to be used for the mapset; whether the maps will be used for input, output, or both; and the extended attributes to be supported. You code a single parameter on the ending macro: TYPE=FINAL.

- A DFHMDI macro marks the beginning of each map in the mapset. Its parameters supply information about the map, such as its size and starting location on the screen.

- Each field in the mapset is defined by one or more DFHMDF macros. The parameters on these macros supply information about the field, such as its size and position; its display attributes; its initial value; and how input and output data should be formatted.

Figure 7-5   The BMS mapset for the CICS/DB2 inquiry program (part 2 of 2)

The symbolic map

Figure 7-6 presents the symbolic map the assembler produced from the mapset in figure 7-5. You'll recall from chapter 6 that the symbolic map is stored as a COBOL copy book. Then, the COBOL compiler includes that copy book when it processes the translated source program.

Notice that the symbolic map uses the same data area for both terminal input and output. The input fields are subordinate to the 01-level item DINMAP1I (page 1 of the output), and the output fields are subordinate to the 01-level item DINMAP1O (page 2 of the output), which is a redefinition of DINMAP1I. The symbolic map defines separate fields for input and output so that you can specify different PICTURE clauses for them. You may want to do that if you're working with numeric data.

For each screen field that's named in the mapset, the symbolic map contains a data field, a length field, an attribute field, and a field that indicates if the value of the field has changed. The names for these fields are created by adding a one-character suffix to the label that was coded on the DFHMDF macro in the mapset. So the name of the input field for the field labeled CUSTNO is CUSTNOI, the name of the length field is CUSTNOL, the name of the attribute field is CUSTNOA, and the name of the field that indicates a change is CUSTNOF. Since the fields that define headings, labels, and instructions aren't named in the mapset, they don't appear in the symbolic map. Typically, you'll name only those fields in a mapset that your program needs to access.

The code for the symbolic map   **Page 1**

```
01  DINMAP1I.
    02   FILLER    PIC X(12).
    02   CUSTNOL   PIC S9(4) COMP.
    02   CUSTNOF   PIC X.
    02   FILLER REDEFINES CUSTNOF.
     03  CUSTNOA   PIC X.
    02   CUSTNOI   PIC X(0006).
    02   LNAMEL    PIC S9(4) COMP.
    02   LNAMEF    PIC X.
    02   FILLER REDEFINES LNAMEF.
     03  LNAMEA    PIC X.
    02   FNAMEI    PIC X(0020).
    02   ADDRL     PIC S9(4) COMP.
    02   ADDRF     PIC X.
    02   FILLER REDEFINES ADDRF.
     03  ADDRA     PIC X.
    02   ADDRI     PIC X(0030).
    02   CITYL     PIC S9(4) COMP.
    02   CITYF     PIC X.
    02   FILLER REDEFINES CITYF.
     03  CITYA     PIC X.
    02   CITYI     PIC X(0020).
    02   STATEL    PIC S9(4) COMP.
    02   STATEF    PIC X.
    02   FILLER REDEFINES STATEF.
     03  STATEA    PIC X.
    02   STATEI    PIC X(0002).
    02   ZIPCODEL  PIC S9(4) COMP.
    02   ZIPCODEF  PIC X.
    02   FILLER REDEFINES ZIPCODEF.
     03  ZIPCODEA  PIC X.
    02   ZIPCODEI  PIC X(0010).
    02   MESSAGEL  PIC S9(4) COMP.
    02   MESSAGEF  PIC X.
    02   FILLER REDEFINES MESSAGEF.
     03  MESSAGEA  PIC X.
    02   MESSAGEI  PIC X(0079).
    02   DUMMYL    PIC S9(4) COMP.
    02   DUMMYF    PIC X.
    02   FILLER REDEFINES DUMMYF.
     03  DUMMYA    PIC X.
    02   DUMMYI    PIC X(0001).
```

Figure 7-6   The symbolic map for the CICS/DB2 inquiry program (part 1 of 2)

In the redefined area for the output fields, you'll notice that only the data fields are named (CUSTNOO, LNAMEO, etc.). The length, attribute, and change indicator fields are coded as FILLER. To change the value of any of these fields for an output operation, then, you have to refer to the fields in the input area.

For the sample program in this chapter, I'll use the symbolic map produced by BMS without any changes. However, notice that the data names in the symbolic map aren't as meaningful as they could be. Also, the format of the code in the BMS-created symbolic map makes it harder to read and use than it needs to be. In the next chapter, I'll show you a customized symbolic map you can use instead of the BMS-generated one.

The code for the symbolic map   **Page 2**

```
01    DINMAP1O REDEFINES DINMAP1I.
      02    FILLER     PIC X(12).
      02    FILLER     PIC X(3).
      02    CUSTNOO    PIC X(0006).
      02    FILLER     PIC X(3).
      02    LNAMEO     PIC X(0030).
      02    FILLER     PIC X(3).
      02    FNAMEO     PIC X(0020).
      02    FILLER     PIC X(3).
      02    ADDRO      PIC X(0030).
      02    FILLER     PIC X(3).
      02    STATEO     PIC X(0002).
      02    FILLER     PIC X(3).
      02    ZIPCODEO   PIC X(0010).
      02    FILLER     PIC X(3).
      02    MESSAGEO   PIC X(0079).
      02    FILLER     PIC X(3).
      02    DUMMYO     PIC X(0001).
```

Description

- A symbolic map is used to access data sent to and received from a terminal screen in a COBOL program. It is created and placed in a COBOL copy library when you assemble the mapset that defines it.

- To use a symbolic map in a COBOL program, you use a COPY statement to include it in the Working-Storage Section.

- A symbolic map includes two 01-level items: one for input and one for output. Because the second item contains a REDEFINES clause, it occupies the same storage as the first item.

- The symbolic map defines separate fields for input and output so you can specify different PICTURE clauses for them. In addition, for each screen field that's named in the mapset, the symbolic map contains a field that indicates the length of the data in the input field, a field that indicates if the user made changes to the input field, and a field that contains the attributes for output operations.

Figure 7-6   The symbolic map for the CICS/DB2 inquiry program (part 2 of 2)

The DFHAID copy book

When the user presses an attention key to indicate that the program should restart, the program must be able to determine which key was pressed. To do that, it uses the code in a COBOL copy book named DFHAID along with a field in the Execute Interface Block (EIB) named EIBAID. Although you have to code a COPY statement for DFHAID to include it in a program, the code that defines the EIB is automatically inserted into the Linkage Section of a program by the CICS translator.

Figure 7-7 presents the DFHAID copy book, which is supplied by IBM. It contains literal values that correspond to the *AID (attention identifier) keys* that the user can press to communicate with the system. The keys that are used by the customer inquiry program are highlighted in this figure. When the user presses one of these keys, CICS passes the corresponding one-byte value in the DFHAID member to the program through the EIBAID field in the EIB. I'll describe this field and some of the other fields in the EIB in just a moment.

To illustrate how the DFHAID fields and EIBAID work, suppose the user presses F12. Then, CICS stores "@," the value of DFHPF12, in EIBAID. Your program can check for F12 explicitly by using an IF statement like this:

```
IF EIBAID = '@'
```

However, you can also use the literal data name from the DFHAID copy member in an IF statement like this:

```
IF EIBAID = DFHPF12
```

Then, your program will be easier to read and understand.

The code for the DFHAID copy book

```
01      DFHAID.
   02   DFHNULL    PIC  X   VALUE IS ' '.
   02   DFHENTER   PIC  X   VALUE IS ''''.
   02   DFHCLEAR   PIC  X   VALUE IS '_'.
   02   DFHCLRP    PIC  X   VALUE IS '('.
   02   DFHPEN     PIC  X   VALUE IS '='.
   02   DFHOPID    PIC  X   VALUE IS 'W'.
   02   DFHMSRE    PIC  X   VALUE IS 'X'.
   02   DFHSTRF    PIC  X   VALUE IS 'h'.
   02   DFHTRIG    PIC  X   VALUE IS ''''.
   02   DFHPA1     PIC  X   VALUE IS '%'.
   02   DFHPA2     PIC  X   VALUE IS ''.
   02   DFHPA3     PIC  X   VALUE IS ','.
   02   DFHPF1     PIC  X   VALUE IS '1'.
   02   DFHPF2     PIC  X   VALUE IS '2'.
   02   DFHPF3     PIC  X   VALUE IS '3'.
   02   DFHPF4     PIC  X   VALUE IS '4'.
   02   DFHPF5     PIC  X   VALUE IS '5'.
   02   DFHPF6     PIC  X   VALUE IS '6'.
   02   DFHPF7     PIC  X   VALUE IS '7'.
   02   DFHPF8     PIC  X   VALUE IS '8'.
   02   DFHPF9     PIC  X   VALUE IS '9'.
   02   DFHPF10    PIC  X   VALUE IS ':'.
   02   DFHPF11    PIC  X   VALUE IS '#'.
   02   DFHPF12    PIC  X   VALUE IS '@'.
   02   DFHPF13    PIC  X   VALUE IS 'A'.
   02   DFHPF14    PIC  X   VALUE IS 'B'.
   02   DFHPF15    PIC  X   VALUE IS 'C'.
   02   DFHPF16    PIC  X   VALUE IS 'D'.
   02   DFHPF17    PIC  X   VALUE IS 'E'.
   02   DFHPF18    PIC  X   VALUE IS 'F'.
   02   DFHPF19    PIC  X   VALUE IS 'G'.
   02   DFHPF20    PIC  X   VALUE IS 'H'.
   02   DFHPF21    PIC  X   VALUE IS 'I'.
   02   DFHPF22    PIC  X   VALUE IS X'5B'.
   02   DFHPF23    PIC  X   VALUE IS '.'.
   02   DFHPF24    PIC  X   VALUE IS ''.
```

Description

- The DFHAID copy book contains literal values that correspond to the *attention identifier (AID) keys* that the user can press to communicate with the system.

- When the user presses an AID key, CICS passes the corresponding one-byte value in the DFHAID member to the program through the EIBAID field in the Execute Interface Block.

Figure 7-7   The DFHAID copy book

The Execute Interface Block

Figure 7-8 presents the code for the Execute Interface Block that the CICS translator includes in every COBOL program. The two fields you'll use most often are EIBAID and EIBCALEN. As you just learned, EIBAID contains the value of the last AID key that was pressed as defined in the DFHAID copy book.

EIBCALEN contains the length of the data that was passed to the program through its communication area. The *communication area* provides a place where a program can move data that it will use in its next execution. That's necessary because when a pseudo-conversational program ends, the contents of its Working-Storage fields are lost. You'll see how to use the communication area when I present the code for the customer inquiry program.

The Execute Interface Block also includes fields that contain the date (EIBDATE) and time (EIBTIME) the task was started; the trans-id that was used to start the task (EIBTRNID); the name of the terminal that's running the task (EIBTRMID); and debugging information (EIBRESP, EIBRESP2, and EIBRCODE). For a description of each of the fields in the EIB, you can refer to the *CICS Application Programming Reference* manual.

The code for the Execute Interface Block

```
01      DFHEIBLK.
  02    EIBTIME      PIC S9(7) COMP-3.
  02    EIBDATE      PIC S9(7) COMP-3.
  02    EIBTRNID     PIC X(4).
  02    EIBTASKN     PIC S9(7) COMP-3.
  02    EIBTRMID     PIC X(4).
  02    DFHEIGDI     PIC S9(4) COMP.
  02    EIBCPOSN     PIC S9(4) COMP.
  02    EIBCALEN     PIC S9(4) COMP.
  02    EIBAID       PIC X(1).
  02    EIBFN        PIC X(2).
  02    EIBRCODE     PIC X(6).
  02    EIBDS        PIC X(8).
  02    EIBREQID     PIC X(8).
  02    EIBRSRCE     PIC X(8).
  02    EIBSYNC      PIC X(1).
  02    EIBFREE      PIC X(1).
  02    EIBRECV      PIC X(1).
  02    EIBFIL01     PIC X(1).
  02    EIBATT       PIC X(1).
  02    EIBEOC       PIC X(1).
  02    EIBFMH       PIC X(1).
  02    EIBCOMPL     PIC X(1).
  02    EIBSIG       PIC X(1).
  02    EIBCONF      PIC X(1).
  02    EIBERR       PIC X(1).
  02    EIBERRCD     PIC X(4).
  02    EIBSYNRB     PIC X(1).
  02    EIBNODAT     PIC X(1).
  02    EIBRESP      PIC S9(8) COMP.
  02    EIBRESP2     PIC S9(8) COMP.
  02    EIBRLDBK     PIC X(1).
```

Description

- The Execute Interface Block is a CICS area that contains information related to the current task, such as the date and time the task was started and the transaction-id that was used to start it.

- The EIBAID field indicates the last AID key that was pressed. You can use the value of this field to determine the processing the user has requested.

- The EIBCALEN field contains the length of the data passed to the program through its *communication area* (DFHCOMMAREA). A length of zero indicates that no data was passed to the program, which means that it's the first execution of the program.

Figure 7-8   The Execute Interface Block

The structure chart

Pseudo-conversational programming complicates program design and coding. That's because each time CICS starts a program, the program has to determine if it should start from scratch or if it's in the middle of an interaction. As a result, programs that run under CICS have designs that are different from what you may expect. To illustrate, consider the structure chart in figure 7-9 for the CICS customer inquiry program.

Each time the program starts, it evaluates the conditions surrounding its execution to determine what to do. For now, assume that the condition is that the user just entered a customer number and pressed the Enter key. In that case, module 0000 invokes module 1000 to process the input map.

Module 1000 starts by performing module 1100 to retrieve the customer-number entry from the screen and module 1200 to edit it. If the edit doesn't detect any problems with the customer number, module 1000 performs module 1300 to issue an SQL statement that retrieves the requested row. If DB2 retrieves the row successfully, it passes it back to the program through CICS. Then, module 1000 performs module 1400 to send the output map to the screen with the data from the row. On the other hand, if either module 1200 or module 1300 detects an error condition, module 1000 performs module 1500 to send an error message to the terminal user.

If module 0000 detects a condition other than the "normal" condition, it can do one of three things. First, it can perform module 1500 to send an error message to the user. Second, it can perform module 2000 to send a "fresh" data entry screen to the terminal to let the user start a new inquiry. Or third, it can end. (There isn't a separate module for this function.)

This is different from the design for the first version of the customer inquiry program that's presented in *Part 1* of this series. That program was structured around a PERFORM-UNTIL loop that prompted the user for a customer number, retrieved the row for that customer, and displayed the data from it. It repeated that process for each customer number entered by the user until the user signaled that the program should end. So, for example, even if a user wanted to review data for six customers, the program would run only once. That program was conversational, not pseudo-conversational.

In contrast, a session with the CICS version of the program to retrieve and display six rows from the table would involve at least eight separate executions of the program. The first execution would display the entry screen, then end. The second through the seventh executions would use the customer number the user entered on the screen to retrieve the requested row from the customer table, then display the data from it and end. If any of the iterations of this process detected an error, such as an invalid key entered by the user or a customer number value that didn't correspond to a row in the customer table, the number of executions would be even greater. The last execution of the program would detect the use of the F3 or F12 key and end.

The structure chart

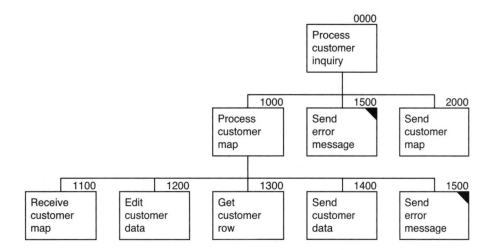

Description

- Because this program is pseudo-conversational, it must determine what processing needs to be done each time it's executed. Module 0000 makes that determination and performs module 1000, 1500, or 2000 based on the results.

- If the program is being executed for the first time, module 2000 is performed to display the customer map on the screen. This module is also executed if the user requests that the screen be refreshed. To do that, the user can press the Clear key.

- If the user presses the Enter key, module 1000 is performed. This module begins by performing module 1100 to receive the customer map. Then, it performs module 1200 to edit the customer number entered by the user to make sure it's valid. If it is, module 1300 is performed to retrieve the row for that customer from the customer table. Finally, module 1400 is performed to display the customer information on the screen.

- If the user presses an invalid key, presses the Enter key without entering a customer number, or enters an invalid customer number, module 1500 is performed. This module displays an error message on the screen.

Figure 7-9   The structure chart for the CICS/DB2 inquiry program

The COBOL listing

Figure 7-10 presents the source code for the CICS version of the customer inquiry program. Like the other DB2 program examples you've seen, this program's Identification, Environment, and Data Divisions are simple. In particular, you should notice that the Environment Division doesn't include any entries. Just as you don't have to include any Environment Division entries for the DB2 tables your programs process, you also don't need to include any entries for the CICS-controlled screens they use.

The Working-Storage Section of this program contains several items. The first 01-level item, SWITCHES, contains one control field: VALID-DATA-SW. You'll see how the program uses this switch when you review the Procedure Division code.

The next field is for data related to the communication area. To use the communication area, you need to provide two definitions for it in your program: one in the Working-Storage Section and one in the Linkage Section. The Working-Storage definition in this program is named COMMUNICATION-AREA, and the Linkage Section definition is named DFHCOMMAREA. Although you can use any name for the Working-Storage field, you must use the name DFHCOMMAREA for the Linkage Section field. You'll see how the customer inquiry program uses the communication area when you review the Procedure Division code that implements the pseudo-conversational design.

You should recognize the next two items in the Working-Storage Section: the SQL INCLUDE statements. The first statement causes the DB2 precompiler to include the DCLGEN-generated host variable definitions for the customer table, and the second statement causes the precompiler to include the SQLCA fields.

Next are two COBOL COPY statements. The first one causes the COBOL compiler to include the symbolic map for the mapset named DINSET1. The second COPY statement causes the compiler to include the DFHAID copy member.

The CICS/DB2 customer inquiry program   Page 1

```
IDENTIFICATION DIVISION.
*
 PROGRAM-ID.     DB2DIN1.
*
 ENVIRONMENT DIVISION.
*
 DATA DIVISION.
*
 FILE SECTION.
*
 WORKING-STORAGE SECTION.
*
 01  SWITCHES.
*
     05  VALID-DATA-SW          PIC X    VALUE 'Y'.
         88  VALID-DATA                  VALUE 'Y'.
*
 01  COMMUNICATION-AREA         PIC X.
*
     EXEC SQL
         INCLUDE CUSTOMER
     END-EXEC.
*
     EXEC SQL
         INCLUDE SQLCA
     END-EXEC.
*
 COPY DINSET1.
*
 COPY DFHAID.
*
 LINKAGE SECTION.
*
 01  DFHCOMMAREA                PIC X.
*
```

Figure 7-10   The COBOL listing for the CICS/DB2 inquiry program (part 1 of 4)

Page two of the COBOL listing presents the top-level module for this program. It contains the logic required to implement the pseudo-conversational design. As you can see, the EVALUATE statement specifies actions for the different conditions the program may encounter when it's started.

The operation of the EVALUATE statement depends on the values CICS makes available to the program through the Execute Interface Block. For example, the first condition in the EVALUATE statement tests the value of EIBCALEN, which contains the length of the data passed to the program through its communication area. If the length is zero, it means that no data was passed to the program, which indicates that there was no previous execution of the program. As a result, module 2000 is performed to send the customer map to the screen.

Note that this program uses the communication area only to determine whether it's executing for the first time. However, a program can also use the communication area to pass data from one execution to the next. You'll see how that works in the program that's presented in the next chapter.

The next four conditions in the EVALUATE statement test for values in the EIBAID field to see if the user pressed a specific attention key. Notice that each condition uses data names from the DFHAID copy member. The program checks EIBAID so it can avoid retrieving data from the terminal if the function it's about to perform doesn't call for it. That reduces network traffic and improves overall system performance.

If the user pressed the Clear key (EIBAID = DFHCLEAR), the program performs module 2000 to restart with a fresh screen. If the user pressed one of the program attention (PA) keys (EIBAID = DFHPA1 OR DFHPA2 OR DFHPA3), no special action is taken. Then, the CONTINUE statement causes program execution to proceed after the EVALUATE statement. If the user pressed the F3 or F12 key (DFHAID = DFHPF3 OR DFHPF12), the program issues a CICS XCTL command, which ends the program. In this case, the XCTL command tells CICS to pass control to the menu named DB2MENU. Finally, if the user pressed the Enter key (DFHAID = DFHENTER), the program performs module 1000 to receive and process the customer map.

If none of the other conditions the EVALUATE statement specifies are true, the last condition, WHEN OTHER, is reached. Then, module 1500 is performed to display an error message. In this case, the error message indicates that an invalid key was pressed.

Unless the XCTL command was executed in response to F3 or F12, program execution continues after the EVALUATE statement with a CICS RETURN command. It causes CICS to invoke the same trans-id (DIN1) the next time the user presses one of the AID keys. It also contains the code necessary to save data from one execution of the program to another in the communication area. In the COMMAREA option, it names the Working-Storage field (COMMUNICATION-AREA) whose contents should be passed forward to the next execution of the program through the CICS communication area. Note that the program never establishes the value of this field, though, because it doesn't matter what its value is. The program checks only its length.

The CICS/DB2 customer inquiry program   **Page 2**

```
 PROCEDURE DIVISION.
*
 0000-PROCESS-CUSTOMER-INQUIRY.
*
     EVALUATE TRUE

         WHEN EIBCALEN = ZERO
             PERFORM 2000-SEND-CUSTOMER-MAP

         WHEN EIBAID = DFHCLEAR
             PERFORM 2000-SEND-CUSTOMER-MAP

         WHEN EIBAID = DFHPA1 OR DFHPA2 OR DFHPA3
             CONTINUE

         WHEN EIBAID = DFHPF3 OR DFHPF12
             EXEC CICS
                 XCTL PROGRAM('DB2MENU')
             END-EXEC

         WHEN EIBAID = DFHENTER
             PERFORM 1000-PROCESS-CUSTOMER-MAP

         WHEN OTHER
             MOVE 'Invalid key pressed.' TO MESSAGEO
             PERFORM 1500-SEND-ERROR-MESSAGE

     END-EVALUATE.

     EXEC CICS
         RETURN TRANSID('DIN1')
                COMMAREA(COMMUNICATION-AREA)
     END-EXEC.
*
```

Figure 7-10   The COBOL listing for the CICS/DB2 inquiry program (part 2 of 4)

If the user presses the Enter key, module 1000 is performed. This module starts by performing module 1100 to get the data the user entered on the screen. Then, it executes module 1200 to edit that data. If the edit doesn't detect an error, the program executes module 1300 to retrieve the requested row from the customer table. If that function is successful, the program displays the retrieved data by invoking module 1400. On the other hand, if an error is detected, the program executes module 1500 to display an error message.

Module 1100 contains a single CICS command: RECEIVE MAP. This command receives data from the terminal using the DINMAP1 map in the DINSET1 mapset. After CICS processes this command, the number for the customer whose table row the user wants to retrieve is stored in the CUSTNOI field in the symbolic map.

The only editing requirement for this program is that the user must enter a customer number. Module 1200 performs this editing by checking the length and input fields for the customer number in the symbolic map. As you can see, the input field (CUSTNOI) is checked to be sure that it doesn't contain spaces. Note, however, that this condition isn't satisfied if the field was blank and the user didn't enter anything or if the user erased the field using the ERASE-EOF key. In both of these cases, no data is transmitted back to CICS. Then, after CICS processes the RECEIVE MAP command, the CUSTNOI field will contain low-values. Because low-values and spaces are different, module 1200 also checks the length field (CUSTNOL) for a value of zero, which would indicate that no data was transmitted.

If either of the two error conditions is true, module 1200 turns the valid-data switch off. As you'll see in a minute, the program uses this switch to determine the processing it does next. This module also moves an error message to the output field in the symbolic map for the screen's MESSAGE field (MESSAGEO).

If module 1200 didn't turn the valid-data switch off, module 1000 invokes module 1300 to issue the SQL statement necessary to retrieve the requested row from the customer table. Note that this SELECT statement is the same as the one in the non-CICS version of the program presented in *Part 1* of this series.

The CICS/DB2 customer inquiry program   **Page 3**

```
1000-PROCESS-CUSTOMER-MAP.
*
    PERFORM 1100-RECEIVE-CUSTOMER-MAP.
    PERFORM 1200-EDIT-CUSTOMER-DATA.
    IF VALID-DATA
        PERFORM 1300-GET-CUSTOMER-ROW
        IF VALID-DATA
            PERFORM 1400-SEND-CUSTOMER-DATA
        ELSE
            PERFORM 1500-SEND-ERROR-MESSAGE
    ELSE
        PERFORM 1500-SEND-ERROR-MESSAGE.
*
 1100-RECEIVE-CUSTOMER-MAP.
*
    EXEC CICS
        RECEIVE MAP('DINMAP1')
                MAPSET('DINSET1')
                INTO(DINMAP1I)
    END-EXEC.
*
 1200-EDIT-CUSTOMER-DATA.
*
    IF       CUSTNOL = ZERO
        OR CUSTNOI = SPACE
        MOVE 'N' TO VALID-DATA-SW
        MOVE 'You must enter a customer number.' TO MESSAGEO.
*
 1300-GET-CUSTOMER-ROW.
*
    EXEC SQL
        SELECT CUSTNO,      FNAME,        LNAME,
               ADDR,        CITY,         STATE,
               ZIPCODE
        INTO   :CUSTNO,   :FNAME,     :LNAME,
               :ADDR,     :CITY,      :STATE,
               :ZIPCODE
        FROM   MM01.CUSTOMER
            WHERE CUSTNO = :CUSTNOI
    END-EXEC.
```

Figure 7-10   The COBOL listing for the CICS/DB2 inquiry program (part 3 of 4)

If the SELECT statement doesn't produce a DB2 error (SQLCODE = 0), module 1300 continues by moving the values returned from DB2 (through the fields in the DCLGEN-generated host variable definitions) into the corresponding output fields in the BMS symbolic map. It also moves spaces to the output field used for messages.

If the SELECT statement in module 1300 isn't successful, the program does one of two things depending on the value of SQLCODE. If SQLCODE is 100, which indicates that the row wasn't found, the program turns the valid-data switch off, prepares an error message, and clears the output fields. If SQLCODE is any non-zero value other than 100, the program issues a CICS ABEND command. The ABEND command terminates the task and returns control to CICS.

If a valid row is retrieved, module 1400 is performed to send the data for that customer to the screen. Otherwise, module 1500 is performed to send an error message to the screen. Both of these modules issue a CICS SEND MAP command. The only difference between them is that the SEND MAP command in module 1500 specifies the ALARM option. ALARM causes an audio beep to sound at the terminal to call the user's attention to the error. Notice that these two SEND MAP commands, like the RECEIVE MAP command in module 1100, specify the mapset DINSET1 and the map DINMAP1. However, instead of the INTO option, SEND MAP uses the FROM option. The FROM option specifies the source of the data to be sent to the terminal. In this case, the source is the output fields in the symbolic map.

The SEND MAP commands in both of these modules specify the DATAONLY option. That means that only the variable data, that is, only the data in the symbolic map, is sent to the terminal; the literals that make up the headings, labels, and instructions don't need to be sent again because they're already there from the previous execution. Using this option improves performance because it reduces the amount of data transmitted between CICS and the users' terminals.

The last module in this program, module 2000, is performed when the program is started for the first time or when the user presses the Clear key to refresh the screen. This module starts by moving LOW-VALUE to the symbolic map to clear any data it contains. Then, it issues a SEND MAP command, much like the ones for modules 1400 and 1500. However, the command in module 2000 contains a different set of options. Instead of DATAONLY, the command in module 2000 specifies ERASE. That causes CICS to clear the screen so any data it contained is removed. Then, because the command does not contain DATAONLY, both literals and variable data fields are sent to the screen.

The CICS/DB2 customer inquiry program   **Page 4**

```
    IF SQLCODE = 0
        MOVE LNAME      TO LNAMEO
        MOVE FNAME      TO FNAMEO
        MOVE ADDR       TO ADDRO
        MOVE CITY       TO CITYO
        MOVE STATE      TO STATEO
        MOVE ZIPCODE    TO ZIPCODEO
        MOVE SPACE      TO MESSAGEO
    ELSE
        IF SQLCODE = 100
            MOVE 'N' TO VALID-DATA-SW
            MOVE 'That customer does not exist.' TO MESSAGEO
            MOVE SPACE TO LNAMEO
                          FNAMEO
                          ADDRO
                          CITYO
                          STATEO
                          ZIPCODEO
        ELSE
            EXEC CICS
                ABEND
            END-EXEC.
*
 1400-SEND-CUSTOMER-DATA.
*
    EXEC CICS
        SEND MAP('DINMAP1')
            MAPSET('DINSET1')
            FROM(DINMAP1O)
            DATAONLY
    END-EXEC.
*
 1500-SEND-ERROR-MESSAGE.
*
    EXEC CICS
        SEND MAP('DINMAP1')
            MAPSET('DINSET1')
            FROM(DINMAP1O)
            DATAONLY
            ALARM
    END-EXEC.
*
 2000-SEND-CUSTOMER-MAP.
*
    MOVE LOW-VALUE TO DINMAP1O.
    EXEC CICS
        SEND MAP('DINMAP1')
            MAPSET('DINSET1')
            FROM(DINMAP1O)
            ERASE
    END-EXEC.
*
```

Figure 7-10   The COBOL listing for the CICS/DB2 inquiry program (part 4 of 4)

Perspective

As you can tell from the program presented in this chapter, there's little difference between the way you process DB2 data in a CICS program and the way you process DB2 data in a batch program. The difference between CICS and batch processing is that with CICS, you have to use pseudo-conversational programming so you don't tie up resources, and you have to use CICS commands to request CICS services.

Keep in mind, though, that CICS programming can be more complicated than the inquiry program in this chapter indicates. In the next chapter, for example, you'll learn how to use CICS to browse a multi-row result table.

8

How to browse DB2 data in a CICS program

The program in the last chapter retrieved and displayed data from a single row in a DB2 table in response to a user inquiry. As a result, it was relatively simple. However, some CICS applications let users make inquiries that return multiple rows. In CICS, this is called *browsing*. Browsing a multi-row result table through a CICS program can present both performance and programming challenges.

An introduction to CICS/DB2 browse programs

A browse program lets a user retrieve a number of items of stored data and examine all of them. Usually, a browse operation involves more data than will fit on a terminal screen at one time. Browsing implies that the user can move, or scroll, from one screen to another and review all of them. As a result, a single browse operation can involve many CICS displays.

How a browse program works

Figure 8-1 illustrates part of a session with a CICS browse program that lets a user retrieve and scroll through information for all customers who live in a specific state. (This example uses a different version of the customer table named VARCUST that contains more rows than the table used in previous examples and whose LNAME column is defined as VARCHAR.) The first screen in this figure prompts the user to enter the state code to be used for the browse. Here, the user entered CA to retrieve data for all customers who live in California.

After the user pressed the Enter key, the program displayed the second screen in this figure. It shows data for 14 customers. If you look at the right side of the screen, you'll see the program reported that it's displaying the first 14 of a total of 75 rows that contain CA as the state code. This follows IBM's *CUA (Common User Access) standard* for displaying information about scrollable data.

The line beneath the count information is also CUA scroll information. It advises the user that there is more data to be displayed. The plus sign in this example indicates that the user can display more data by scrolling forward (down). The CUA standard keys for scrolling data are F7 (for scrolling backward, or up) and F8 (for scrolling forward, or down). The bottom line of the screen reminds the user of these options.

The opening screen for the customer browse program

From this screen, the user can enter the state code for the customers to be displayed.

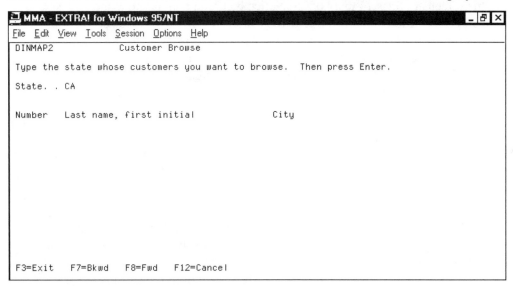

The screen after the user enters a state code

After the user enters a state code and presses the Enter key, the first screen of customers in that state is displayed. From this screen, the user can press F8 to scroll forward through the list of customers.

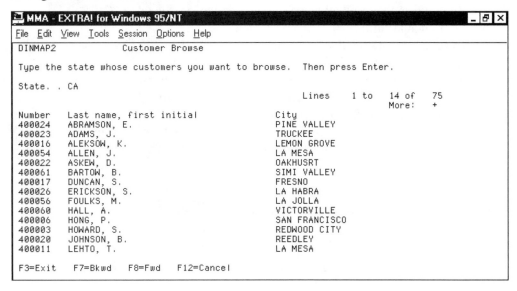

Figure 8-1   How the customer browse program works (part 1 of 2)

When the user pressed the F8 key from the second screen in this figure, the third screen appeared. The scroll information lines here report that the rows on this screen are lines 14 to 27 of 75. Notice that both a minus sign and a plus sign follow "More:" in this screen. They indicate that the user can scroll both forward and backward from this screen. Also notice that the last line of data displayed in the second screen in this figure is the first line of data displayed in the third screen. That's because CUA standards suggest that when data scrolls in blocks, one item from the previous group should remain on the screen to orient the user.

How CICS and DB2 operations conflict with each other

As the customer browse program illustrates, a single browse operation can involve many CICS displays. And, if the program is written using pseudo-conversational programming, the operation may involve many separate executions of the program.

Unfortunately, DB2 operations and CICS operations come into conflict when multi-row result tables need to be browsed. That's because when a pseudo-conversational program ends, DB2 drops the result table it was using for the browse operation. Although the program could recreate the result table each time it's executed, the system resources required to do that can be excessive. On the other hand, if the program were written using conversational programming so the result table was created only once, the whole CICS subsystem would suffer.

The conflict between the operating modes of CICS and DB2 is so serious that some shops prohibit CICS/DB2 browse programs or limit their number and operations. For applications that could involve huge numbers of rows, limiting CICS/DB2 browsing is certainly reasonable. If an online table contains millions of rows, for example, it would be unreasonable not to prohibit browse operations. However, for result tables that contain a modest number of rows, browsing with a CICS program may be reasonable if you adopt an appropriate programming strategy.

Programming strategies for CICS/DB2 browse programs

Figure 8-2 lists three programming strategies you can use for developing CICS/DB2 browse programs. As you'll see, all of them are costly. They differ largely by how the CICS and DB2 subsystems share the processing burden. Whichever strategy you use, though, you should follow two general guidelines to reduce the burden. First, you should minimize the number of rows DB2 includes in the result table it produces. And second, you should reduce the number of screen interactions that are required by displaying as much data as you can on each screen.

The screen after the user presses F8 to scroll forward

When the user scrolls forward to display additional customers, the last customer on the previous screen is displayed at the top of the list. From this screen, the user can press F7 to scroll backward or F8 to scroll forward.

```
┌─────────────────────────────────────────────────────────────────────────┐
│ 🖳 MMA - EXTRA! for Windows 95/NT                              _ □ ✕       │
├───────────────────────────────────────────────────────────────────────── │
│ File  Edit  View  Tools  Session  Options  Help                           │
│ DINMAP2              Customer Browse                                       │
│                                                                           │
│ Type the state whose customers you want to browse.  Then press Enter.     │
│                                                                           │
│ State. . CA                                                               │
│                                          Lines   14 to   27 of   75       │
│                                                      More: - +            │
│ Number    Last name, first initial       City                            │
│ 400011    LEHTO, T.                       LA MESA                         │
│ 400015    MENDOZA, M.                     SAN FRANCISCO                    │
│ 400025    PINON, I.                       CULVER CITY                      │
│ 400014    RALSTON, J.                     SAN DIEGO                        │
│ 400021    ROBERT, J.                      SELMA                           │
│ 400005    ROBERTS, E.                     CERRITOS                        │
│ 400019    RUBBLE, B.                      STONE                           │
│ 400027    SMITH, J.                       SALIDA                          │
│ 400057    SNOW, R.                        TEMECULA                        │
│ 400018    THUMB, T.                       TURLOCK                         │
│ 400058    WELCH, S.                       SANTEE                          │
│ 400055    WHITE, T.                       SANTA BARBARA                    │
│ 400013    ZOLEZZI, R.                     LA MESA                         │
│ 400012    ZOPFI, D.                       SELMA                           │
│                                                                           │
│ F3=Exit   F7=Bkwd   F8=Fwd   F12=Cancel                                   │
└─────────────────────────────────────────────────────────────────────────┘
```

Notes

- The user can enter a new state code at any time to display the customers from that state. To end the program, the user must press F3 or F12.

- The browse program also displays an indication of the lines that are currently displayed, the total number of lines to be displayed, and whether the user can scroll forward (More: +), backward (More -), or both (More - +) to display more lines. This information is displayed above and to the right of the customer lines.

Figure 8-1   How the customer browse program works (part 2 of 2)

The first strategy is to perform a query each time the program is executed. Then, the program can store values between executions to indicate the scroll position so that a single screen of data can be retrieved and displayed with each execution. Although this is the most efficient strategy from the CICS perspective, it can be a burden on DB2. In fact, this strategy may be unacceptable in busy interactive systems where contention for access to DB2 data is high. That's because this kind of process monopolizes a thread longer and more often than an average program and causes extensive DB2 locking activity.

The second strategy is to avoid pseudo-conversational programming altogether and code a conversational program. This strategy is efficient in terms of DB2 since the query is performed only once. But it's inefficient in terms of CICS resources. Since long browse operations implemented in this way tie up resources in both the CICS and DB2 subsystems, it's an unusual approach.

The third strategy is to code a pseudo-conversational program, but to create the result table at the beginning of the browse operation and save the results in a temporary area. Then, subsequent executions of the program can use the data in the temporary area to perform the browse operation rather than using the data in the base table. One way to do that is to perform a mass insert to construct a work table that contains only the data that satisfies the selection condition. Then, the program can create a cursor-controlled result table from the work table each time it's executed, instead of from the base table. When the browse is completed, the program deletes the data from the temporary work table.

Although this strategy doesn't reduce the number of SQL operations the program performs, it can improve efficiency because it reduces access to the base tables. In addition, the DB2 locks that are generated won't block other programs' requests since your program is the only one that will access your temporary work table. The disadvantage of this approach is the extra overhead it requires, both in terms of disk space and processor time. And it still doesn't eliminate the fundamental conflict between CICS and DB2.

Two other approaches to this strategy involve creating a working set of the selected table data outside DB2. To do this, your program would fetch each row from a cursor-controlled result table at the start of a browse operation, then write its contents at another location that's accessible to CICS. One option is to use a VSAM data set. Then, after you transfer the data into the VSAM data set, you can use CICS's browse commands (STARTBR, READNEXT, READPREV, ENDBR, and RESETBR) to retrieve the data for display. This approach is much more efficient in terms of processor time because it's less costly to browse VSAM data than it is to browse DB2 data. Still, this approach may be unacceptable for performance reasons.

A variation of this approach is to store the contents of the result table in a CICS storage area called *temporary storage*. CICS provides temporary storage for your programs through a VSAM data set it manages for you. CICS also provides special commands for saving and retrieving data from temporary storage. Because this approach is simple and straightforward, it's the approach that's illustrated in the program example you'll see next.

Strategy 1: Do a separate query for each execution of the program

- This strategy may be acceptable if the number of rows to be browsed is small. It is most efficient from the CICS perspective, but imposes a burden on DB2.

- To implement this strategy, the program needs to store values between executions to indicate the scroll position. Then, the next time the program is executed, those values can be used to determine which rows to retrieve, format, and display.

Strategy 2: Do a single query and browse in a conversational style

- A *conversational program* is one that doesn't end and pass control back to CICS with each user interaction. Instead, the operator must make a special entry to signal the end of the program.

- This strategy is most appropriate when the DB2 costs for doing browse operations in a pseudo-conversational program are excessive and the application is critical. Because long browse operations implemented this way tie up resources in both the CICS and DB2 subsystems, this strategy is unusual.

Strategy 3: Do a single query and save the results in a temporary area between pseudo-conversational executions

- One approach is to perform a mass insert at the beginning of the browse operation to create a DB2 work table that contains only the rows to be browsed. Then, each execution of the program can create a cursor-controlled result table from the work table instead of the base table. This improves program efficiency, but requires extra overhead in terms of disk space and processor time.

- Another approach is to create a cursor-controlled result table at the beginning of the browse operation, and write its contents to a VSAM data set. Then, you can use CICS's browse commands to retrieve the data for the display. This approach is more efficient in terms of processor time, but may be unacceptable for performance reasons.

- A final approach is to write the contents of a cursor-controlled result table created at the beginning of the browse operation to a CICS storage area called *temporary storage*. CICS provides special commands for saving and retrieving data from temporary storage. This is a simple and straightforward approach.

Note

- To reduce the burden imposed by any browse operation, you should minimize the number of rows included in the result set and display as much data as you can on each screen.

Figure 8-2   Programming strategies for CICS/DB2 browse programs

A CICS/DB2 program that browses the customer table

To illustrate how you can implement a browse application in CICS, this chapter now presents a program that does the customer browse described at the start of this chapter. This program prompts the user for a state code, then retrieves data from all the rows in the customer table for customers who live in that state. As it retrieves the data, it stores it in CICS temporary storage. Then, the program formats and displays the data in groups of 14 rows. The user can scroll forward and backward from group to group to view all of the data that satisfied the selection request.

The BMS mapset

The BMS mapset for the browse program is more complicated than the one for the inquiry program you saw in the last chapter. However, the difference isn't in the complexity of the features it uses; it's just in the number of fields it defines. In fact, the entries in part 1 of figure 8-3 are much like the ones I described for the inquiry application's mapset.

The first DFHMSD macro defines the mapset, which is named DINSET2. Then, the DFHMDI macro defines the only map in the mapset, which is named DINMAP2. The next five DFHMDF macros that follow define the first three heading lines at the top of the screen. These macros are followed by two more DFHMDF macros that define the input field where the user will enter the state code for the browse operation.

The last two DFHMDF macros in part 1 of this figure define the fields that contain the scrolling messages that appear on the right side of the display. The first one, named LINEMSG, is used for the messages like:

```
Lines    14 to     27 of     75
```

and the one beneath it, MOREMSG, is used for the messages like:

```
More: - +
```

Notice that neither of these fields has an initial value. Instead, the application program provides their values each time it sends this map to the terminal.

The code for the BMS mapset   Page 1

```
          PRINT NOGEN
DINSET2   DFHMSD TYPE=&SYSPARM,                                           X
                 LANG=COBOL,                                              X
                 MODE=INOUT,                                              X
                 TERM=3270-2,                                             X
                 CTRL=FREEKB,                                             X
                 MAPATTS=COLOR,                                           X
                 STORAGE=AUTO,                                            X
                 TIOAPFX=YES
**********************************************************************
DINMAP2   DFHMDI SIZE=(24,80),                                           X
                 LINE=1,                                                  X
                 COLUMN=1
**********************************************************************
          DFHMDF POS=(1,1),                                              X
                 LENGTH=7,                                               X
                 ATTRB=(NORM,PROT),                                      X
                 COLOR=BLUE,                                             X
                 INITIAL='DINMAP2'
          DFHMDF POS=(1,20),                                             X
                 LENGTH=15,                                              X
                 ATTRB=(NORM,PROT),                                      X
                 COLOR=BLUE,                                             X
                 INITIAL='Customer Browse'
**********************************************************************
          DFHMDF POS=(3,1),                                              X
                 LENGTH=39,                                              X
                 ATTRB=(NORM,PROT),                                      X
                 COLOR=GREEN,                                            X
                 INITIAL='Type the state whose customers you want'
          DFHMDF POS=(3,41),                                             X
                 LENGTH=29,                                              X
                 ATTRB=(NORM,PROT),                                      X
                 COLOR=GREEN,                                            X
                 INITIAL='to browse.   Then press Enter.'
          DFHMDF POS=(5,1),                                              X
                 LENGTH=8,                                               X
                 ATTRB=(NORM,PROT),                                      X
                 COLOR=GREEN,                                            X
                 INITIAL='State. .'
STATE     DFHMDF POS=(5,10),                                             X
                 LENGTH=2,                                               X
                 ATTRB=(NORM,UNPROT,IC),                                 X
                 COLOR=TURQUOISE,                                        X
                 INITIAL='__'
          DFHMDF POS=(5,13),                                             X
                 LENGTH=1,                                               X
                 ATTRB=ASKIP
**********************************************************************
LINEMSG   DFHMDF POS=(6,53),                                             X
                 LENGTH=26,                                              X
                 ATTRB=(NORM,PROT),                                      X
                 COLOR=BLUE
MOREMSG   DFHMDF POS=(7,69),                                             X
                 LENGTH=9,                                               X
                 ATTRB=(NORM,PROT),                                      X
                 COLOR=WHITE
**********************************************************************
```

Figure 8-3   The BMS mapset for the CICS/DB2 browse program (part 1 of 2)

In contrast to the first part of the BMS mapset, the second part of this mapset is significantly different from the one for the inquiry program. The first two DFHMDF macros shown in part 2 of the figure define the column headings for the lines of customer information the screen displays. Then, the mapset contains 14 groups of macros, one for each of the customer data lines that can appear on the screen. (Only the first 2 of these 14 groups are shown in this figure.) Each group contains three DFHMDF macros. The first macro defines the customer number field, the second defines the name field, and the third defines the city field.

The last three macros in the mapset are similar to those in the mapset for the inquiry program you saw in the last chapter. The only difference is the initial value of the second field, which contains instructions for the user. Here, the instructions include the functions of the F7 and F8 keys, which let the user scroll backward and forward through the display.

The code for the BMS mapset   Page 2

```
              DFHMDF POS=(8,1),                                      X
                     LENGTH=33,                                      X
                     ATTRB=(NORM,PROT),                              X
                     COLOR=BLUE,                                     X
                     INITIAL='Number   Last name, first initial'
              DFHMDF POS=(8,48),                                     X
                     LENGTH=4,                                       X
                     ATTRB=(NORM,PROT),                              X
                     COLOR=BLUE,                                     X
                     INITIAL='City'
*        Customer Line 1     ****************************************
CUST1         DFHMDF POS=(9,1),                                      X
                     LENGTH=6,                                       X
                     COLOR=TURQUOISE,                                X
                     ATTRB=(NORM,PROT)
NAME1         DFHMDF POS=(9,10),                                     X
                     LENGTH=34,                                      X
                     COLOR=TURQUOISE,                                X
                     ATTRB=(NORM,PROT)
CITY1         DFHMDF POS=(9,48),                                     X
                     LENGTH=20,                                      X
                     COLOR=TURQUOISE,                                X
                     ATTRB=(NORM,PROT)
*        Customer Line 2     ****************************************
CUST2         DFHMDF POS=(10,1),                                     X
                     LENGTH=6,                                       X
                     COLOR=TURQUOISE,                                X
                     ATTRB=(NORM,PROT)
NAME2         DFHMDF POS=(10,10),                                    X
                     LENGTH=34,                                      X
                     COLOR=TURQUOISE,                                X
                     ATTRB=(NORM,PROT)
CITY2         DFHMDF POS=(10,48),                                    X
                     LENGTH=20,                                      X
                     COLOR=TURQUOISE,                                X
                     ATTRB=(NORM,PROT)
              .
              .
    Twelve more sets of field definitions for customer lines 3 through 14.
              .
              .
**********************************************************************
MESSAGE       DFHMDF POS=(23,1),                                     X
                     LENGTH=79,                                      X
                     ATTRB=(BRT,PROT),                               X
                     COLOR=YELLOW
              DFHMDF POS=(24,1),                                     X
                     LENGTH=39,                                      X
                     ATTRB=(NORM,PROT),                              X
                     COLOR=BLUE,                                     X
                     INITIAL='F3=Exit   F7=Bkwd   F8=Fwd   F12=Cancel'
DUMMY         DFHMDF POS=(24,79),                                    X
                     LENGTH=1,                                       X
                     ATTRB=(DRK,PROT,FSET),                          X
                     INITIAL=' '
**********************************************************************
              DFHMSD TYPE=FINAL
              END
```

Figure 8-3   The BMS mapset for the CICS/DB2 browse program (part 2 of 2)

The BMS-generated symbolic map

In the last chapter, I mentioned that you can code your own symbolic map instead of using the symbolic map BMS generates. That's what I did in this program. If you code your own symbolic maps, you should use the BMS-generated maps as a guide. That way, you'll be sure to include the same number and types of fields.

To start, figure 8-4 presents the BMS-generated symbolic map for the browse program. In the first part of this figure, you can see the input definitions for the fields named in the mapset. Notice that separate fields are defined in the symbolic map for each customer that's defined in the mapset. In just a moment, you'll see that there's a much easier way to code these repeating fields in a customized symbolic map.

The BMS-generated code for the symbolic map   Page 1

```
01  DINMAP2I.
    02  FILLER     PIC X(12).
    02  STATEL     PIC S9(4) COMP.
    02  STATEF     PIC X.
    02  FILLER REDEFINES STATEF.
     03 STATEA     PIC X.
    02  STATEI     PIC X(0002).
    02  LINEMSGL   PIC S9(4) COMP.
    02  LINEMSGF   PIC X.
    02  FILLER REDEFINES LINEMSGF.
     03 LINEMSGA   PIC X.
    02  LINEMSGI   PIC X(0026).
    02  MOREMSGL   PIC S9(4) COMP.
    02  MOREMSGF   PIC X.
    02  FILLER REDEFINES MOREMSGF.
     03 MOREMSGA   PIC X.
    02  MOREMSGI   PIC X(0009).
    02  CUST1L     PIC S9(4) COMP.
    02  CUST1F     PIC X.
    02  FILLER REDEFINES CUST1F.
     03 CUST1A     PIC X.
    02  CUST1I     PIC X(0006).
    02  NAME1L     PIC S9(4) COMP.
    02  NAME1F     PIC X.
    02  FILLER REDEFINES NAME1F.
     03 NAME1A     PIC X.
    02  NAME1I     PIC X(0034).
    02  CITY1L     PIC S9(4) COMP.
    02  CITY1F     PIC X.
    02  FILLER REDEFINES CITY1F.
     03 CITY1A     PIC X.
    02  CITY1I     PIC X(0020).
    02  CUST2L     PIC S9(4) COMP.
    02  CUST2F     PIC X.
    02  FILLER REDEFINES CUST2F.
     03 CUST2A     PIC X.
    02  CUST2I     PIC X(0006).
    02  NAME2L     PIC S9(4) COMP.
    02  NAME2F     PIC X.
    02  FILLER REDEFINES NAME2F.
     03 NAME2A     PIC X.
    02  NAME2I     PIC X(0034).
    02  CITY2L     PIC S9(4) COMP.
    02  CITY2F     PIC X.
    02  FILLER REDEFINES CITY2F.
     03 CITY2A     PIC X.
    02  CITY2I     PIC X(0020).
          .
          .
```

Twelve more sets of field definitions for customer lines 3 through 14.

```
          .
          .
```

Figure 8-4   The BMS-generated symbolic map for the CICS/DB2 browse program
              (part 1 of 2)

You can see the output definitions for the fields in the mapset in part 2 of this figure. Like the BMS-generated mapset in chapter 7, the output area of the mapset redefines the input area. Separate input and output fields are defined so you can give them different pictures if necessary. When you create your own symbolic maps, though, you may not need separate output fields.

The BMS-generated code for the symbolic map   **Page 2**

```
    02    MESSAGEL  PIC S9(4) COMP.
    02    MESSAGEF  PIC X.
    02    FILLER REDEFINES MESSAGEF.
     03   MESSAGEA  PIC X.
    02    MESSAGEI  PIC X(0079).
    02    DUMMYL    PIC S9(4) COMP.
    02    DUMMYF    PIC X.
    02    FILLER REDEFINES DUMMYF.
     03   DUMMYA    PIC X.
    02    DUMMYI    PIC X(0001).
01  DINMAP2O REDEFINES DINMAP2I.
    02    FILLER    PIC X(12).
    02    FILLER    PIC X(3).
    02    STATEO    PIC X(0002).
    02    FILLER    PIC X(3).
    02    LINEMSGO  PIC X(0026).
    02    FILLER    PIC X(3).
    02    MOREMSGO  PIC X(0009).
    02    FILLER    PIC X(3).
    02    CUST1O    PIC X(0006).
    02    FILLER    PIC X(3).
    02    NAME1O    PIC X(0034).
    02    FILLER    PIC X(3).
    02    CITY1O    PIC X(0020).
    02    FILLER    PIC X(3).
    02    CUST2O    PIC X(0006).
    02    FILLER    PIC X(3).
    02    NAME2O    PIC X(0034).
    02    FILLER    PIC X(3).
    02    CITY2O    PIC X(0020).
    02    FILLER    PIC X(3).
        .
        .
        .
```

Twelve more sets of field definitions for customer lines 3 through 14.

```
        .
        .
    02    MESSAGEO  PIC X(0079).
    02    FILLER    PIC X(3).
    02    DUMMYO    PIC X(0001).
```

Figure 8-4   The BMS-generated symbolic map for the CICS/DB2 browse program
             (part 2 of 2)

The customized symbolic map

Figure 8-5 presents the customized map that I coded for the inquiry program instead of using the BMS-generated map. Notice in this map that I gave the 01-level item a meaningful name (STATE-INQUIRY-MAP). Then, I used an abbreviation of that name as the prefix for all of the data names subordinate to it: SIM.

For each of the map fields, I coded three data names in the symbolic map: one for the length field, one for the attribute field, and one for the data field itself. To distinguish these three fields, I included the characters -L- for the length field, -A- for the attribute field, and -D- for the data field. These names parallel the ones in the BMS-generated map in figure 8-4, but they're more understandable.

The biggest difference between the customized symbolic map in this figure and the BMS-generated map in figure 8-4 is in how the fields for the customer data lines are defined. In the BMS-generated version, separate data names are used for the elements in each of those lines. But if you use an OCCURS structure instead, the symbolic map is shorter and easier to understand. More important, it makes it easier to code the program statements that move data to the symbolic map.

Also notice that I omitted the output area from this symbolic map. Because the same picture is used for both input and output, a separate output area isn't necessary.

The customized code for the symbolic map

```
01  STATE-INQUIRY-MAP.
*
    05  FILLER                PIC X(12).
*
    05  SIM-L-STATE           PIC S9(4)     COMP.
    05  SIM-A-STATE           PIC X.
    05  SIM-D-STATE           PIC XX.
*
    05  SIM-L-LINEMSG         PIC S9(4)     COMP.
    05  SIM-A-LINEMSG         PIC X.
    05  SIM-D-LINEMSG         PIC X(26).
*
    05  SIM-L-MOREMSG         PIC S9(4)     COMP.
    05  SIM-A-MOREMSG         PIC X.
    05  SIM-D-MOREMSG         PIC X(9).
*
    05  SIM-CUSTOMER-LINE     OCCURS 14.
*
        10  SIM-L-CUSTNO      PIC S9(4)     COMP.
        10  SIM-A-CUSTNO      PIC X.
        10  SIM-D-CUSTNO      PIC X(6).
*
        10  SIM-L-NAME        PIC S9(4)     COMP.
        10  SIM-A-NAME        PIC X.
        10  SIM-D-NAME        PIC X(34).
*
        10  SIM-L-CITY        PIC S9(4)     COMP.
        10  SIM-A-CITY        PIC X.
        10  SIM-D-CITY        PIC X(20).
*
    05  SIM-L-MESSAGE         PIC S9(4)     COMP.
    05  SIM-A-MESSAGE         PIC X.
    05  SIM-D-MESSAGE         PIC X(79).
*
    05  SIM-L-DUMMY           PIC S9(4)     COMP.
    05  SIM-A-DUMMY           PIC X.
    05  SIM-D-DUMMY           PIC X.
*
```

Figure 8-5   The customized symbolic map for the CICS/DB2 browse program

The structure chart

Figure 8-6 presents the structure chart for the browse program. Like the inquiry program in chapter 7, the browse program is pseudo-conversational. So each time the program is executed, it has to figure out what it should do. As you can see from the structure chart, the possibilities are to start a new browse (module 1000), delete the temporary storage queue (module 1100), send an error message (module 1600), scroll the browse display (module 2000), and send a new map to the terminal (module 3000).

To start a new browse, the user presses the Enter key. Then, module 1000 performs module 1100 to delete the program's CICS temporary storage area, called a *temporary storage queue*, or *TS queue*. The program deletes this queue so it doesn't contain data from a previous browse. (There's no way to delete the data from a queue without deleting the queue.) After the queue is deleted, module 1200 receives the screen map to get the state code that will be used for the browse, and module 1300 checks to make sure the user entered an acceptable state code value.

If the state code value is acceptable, the program invokes module 1400 to retrieve all the rows from the customer table whose state column contains that value. Module 1400 generates the appropriate result table by first opening the cursor using the new state code value (module 1410). Then, if that was successful, module 1400 performs module 1420 repeatedly to fetch the current row from the result table (module 1430) and store the data it contains in the temporary storage queue (module 1440). When module 1430 tries to fetch a row beyond the last row in the result table, module 1400 stops invoking 1420 and closes the cursor (module 1450). Since all the data needed to perform the browse operation is now stored outside of DB2, DB2's work is complete.

The next step is for module 1500 to prepare the first screen of data for the new browse. It invokes module 1510 14 times to fill in the symbolic map fields with data for the first 14 records retrieved from the TS queue. After it has prepared the symbolic map, module 1500 performs module 1520 to issue the CICS SEND MAP command to display the data.

If one of module 1000's subordinates detects a processing error, module 1000 performs module 1600 to send an error message to the terminal. But first, module 1600 performs module 1610 14 times to clear the customer line fields in the symbolic map. That insures that no data remains on the screen.

If the program has already retrieved the data for a browse, the user may press the F7 or F8 key to scroll the customer lines on the screen. To process a scroll request, the program performs module 2000, which uses the same subordinates as module 1500. First, it invokes module 1510 14 times to move the appropriate data from the temporary storage queue to the symbolic map. Then, it performs module 1520 to send the map.

The structure chart

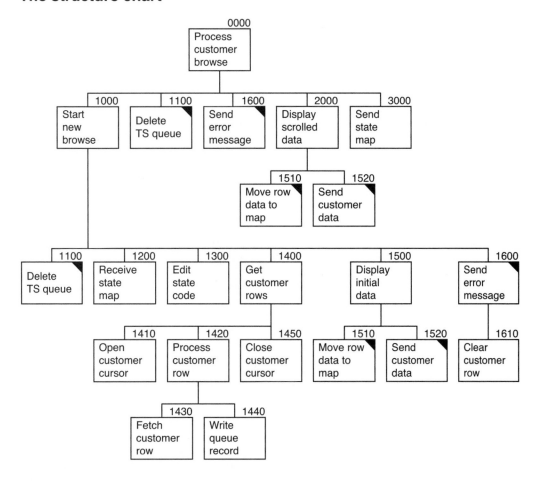

Description

- Because this program is pseudo-conversational, module 0000 must determine the processing to be done each time it's executed. If the program is being executed for the first time, module 3000 is executed to display the state map you saw in figure 8-1.

- If the user presses the Enter key, module 1000 is performed. This module starts by performing module 1100 to delete the temporary queue used by the program. Then, it performs module 1200 to receive the state map and module 1300 to edit the state code entered by the user.

- If the state code is valid, module 1000 continues by performing module 1400 to retrieve the customers in that state and write them to the temporary queue and module 1500 to display the first group of customers. If an error occurs during this processing, module 1600 is performed to display an error message and clear the customer data from the display.

- If the user presses F3 or F12 to end the program, module 1000 performs module 1100 to delete the temporary queue. Then, the program ends.

- If the user presses F7 or F8, module 1000 performs module 2000 to scroll the data on the display. If the user presses any other key, module 1600 is performed to display an error message and clear the customer data from the display.

Figure 8-6   The structure chart for the CICS/DB2 browse program

Other design approaches to the customer browse program

As I designed this program, I tried to keep it as easy to understand as possible. Because I took this approach, I didn't include some features in the program that could make it operate more efficiently. Figure 8-7 presents three of those features.

First, I could have designed the program so it stored more data in each temporary storage record. As this program's design suggests, it stores each row it fetches in a single temporary storage record. Then, to display scrolled data, it retrieves the proper 14 records from the temporary storage in 14 separate operations. A more efficient approach would be to design the temporary storage records so they contain all the data for a complete screen. In other words, each record would contain 14 rows of data. That would reduce the number of CICS requests the program would have to make to store and retrieve data from temporary storage. However, that would also fix the scroll size to a full screen. By using a separate record for each customer line, the program can easily be adjusted to let the user scroll a specific number of lines.

Second, I could have designed the program so that if the user presses the Enter key without changing the state code, the program doesn't start a new browse. To do that, the program would have to compare the state code the user entered with the state code used for the current browse to determine what processing it would do next. This would be more efficient and wouldn't penalize the user for a simple keying error.

Third, I could have combined the functions of modules 1400 and 1500. Under the design in figure 8-6, the program first fetches and stores all of the retrieved data (module 1400). Then, it goes back to the temporary storage queue to get the data for the first 14 rows to format the display (module 1500). I used this approach because I think it makes it easier to understand the programming techniques that accomplish these two tasks. However, a more efficient approach would be for the program to prepare the symbolic map fields for the first screen of a new browse as it loads the temporary storage queue.

If you put your mind to it, I'm sure you can think of still other ways the program could operate. In practice, CICS program development depends on a high degree of finesse that varies with the specifics of the application, the users, the execution environment, and the data itself. So, what may be the best approach in one situation may not be the best in another.

Store data in the TS queue in larger chunks

*   Store a full screen of data (14 records) in each temporary storage queue record.

*   This approach reduces the number of CICS requests the program has to make to store and retrieve data from the queue. However, it also restricts scrolling to a full screen.

Allow the program to restart a browse

*   If the user presses the Enter key without changing the state code, restart the browse by displaying the first 14 records. To do that, the program has to compare the state code retrieved from the screen with the state code used by the current browse to determine if the code has changed.

*   This approach is more efficient since the temporary storage queue doesn't need to be deleted and recreated, so it doesn't penalize the user in terms of response time for a simple keying error.

Combine the data retrieval and initial display functions

*   As the first 14 records are loaded into the temporary storage queue, prepare the customer lines in the symbolic map for those records.

*   This approach is more efficient because the program doesn't have to go back to the temporary storage queue to retrieve the first 14 records after it loads all the records. However, the program is easier to understand with these two tasks coded separately.

Figure 8-7   Other design approaches to the customer browse program

The COBOL listing

Figure 8-8 presents the source code for the browse program. As you can see in part 1 of this figure, this program requires a number of Working-Storage fields. I'll describe some of those fields now, and you'll see how the others are used as I describe the code in the Procedure Division of the program.

The first thing you should notice in the Working-Storage Section is that the communication area is defined with three fields. The first field will contain the state code that's used by the current browse operation, the second field will contain the total number of customer records for that state, and the third field will contain the number of the first record that's currently displayed on the screen. These fields will be passed from one execution of the program to the next through the DFHCOMMAREA field defined in the Linkage Section and will be used to determine the data that's displayed on the screen. If you look ahead to part 2 of this figure, you'll see that DFHCOMMAREA is defined as a 6-character field, which corresponds to the definition in the Working-Storage Section.

The fields that are subordinate to the 01-level item named TEMPORARY-STORAGE-FIELDS are used to work with the records in the temporary storage queue. The first field, TS-QUEUE-NAME, defines the name that's used for the queue. Because your program names the TS queue it uses, you should use a unique identifier as part of the name. That way, you'll avoid naming conflicts with other users' temporary storage queues. Although in many cases an application can benefit by sharing the data in a single TS queue among its users, the customer browse program needs exclusive use of the storage area where it keeps the data it retrieves.

A simple, effective way to create a unique queue name is to combine the CICS identification for the terminal where the user is running the transaction with the name of the transaction itself. Notice in this program that the name of the transaction, DIN2, is coded as a literal, but the name of the terminal will vary. The program can retrieve that name from the field named EIBTRMID in the Execute Interface Block, as you'll see later in this program.

To retrieve a record from a temporary storage queue, you must specify its position in the queue. The first record, for example, is stored in position number 1, the second record in position number 2, and so on. That's what the TS-ITEM-NUMBER field is used for. The last temporary storage field, TS-CUSTOMER-ROW, is used to hold the data for a single record in the temporary storage queue.

The CICS/DB2 browse program   **Page 1**

```
IDENTIFICATION DIVISION.
*
PROGRAM-ID.    DB2DIN2.
*
ENVIRONMENT DIVISION.
*
DATA DIVISION.
*
FILE SECTION.
*
WORKING-STORAGE SECTION.
*
01  SWITCHES.
*
    05  VALID-DATA-SW             PIC X    VALUE 'Y'.
        88  VALID-DATA                     VALUE 'Y'.
    05  END-OF-CUSTOMERS-SW       PIC X    VALUE 'N'.
        88  END-OF-CUSTOMERS               VALUE 'Y'.
    05  CLEAR-CUSTOMER-ROWS-SW    PIC X    VALUE 'N'.
        88  CLEAR-CUSTOMER-ROWS            VALUE 'Y'.
*
01  COMMUNICATION-AREA.
*
    05  CA-STATE-CODE             PIC XX.
    05  CA-TS-RECORD-COUNT        PIC S9(4)   COMP.
    05  CA-FIRST-RECORD-ON-DISPLAY PIC S9(4)  COMP.
*
01  RESPONSE-CODE                 PIC S9(8)   COMP.
*
01  TEMPORARY-STORAGE-FIELDS.
*
    05  TS-QUEUE-NAME.
        10  TS-TERMINAL-ID        PIC X(4).
        10  FILLER                PIC X(4)   VALUE 'DIN2'.
    05  TS-ITEM-NUMBER            PIC S9(4) COMP VALUE ZERO.
    05  TS-CUSTOMER-ROW.
        10  TS-CUSTNO             PIC X(6).
        10  TS-CNAME              PIC X(34).
        10  TS-CITY               PIC X(20).
*
01  POSITION-MESSAGE.
*
    05  FILLER                    PIC X(6) VALUE 'Lines '.
    05  PM-START                  PIC ZZZ9.
    05  FILLER                    PIC X(4) VALUE ' to '.
    05  PM-END                    PIC ZZZ9.
    05  FILLER                    PIC X(4) VALUE ' of '.
    05  PM-TOTAL                  PIC ZZZ9.
*
01  WORK-FIELDS.
*
    05  TOP-ROW-PLUS-13           PIC S9(4) COMP.
    05  STATE-MAP-ROW             PIC S9(4) COMP.
*
```

Figure 8-8   The COBOL listing for the CICS/DB2 browse program (part 1 of 7)

At the top of page 2 of this program, you can see the definition of a row that's retrieved from the customer table. This definition is included instead of the DCLGEN output for the customer table because the DCLGEN output isn't compatible with the data that's retrieved from the table. If you look at the DECLARE CURSOR statement that defines the columns that are included in the cursor, you'll see why that is.

The DECLARE CURSOR statement defines a three-column result table. The first column will contain the customer number, and the third column will contain the customer city. The second column, though, will contain a concatenation that includes the customer's last name followed by a comma and a space, followed by the first letter of the customer's first name and a period. Because the last name field can have a maximum of 30 characters (remember, it's defined as a variable-length column), the concatenated column can have a maximum of 34 characters. You can see the result of this concatenation in the screen in figure 8-1.

The next thing you should notice in the DECLARE CURSOR statement is the SELECT component's WHERE clause. It specifies that data should be selected from the rows in the VARCUST table where the value of the STATE column is equal to the value of the program host variable SIM-D-STATE, which contains the state code the user entered. Note that although STATE isn't one of the columns that are retrieved into the result table, it can still be used to select the rows that are retrieved.

Finally, notice that the DECLARE CURSOR statement includes an ORDER BY clause. It specifies that the rows in the cursor-controlled result table should be put into ascending sequence by the contents of the second column. Because that column contains the last name/first initial concatenation, the result table will be in alphabetical order.

Like the inquiry program in chapter 7, the top-level module in this program starts with an EVALUATE statement that determines which of several functions the current execution of the program should perform. The first two conditions in the EVALUATE statement cause the program to invoke module 3000 to send a fresh screen to the terminal. This happens the first time the program is executed during a terminal session (EIBCALEN = ZERO) and when the user presses the Clear key to reset the screen display (EIBAID = DFHCLEAR).

The third condition in the EVALUATE statement in module 0000 (EIBAID = DFHPA1 OR DFHPA2 OR DFHPA3) is the same as in the inquiry program. It specifies literal values from the DFHAID copy member to detect if the user pressed one of the program attention keys (PA1, PA2, or PA3). CONTINUE directs the program to skip the rest of the EVALUATE structure and continue execution with the next statement.

The fourth condition (EIBAID = DFHPF3 OR DFHPF12) causes the program to issue a CICS XCTL command to pass control back to the menu program named DB2MENU when the user presses either F3 or F12. Before it does that, though, it performs module 1100. This module deletes the TS queue the program used for previous browse operations.

The fifth EVALUATE condition (EIBAID = DFHPF7 OR DFHPF8) causes the program to invoke module 2000 to scroll the lines displayed on the screen. And the sixth condition (EIBAID = DFHENTER) causes the program to start a new browse by invoking module 1000.

The CICS/DB2 browse program   **Page 2**

```
01   CUSTOMER-ROW.
*
     05   CUSTNO                   PIC X(6).
     05   CNAME                    PIC X(34).
     05   CITY                     PIC X(20).
*
     EXEC SQL
         INCLUDE SQLCA
     END-EXEC.
*
 COPY DINSET2.
*
 COPY DFHAID.
*
     EXEC SQL
         DECLARE CUST CURSOR FOR
             SELECT CUSTNO,
                 (LNAME || ', ' ||
                  SUBSTR(FNAME,1,1) || '.'),
                  CITY
                FROM MM01.VARCUST
                WHERE STATE = :SIM-D-STATE
             ORDER BY 2
     END-EXEC.
*
 LINKAGE SECTION.
*
 01   DFHCOMMAREA     PIC X(6).
*
 PROCEDURE DIVISION.
*
 0000-PROCESS-CUSTOMER-BROWSE.
*
     EVALUATE TRUE

         WHEN EIBCALEN = ZERO
             PERFORM 3000-SEND-STATE-MAP

         WHEN EIBAID = DFHCLEAR
             PERFORM 3000-SEND-STATE-MAP

         WHEN EIBAID = DFHPA1 OR DFHPA2 OR DFHPA3
             CONTINUE

         WHEN EIBAID = DFHPF3 OR DFHPF12
             PERFORM 1100-DELETE-TS-QUEUE
             EXEC CICS
                 XCTL PROGRAM('DB2MENU')
             END-EXEC

         WHEN EIBAID = DFHPF7 OR DFHPF8
             PERFORM 2000-DISPLAY-SCROLLED-DATA

         WHEN EIBAID = DFHENTER
             PERFORM 1000-START-NEW-BROWSE
```

Figure 8-8   The COBOL listing for the CICS/DB2 browse program (part 2 of 7)

Finally, if the user pressed an AID key other than those the EVALUATE conditions specify, the code in the WHEN OTHER clause shown on page 3 of this program is executed. The first statement in this clause gets the contents of the communication area from the previous execution of the program. To do that, it moves the DFHCOMMAREA field in the Linkage Section to the COMMUNICATION-AREA group item in the Working-Storage Section. Next, it moves LOW-VALUE to the symbolic map to clear its contents. Then, it sets the value of the map's error message field to "Invalid key pressed." to advise the user of the error, and it moves the state code value for the current browse to the state field in the symbolic map. That way, if the user changed the state code before pressing an invalid key, the state code for the customer rows currently on display will reappear when the map is sent to the terminal. Finally, the program performs module 1600 to send the map to the terminal. This module contains a SEND MAP command with the ALARM option.

Unless the user pressed F3 or F12, program execution continues with the CICS RETURN command that follows EVALUATE. This command passes control back to CICS and causes the current execution of the program to end. However, it specifies that the next time the terminal user presses an AID key, CICS should execute the program associated with the transaction identifier DIN2. That's the browse program this chapter presents. The RETURN command also specifies that the contents of the Working-Storage field COMMU-NICATION-AREA should be retained in the CICS communication area. So, the next time this program runs, that data will be available through DFHCOMMAREA.

Page 3 of this program also shows module 1000, which is performed when the user presses the Enter key to start a new browse. Its functions fall into five categories: (1) clearing data stored by a previous browse, (2) getting a valid state code for the new browse, (3) retrieving all the data for the new browse into temporary storage, (4) preparing and displaying the first screen of browse data, and (5) displaying an error message, if necessary.

Module 1100 clears the data stored by a previous browse. To do that, it uses the CICS DELETEQ TS command. This command causes CICS to delete the temporary storage queue the statement names. Before this command is issued, then, the EIBTRMID field in the EIB is moved to the TS-TERMINAL-ID field. If you look back to part 1 of this figure, you'll see that the TS-TERMINAL-ID field is part of the TS-QUEUE-NAME field that's used in the DELETEQ TS command.

The RESP option that's included on the DELETEQ TS command specifies a Working-Storage field that will contain a response-code value CICS returns to report the success or failure of the command. The compound IF statement that immediately follows the command checks the response code. First, it checks to see whether errors occurred:

```
RESPONSE-CODE NOT = DFHRESP(NORMAL)
```

And if an error did occur, it checks to see if the error was an invalid queue name:

```
RESPONSE-CODE NOT = DFHRESP(QIDERR)
```

The CICS/DB2 browse program   **Page 3**

```
          WHEN OTHER
               MOVE DFHCOMMAREA TO COMMUNICATION-AREA
               MOVE LOW-VALUE TO STATE-INQUIRY-MAP
               MOVE 'Invalid key pressed.' TO SIM-D-MESSAGE
               MOVE CA-STATE-CODE TO SIM-D-STATE
               PERFORM 1600-SEND-ERROR-MESSAGE

      END-EVALUATE.

      EXEC CICS
          RETURN TRANSID('DIN2')
                  COMMAREA(COMMUNICATION-AREA)
      END-EXEC.
*
 1000-START-NEW-BROWSE.
*
      MOVE LOW-VALUE TO STATE-INQUIRY-MAP.
      MOVE SPACE       TO SIM-D-MESSAGE.
      PERFORM 1100-DELETE-TS-QUEUE.
      PERFORM 1200-RECEIVE-STATE-MAP.
      PERFORM 1300-EDIT-STATE-CODE.
      IF VALID-DATA
          MOVE ZERO TO CA-TS-RECORD-COUNT
          PERFORM 1400-GET-CUSTOMER-ROWS.
      IF VALID-DATA
          IF CA-TS-RECORD-COUNT > 0
              PERFORM 1500-DISPLAY-INITIAL-DATA
          ELSE
              MOVE 'There are no customers in that state.'
                         TO SIM-D-MESSAGE
              MOVE SPACE TO SIM-D-LINEMSG
                              SIM-D-MOREMSG
              MOVE 'Y'    TO CLEAR-CUSTOMER-ROWS-SW
              MOVE 'N'    TO VALID-DATA-SW.
      IF NOT VALID-DATA
          PERFORM 1600-SEND-ERROR-MESSAGE.
*
 1100-DELETE-TS-QUEUE.
*
      MOVE EIBTRMID TO TS-TERMINAL-ID.
      EXEC CICS
          DELETEQ TS QUEUE(TS-QUEUE-NAME)
                      RESP(RESPONSE-CODE)
      END-EXEC.
      IF        RESPONSE-CODE NOT = DFHRESP(NORMAL)
          AND RESPONSE-CODE NOT = DFHRESP(QIDERR)
          EXEC CICS
              ABEND
          END-EXEC.
*
```

Figure 8-8   The COBOL listing for the CICS/DB2 browse program (part 3 of 7)

This condition will occur for the first browse request, since no queue was previously created. (A TS queue is created automatically when your program writes to it.) If an error occurred and the queue name wasn't invalid, it indicates a more serious error. Then, module 1100 issues a CICS ABEND command to end the program immediately.

After module 1100 deletes the program's temporary storage queue, execution continues as module 1000 invokes module 1200. This module issues a CICS RECEIVE MAP command to get the data the user entered to start the browse. It is much like the RECEIVE MAP command you saw in the inquiry program in the last chapter. However, the INTO option specifies the name of the customized symbolic map (STATE-INQUIRY-MAP).

Next, module 1000 performs module 1300 to edit the state code value the user entered. Here again, the browse program is similar to the inquiry program. If the length of the user's entry (returned in the SIM-L-STATE field) is greater than zero and the entry itself (the value of SIM-D-STATE) isn't spaces, the entry is valid. A more sophisticated version of this program might include a table look-up to verify that a non-blank entry really is a valid state code.

If the state code isn't valid, the program turns the valid-data switch off and turns the clear-customer-rows switch on. You'll see how the program uses these switches in later modules. The program also moves an error message to the message field in the symbolic map (SIM-D-MESSAGE).

After module 1300 finishes, module 1000 checks the setting of the valid-data switch to determine if the program should proceed by retrieving data from the customer table. If this switch is on, module 1000 performs module 1400.

Module 1400 manages all of this program's SQL operations. First, it performs module 1410 to open a cursor for the browse. The SQL OPEN statement in module 1410 names CUST as the cursor. You can look back to part 2 of the figure to see the DECLARE CURSOR statement that specifies CUST.

If the OPEN statement in module 1410 returns a non-zero SQLCODE value, it indicates some serious processing error occurred. In that case, module 1410 supplies an appropriate error message and sets switches that control later processing. Otherwise, the cursor-controlled result table is ready for the program to access, and module 1400 continues.

Module 1400 uses a PERFORM UNTIL statement to execute module 1420 repeatedly, and module 1420 has two subordinates of its own. Module 1430 issues an SQL FETCH statement to retrieve a row from the cursor-controlled result table. Its INTO clause names the three fields in the host structure for the operation: CUSTNO, CNAME, and CITY. Module 1430 also performs error checking similar to module 1410's.

The CICS/DB2 browse program   **Page 4**

```
1200-RECEIVE-STATE-MAP.
*
    EXEC CICS
        RECEIVE MAP('DINMAP2')
               MAPSET('DINSET2')
               INTO(STATE-INQUIRY-MAP)
    END-EXEC.
*
1300-EDIT-STATE-CODE.
*
    IF       SIM-L-STATE = ZERO
         OR SIM-D-STATE = SPACE
        MOVE 'N' TO VALID-DATA-SW
        MOVE 'Y' TO CLEAR-CUSTOMER-ROWS-SW
        MOVE 'You must enter a state code.' TO SIM-D-MESSAGE
    ELSE
        MOVE SIM-D-STATE TO CA-STATE-CODE.
*
1400-GET-CUSTOMER-ROWS.
*
    PERFORM 1410-OPEN-CUSTOMER-CURSOR.
    IF VALID-DATA
        PERFORM 1420-PROCESS-CUSTOMER-ROW
            UNTIL END-OF-CUSTOMERS
        PERFORM 1450-CLOSE-CUSTOMER-CURSOR.
*
1410-OPEN-CUSTOMER-CURSOR.
*
    EXEC SQL
        OPEN CUST
    END-EXEC.
    IF SQLCODE NOT = 0
        MOVE 'Y' TO CLEAR-CUSTOMER-ROWS-SW
        MOVE 'DB2 open error.' TO SIM-D-MESSAGE
        MOVE 'N' TO VALID-DATA-SW.
*
1420-PROCESS-CUSTOMER-ROW.
*
    PERFORM 1430-FETCH-CUSTOMER-ROW.
    IF NOT END-OF-CUSTOMERS
        PERFORM 1440-WRITE-QUEUE-RECORD.
*
1430-FETCH-CUSTOMER-ROW.
*
    EXEC SQL
        FETCH CUST
            INTO :CUSTNO, :CNAME, :CITY
    END-EXEC.
    IF SQLCODE NOT = 0
        MOVE 'Y' TO END-OF-CUSTOMERS-SW
        IF SQLCODE NOT = 100
            MOVE 'Y' TO CLEAR-CUSTOMER-ROWS-SW
            MOVE 'DB2 fetch error.' TO SIM-D-MESSAGE
            MOVE 'N' TO VALID-DATA-SW.
*
```

Figure 8-8   The COBOL listing for the CICS/DB2 browse program (part 4 of 7)

If the FETCH succeeds, module 1420 performs module 1440. This module begins by incrementing the counter field that keeps track of how many rows are returned through the cursor-controlled result table: CA-TS-RECORD-COUNT.

Then, it moves the fetched data into the Working-Storage fields that will make up the record that's stored in the temporary storage queue. Finally, module 1440 issues a CICS WRITEQ TS command to write the record to the temporary storage queue. This command's first option, TS-QUEUE-NAME, is the same name the program used in module 1100. The second option, TS-CUSTOMER-ROW, is the name of the group item that contains the data this command writes to the temporary storage queue.

After the program fetches all the rows in the CUST table that have the specified state code and writes them to the TS queue, module 1400 executes module 1450. This module issues an SQL CLOSE statement to close the CUST cursor. Then, it performs some error checking. From this point on, the program manages the browse without issuing another SQL statement.

If no unexpected errors occur during the processing of module 1400, module 1000 invokes module 1500 to display the first screen of data for the new browse. This module performs module 1510 14 times, once for each customer row on the screen. Module 1510 issues a CICS READQ TS command to retrieve a stored record from the temporary storage queue. The third option in this command, ITEM, names a program field whose value specifies the number of the record in the queue that should be returned into TS-CUSTOMER-ROW. Module 1500 sets the value of TS-ITEM-NUMBER to 1 before it executes module 1510. And module 1510 increments its value each time it retrieves a record from the queue.

Notice that module 1510 issues the CICS READQ TS command only if the number of the queue item that's about to be read is not greater than the total number of rows that were fetched from the VARCUST table and saved in the TS queue. Then, after this module retrieves the item, it moves the data to the appropriate fields in the symbolic map. Otherwise, it moves spaces to those fields.

After it performs module 1510 to format each of the 14 customer lines in the symbolic map, module 1500 prepares the contents of the scroll information lines. Here, the program stores the information for the first line in a group item named POSITION-MESSAGE. It sets the value of the first row displayed (PM-START) to 1 and the value of the total number of rows retrieved (PM-TOTAL) to the value of CA-TS-RECORD-COUNT. Then, if the program stored more than 14 records in the TS queue for the browse, it sets the value of the last row displayed (PM-END) to 14. If the program stored 14 or fewer records in the TS queue, it sets the value of PM-END to CA-TS-RECORD-COUNT.

Module 1500 also provides a literal value for the scrolling direction message field in the symbolic map (SIM-D-MOREMSG). If the program stored 14 or fewer records in the TS queue, it sets the value of SIM-D-MOREMSG to space; no scrolling is possible, either up or down. Otherwise, it sets the value of SIM-D-MOREMSG to indicate that the user can scroll forward. After the condition ends, the program moves the entire line-count message (POSITION-MES-SAGE) to the SIM-D-LINEMSG field in the symbolic map.

The CICS/DB2 browse program   **Page 5**

```
 1440-WRITE-QUEUE-RECORD.
*
     ADD 1          TO CA-TS-RECORD-COUNT.
     MOVE CUSTNO  TO TS-CUSTNO.
     MOVE CNAME   TO TS-CNAME.
     MOVE CITY    TO TS-CITY.
     EXEC CICS
         WRITEQ TS QUEUE(TS-QUEUE-NAME)
                   FROM(TS-CUSTOMER-ROW)
     END-EXEC.
*
 1450-CLOSE-CUSTOMER-CURSOR.
*
     EXEC SQL
         CLOSE CUST
     END-EXEC.
     IF SQLCODE NOT = 0
         MOVE 'Y' TO CLEAR-CUSTOMER-ROWS-SW
         MOVE 'DB2 close error.' TO SIM-D-MESSAGE
         MOVE 'N' TO VALID-DATA-SW.
*
 1500-DISPLAY-INITIAL-DATA.
*
     MOVE SPACE TO SIM-D-MESSAGE.
     MOVE 1 TO CA-FIRST-RECORD-ON-DISPLAY
               TS-ITEM-NUMBER.
     PERFORM 1510-MOVE-ROW-DATA-TO-MAP
         VARYING STATE-MAP-ROW FROM 1 BY 1
         UNTIL STATE-MAP-ROW > 14.
     MOVE 1 TO PM-START.
     MOVE CA-TS-RECORD-COUNT TO PM-TOTAL.
     IF CA-TS-RECORD-COUNT > 14
         MOVE 14 TO PM-END
         MOVE 'More:    +' TO SIM-D-MOREMSG
     ELSE
         MOVE CA-TS-RECORD-COUNT TO PM-END
         MOVE SPACE TO SIM-D-MOREMSG.
     MOVE POSITION-MESSAGE TO SIM-D-LINEMSG.
     PERFORM 1520-SEND-CUSTOMER-DATA.
*
 1510-MOVE-ROW-DATA-TO-MAP.
*
     IF TS-ITEM-NUMBER <= CA-TS-RECORD-COUNT
         EXEC CICS
             READQ TS QUEUE(TS-QUEUE-NAME)
                      INTO (TS-CUSTOMER-ROW)
                      ITEM(TS-ITEM-NUMBER)
         END-EXEC
         MOVE TS-CUSTNO TO SIM-D-CUSTNO(STATE-MAP-ROW)
         MOVE TS-CNAME  TO SIM-D-NAME(STATE-MAP-ROW)
         MOVE TS-CITY   TO SIM-D-CITY(STATE-MAP-ROW)
         ADD 1 TO TS-ITEM-NUMBER
     ELSE
```

Figure 8-8   The COBOL listing for the CICS/DB2 browse program (part 5 of 7)

After it has prepared the entire symbolic map, module 1500 performs module 1520. This module issues a CICS SEND MAP command with the DATAONLY option. The command transmits the contents of the symbolic map to the terminal without headings and captions. Those literal values are already present on the screen.

If one of module 1000's subordinates detects an unmanageable error condition, it turns the valid-data switch off. The last thing module 1000 does is check the value of that switch. If it indicates an error, module 1000 invokes module 1600, which performs module 1610 14 times to clear the contents of the customer lines in the symbolic map. Note, however, that this module is executed only if the clear-customer-rows switch is true, which is the case if any errors occur in a module subordinate to module 1000. The only time this condition isn't true is when module 1600 is executed from module 0000. After module 1600 performs module 1610, it issues a SEND MAP command with the ALARM option to send the error message.

When a browse is in progress, the user may be able to press F7 or F8 to scroll backward or forward on the screen. If the EVALUATE statement in module 0000 detects either of those PF keys, it performs module 2000 to scroll the display as indicated by the user.

The operation of module 2000 depends on the values CICS passed to the current execution of the program from the previous execution through the communication area. So, the first thing module 2000 does is move the contents of DFHCOMMAREA to the Working-Storage group item named COMMUNI-CATION-AREA. The scroll operations in this module depend on the CA-TS-RECORD-COUNT field in this group, which contains the total number of records in temporary storage, and the CA-TS-FIRST-RECORD-ON-DISPLAY field, which contains the number of the temporary storage record that's currently the first customer line on the screen.

After module 2000 sets the values of some data items, it determines which record in the temporary storage queue should appear at the top of the screen after the scroll operation is completed. To do that, it starts by checking the EIBAID field to determine if the user pressed PF7 to display the 13 rows that precede those currently on the screen or PF8 to display the 13 rows that follow those currently on the screen. (Remember, the program scrolls the display 13 rows rather than 14 so that one item from the previous group remains on the screen to orient the user.) If the user pressed PF7, the program then checks to see if the first record that's displayed is the fourteenth or later record. If so, it subtracts 13 from the CA-FIRST-RECORD-ON-DISPLAY field. If not, it indicates that the first screen of customers is already displayed and no processing is performed.

If the program determines that the user pressed PF8, similar processing is performed. This time, though, the program checks to be sure that the last screen of data isn't already displayed. To do that, it adds 13 to the value of the CA-FIRST-RECORD-ON-DISPLAY field and compares it with the value of the CA-TS-RECORD-COUNT field. If the first value is less than the second, it means that there are more records to be displayed. Then, 13 is added to the CA-FIRST-RECORD-ON-DISPLAY field. If all of the records have already been displayed, no processing is performed.

The CICS/DB2 browse program   **Page 6**

```
                MOVE SPACE       TO SIM-D-CUSTNO(STATE-MAP-ROW)
                                    SIM-D-NAME(STATE-MAP-ROW)
                                    SIM-D-CITY(STATE-MAP-ROW).
*
 1520-SEND-CUSTOMER-DATA.
*
     EXEC CICS
         SEND MAP('DINMAP2')
              MAPSET('DINSET2')
              FROM(STATE-INQUIRY-MAP)
              DATAONLY
     END-EXEC.
*
 1600-SEND-ERROR-MESSAGE.
*
     IF CLEAR-CUSTOMER-ROWS
         PERFORM 1610-CLEAR-CUSTOMER-ROW
             VARYING STATE-MAP-ROW FROM 1 BY 1
             UNTIL STATE-MAP-ROW > 14.
     EXEC CICS
         SEND MAP('DINMAP2')
              MAPSET('DINSET2')
              FROM(STATE-INQUIRY-MAP)
              DATAONLY
              ALARM
     END-EXEC.
*
 1610-CLEAR-CUSTOMER-ROW.
*
     MOVE SPACE TO SIM-D-CUSTNO(STATE-MAP-ROW)
                   SIM-D-NAME(STATE-MAP-ROW)
                   SIM-D-CITY(STATE-MAP-ROW).
*
 2000-DISPLAY-SCROLLED-DATA.
*
     MOVE DFHCOMMAREA    TO COMMUNICATION-AREA.
     MOVE EIBTRMID       TO TS-TERMINAL-ID.
     MOVE LOW-VALUE      TO STATE-INQUIRY-MAP.
     MOVE SPACE          TO SIM-D-MESSAGE.
     MOVE CA-STATE-CODE TO SIM-D-STATE.
     IF CA-TS-RECORD-COUNT = 0
         MOVE 'No customers selected.' TO SIM-D-MESSAGE
     ELSE
         IF EIBAID = DFHPF7
             IF CA-FIRST-RECORD-ON-DISPLAY > 13
                 SUBTRACT 13 FROM CA-FIRST-RECORD-ON-DISPLAY
             END-IF
         ELSE
             IF CA-FIRST-RECORD-ON-DISPLAY + 13 <
                     CA-TS-RECORD-COUNT
                 ADD 13 TO CA-FIRST-RECORD-ON-DISPLAY
             END-IF
         END-IF
     MOVE CA-FIRST-RECORD-ON-DISPLAY TO TS-ITEM-NUMBER
```

Figure 8-8   The COBOL listing for the CICS/DB2 browse program (part 6 of 7)

After it determines what queue record should appear in the first line on the next screen of data, the program moves the number of that record to the Working-Storage field named TS-ITEM-NUMBER. Then, it uses a PERFORM VARYING statement to invoke module 1510 repeatedly. This is the same module that was used to format and display the initial screen for a browse. It retrieves records from temporary storage and moves the data they contain to the proper fields in the symbolic map.

The rest of the code in module 2000 prepares the contents of the scroll information lines so they contain the proper line numbers and the right scrolling message for the new screen. Then, the symbolic map is complete, and module 2000 performs module 1520 to send the data to the terminal.

The last module in the program, module 3000, sends a fresh screen to the terminal. To do that, it moves LOW-VALUE to the symbolic map, then issues a SEND MAP command with the ERASE option. This module is performed from module 0000 the first time the program is executed and when the user presses the Clear key.

The CICS/DB2 browse program   **Page 7**

```
            PERFORM 1510-MOVE-ROW-DATA-TO-MAP
                VARYING STATE-MAP-ROW FROM 1 BY 1
                UNTIL STATE-MAP-ROW > 14
            MOVE CA-FIRST-RECORD-ON-DISPLAY  TO PM-START
            MOVE CA-TS-RECORD-COUNT          TO PM-TOTAL
            ADD 13 TO CA-FIRST-RECORD-ON-DISPLAY
                GIVING TOP-ROW-PLUS-13
            IF CA-FIRST-RECORD-ON-DISPLAY = 1
                IF TOP-ROW-PLUS-13 < CA-TS-RECORD-COUNT
                    MOVE TOP-ROW-PLUS-13    TO PM-END
                    MOVE 'More:    +'       TO SIM-D-MOREMSG
                ELSE
                    MOVE CA-TS-RECORD-COUNT TO PM-END
                    MOVE SPACE              TO SIM-D-MOREMSG
                END-IF
            ELSE
                IF TOP-ROW-PLUS-13 < CA-TS-RECORD-COUNT
                    MOVE TOP-ROW-PLUS-13    TO PM-END
                    MOVE 'More: - +'        TO SIM-D-MOREMSG
                ELSE
                    MOVE CA-TS-RECORD-COUNT TO PM-END
                    MOVE 'More: -  '        TO SIM-D-MOREMSG
                END-IF
            END-IF
            MOVE POSITION-MESSAGE TO SIM-D-LINEMSG.
        PERFORM 1520-SEND-CUSTOMER-DATA.
    *
     3000-SEND-STATE-MAP.
    *
        MOVE LOW-VALUE TO STATE-INQUIRY-MAP.
        EXEC CICS
            SEND MAP('DINMAP2')
                MAPSET('DINSET2')
                FROM(STATE-INQUIRY-MAP)
                ERASE
        END-EXEC.
```

Figure 8-8   The COBOL listing for the CICS/DB2 browse program (part 7 of 7)

Perspective

The program example in this chapter presents a simple and straightforward approach to browsing DB2 data in a CICS program. Even so, it should give you an idea of the complexity that's involved in developing browse applications. In particular, this program illustrates the techniques for implementing the basic browse functions: displaying multiple rows of data on the screen at one time, and letting the user scroll from one screen to another to display all the records in the set.

Beyond that, this chapter should help you understand the basic conflict between CICS and DB2 operations, how that conflict affects the strategies you can use to develop a browse application, and the tradeoffs involved in using each of those strategies. Keep in mind, however, that regardless of the strategy you use, browses are always costly in terms of the overall performance of an online transaction processing system. So you should use browse applications only when they provide a critical function.

The intent of the chapters in this section has been to present the basic design and programming considerations for developing CICS programs that access DB2 data. But there's a lot more to know about CICS than what's presented in this section. So for complete coverage of developing COBOL programs that run under CICS, we recommend our books *CICS for the COBOL Programmer, Part 1* and *Part 2*.

Section 4

Database administration

In most OS/390 shops, the database administrator is responsible for designing, defining, and managing the DB2 databases in the production environment. As an application programmer or programmer/analyst, however, you may be responsible for designing, defining, and managing the databases in your testing or quality assurance environment. If so, you'll want to know about the topics related to database administration presented in the chapters in this section. Even if you're not responsible for database administration, though, you may want to read these chapters because they can help you work more productively and professionally.

Chapter 9 presents concepts for designing DB2 data structures. Chapter 10 presents the SQL Data Definition Language (DDL) statements you can use to create and manage DB2 objects as you test your programs. Chapter 11 presents the DB2 commands and utilities you can use to work with database objects. Chapter 12 describes the information you can get from some of the system tables that comprise the DB2 catalog. And chapter 13 covers the SQL EXPLAIN statement that you can use to get performance analysis data about your program.

Although the intent of this section is to give you an overview of DB2 features related to database administration, the information presented here should be enough to get you started if you ever need to use any of these features. If you need to create the tables that you use to test the application programs you develop, for example, you can do that using the information on the CREATE TABLE statement that's presented in chapter 10. If you need to find out about the organization of an existing table or about the relationships between tables, you can display information from DB2's catalog tables as described in chapter 12. And if you need information about the performance of a specific SQL statement, you can use the EXPLAIN statement to display that information as described in chapter 13.

9

How to design a DB2 database

To develop programs that process DB2 data, you need to have a basic understanding of relational database design. Specifically, you need to understand how a relational table is organized and how the tables in a relational database are related. *Part 1* of this series presented those concepts, and they have been illustrated by the tables used for the programs throughout *Part 1* and *Part 2*.

Now, this chapter presents some additional concepts related to database design. Specifically, it describes the process of normalization, which insures that the data is stored in the most efficient and practical way possible. Although most programmers aren't responsible for designing databases, you'll be able to work more effectively and confidently as a programmer if you have a basic understanding of the normalization process.

An introduction to database design

Figure 9-1 lists the three basic steps for designing a database. To start, you identify all the data that will be stored in the database. In general, you do that by looking at the output that will be produced from the data in the database. For example, most of the data that will be stored in the orders database used as an example in this chapter appears on the invoice form shown in this figure.

Before you can look at the output requirements for a database, of course, you must have the specifications for the applications that will use the database. That means you need to know what processing they will perform, what input they will receive, and what output they will produce. This chapter assumes that you have that information and you can readily identify the data that the database will contain.

Once you identify the data requirements, you can organize the data into normalized tables. You'll see how to do that in the topics that follow. For now, just realize that normalized data uses storage efficiently and is easy to maintain.

After you design the tables of the database, you still need to identify the indexes and views that will be used to access the data they contain. You can usually do that by studying the specifications for the programs that access the database. If all the program specifications aren't available, though, or new programs are added after you've designed the database, don't worry. You can always add indexes and views to the database at a later time. In fact, you can add new columns of data to the database later too if you discover that you've left some information out. In general, though, it's best if you get the most complete specifications you can before you create the tables, views, and indexes.

In the past, database design was mostly a manual process where you wrote out the specifications by hand or, more recently, using a word processing program. Today, other programs are available that let you design a database using a visual interface. Most of these programs are designed to run on PCs under the Windows operating system.

In this chapter, you'll see the design of the orders database in Microsoft Access. Although this tool wasn't developed for designing DB2 databases, it is a relational database management tool. So you can use it to analyze and organize the data for a DB2 database.

Three basic steps for designing a database

Step 1:   Identify the data requirements

Step 2:   Organize the data into normalized tables

Step 3:   Identify the indexes and views that will be used to access the data

An invoice form that identifies most of the data requirements for the order database

Invoice number	999999
Invoice date	99-99-99

Customer Number	999999
Name	XXXXXXXXXXXXXXXXXX XXXXXXXXXXXXXXXXXXXXXXXXXXXXX
Address	XXXXXXXXXXXXXXXXXXXXXXXXXXXX
City State Zip	XXXXXXXXXXXXXXXXXXXX XX 99999-9999

Product	Description	Quantity	Unit price	Discount	Extension
XXXXXXXXXX	XXXXXXXXXXXXXXXXXXXXXXXXXXXXXXXX	9999999	99999.99	99999.99	99999.99
XXXXXXXXXX	XXXXXXXXXXXXXXXXXXXXXXXXXXXXXXXX	9999999	99999.99	99999.99	99999.99
XXXXXXXXXX	XXXXXXXXXXXXXXXXXXXXXXXXXXXXXXXX	9999999	99999.99	99999.99	99999.99
XXXXXXXXXX	XXXXXXXXXXXXXXXXXXXXXXXXXXXXXXXX	9999999	99999.99	99999.99	99999.99
XXXXXXXXXX	XXXXXXXXXXXXXXXXXXXXXXXXXXXXXXXX	9999999	99999.99	99999.99	99999.99
XXXXXXXXXX	XXXXXXXXXXXXXXXXXXXXXXXXXXXXXXXX	9999999	99999.99	99999.99	99999.99
XXXXXXXXXX	XXXXXXXXXXXXXXXXXXXXXXXXXXXXXXXX	9999999	99999.99	99999.99	99999.99
XXXXXXXXXX	XXXXXXXXXXXXXXXXXXXXXXXXXXXXXXXX	9999999	99999.99	99999.99	99999.99
XXXXXXXXXX	XXXXXXXXXXXXXXXXXXXXXXXXXXXXXXXX	9999999	99999.99	99999.99	99999.99
XXXXXXXXXX	XXXXXXXXXXXXXXXXXXXXXXXXXXXXXXXX	9999999	99999.99	99999.99	99999.99
XXXXXXXXXX	XXXXXXXXXXXXXXXXXXXXXXXXXXXXXXXX	9999999	99999.99	99999.99	99999.99
XXXXXXXXXX	XXXXXXXXXXXXXXXXXXXXXXXXXXXXXXXX	9999999	99999.99	99999.99	99999.99
XXXXXXXXXX	XXXXXXXXXXXXXXXXXXXXXXXXXXXXXXXX	9999999	99999.99	99999.99	99999.99
XXXXXXXXXX	XXXXXXXXXXXXXXXXXXXXXXXXXXXXXXXX	9999999	99999.99	99999.99	99999.99
XXXXXXXXXX	XXXXXXXXXXXXXXXXXXXXXXXXXXXXXXXX	9999999	99999.99	99999.99	99999.99
XXXXXXXXXX	XXXXXXXXXXXXXXXXXXXXXXXXXXXXXXXX	9999999	99999.99	99999.99	99999.99
XXXXXXXXXX	XXXXXXXXXXXXXXXXXXXXXXXXXXXXXXXX	9999999	99999.99	99999.99	99999.99
XXXXXXXXXX	XXXXXXXXXXXXXXXXXXXXXXXXXXXXXXXX	9999999	99999.99	99999.99	99999.99
XXXXXXXXXX	XXXXXXXXXXXXXXXXXXXXXXXXXXXXXXXX	9999999	99999.99	99999.99	99999.99
XXXXXXXXXX	XXXXXXXXXXXXXXXXXXXXXXXXXXXXXXXX	9999999	99999.99	99999.99	99999.99

Subtotal	9999999.99
Shipping	99999.99
Sales tax	99999.99
TOTAL DUE	9999999.99

Figure 9-1   The basic steps for designing a database

How to normalize a data structure

Normalization results in a data design that's appropriate for DB2 tables, that's easy to understand, and that will be relatively efficient. The normalization process has several steps, and the table design that results from each of the steps is called a *normal form*. For example, the result of the first step is called the first normal form, the result of the second step is called the second normal form, and so on. Although database designers sometimes use five levels of normalization, three levels are adequate for most databases.

The essence of normalization is that the data stored in a row of a table should be identifiable by a key, and all the columns in the table should relate directly to that key. For example, the key values for a customer table identify specific rows in the table, and all the data elements in a row relate to the entity represented by the key value, in this case, a customer. In this chapter, you'll see how to apply the normalization process to the data for the order database. But first, I want you to see an unnormalized structure for the order data so you can compare it with the normalized data structure you'll see later.

An unnormalized data structure for the order data

Figure 9-2 presents a COBOL record description for the unnormalized order data. Except for the last field, IR-INVPROM, all of the information in this record was extracted from the invoice form you saw in the previous figure. The IR-INVPROM field contains a promotion code for the invoice, which would be entered with the other invoice information and could appear on other output documents or displays.

If you review the fields in this record description, you'll notice two problems with this structure. First, if the same customer has two or more invoices, the information for that customer is stored in each invoice. So if any of that information changes, it would have to be changed in all of the invoices. Otherwise, the data would be inconsistent. A similar problem exists with the product information, since the product description is stored in each line item for each invoice.

The second problem is that each invoice can contain a maximum of 20 line items as specified by the OCCURS clause, which makes this structure inflexible. In addition, repeating groups like this aren't supported by relational databases, so you couldn't actually implement this structure in DB2.

In a minute, you'll see how these problems are eliminated by the first three normal forms. But first, you should know that you would never start a database design by creating a structure like the one in this figure. Instead, you'd start by breaking the data into recognizable entities, like customer data, invoice data, and product data. Then, you'd apply the rules of normalization to each of those entities. To illustrate the complete process of normalization, though, I'll start with the unnormalized data structure shown in this figure.

A COBOL record description for the unnormalized order data

```
01  INVOICE-RECORD
*
    05  IR-INVNO            PIC X(6).
    05  IR-INVDATE          PIC X(8).
    05  IR-CUSTNO           PIC X(6).
    05  IR-FNAME            PIC X(20).
    05  IR-LNAME            PIC X(30).
    05  IR-ADDR             PIC X(30).
    05  IR-CITY             PIC X(20).
    05  IR-STATE            PIC XX.
    05  IR-ZIPCODE          PIC X(10).
    05  IR-LINE-ITEM  OCCURS 20 TIMES.
        10  IR-PCODE        PIC X(10).
        10  IR-DESC         PIC X(30).
        10  IR-QTY          PIC S9(7)     COMP-3.
        10  IR-PRICE        PIC S9(5)V99  COMP-3.
        10  IR-DISC         PIC S9(5)V99  COMP-3.
        10  IR-EXT          PIC S9(5)V99  COMP-3.
    05  IR-INVSUBT          PIC S9(7)V99  COMP-3.
    05  IR-INVSHIP          PIC S9(5)V99  COMP-3.
    05  IR-INVTAX           PIC S9(5)V99  COMP-3.
    05  IR-INVTOTAL         PIC S9(7)V99  COMP-3.
    05  IR-INVPROM          PIC X(10).
```

Problems caused by an unnormalized data structure

- An unnormalized data structure can contain information on two or more entities. For example, the unnormalized order structure contains information on both invoices and customers. That means that if a customer has two or more invoices, the information for that customer is repeated in each invoice. And that can cause storage and maintenance problems.

- An unnormalized data structure that contains a repeating group can include a limited number of items in that group. The line item group in the unnormalized invoice structure, for example, can contain a maximum of 20 items.

Note

- DB2 doesn't support repeating groups like the one used for the invoice line items. Because of that, you can't implement this structure in DB2.

Figure 9-2   An unnormalized data structure for the order data

How to create a data structure in first normal form

To create a data structure in *first normal form*, you store the elements of a repeating group in a separate table. In figure 9-3, for example, you can see that the database consists of two tables. The invoice table contains general invoice information, and the line item table contains information about the line items for each invoice.

The line between the invoice and line item table in this figure indicates that the tables have a one-to-many relationship. In other words, each row in the invoice table can be related to one or more rows in the line item table. Here, the invoice number column in the line item table is a foreign key, and it identifies the invoice in the invoice table that it's related to. The invoice number column in the invoice table is the primary key of that table.

If you read *Part 1* of this series, you may recall that foreign keys are central to maintaining referential integrity. *Referential integrity* means that references from one table to another (such as from the line item table to the invoice table) are valid. DBAs can specify that DB2 should automatically enforce referential integrity rules when they define related tables. You'll learn how to define the foreign keys that enforce referential integrity in the next chapter.

Because the line item table can contain more than one row for each invoice, the invoice number column in that table doesn't uniquely identify a row in that table. To do that, you need to include the product code column as part of the primary key. In other words, the primary key for the line item table is a *composite key* that consists of the invoice number and product code columns. That's what the boldfaced column names in this diagram indicate. For that to work, you have to assume that the same product can't be referred to in more than one line item in the same invoice. That constraint would probably be implemented by the program that accepted the order information.

You should also notice that the extension data that's included in the invoice form in figure 9-1 and the unnormalized data structure in figure 9-2 isn't included in the line item table in this figure. That's because the extension can be calculated based on other data elements in the row, and it would be redundant to include it. If this information is used frequently, though, it may be more efficient to include than it would be to calculate it each time it's needed. That's the type of decision you have to make as you study the specifications for the programs that will use the database.

The order data in first normal form

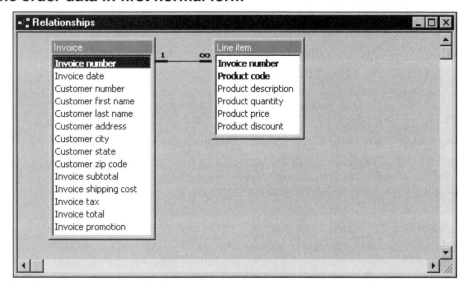

Description

- To create a data structure in *first normal form*, you store the elements of a repeating group, like the line items in the order database, in a separate table. Then, each row in the original table has a one-to-many relationship with the rows in the new table.

- Each row in the table on the "one" side of a one-to-many relationship must have a unique key that can be used to identify it. That key is then included in each related row in the table on the "many" side of the relationship as a foreign key.

- With version 5 of DB2, you can define a relationship between a foreign key in one table and any unique key in another table, including the primary key. Before version 5, relationships could only be defined between a foreign key and a primary key.

- Two or more columns can be used to uniquely identify each row in a table. When a key consists of more than one column, it's called a *composite key*.

Note

- The boldfaced column names in each table above make up the primary key for the table. The line between the tables indicates the relationship between the tables, where the number 1 represents the one side of the relationship and the infinity symbol represents the many side of the relationship.

Figure 9-3   How to create a data structure in first normal form

How to create a data structure in second normal form

The next step in the normalization process is to separate data items from a table with a composite key if the items only depend on part of the key. For example, the complete key for the line item table in figure 9-3 consists of both the invoice number and the product code columns. However, one of the line item data elements, product description, depends only on the product code component of the composite key. It doesn't depend on the invoice number component because its value doesn't change from one invoice to another. As a result, this table needs to be modified to be in *second normal form.*

Figure 9-4 shows the tables in the order database in second normal form. Here, the product description column has been removed from the line item table and put it in a separate product table. The product code column is also included in the product table as the primary key, which establishes the relationship between the product table and the line item table. Now, all of the data elements in the line item table depend on the complete composite key. If you reflect on the data structure in this figure, you'll notice that the line item table is an implementation of the many-to-many association between invoices and products.

You should realize that there are performance trade-offs involved in refining a table to second normal form. That's because the more you split the data into separate tables, the more system resources it takes to retrieve and join the data. So, the data structure in this figure will be less efficient than the simpler structure in figure 9-3. On the other hand, with the second normal form design, product description information is stored in just one place. That saves storage space, makes maintenance easier, and reduces the chances of storing inconsistent data. In general, then, it's worth the extra cost of joining related data.

At this point, it should be clear how heavily normalized table structures rely on relationships implemented through keys. For this to work, though, it's essential for equal key values to represent the same entity. Although that may seem obvious, remember that DB2 can join data elements even if they don't make sense in the context of the application.

The order data in second normal form

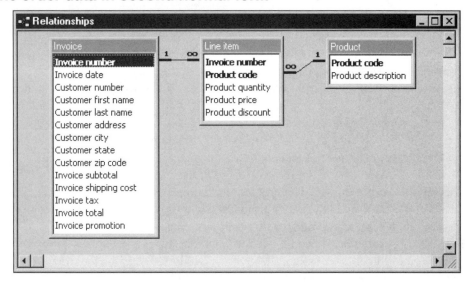

Description

- To create a data structure in second normal form, you separate data items from a table with a composite key if the items only depend on part of the key. For the order database, that means storing the product description in a separate table since it depends only on the product code and not the invoice number.

- When you split data into separate tables, it takes more system resources to retrieve and join the data. However, storing information in a separate table rather than in every row of the related table saves storage space, makes maintenance easier, and reduces the chances of storing inconsistent data.

Figure 9-4   How to create a data structure in second normal form

How to create a data structure in third normal form

The data structure in figure 9-4 can be improved further by taking it to *third normal form*. In third normal form, the data in non-key columns must depend *only* on the key. In other words, they must have a one-to-one relationship with the key. If a non-key data item depends on another non-key data item, the structure isn't in third normal form.

In the data structure in figure 9-4, for example, the name and address information for the customer associated with an invoice isn't dependent on the invoice number. It's dependent on the customer number. As a result, the invoice table isn't in third normal form. The problem with this is that if a customer had two invoices, the name and address information could be changed in one invoice, but not the other. And this would result in inconsistency.

To avoid this problem, you can move the customer name and address data from the invoice table into a customer table as shown in figure 9-5. Here, the primary key for the customer table is the customer number column. To maintain the relationship between the invoice and customer tables, the customer number column remains in the invoice table as a foreign key that identifies the associated row in the customer table.

The order data in third normal form

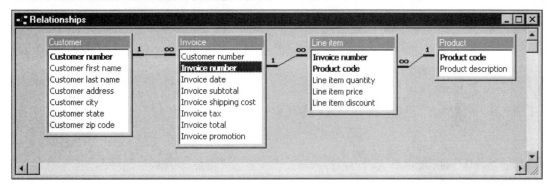

Description

- To create a data structure in third normal form, you make sure that the data in non-key columns depends only on the key.

- If the data in a column depends on another non-key column, the data should be moved to a separate table. Then, it can be related to the original table through the non-key column it depends on. For the order database, that means moving the customer name and address to a separate table and relating it to the invoice table through the customer number.

Figure 9-5   How to create a data structure in third normal form

The COBOL host structures for the normalized order data

Figure 9-6 presents the host structure definitions for the rows of the tables in the data structure shown in figure 9-5. These definitions should look familiar since they're the ones used for the sample programs in this book and in *Part 1* of this series. Now, you should understand why these tables are designed the way they are.

When and how to denormalize a data structure

If necessary, database designers can continue the normalization process beyond the third normal form. For instance, the fourth and fifth normal forms may be appropriate when a data structure involves one-to-many and many-to-many associations. However, few situations require the fourth and fifth normal forms. Moreover, these forms can result in fragmented data structures that consist of many small tables, all related by keys.

Often, the performance costs of normalization beyond the third normal form are too high for the benefits they yield. And in some cases, even normalizing data completely to the second or third normal form will lead to an inefficient design. As a result, DBAs sometimes choose to *denormalize* stored data. A DBA who denormalizes data does it by choosing not to normalize data as far a possible.

Although denormalized data structures involve fewer tables, fewer rows, and fewer keys than fully normalized structures, they have their drawbacks too. Denormalization results in greater redundancy of stored data, the need for extra storage for the redundant data, and the potential for inconsistency because of the redundant data. So weighing the costs of normalizing against the risks of denormalizing is a critical system design concern. In practice, though, most databases are designed to the third normal form, or 3NF.

The Customer table

```
*
 01    CUSTOMER-ROW.
*
       05    CUSTNO              PIC  X(6).
       05    FNAME               PIC  X(20).
       05    LNAME               PIC  X(30).
       05    ADDR                PIC  X(30).
       05    CITY                PIC  X(20).
       05    STATE               PIC  XX.
       05    ZIPCODE             PIC  X(10).
```

The Invoice table

```
*
 01    INVOICE-ROW.
*
       05    INVCUST             PIC  X(6).
       05    INVNO               PIC  X(6).
       05    INVDATE             PIC  X(10).
       05    INVSUBT             PIC  S9(7)V99    COMP-3.
       05    INVSHIP             PIC  S9(5)V99    COMP-3.
       05    INVTAX              PIC  S9(5)V99    COMP-3.
       05    INVTOTAL            PIC  S9(7)V99    COMP-3.
       05    INVPROM             PIC  X(10).
```

The Line item table

```
*
 01    LINE-ITEM-ROW.
*
       05    LIINVNO             PIC  X(6).
       05    LIPCODE             PIC  X(10).
       05    LIQTY               PIC  S9(7)       COMP-3.
       05    LIPRICE             PIC  S9(5)V99    COMP-3.
       05    LIDISC              PIC  S9(5)V99    COMP-3.
```

The Product table

```
*
 01    PRODUCT-ROW.
*
       05    PCODE               PIC  X(10).
       05    PDESC               PIC  X(30).
```

Figure 9-6   The COBOL host structures for the normalized order data

Perspective

The main purpose of this chapter has been to give you a better understanding of and an appreciation for the database design process. In addition, if you ever need to design your own database, the information presented here should be enough to get you started. Keep in mind, though, that before you design a database, you need a thorough understanding of the applications that will use it. So be sure you have all the information that's available before you start the design process.

Whether or not you design your own databases, you may have to create and manage the tables, indexes, and views for the databases you use to test your programs. In the next chapter, you'll learn the SQL statements you need to do that. Then, in the remaining chapters of this section, you'll learn how to get information about existing DB2 databases and the SQL statements you issue against them.

10

How to manage DB2 objects with SQL's Data Definition Language

To create and modify tables and other DB2 objects, you use DB2's *Data Definition Language*, or *DDL*. DDL is a subset of SQL just like DB2's Data Manipulation Language, or DML. Although database administrators are much more likely to use DDL than programmers, programmers may need to use DDL statements to define the objects they need to test their applications.

How DB2 objects are stored

A DB2 object is anything that can be created and manipulated with SQL, like a database, table, view, or index. Although you already know about most of these objects, one you may not be familiar with is the *storage group*. That's the set of DASD volumes that can be used to store the objects in a database.

How storage is provided for the objects in a database

It may surprise you, but databases don't have storage space allocated to them directly. Instead, DB2 allocates disk storage as users add data to and delete data from objects "owned" by a database. DB2 allocates that storage from one or more disk volumes that make up a storage group. When a database is created, the DBA specifies the storage group that will be used for the objects in the database. But as far as users are concerned, allocation of disk space for the objects is automatic and transparent.

A storage group is a set of disk volumes that contain the VSAM data sets where the objects associated with a database are stored. For example, figure 10-1 shows a storage group named BILLSG that contains the objects that belong to a database named BILLDB. This database contains the four tables that were used as examples in the last chapter. In this example, the storage group consists of two disk volumes, but a storage group can consist of up to 133 volumes.

Within the disk volumes associated with a storage group, DB2 automatically defines and manages VSAM data sets to provide storage for objects like tables and indexes. Because of that, programmers are insulated from the details of data management, so they don't have to know what database contains a table or what storage group a table is associated with to access the table.

The BILLDB database and its associated storage group

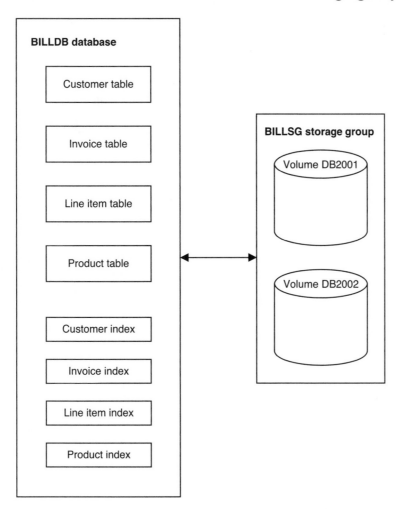

Description

- A database can contain other DB2 objects like tables and indexes. What a specific database contains depends on how the DBA creates, names, and manages those objects.

- Databases don't have storage space allocated to them directly. Instead, DB2 provides storage as necessary from the storage group associated with the database.

- A *storage group* is a set of disk volumes that contain the VSAM data sets where the objects associated with a database are stored. DB2 automatically defines and manages the required VSAM data sets.

Figure 10-1   How storage is provided for the objects in a database

How table spaces map to VSAM data sets

In *Part 1* of this series and in chapter 2 of this book, you learned about the different types of table spaces and the effects they have on locking. Now, you'll learn how tables spaces are mapped to the VSAM data sets that reside on the volumes associated with a storage group. Figure 10-2 illustrates this concept.

This figure shows the tables in the BILLDB database and the table spaces that contain them. Notice that the Customer and Product tables are each stored in their own table space, but the Invoice and Line item tables share a table space. Each of these table spaces consists of one or more data sets on the volumes in the BILLSG storage group, and each table space can include data sets from more than one volume. It's up to DB2 to keep track of where the data for each table and table space is stored.

Although it's not illustrated in this figure, indexes occupy their own index spaces just as tables occupy table spaces. Like table spaces, index spaces consist of one or more VSAM data sets. Unlike table spaces, DB2 manages index spaces in a way that's completely transparent to programmers.

The tables spaces in the BILLDB database and the data sets allocated to them

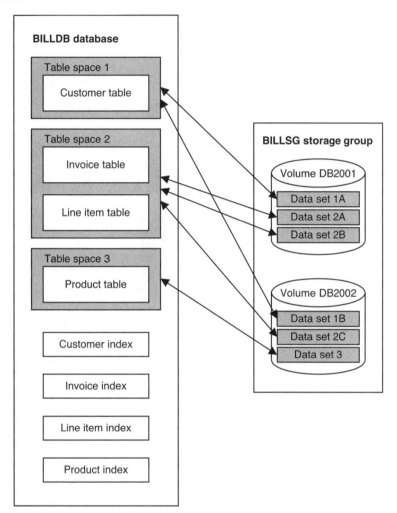

Figure 10-2   How table spaces map to VSAM data sets

Description

- A table space consists of one or more VSAM data sets that reside on the volumes associated with a storage group. DB2 supports different types of table spaces as described in chapter 2.
- A single table space can contain one or more tables. The table space that a table will use can be defined when the table is created. If it's not, DB2 automatically creates a new table space for the table.

A programmer's subset of DDL

In this section, I'll present the DDL statements you're most likely to need as an application programmer. These are the statements you'll use to create and delete the databases and table spaces you need for testing; to create, modify, and delete the tables in those databases and table spaces; and to create and delete the indexes and views for those tables.

A summary of the DDL statements

Figure 10-3 presents a summary of the DDL statements for working with DB2 objects. The statements in the first table let you create, modify, and delete these objects. At this point, you should be familiar with all of these objects except for synonyms and temporary tables. Since these objects aren't described anywhere else in this book, I'll describe them briefly now.

A *synonym* is an alternative name for a table or view. A synonym is similar to an alias, which you learned about in chapter 4. The difference is that a synonym can only be used from the subsystem where it's defined, and an alias can be used from either a local or a remote subsystem. As a result, you're more likely to create an alias than a synonym.

A *temporary table* is one that exists only during the execution of an application. Temporary tables are particularly useful for storing the data in an intermediate result set. For example, you can store the results of a query in a temporary table, then perform another query on the temporary table. Temporary tables can be more efficient to use than permanent tables because DB2 doesn't log changes to temporary tables. In addition, they can be accessed only by the applications that create them, so lock contention isn't a concern. Temporary tables became available with version 5 of DB2.

The two statements in the second table in this figure—COMMENT ON and LABEL ON—can be used to add comments to a table, view, alias, or column. These comments are stored in the DB2 catalog tables, which you'll learn more about in chapter 12. The difference between these two statements is in the length of the comment they can specify.

The statements in the third table let you work with processing privileges and authorization-ids. The DBA typically uses these statements to determine who can access the objects in a database and what they can do with them. The statements in the last table perform a variety of functions that are usually handled by the DBA.

In this chapter, you'll learn how to use the statements that are shaded in this figure. These are the statements you'll use most often as an application programmer. If you want to find out more about a statement that's not presented in this chapter, you can refer to the IBM *SQL Reference* manual for more details.

DDL statements to create, modify, and delete objects

CREATE DATABASE	Defines a new database.
CREATE STOGROUP	Defines a new storage group.
CREATE TABLESPACE	Defines a new table space.
CREATE TABLE	Defines a new table.
CREATE INDEX	Defines a new index.
CREATE VIEW	Defines a new view.
CREATE SYNONYM	Defines a new synonym.
CREATE ALIAS	Defines a new alias.
CREATE GLOBAL TEMPORARY TABLE	Defines a temporary table (version 5 only).
ALTER DATABASE	Modifies the attributes of a specified database.
ALTER STOGROUP	Modifies the attributes of a specified storage group.
ALTER TABLESPACE	Modifies the attributes of a specified table space.
ALTER TABLE	Modifies the attributes of a specified table.
ALTER INDEX	Modifies the attributes of a specified index.
RENAME	Renames a specified table.
DROP	Deletes a specified object.

DDL statements to add comments or labels to catalog definitions of objects

COMMENT ON	Specifies an informational text string, up to 254 characters, for an object.
LABEL ON	Specifies an informational text string, up to 80 characters, for an object.

DDL statements to manage processing privileges and authorization-ids

GRANT	Grants specified processing privileges to specified authorization-ids.
REVOKE	Revokes specified processing privileges for specified authorization-ids.
SET CURRENT SQLID	Specifies the authorization-id of the current user.

Miscellaneous DDL statements

SET CURRENT DEGREE	Specifies the degree of parallelism for queries that are executed dynamically.
SET CURRENT PACKAGESET	Specifies the collection ID of the package or packages that will be used to execute SQL statements.
SET CURRENT RULES	Specifies whether DB2 or standard SQL rules are used to execute some SQL statements.

Figure 10-3   A summary of the DDL statements

How to create a database

Figure 10-4 presents the syntax of the CREATE DATABASE statement that you use to create a new database. For a test database, you'll usually just specify the name of the database you want to create on this statement. Sometimes, though, you may need to specify the default buffer pool or the storage group for the database. The statement shown in this figure, for example, creates a database named MMADBV, which stores its objects on the disk volumes associated with the storage group named MMASG.

Before I go on, you should know that the CREATE DATABASE statement has other options that aren't included in the syntax in this figure. You're not likely to need these options for program testing purposes, though.

You should also notice that I didn't include EXEC SQL and END-EXEC delimiters for the CREATE DATABASE statement in this figure. That's appropriate, because you're most likely to enter this statement, and the other statements presented in this chapter, interactively through SPUFI. In that case, you end the statement with a semicolon as shown. However, you should know that you can embed these statements in an application program if you need to. If you do, be sure to include the EXEC SQL and END-EXEC delimiters and omit the semicolon.

The syntax of the CREATE DATABASE statement

```
CREATE DATABASE database-name
    [BUFFERPOOL bp-name]
    [STOGROUP stogroup-name]
```

Explanation

database-name	The name DB2 will use for the new database. The name must be unique within the DB2 subsystem.
bp-name	The default buffer pool that will be used for the table spaces and indexes in the database. If omitted, the default buffer, BP0, will be used.
stogroup-name	The name of the storage group where the objects associated with the database will be stored. If omitted, the default storage group, SYSDEFLT, will be used.

A CREATE DATABASE statement that creates a database named MMADBV in a storage group named MMASG

```
CREATE DATABASE MMADBV
    STOGROUP MMASG;
```

Note

- If you try to create a database, or any other DB2 object, with a name that already exists in the DB2 subsystem, you'll get an SQLCODE of -601.

Figure 10-4   How to create a database

How to create a table space

As you'll learn in the next topic, if you don't specify the name of a table space when you create a new table, DB2 creates a simple table space for the table. Although that's usually fine for the tables in your test environment, you won't want to use simple table spaces in a quality assurance environment. Instead, you'll want to use the same types of table spaces that will be used in the production environment.

Figure 10-5 presents the syntax of the CREATE TABLESPACE statement you use to create a simple, partitioned, or segmented table space. To create a segmented table space, you code the SEGSIZE option as shown in the sample statement in this figure. In this case, each segment in the table space will contain four pages, which is the minimum number of pages in a segment.

To create a partitioned table space, you code the NUMPARTS option. This option specifies the number of partitions that the table space will contain. You can also code the LOCKPART option for a partitioned table space. If you code LOCKPART YES, DB2 can lock the table space at the partition level. If you code LOCKPART NO or omit the LOCKPART option, individual partitions can't be locked.

In most cases, you won't need to code a CREATE TABLESPACE statement to create a simple table space. Instead, you'll just let DB2 create the table space automatically for each table you create. You may want to code a CREATE TABLESPACE statement, though, to create a simple table space that uses a lock size other than the default (ANY), or to create a simple table space that will contain more than one table. To create a simple table space, you simply omit the NUMPARTS and SEGSIZE options.

The syntax of the CREATE TABLESPACE statement

```
CREATE TABLESPACE [LARGE] tablespace-name
    [IN database-name]
    [NUMPARTS integer]
    [SEGSIZE integer]
    [LOCKSIZE {ANY | TABLESPACE | TABLE | PAGE | ROW}]
    [LOCKPART {YES | NO}]
```

Explanation

LARGE	Indicates that the table space should be able to hold more than 64GB of data. A large table space must be partitioned (NUMPARTS must be specified).
tablespace-name	The name DB2 will use for the new table space. The name must be unique within the specified database.
database-name	The name of the database that will contain the new table space. If omitted, the table space is created in the default database, DSNDB04.
NUMPARTS	Indicates that the table space will be partitioned, and specifies the number of partitions. If the number of partitions you specify is greater than 64, DB2 will create a large table space even if you omit the LARGE option.
SEGSIZE	Indicates that the table space will be segmented, and specifies the number of pages in each segment. The number of pages must be a multiple of four.
LOCKSIZE	Specifies the size of the locks that will be used within the table space. LOCKSIZE ANY indicates that DB2 will determine the size of the locks that are taken. ANY is the default.
LOCKPART	Indicates whether or not a partitioned table space can be locked at the partition level. LOCKPART YES can't be coded with LOCKSIZE TABLESPACE. LOCKPART NO is the default.

A CREATE TABLESPACE statement that creates a segmented table space named MMATS1 in the MMADBV database

```
CREATE TABLESPACE MMATS1
    IN MMADBV
    SEGSIZE 4
    LOCKSIZE ANY;
```

Figure 10-5   How to create a table space

The basic syntax of the CREATE TABLE statement

To define a new table, you use the CREATE TABLE statement. Figure 10-6 presents the basic syntax of this statement. Although it's not obvious in this figure, you can use two different approaches to defining a new table. First, you can create a table based on an existing table or view. Second, you can create a table by defining it explicitly.

Whichever approach you use, you can code the IN clause on the CREATE TABLE statement to identify the database, or alternatively, the table space, that will contain the new table. For the test tables you create, you'll usually omit this clause or specify just the database name. If you omit it, the table will be stored in the default database, DSNDB04, and DB2 will create a simple table space for the table. DB2 also creates a simple table space for the table if you specify just the database name.

To create a table that has the same characteristics as an existing table or view, you code the LIKE clause to identify that table or view. Then, the new table will have the same column definitions as the table or view you specify. Note, however, that if the new table is based on a table that's defined with a primary key, foreign keys, or other constraints, these keys and constraints are not defined in the new table. To add them to the table, you have to use the ALTER TABLE statement presented later in this chapter.

To define a table explicitly, you have to include all the detailed information about the table definition on the CREATE TABLE statement. As you can see in this figure, that information includes the definition of each column, unique constraint, referential constraint, and check constraint in the table. In the next two topics, you'll see the clauses that you code to define these items. But first, I want to be sure you understand the different types of constraints.

A *unique constraint* defines a key that uniquely identifies the rows in a table. If a table has a primary key, for example, it is a unique constraint. But a table can be defined with unique keys other than the primary key. For example, the primary key for a table of employees might be the employee number. But if that table contains social security numbers for the employees, that number could also be defined as a unique key.

A *referential constraint* is a constraint that's used to maintain the referential integrity between a parent table and a dependent table. In other words, it identifies the foreign key in the dependent table that identifies the related row in the parent table. It also identifies the action DB2 takes when an application tries to delete a row from the parent table.

A *check constraint* identifies a condition that must be satisfied before a new row can be added to a table or an existing row can be modified. For example, a check constraint for an employee table might specify that the bonus pay for an employee can't exceed twice the employee's salary. When you see the syntax for a column definition, you'll see that you can also code check constraints for individual columns. When you do that, though, the constraint can refer only to the column it's defined for. In contrast, a check constraint

The basic syntax of the CREATE TABLE statement

```
CREATE TABLE table-name
    ([column-definition[,column-definition]…]
     [unique-constraint[,unique-constraint]…]
     [referential-constraint[,referential-constraint]…]
     [check-constraint[,check-constraint]…])
     [LIKE {existing-table | existing-view}]
  [IN {DATABASE database-name | [database-name.]tablespace-name}]
```

Explanation

table-name	The name DB2 will use for the new table. The table name, qualified by the authorization-id, must be unique within the DB2 subsystem.
column-definition	The definition of a column that will be included in the table (see figure 10-7).
unique-constraint	The definition of a unique constraint for the table, including the primary key (see figure 10-8).
referential-constraint	The definition of a referential constraint for the table (see figure 10-8).
check-constraint	The definition of a check constraint for the table (see figure 10-8).
existing-table	The name of an existing table whose structure will be copied for the new table.
existing-view	The name of an existing view whose structure will be copied for the new table.
database-name	The database that will contain the new table.
tablespace-name	The table space that will contain the new table. The table space must be owned by the database you specify or by your DB2 system's default database.

Description

- You use the CREATE TABLE statement to create a table that contains one or more columns, unique constraints, referential constraints, and check constraints.

- A *unique constraint* is a primary or non-primary key that uniquely identifies the records in the table.

- A *referential constraint* is a foreign key that identifies a row in another table.

- A *check constraint* is a condition that must be satisfied before a record can be added or modified. When it's defined at the table level, it can refer to one or more columns in the table. When it's defined at the column level, it can refer only to that column.

- You can use the LIKE clause to create a table that has the same columns, with the same data types and names, as an existing table or view. When you code this clause, you cannot code the clauses that define columns or constraints.

- If you omit the IN clause, DB2 will add the table to the default database, DSNDB04. If you omit the IN clause or specify a database name without a table space name, DB2 will create a simple table space for the table.

Figure 10-6   The basic syntax of the CREATE TABLE statement that's defined at the table level can refer to any number of columns in the table. In addition, a column can be defined with a single check constraint, but a table can be defined with as many constraints as are necessary. For those reasons, check constraints are typically coded at the table level.

Like the other statements presented in this chapter, the CREATE TABLE statement has other options that aren't included here. These options let you specify more exotic features like edit procedures and auditing actions. For program testing purposes, though, you won't need these options.

How to define a table column

Figure 10-7 presents the syntax for defining a table column. The two options that are required for each column are column-name and data-type, which specify the name DB2 will use for the column and the type of data the column will contain. The values you can specify for the data-type option are also presented in this figure.

By default, the columns you define for a table can contain null values. If you don't want a column to contain null values, you can code the NOT NULL option. Then, an error will occur if you try to store a null value in that column, unless it's also defined with the WITH DEFAULT option. This option lets you specify the value that's assigned to a column if one isn't supplied. You can also code WITH DEFAULT without specifying a default value. In that case, DB2 assigns a value according to the data type of the column. If a column has a numeric data type, for example, it's assigned a value of zero. And if a column contains fixed-length character data, it's assigned a blank value. If you omit both the NOT NULL and WITH DEFAULT options, the default is always a null value.

If the primary key of a table consists of a single column, you can code the PRIMARY KEY option on the definition of that column to identify it as the primary key. You can also identify a column as a unique key by coding the UNIQUE option on its definition. Alternatively, you can identify a primary or unique key using the PRIMARY KEY or UNIQUE clause of the CREATE TABLE statement as shown in the next figure. That figure will also show you the syntax for coding a check constraint, which you can include in the definition for each column of a table.

The syntax for defining a table column

```
column-name data-type [NOT NULL] [{PRIMARY KEY | UNIQUE}]
   [[WITH] DEFAULT [default-value]] [check-constraint]
```

Explanation

column-name	The name of a column that will be included in the table. The name can contain a maximum of 18 characters.
data-type	The type of data the column will contain as listed below.
NOT NULL	Specifies that the column can not contain null values.
PRIMARY KEY	Specifies that the column contains the primary key value.
UNIQUE	Specifies that the column contains a unique constraint.
default-value	The value that's assigned to the column if a value isn't specified. If DEFAULT is coded without a value, the value it's assigned depends on the data type of the column.
check-constraint	The definition of a check constraint for the column (see figure 10-8).

The data-type values you can specify for a column

Data type	Description
CHARACTER(n)	A fixed-length string column, where n is its length. CHARACTER can be abbreviated as CHAR.
VARCHAR(n) CHARACTER VARYING(n)	A variable-length string column, where n is its maximum length. CHARACTER can be abbreviated as CHAR.
LONG VARCHAR	A variable-length string column. Its maximum length is determined by the amount of space available in the page where a row is stored.
DATE, TIME, TIMESTAMP	A date, time, or timestamp column.
INTEGER	A large integer column. INTEGER can be abbreviated as INT.
SMALLINT	A small integer column.
DECIMAL(p,s) NUMERIC(p,s)	A packed-decimal numeric column, where p is its precision and s is its scale. DECIMAL can be abbreviated as DEC.
FLOAT(21) REAL	A single-precision floating-point numeric column.
FLOAT(53) FLOAT DOUBLE DOUBLE PRECISION	A double-precision floating-point numeric column.
GRAPHIC(n)	A fixed-length graphic (Double-Byte Character Set) column, where n is its length.
VARGRAPHIC(n)	A variable-length DBCS column, where n is its maximum length.
LONG VARGRAPHIC	A variable-length DBCS column. Its maximum length is determined by the amount of space available in the page where a row is stored.

Figure 10-7   How to define a table column

How to define table constraints

Each table you define can include one or more unique constraints, referential constraints, and check constraints. The clauses you use to define these constraints are presented in figure 10-8.

As you know, a unique constraint can be defined as either a primary key or a unique, non-primary, key. To define a primary key, you use the PRIMARY KEY clause. To define a unique, non-primary key, you use the UNIQUE clause. For either clause, you include the names of one or more columns that make up the key. Although a table can contain a single primary key, it can contain one or more unique keys.

To define a table's foreign keys, you use the FOREIGN KEY clause. On this clause, you specify the names of the columns that make up the key along with an optional constraint name. Although the constraint name isn't required, some shops use it to identify the column in the parent table that enforces the relationship. You'll see an example of that in the next figure. For now, just realize that the only time you need to know the name of the constraint is if you want to delete it.

To identify the parent table that the new table is related to, you code the REFERENCES option. Then, DB2 will enforce referential integrity between the two tables using the foreign key of the dependent table (the new table) and the primary key of the parent table.

With version 5 of DB2, you can also code the names of the columns in the parent table that identify the relationship on the REFERENCES option. If you omit the column names, DB2 assumes that the foreign key columns are related to the primary key columns of the parent table. So the only time you need to code the column names is if the foreign key is related to a unique key of the parent table other than the primary key. On the other hand, the column names can provide helpful documentation, so you may want to include them even if they identify the primary key. You'll see an example of this in the next figure.

The ON DELETE option of the FOREIGN KEY clause determines what happens when DB2 receives a request to delete a row in the parent table whose primary key value matches the foreign key value of one or more rows in the dependent table (the table you're creating). If you code the RESTRICT or NO ACTION option, the delete operation is not performed. If you code the CAS-CADE option, the parent row and all related rows in the dependent table are deleted. And if you code the SET TO NULL option, the foreign keys in all related rows are set to null values. For this to work, of course, the columns that make up the foreign key must allow null values.

To define a check constraint, you use the CHECK clause. Like a foreign key, you can name a check constraint if you think you may need to delete it later. To do that, you code the CONSTRAINT option. Otherwise, you simply code the condition for the constraint after the CHECK keyword as shown in the sample constraint in this figure. This constraint checks to be sure that the value of the INVTOTAL column in the invoice table is greater than zero.

The syntax for defining a unique constraint

```
{PRIMARY KEY | UNIQUE}(column-name[,column-name]…)
```

The syntax for defining a referential constraint

```
FOREIGN KEY [constraint-name] (column-name[,column-name]…)
    REFERENCES parent-table-name
        [(pkey-column-name[,pkey-column-name]…)]
    ON DELETE {RESTRICT | CASCADE | SET NULL | NO ACTION}
```

The syntax for defining a check constraint

```
[CONSTRAINT constraint-name] CHECK (check-condition)
```

Explanation

column-name	The name of a column whose value will be used as the constraint or part of the constraint. You can specify a maximum of 64 columns or 254 characters. For a unique constraint, the column must be defined as NOT NULL.
constraint-name	The name of a referential or check constraint defined by a FOREIGN KEY or CONSTRAINT clause. If omitted, a name is derived from the name of the first column in the constraint.
parent-table-name	The name of the table that is the parent of the new table.
pkey-column-name	The name of a column in the parent table that is part of the unique key that the foreign key is related to. This option was introduced with version 5.
RESTRICT CASCADE SET NULL NO ACTION	Specifies the referential constraint for the relationship the FOREIGN KEY clause defines. If you code RESTRICT or NO ACTION, DB2 won't delete a row in the parent table if there are rows with matching foreign keys in the dependent table. If you code CASCADE, the parent row and all matching rows in the dependent table are deleted. And if you code SET NULL, the foreign keys in the matching rows are set to null values.
check-condition	A condition that one or more columns in the table must satisfy.

A check constraint that insures that the value of the INVTOTAL column is greater than zero

```
CHECK (INVTOTAL > 0)
```

Note

- A table can contain only one primary key. However, it can contain as many unique keys as are necessary.

Figure 10-8   How to define table constraints

CREATE TABLE statement examples

Figure 10-9 presents three CREATE TABLE statement examples. The first statement creates the line item table described in the last chapter. The name of this table is LINEITEM, and in this statement, it's qualified with my authorization-id, MM01. The IN clause indicates that the table will be stored in the MMATS1 table space in the MMADBV database.

As you can see, the line item table consists of five columns, and none of them can contain nulls. The primary key for the line item table is a composite key that consists of both an invoice number (LIINVNO) and a product code (LIPCODE). Both of these columns are also foreign keys. The value of LIINVNO identifies a row in the INVOICE table, and the value of LIPCODE identifies a row in the PRODUCT table. Notice that I included names for both of these constraints, and the names are the same as the primary key columns that enforce the constraint. Although that's not necessary, this is one way to document the relationship between the two tables.

The second CREATE TABLE statement in this figure creates the invoice table that the line item table is related to. Like the line item table, none of the columns in the invoice table can contain nulls. Notice, however, that the column named INVPROM is defined with the WITH DEFAULT option. Since this column is defined with the CHAR data type, that means that DB2 will assign a blank value to it if a value isn't provided. Also notice that the field named INVNO is defined with the PRIMARY KEY option. Since the key consists of a single column, this option can be coded in place of the PRIMARY KEY clause.

The invoice table also contains one foreign key and one check constraint. The foreign key consists of the INVCUST column, which identifies a row in the customer table. Notice that the REFERENCES option includes the name of the column in the parent table that enforces the constraint. That makes it clear what columns are involved in the relationship and can be helpful for documentation. Remember, though, that you can't code the parent column names if you're working with DB2 version 4. That feature became available with version 5.

The check constraint ensures that the value in the INVTOTAL column is greater than or equal to the value in the INVSUBT column. Note that since this restraint refers to more than one column in the table, it must be coded as a table constraint rather than as a column constraint.

The last statement in this figure shows how easy it is to create a new table based on the characteristics of an existing table. Here, a new table named CUSTCOPY will be created based on the customer table. That means that the new table will contain the same columns with the same data types as the customer table. Remember, though, that the new table won't inherit the constraints defined in the existing table. You have to define the constraints, including the primary key, separately.

Also notice that the IN clause on this statement specifies only a database name. Because a table space name isn't specified, DB2 will create a simple table space for the table.

A statement that creates a line item table with a composite primary key and two foreign keys

```
CREATE TABLE MM01.LINEITEM
    (LIINVNO   CHAR(6)      NOT NULL,
     LIPCODE   CHAR(10)     NOT NULL,
     LIQTY     DECIMAL(7)   NOT NULL,
     LIPRICE   DECIMAL(7,2) NOT NULL,
     LIDISC    DECIMAL(7,2) NOT NULL,
     PRIMARY KEY(LIINVNO,LIPCODE),
     FOREIGN KEY INVNO (LIINVNO)
         REFERENCES MM01.INVOICE ON DELETE RESTRICT,
     FOREIGN KEY PCODE (LIPCODE)
         REFERENCES MM01.PRODUCT ON DELETE RESTRICT)
     IN MMADBV.MMATS1;
```

A statement that creates an invoice table with a primary key, a foreign key, and a check constraint

```
CREATE TABLE MM01.INVOICE
    (INVCUST   CHAR(6)      NOT NULL,
     INVNO     CHAR(6)      NOT NULL  PRIMARY KEY,
     INVDATE   DATE         NOT NULL,
     INVSUBT   DECIMAL(9,2) NOT NULL,
     INVSHIP   DECIMAL(7,2) NOT NULL,
     INVTAX    DECIMAL(7,2) NOT NULL,
     INVTOTAL  DECIMAL(9,2) NOT NULL,
     INVPROM   CHAR(10)     NOT NULL  WITH DEFAULT,
     FOREIGN KEY (INVCUST)
         REFERENCES MM01.CUSTOMER (CUSTNO) ON DELETE RESTRICT,
     CHECK (INVTOTAL >= INVSUBT))
     IN MMADBV.MMATS1;
```

A statement that creates a table with the same structure as the customer table

```
CREATE TABLE MM01.CUSTCOPY
    LIKE MM01.CUSTOMER
    IN DATABASE MMADBV;
```

Figure 10-9   CREATE TABLE statement examples

Although basing a table on an existing table is an easy way to create a new table, this approach isn't used much in practice. Instead, you can create the table using the same statement that was used to create the original table and simply modify it by changing the table name. Then, the new table will be created with the same constraints, as well as the same column definitions, as the existing table. To use this technique, of course, the statement used to create the original table must have been saved so it can be reused. This is a common practice in many shops.

How to create an index

For each primary and unique key you define in a table, you must create a unique index to enforce the uniqueness of that key. You may also want to create indexes for other columns in a table if you frequently access the table using the values in those columns.

Figure 10-10 presents the syntax of the CREATE INDEX statement with the options you're most likely to use. The options I didn't include are related to optimizing the performance of the index, which is usually the responsibility of the DBA.

The first option on the CREATE INDEX statement, TYPE, indicates whether a type 1 or type 2 index will be created. In most cases, TYPE 2 is the default so you can omit this option.

You use the next option, UNIQUE, when you want DB2 to insure that the values of the index in each row are unique. This option is required for indexes that are based on primary or unique keys. If the index is defined with the UNIQUE option and one or more columns in the key can contain null values, the WHERE NOT NULL option determines how DB2 handles nulls. If you include this option, any number of rows can contain a null value in one or more columns of the index. In other words, DB2 won't treat the nulls as duplicate values. If you omit the WHERE NOT NULL option, DB2 won't allow duplicate null values in the index. Note that WHERE NOT NULL is available only for type 2 indexes.

After you specify the name of the index and the table it's associated with, you specify the names of the columns to be included in the index. You can also specify the sequence in which you want each column in the index sorted. The statement at the bottom of this figure, for example, creates an index for the LIINVNO and LIPCODE columns in the line item table. Since I didn't specify a sort order for either column, they'll both be sorted in ascending sequence since that's the default.

I also coded the UNIQUE option on this statement, since the two columns in the index make up the primary key of the line item table. You can look back to the first CREATE TABLE statement in figure 10-9 to see the definition of this primary key. I omitted the TYPE option from the CREATE INDEX statement, however, since the default is TYPE 2, which is what I wanted.

The syntax of the CREATE INDEX statement

```
CREATE [TYPE {1 | 2}] [UNIQUE [WHERE NOT NULL]] INDEX index-name
    ON table-name
    (column-name [{ASC | DESC}][,column-name [{ASC | DESC}]]…)
```

Explanation

TYPE	The type of index you want to create.
UNIQUE	Specifies that the table should not contain more than one row with a given value of the index column(s). If WHERE NOT NULL is specified, two or more rows can contain a null index value. Otherwise, only one row can contain a null index value. WHERE NOT NULL can be specified only for type 2 indexes.
index-name	The name DB2 will use for the index. The index name, qualified by the authorization-id, must be unique within the DB2 subsystem.
table-name	The name of the table that's associated with the index.
column-name	The name of a column in the specified table whose value will be used as the index or part of the index. You can specify up to 64 columns for an index.
ASC I DESC	Specifies whether the entries should be in ascending or descending sequence. ASC is the default.

A CREATE INDEX statement that creates a composite index on the line item table

```
CREATE UNIQUE INDEX MM01.XLITEM ON MM01.LINEITEM
    (LIINVNO,LIPCODE);
```

Notes

- An index consists of a set of pointers to the data in a related DB2 table. These pointers are organized into a hierarchy of pages, where the entries in the upper levels point to additional pages, and the entries in the lowest level point directly to rows in the table.

- DB2 introduced type 2 indexes with version 4.1. Prior to that, DB2 used type 1 indexes exclusively.

- With type 1 indexes, the pages in the index are locked when the related data in a table space is locked, which can cause frequent timeouts and suspensions. With type 2 indexes, only the key for each row that's locked in a table space is locked in the index.

Figure 10-10   How to create an index

How to add elements to a table

One way to change the definition of an existing object is to delete it (with the DROP statement) and recreate it with an updated definition. In fact, that's the approach I suggest you take for simple tables and for other objects like indexes and views. When you delete an object, however, keep in mind that you lose any data it contains. So if you need to adjust the structure of a table without deleting its contents, you'll want to use the ALTER TABLE statement instead.

Figure 10-11 presents the syntax of ALTER TABLE for the functions you're most likely to need. These four functions let you add a column, a primary key, a foreign key, or a check constraint to a table. To add these elements, you use the same clauses that are presented in figures 10-7 and 10-8 for use with the CREATE TABLE statement with one exception: You can't code the PRIMARY KEY or UNIQUE option on a column definition. To create a primary key, you have to use the PRIMARY KEY clause. And you can't create a unique key using the ALTER TABLE statement. To do that, you have to use the CREATE TABLE statement.

Figure 10-11 also presents examples of two ALTER TABLE statements. The first statement adds a column named INVCOMMENTS to the invoice table. Notice that this column allows null values and doesn't have a default value since the NOT NULL and WITH DEFAULT options are omitted. Because of that, DB2 assigns a null value to the column. The second statement adds a primary key to the same table. Here, the key consists of a single column named INVNO.

If you've ever had to add a field to a standard file, you'll appreciate the simplicity of using the ALTER TABLE statement with a DB2 database. With a standard file, you have to move all the data stored in the old file to a file with the new definition. Then, at the least, you have to recompile every program that uses that file. When you use the ALTER TABLE statement, though, you simply issue the statement and DB2 does the rest for you.

The syntax of the ALTER TABLE statement for adding elements to a table definition

```
ALTER TABLE table-name
    [ADD column-definition]
    [[ADD] PRIMARY KEY (column-name[,column-name]…)]
    [[ADD] referential-constraint]
    [ADD check-constraint]
```

Explanation

table-name	The name of the table to be altered.
column-definition	The definition of the column to be added to the table. The syntax of the column definition is the same as that for the CREATE TABLE statement presented in figure 10-7 except that you can't include the PRIMARY KEY or UNIQUE keywords. The column is added to the end of the table.
column-name	The name of a column whose value is to be used as the primary key or part of the primary key. You can specify a maximum of 64 columns or 254 characters. Each column in the key must be defined as NOT NULL.
referential-constraint	The definition of a referential constraint for the table (see figure 10-8).
check-constraint	The definition of a check constraint for the table (see figure 10-8).

An ALTER TABLE statement that adds a column to a table

```
ALTER TABLE MM01.INVOICE
    ADD INVCOMMENTS VARCHAR(254);
```

An ALTER TABLE statement that adds a primary key to a table

```
ALTER TABLE MM01.INVOICE
    ADD PRIMARY KEY (INVNO);
```

Note

- You can code one or more ADD clauses on an ALTER TABLE statement. However, you can code only one clause of each type.

Figure 10-11   How to add elements to a table

How to create a view

Figure 10-12 presents the syntax of the CREATE VIEW statement. As you know, a view is simply a definition of a result set that's stored with a database. For example, the view definition in this figure defines a result set that includes eight columns extracted from four different tables. Although you could just code a SELECT statement to create this result set in each application program that needs it, it makes more sense to save the SELECT statement in a view. Then, you can use the view from any application that needs the result set it defines, and you can use it just as if it was a table.

When you create a view, you specify the name of the view and the SELECT statement that defines the contents of the view. You can also include the names you want to use for the columns that are returned by the SELECT statement. If you omit the column names, the names of the columns in the SELECT statement will be inherited by the columns in the view.

The CREATE VIEW statement shown in this figure will create a result set that contains information from four tables. Specifically, it will contain the customer number and name for each customer in the customer table; the invoice number and date for each invoice for those customers; the product code and quantity for each line item for those invoices; and the product description for each line item product.

To use this view, you can code a SELECT statement like the one shown in this figure in an application program. Notice that this statement includes a WHERE clause that specifies that only those rows in the result set created by the view that have a product code of "SLE40025XL" should be returned to the program. Keep in mind, though, that although only those rows that match this criteria are returned to the program, the result set created by the view contains all the records defined by the view. Because that result set can contain a large number of rows, this can be inefficient.

A more efficient way to get only the data for a specific product would be to create a stored procedure that accepts the product code as a parameter. Then, the stored procedure could create a result set that consists of only the requested rows. To learn more about creating and using stored procedures, you can read chapter 5.

Although views can simplify the code for an application, they can also be used to restrict the data that a user is allowed to access. If, for example, you want to restrict the access to payroll information in an employee table, you can create a view that doesn't include the sensitive salary information. Then, you can allow users to access the table only through that view. You can also use views to present the data in a database in a form that's familiar to the user. Then, even if the structure of the database changes, the view can remain the same.

The syntax of the CREATE VIEW statement

```
CREATE VIEW view-name [(column-name,[column-name]…)]
    AS subselect
```

Explanation

view-name	The name DB2 will use for the view. The view name, qualified by the authorization-id, must be unique within the DB2 subsystem.
column-name	The name of a column in the view. If you specify column names, you must include the same number that the subselect returns. If you omit the list of column names, DB2 uses the names from the subselect.
subselect	A SELECT statement that defines the contents of the view. The subselect may not name more than 15 base tables.

A CREATE VIEW statement that joins data from four tables

```
CREATE VIEW MM01.V_CUSTPROD
                ( VCUSTNO, VFNAME, VLNAME, VPCODE,
                  VPDESC,  VQTY,    VINVNO, VINVDATE )
    AS SELECT   CUSTNO,  FNAME,  LNAME,  PCODE,
                PDESC,   LIQTY,  INVNO,  INVDATE
         FROM  MM01.CUSTOMER,
               MM01.INVOICE,
               MM01.LINEITEM,
               MM01.PRODUCT
        WHERE CUSTNO  = INVCUST AND
              INVNO   = LIINVNO AND
              LIPCODE = PCODE;
```

A SELECT statement that accesses the view

```
SELECT VCUSTNO, VFNAME, VLNAME, VPCODE,
       VPDESC,  VQTY,    VINVNO, VINVDATE
    FROM MM01.V_CUSTPROD
    WHERE VPCODE = 'SLE40025XL'
```

Note

- Not all SQL operations are allowed for all views. In particular, DB2 won't process INSERT, UPDATE, or DELETE statements issued against a read-only view. A *read-only view* is one that involves more than one base table, or one whose definition includes a column function, a GROUP BY clause, a HAVING clause, or a DISTINCT clause.

Figure 10-12   How to create a view

How to delete a database object

Figure 10-13 presents the syntax of the DROP statement, which you can use to delete any of the objects in a database. Here, I've presented just the syntax for deleting a database, table space, table, index, or view, since these are the objects you'll work with most often. To delete one of these objects, you just specify the keyword that indicates the type of object you want to delete and the name of the object. The statement in this figure, for example, deletes the V_CUSTPROD view that was created by the example in figure 10-12.

Although, you can use the DROP statement to delete any of the objects you create, remember that when you delete an object, all of the data associated with it is deleted too. So you should be sure that's what you want to do before you delete an object.

The syntax of the DROP statement for deleting a database, table space, table, index, or view

```
DROP {DATABASE database-name |
      TABLESPACE [database-name.]tablespace-name |
      TABLE table-name |
      INDEX index-name |
      VIEW view-name}
```

Explanation

database-name	The name of the database you want DB2 to delete, or the name of the database that contains the table space you want DB2 to delete.
tablespace-name	The name of the table space you want DB2 to delete. If you omit the database name, DB2 assumes that the table space is in the default database (DSNDB04).
table-name	The name of the table you want DB2 to delete.
index-name	The name of the index you want DB2 to delete.
view-name	The name of the view you want DB2 to delete.

A DROP statement that deletes the view created in figure 10-12

```
DROP VIEW MM01.V_CUSTPROD;
```

Figure 10-13   How to delete a database object

Perspective

More and more, application programmers are responsible for creating and managing the database objects they need to test the programs they develop. Now, with what you've learned in this chapter about DB2's Data Definition Language, you should have the skills you need to do that. If you're creating a database from scratch, though, be sure to use the skills presented in chapter 9 to help you design the database before you create the objects it contains.

On the other hand, if you're creating a test database based on a production database, be sure to check with your DBA to see if the CREATE statements that were used to create the objects in the production database are available. If they are, you can use those statements with minor modifications to create the objects for your test database. Then, you can be sure that the objects in the test database are identical to the objects in the production database. If these statements aren't available, you can use the CREATE TABLE statement with the LIKE option to create test tables with the same characteristics as the production tables, and you can use the ALTER TABLE statement to add the necessary keys and constraints to those tables.

Although this chapter presents the essential skills for creating and managing database objects, there's a lot more you could learn about database administration. For example, DBAs spend a lot of time and energy working with indexes to optimize system performance. Usually, that means balancing the performance improvements indexes offer with what are often substantial costs of maintaining them. For more information about indexes and other objects, you can turn to the following IBM manuals: *DB2 for OS/390 V5 Application Programming and SQL Guide* and *DB2 for OS/390 V5 Administration Guide*.

11

How to use DB2's commands and utilities

In the last chapter, you learned how to create the DB2 objects you need to test the applications you develop. In this chapter, you'll learn how to use DB2's commands and utilities to manage those objects. Because many of these commands and utilities are used primarily by DBAs who are responsible for managing production environments, this chapter presents the details of only a small subset of those commands and utilities. These are the commands and utilities you're most likely to use as you test your application programs.

How to use DB2 commands

DB2 provides a variety of commands that you can use to display information about DB2 objects and resources and to manage those objects and resources. In the following topics, you'll learn about the DB2 commands you're most likely to use as a programmer. If you want to learn more about these commands, or if you want to learn about any of the commands that aren't presented in this chapter, you can refer to the IBM manual *DB2 for OS/390 V5 Command Reference*.

A summary of the DB2 commands

Figure 11-1 summarizes all of the DB2 commands. Except for the ALTER UTILITY command, these commands are available with both versions 4 and 5 of DB2. The ALTER UTILITY command is new to DB2 version 5.

The three commands you'll learn about in this chapter are shaded in this figure. You can use these commands to display information about the databases you create and to start and stop those databases. The other commands are more useful to DBAs and system administrators for performing the day-to-day tasks of managing the system.

DB2 commands

Command	Description
-ALTER BUFFERPOOL	Alters buffer pool attributes.
-ALTER GROUPBUFFERPOOL	Alters group buffer pool attributes.
-ALTER UTILITY	Alters REORG utility parameter values. New to version 5.
-ARCHIVE LOG	Archives the current DB2 log.
-CANCEL THREAD	Cancels processing for a local or distributed DB2 thread.
-DISPLAY ARCHIVE	Displays information about the archive log.
-DISPLAY BUFFERPOOL	Displays information about buffer pools.
-DISPLAY DATABASE	Displays database status information.
-DISPLAY GROUP	Displays information about the data sharing group.
-DISPLAY GROUPBUFFERPOOL	Displays status information about group buffer pools.
-DISPLAY LOCATION	Displays status information about distributed threads.
-DISPLAY PROCEDURE	Displays status information about stored procedures.
-DISPLAY RLIMIT	Displays status information about the Resource Limit Facility.
-DISPLAY THREAD	Displays information about DB2 threads.
-DISPLAY TRACE	Displays information about DB2 traces.
-DISPLAY UTILITY	Displays status information about one or more DB2 utilities.
-MODIFY TRACE	Modifies the trace events for a specified trace.
-RECOVER BSDS	Re-establishes dual bootstrap data sets after a data set error.
-RECOVER INDOUBT	Recovers in-doubt threads.
-RESET GENERICLU	Purges information stored by VTAM in the Coupling Facility.
-RESET INDOUBT	Purges information from the thread report about in-doubt threads.
-SET ARCHIVE	Sets parameters for archive log processing.
-START DATABASE	Starts a specified database, table space, partition, or index so it's available for use or changes the status of a started object.
-START DB2	Initializes the DB2 subsystem.
-START DDF	Starts the Distributed Data Facility (DDF).
-START PROCEDURE	Starts a stored procedure that has been stopped or cached.
-START RLIMIT	Starts the Resource Limit Facility.
-START TRACE	Starts DB2 trace activity.
-STOP DATABASE	Stops a specified database, table space, partition, or index so it's not available for use.
-STOP DB2	Stops the DB2 subsystem.
-STOP DDF	Stops the Distributed Data Facility (DDF).
-STOP PROCEDURE	Stops a stored procedure so it can't be executed.
-STOP RLIMIT	Stops the Resource Limit Facility.
-STOP TRACE	Stops DB2 trace activity.
-TERM UTILITY	Terminates the execution of one or more DB2 utilities.

Figure 11-1   A summary of the DB2 commands

How to issue DB2 commands

Like the other statements and commands you've learned about in this book, DB2 commands have a basic structure you have to follow when you code them. That's true whether you code them within a job stream or from the DB2 Commands panel that you'll learn about in a minute. The basic structure of a DB2 command is presented at the top of figure 11-2.

To identify a DB2 command, you must prefix it with a recognition character. When you enter the command from DB2I, that character is a hyphen. When you enter the command within a job stream, the recognition character is the command prefix. The command prefix is set when DB2 is installed, so you'll want to check with your DBA to find out what it is. Usually, though, the command prefix is just a hyphen.

After the recognition character, you code the command name followed by the primary keyword and any parameters it requires. Then, you can code any optional keywords along with their parameter values. You can separate the keyword and parameter pairs, called *operands*, with one or more spaces, a comma, or both. You can also separate a keyword from its parameters with one or more spaces.

If a keyword requires two or more parameters, you must also separate them with commas or spaces and enclose them in parentheses. If a keyword requires a single parameter, you can code it in parentheses, or you can separate the keyword and parameter with an equals sign. The sample statements shown in the DB2 Commands panel in this figure illustrate these various coding techniques.

To display the DB2 Commands panel, you can select option 7 (DB2 Commands) from the DB2I Primary Option Menu. As you can see, this panel lets you enter up to seven commands. To execute any of the commands you enter, you just move the cursor to the line that contains the command and press the Enter key.

You can also abbreviate the names of the DB2 commands and some of the keywords as shown in the last example in this figure. Here, the command name STOP has been abbreviated as STO, and the keyword DATABASE has been abbreviated as DB. For more information on the valid abbreviations, see the *DB2 for OS/390 V5 Command Reference* manual.

The parts of a DB2 command

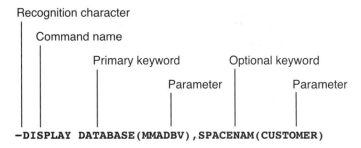

```
            Recognition character
              |
               Command name
               |    |
                    |        Primary keyword          Optional keyword
                    |         |                         |
                    |         |       Parameter         |        Parameter
                    |         |        |                |         |
            -DISPLAY DATABASE(MMADBV),SPACENAM(CUSTOMER)
```

The DB2 Commands panel

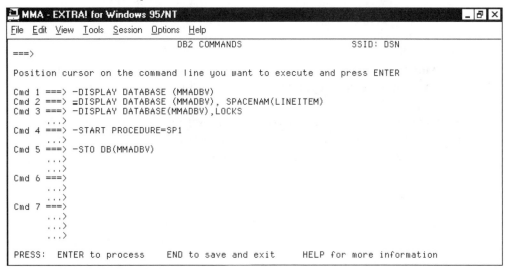

```
MMA - EXTRA! for Windows 95/NT                                      _ 日 ×
File  Edit  View  Tools  Session  Options  Help
                             DB2 COMMANDS                    SSID: DSN
===>

Position cursor on the command line you want to execute and press ENTER

Cmd 1 ===> -DISPLAY DATABASE (MMADBV)
Cmd 2 ===> =DISPLAY DATABASE (MMADBV), SPACENAM(LINEITEM)
Cmd 3 ===> -DISPLAY DATABASE(MMADBV),LOCKS
      ...>
Cmd 4 ===> -START PROCEDURE=SP1
      ...>
Cmd 5 ===> -STO DB(MMADBV)
      ...>
      ...>
Cmd 6 ===>
      ...>
      ...>
Cmd 7 ===>
      ...>
      ...>
      ...>

PRESS:  ENTER to process   END to save and exit   HELP for more information
```

Description

- A DB2 command consists of a recognition character (usually a hyphen), followed by the command name and one or more *operands*. Each operand consists of a keyword and one or more parameters.

- You can separate command operands with a comma or one or more blank spaces. You can also separate a keyword and its parameters with one or more spaces, but that's not necessary.

- If two or more parameters are specified, they must be separated by a comma or one or more spaces and enclosed in parentheses. If a single parameter is specified, it can be enclosed in parentheses, or you can separate it from its keyword with an equals sign.

- You can use the DB2 Commands panel to enter up to seven DB2 commands. To execute a command, place the cursor under it and press the Enter key.

- When you exit from this panel, the commands you've entered are saved so you can issue them again without re-entering them.

Figure 11-2   How to issue DB2 commands

How to use the DISPLAY DATABASE command

Figure 11-3 presents the syntax of the DISPLAY DATABASE command. This command lets you display information about the status of one or more DB2 databases, table spaces, tables, index spaces, or partitions. The specific information that's displayed depends on the options you code. In the next figure, for example, you'll see the output of the command shown at the bottom of this figure. This statement displays basic status information about the table space named LINEITEM in the MMADBV database.

The DISPLAY DATABASE command also provides three options you can use to display information about the application and subsystems that are accessing the database or space, remote threads that are accessing the database, and the locks and claims that are held on the objects in the database. (A *claim* is a registration with DB2 that an object is being accessed.) The information provided by these options—USE, LOCKS, and CLAIMERS—can be useful if you're trying to find out what's causing slow response times. You may want to experiment with these options to get a better idea of the information they provide.

Although this figure presents most of the options that are available for the DISPLAY DATABASE command, you should know that there are others. As an application programmer, though, you're not likely to use them.

The syntax of the DISPLAY DATABASE command

```
-DISPLAY DATABASE(database-name [,database-name]… | name* |
                  name1:name2 | *)
    [SPACENAM(space-name [,space-name]… | name* | name1:name2 | *)
        [PART(integer [,integer]… | integer1:integer2)]]
    [USE]
    [LOCKS]
    [CLAIMERS]
    [AFTER]
    [LIMIT(* | integer)]
```

Explanation

DATABASE	Specifies the databases you want to display status information for. You can specify a list of database names, a string that all the database names must start with (*name**), a range of database names (*name1:name2*), or an asterisk (*) to display information on all the databases you have access to.
SPACENAM	Specifies the table or index spaces within the specified database that you want to display status information for. You can specify a list of space names, a string that all the space names must start with, a range of space names, or an asterisk to display information on all the table and index spaces in the database. You can use the SPACENAM option only if you specify a single database name on the DATABASE operand.
PART	Specifies the partitions within the table or index space that you want to display status information for. You can specify a list or range of partition numbers.
USE	Displays information about the applications, subsystems, and threads that are currently accessing the database or table space.
LOCKS	Displays information similar to that displayed by the USE option, along with more detailed information about the locks that are held. LOCKS overrides USE.
CLAIMERS	Displays information similar to that displayed by the LOCKS option, along with information about logical partitions and claims. CLAIMERS overrides both LOCKS and USE.
AFTER	If a single database name is specified, information about that database and all databases whose names are greater than the specified name is displayed. If a single table space or index space name is specified, information about that space and all other spaces in the same database whose names are greater than the specified name is displayed.
LIMIT	Specifies the maximum number of messages that can be displayed. If you code an asterisk, the messages are limited to the space that's available. If you code an integer, the messages are limited to that number or to the space that's available, whichever is less. The default maximum number of messages is 50.

A DISPLAY DATABASE command that displays the status information for the LINEITEM table space

```
-DISPLAY DATABASE(MMADBV),SPACENAM(LINEITEM)
```

Figure 11-3   How to use the DISPLAY DATABASE command

How to interpret DISPLAY DATABASE output

Figure 11-4 presents the output of the DISPLAY DATABASE command shown in figure 11-3. This output indicates that the table space (TS) named LINEITEM is started for read/write (RW) activity and is in the check pending (CHKP) state. This state indicates that the table space may contain rows that violate referential or check constraints. That can happen if a table is loaded without checking for these constraints, or if a table is recovered to a previous state and is inconsistent with related tables.

When a table space is in check pending state, none of the tables it contains can be used for SELECT, INSERT, UPDATE, or DELETE operations; the table space can't be the object of a COPY, REORG, or QUIESCE utility job; and INSERT, UPDATE, and DELETE operations on related tables in other table spaces won't execute. Later in this chapter, you'll see how you can use the CHECK DATA utility to identify and remove the violating rows.

The blank in the PART column in this output indicates that the table space is not partitioned. If it were, the output would include status information for each partition in the table space. The other columns in the output indicate the location of physical errors. In this example, no physical errors were found so these columns are blank.

Notice that the output also includes information about the database that contains the LINEITEM table space. In this case, the output indicates that the MMADBV database is started for read/write activity. It also indicates the length of the *DBD* (*database descriptor*). The DBD contains information about the database, including definitions of the table spaces, tables, and indexes it contains.

Before I go one, I want to point out that most of the tables that are used in the examples throughout this book are each stored in a separate table space. Because of that, each table space was given the same name as the table it contains. Although that works fine for a simple test database, this practice isn't recommended for production databases.

The DISPLAY DATABASE command can display a variety of status codes as summarized in this figure. The ones you should be most concerned about are those that indicate possible unreliable data. You already know about the CHKP status code. Other status codes that indicate possible problems are COPY, GRECP, and PSRCP.

The COPY status code indicates that the table space or partition is in the copy pending state. That can happen when the COPY utility is stopped in the middle of its process. To remove the copy pending flag so the data can be used, the copy must be completed.

The GRECP status code indicates that a group buffer pool recovery is pending and the object is GBP-dependent. This is caused by a problem with the Coupling Facility. DB2 version 5 corrects this recovery pending state automatically. Prior to version 5, you had to use the RECOVER utility to correct it.

The output of the DISPLAY DATABASE command in figure 11-3

```
MMA - EXTRA! for Windows 95/NT                                    _ |8|X
File  Edit  View  Tools  Session  Options  Help
DSNT360I - ************************************
DSNT361I - *   DISPLAY DATABASE SUMMARY
           *      GLOBAL
DSNT360I - ************************************
DSNT362I -     DATABASE = MMADBV   STATUS = RW
               DBD LENGTH = 28256
DSNT397I -
NAME     TYPE PART STATUS              PHYERRLO PHYERRHI CATALOG  PIECE
-------- ---- ---- ------------------  -------- -------- -------- -----
LINEITEM TS        RW,CHKP
******* DISPLAY OF DATABASE MMADBV    ENDED       *********************
DSN9022I - DSNTDDIS 'DISPLAY DATABASE' NORMAL COMPLETION
*** _
```

DISPLAY DATABASE message status information

Status code	Description
CHKP	The table space or table space partition is in the check pending state.
COPY	The table space or table space partition is in the copy pending state.
GRECP	The object is GBP-dependent and a group buffer pool recovery is pending.
LPL	The object has entries in the logical page list.
LSTOP	The logical partition of a nonpartitioned index is stopped.
PSRCP	The index space is in a page set recover pending state.
RECP	The table space, table space partition, index space, index partition, or logical index partition is in the recover pending state.
RECP*	The logical index partition is in the recover pending state, and the entire index is inaccessible to SQL applications.
REST	The table space or index space is being restarted.
RO	The database, table space, table space partition, index space, or index space partition is started for read-only activity.
RW	The database, table space, table space partition, index space, or index space partition is started for read and write activity.
STOP	The database, table space, table space partition, index space, or index space partition is stopped.
STOPE	The table space or index space was implicitly stopped because there is a problem with the log RBA in a page.
STOPP	A stop is pending for the database, table space, table space partition, index space, or index space partition.
UT	The database, table space, table space partition, index space, or index space partition is started for utility processing only.
UTRO	A utility is in process on a table space, table space partition, index space, or index space partition that allows only RO access.
UTRW	A utility is in process on a table space, table space partition, index space, or index space partition that allows RW access.
UTUT	A utility is in process on a table space, table space partition, index space, or index space partition that allows only UT access.

Note

- The first four columns in the output shown above—Name, Type, Part, and Status—are always displayed as part of the DISPLAY DATABASE output. The other columns that are displayed depend on the options that are specified on the command. The columns shown above are displayed by default.

Figure 11-4   DISPLAY DATABASE output and status code information

The PSRCP status code indicates that an index has been placed in a page set recover pending state. That usually occurs when one or more of the VSAM data sets within the page set encounter problems. To correct this problem, the entire page set must be recovered using the RECOVER utility.

How to use the START DATABASE command

Figure 11-5 presents the syntax of the START DATABASE command. You use this command to start a database so it's available for use. You'll need to do that after you create a new database; after you stop a database using the STOP DATABASE command presented in the next topic; or after pages are written to the logical page list (LPL) indicating that a logical error has occurred on the page. Usually, a logical error occurs when a connection to the Coupling Facility or DASD is lost.

As the syntax in this figure indicates, you can use the START DATABASE command to start one or more databases at the same time. Note that to start a system database or a work file database, you have to specify its name explicitly. The two system databases you'll work with are DSNDB01, which contains the DB2 directory, and DSNDB06, which contains the DB2 catalog. The work file database can be used as working storage for table spaces that require it. For non-data sharing installations, the name of the work file database is DSNDB07. For data sharing installations, the name is defined by the administrator.

You can also use the START DATABASE command to start one or more table or index spaces within a single database. To do that, you code the SPACENAM option. If you specify the name of a partitioned table or index space on this option, you can also code the PART option to start one or more partitions within that space.

You use the ACCESS option of the START DATABASE command to specify the level of access you want programs to have to the objects you're starting. The RW parameter indicates read/write access, the RO parameter indicates read only access, and the UT parameter indicates that only online utility programs can access the object. You'll learn about some of the online utilities you can use later in this chapter.

The last ACCESS parameter, FORCE, makes the specified table space, index, or partition available regardless of its state. It also resets the check pending, copy pending, and recovery pending status flags if necessary so the data is fully accessible. You may need to use this parameter after an error occurs and the data is restored to a previous level. Because it's up to the user to insure the consistency of the data when FORCE is used, its use in a production environment is discouraged.

The sample statement at the bottom of this figure shows how you can start specific partitions within a partitioned table space. Here, partitions two through five of a table space named MMAPTS1 in the MMADBV database are started. Because RO is specified for the ACCESS parameter, programs will be able to read data from, but not write data to, these partitions.

The syntax of the START DATABASE command

```
-START DATABASE (database-name [,database-name]… | *)
    [SPACENAM (space-name [,space-name]… | *)
        [PART (integer [,integer]… | integer1:integer2)]]
    [ACCESS (RW | RO | UT | FORCE)]
```

Explanation

DATABASE	Specifies the names of the databases you want to start. You can specify a list of names, or you can specify an asterisk (*) to start all the databases you're authorized to maintain. To start a system database (DSNDB01 or DSNDB06) or a work file database (such as DSNDB07), you must specify its name explicitly.
SPACENAM	Specifies the names of the table or index spaces within the specified database that you want to start. You can specify a list of names, or you can specify an asterisk to start all table and index spaces in the specified database. You can use the SPACNAM option only if you specify a single database name on the DATABASE operand.
PART	Specifies the partitions within the specified table or index space that you want to start. You can specify a list or range of partition numbers.
ACCESS(RW)	Indicates that programs can read from or write to the specified databases, table spaces, indexes, or partitions. This is the default.
ACCESS(RO)	Indicates that programs can only read from the specified databases, table spaces, indexes, or partitions.
ACCESS(UT)	Indicates that only DB2 online utilities can access the specified databases, table spaces, indexes, or partitions.
ACCESS(FORCE)	Resets any indications that a table space, index, or partition is unavailable. Also resets the check pending, copy pending, and recovery pending states. You can use this option only if you specify a single database and you specify the SPACENAM option with an explicit list of table space and index space names.

A START DATABASE command that starts partitions 2 through 5 in table space MMAPTS1 of database MMADBV in read-only mode

```
-START DATABASE(MMADBV) SPACENAM(MMAPTS1) PART(2:5) ACCESS(RO)
```

Figure 11-5   How to use the START DATABASE command

How to use the STOP DATABASE command

Before you can make changes to the definition of a database, table space, index, or partition, you need to stop the object and close its data sets so they can't be accessed by other programs. To do that, you use the STOP DATABASE command. The syntax of this command is shown in figure 11-6.

The syntax of the DATABASE operand for this command is the same as the DATABASE operand of the START command. You use it to specify the databases, table spaces, index spaces, and partitions you want to stop.

The last operand, AT, determines when the object is stopped. If you omit this operand, the object is stopped immediately, which will cause errors to occur in any programs that are currently accessing the object. To avoid that problem, you can code the AT(COMMIT) option. This option does two things. First, it marks the object as being in the stop pending state so that no additional programs can access it. Second, it allows any program that's currently accessing the object to continue using it until the program reaches its next commit point. Then, no further access by the application is allowed. When no more applications are accessing the object, the object is stopped.

To check the status of an object, you can use the DISPLAY DATABASE command presented earlier in this chapter. A status code of STOPP indicates that the object is in the process of being stopped. And a status code of STOP indicates that the stop has completed and the object is in a stopped state.

This figure presents three STOP DATABASE examples. In the first example, all databases except the system databases (DSNDB01 and DSNDB06) and any work file databases (such as DSNDB07) are stopped. To stop a system or work file database, you must specify its name explicitly on the STOP DATABASE command.

The second example in this figure places all databases in a stop pending state. The databases are stopped only after all programs that are accessing the databases commit their work.

The third example in this figure stops the second partition within the MMAPTS1 partitioned table space. Note that to restart this partition, you'll need to identify the table space explicitly on a START DATABASE statement. You can't use the SPACENAM(*) option to restart it.

The syntax of the STOP DATABASE command

```
-STOP DATABASE (database-name [,database-name]… | *)
    [SPACENAM (space-name [,space-name]… | *)
        [PART (integer [,integer]… | integer1:integer2)]]
    [AT (COMMIT)]
```

Explanation

DATABASE	Specifies the names of the databases you want to stop. You can specify a list of names, or you can specify an asterisk (*) to stop all databases you're authorized to maintain. To stop a system database (DSNDB01 or DSNDB06) or a work file database (such as DSNDB07), you must specify its name explicitly.
SPACENAM	Specifies the names of the table or index spaces within the specified database that you want to stop. You can specify a list of names, or you can specify an asterisk to stop all table and index spaces in the specified database. You can use the SPACENAM option only if you specify a single database name on the DATABASE operand.
PART	Specifies the partitions within the specified table or index space that you want to stop. You can specify a list or range of partition numbers.
AT(COMMIT)	Marks the specified object as being in a stop pending state to prevent other applications from accessing it. If another application is currently accessing the object, it's allowed to continue until its next commit point. The object is stopped when all claims and locks on it are released.

A STOP DATABASE command that stops all databases (except DSNDB01, DSNDB06, and work file databases)

```
-STOP DATABASE(*)
```

A STOP DATABASE command that stops all databases when all the claims and locks on them are released

```
-STOP DATABASE(*) AT(COMMIT)
```

A STOP DATABASE command that stops partition number 2 of the MMAPTS1 table space in the MMADBV database

```
-STOP DATABASE(MMADBV) SPACENAM(MMAPTS1) PART(2)
```

Notes

- You can stop a system or work file database only by coding its name explicitly on the DATABASE operand.
- To start a table space or index space that was stopped explicitly using the SPACENAM operand of the STOP DATABASE command, you must use the SPACENAM operand of the START DATABASE command. START DATABASE(*) won't start table or index spaces that have been stopped explicitly.

Figure 11-6   How to use the STOP DATABASE command

How to use DB2 utilities

DB2 provides two types of utilities. In the following topics, you'll learn about the DB2 *online utilities*, commonly referred to as just *utilities*. These utilities run as standard MVS batch jobs, and DB2 must be running when you execute them. In contrast, the DB2 *stand-alone utilities* run as batch jobs independent of DB2. Because the stand-alone utilities perform functions that you're not likely to need as a programmer, they aren't presented in this chapter.

A summary of the DB2 utilities

Figure 11-7 presents a summary of the DB2 utilities. In general, DBAs use these utilities to perform maintenance functions on the objects in a database. For example, the COPY utility can be used to create an image copy of a table space that can be used to recover the table space in the event of an error. And the REORG utility can be used to defragment a table space, index space, or partition.

The four utilities that are shaded in this figure are the ones you're most likely to use as a programmer, and they're the ones you'll learn about in the following topics. To find out more about the other utilities, you can refer to the IBM manual *DB2 for OS/390 V5 Utility Guide and Reference*.

DB2 utilities

Utility	Description
CATMAINT	The UPDATE function updates the catalog so it conforms to a new release of DB2. The CONVERT function converts catalog and directory indexes from type 1 to type 2 or vice versa.
CHECK DATA	Checks for records that violate referential and check constraints.
CHECK INDEX	Checks indexes to be sure that they're consistent with the data they index.
COPY	Creates image copies of all the pages in a table space or of a data set within a table space.
DIAGNOSE	Creates output that can be useful in diagnosing system problems.
LOAD	Loads records into one or more tables of a table space and updates the related indexes.
MERGECOPY	Merges image copies created using the COPY utility or inline copies created using the LOAD or REORG utility.
MODIFY	Deletes outdated information from the SYSIBM.SYSCOPY table, along with related log records in the SYSIBM.SYSLGRNX directory tables and entries in the DBD. The name of this utility changed from MODIFY RECOVERY in version 4 of DB2 to just MODIFY in version 5.
QUIESCE	Establishes a quiesce point (the current log RBA) for a table space, a partition, or a list of table spaces, and records it in the SYSIBM.SYSCOPY catalog table.
RECOVER INDEX	Recreates one or more indexes for the tables in a table space.
RECOVER TABLESPACE	Recovers a table space, a partition or data set, pages within an error range, or a single page from image copies of a table space or from log records containing changes to the table space.
REORG	Reorganizes a table space, index space, or partition to reclaim fragmented space.
REPAIR	Repairs data by replacing invalid data with valid data.
REPORT	The TABLESPACESET function provides information about all the table spaces and tables in a referential structure. The RECOVERY function provides information necessary for recovering a table space.
RUNSTATS	Provides summary information about the characteristics of the data in table spaces, indexes, and partitions.
STOSPACE	Updates the DB2 catalog columns that indicate how much space is allocated for storage groups and their related table spaces and indexes.

Figure 11-7   A summary of the DB2 utilities

How to execute DB2 utilities

Before you can execute a DB2 utility, you have to create the control statement that describes the utility you want to perform. To do that, you use the ISPF editor. The following topics present the syntax of the control statements for the four utilities you'll learn about in this chapter.

After you create the control statement for the utility, you can execute it using one of four techniques. First, you can use the DSNUPROC procedure. This procedure uses the parameters you supply to build an EXEC statement that invokes the utility. Second, you can use the DSNU CLIST under TSO to generate the JCL needed to invoke the DSNUPROC procedure and execute the online utility as a batch job. Third, you can create the JCL for invoking the utility yourself. And fourth, you can use the DB2 Utilities panel to create the appropriate JCL and submit the job. Because using the DB2 Utilities panel is the easiest and most straightforward way of executing a utility, this topic will describe it in more detail.

Figure 11-8 presents the DB2 Utilities panel. You can display this panel by selecting option 8 (Utilities) from the DB2I Primary Option Menu. As you can see from the first numbered field on this panel (Function), you can use it to perform four functions. If you choose the SUBMIT function, the JCL necessary to execute the utility you specify in field 3 (Utility) using the control statement in the data set specified in field 4 (Control Cards Data Set) is generated and submitted for execution.

If you want to edit the JCL before it's submitted, you can use the EDITJCL function. This function displays the generated JCL in the ISPF editor. After you edit the JCL, you can submit it from the editor.

The DISPLAY function lets you display the results of the utility. Although results are displayed at your terminal as the utility executes, the DISPLAY function makes it easy to scroll through and review the detailed output.

The last function, TERMINATE, lets you stop the execution of the utility before it's complete. It also clears the UTUT status code that's placed on an object while a utility is processing that object. This function is particularly useful for clearing the status code after a utility abends.

If you want to restart a utility after you terminate it, you can do that by setting field 5 (Restart) in the DB2 Utilities panel to CURRENT or PHASE and issuing the SUBMIT function again. If you set the Restart field to CURRENT, the utility is restarted where it left off. If you set this field to PHASE, the utility is restarted at the beginning of the current phase. (Most of the utilities are divided into two or more phases that perform specific functions.) Note that not all of the utilities can be restarted at the current location or phase. See the IBM manual for specific information on each utility.

The DB2 Utilities panel

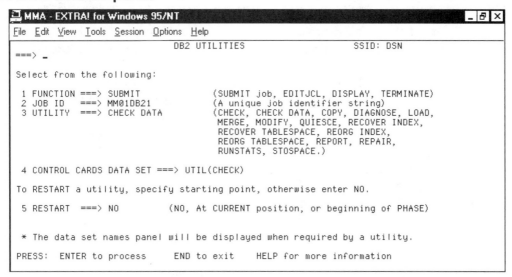

```
🖳 MMA - EXTRA! for Windows 95/NT                                    _ ⊡ ✕
File  Edit  View  Tools  Session  Options  Help
                          DB2 UTILITIES                    SSID: DSN
===>  _

Select from the following:

 1 FUNCTION ===> SUBMIT           (SUBMIT job, EDITJCL, DISPLAY, TERMINATE)
 2 JOB ID   ===> MM01DB21         (A unique job identifier string)
 3 UTILITY  ===> CHECK DATA       (CHECK, CHECK DATA, COPY, DIAGNOSE, LOAD,
                                   MERGE, MODIFY, QUIESCE, RECOVER INDEX,
                                   RECOVER TABLESPACE, REORG INDEX,
                                   REORG TABLESPACE, REPORT, REPAIR,
                                   RUNSTATS, STOSPACE.)

 4 CONTROL CARDS DATA SET ===> UTIL(CHECK)

To RESTART a utility, specify starting point, otherwise enter NO.

 5 RESTART  ===> NO         (NO, At CURRENT position, or beginning of PHASE)


 * The data set names panel will be displayed when required by a utility.

PRESS:  ENTER to process    END to exit    HELP for more information
```

Description

- The DB2 Utilities panel lets you perform four functions related to utility processing as indicated by the options for field 1. The SUBMIT function creates the JCL to execute the utility and submits it automatically. The EDITJCL function displays the ISPF editor, where you can edit the generated JCL and submit it manually. The DISPLAY function displays the results of a utility. And the TERMINATE function ends the utility and clears the UTUT status code from the object the utility was processing.

- To identify a job, you enter a unique job identifier in field 2. The default is TEMP.

- To identify the utility you want to work with, enter its name in field 3.

- Before you can run a utility, you must create a control statement that specifies the operation you want to perform and save it in a sequential or partitioned data set. Then, you enter the name of the data set in field 4 of this panel. The default data set name is UTIL. TSO will prefix the data set name with your user-id unless you enclose the name in single quotes.

- To restart a utility you previously stopped using the TERMINATE function, enter CURRENT in field 5 to restart the utility at the current position or PHASE to restart it at the beginning of the current phase. The default is NO.

- If you're running the COPY, LOAD, MERGECOPY, or REORG TABLESPACE utility, the Data Set Names panel is displayed. On this panel, you enter the names of the data sets the utility will use.

Note

- If you need help completing the DB2 Utilities panel or the Data Set Names panel, you can press the Help key. The Help panels explain the parameters and present the syntax and sample control statements for each utility.

Figure 11-8   How to use the DB2 Utilities panel

How to use the CHECK INDEX utility

Figure 11-9 presents the basic syntax of the control statement for the CHECK INDEX utility. You can use this utility to check one or more indexes or index partitions in a table space to be sure that they're consistent with the data they index. You'll want to do that before you use the CHECK DATA utility presented later in this chapter, since CHECK DATA uses the indexes to check for referential constraints.

The sample statement shown in this figure checks all indexes in the LINEITEM table space. Since this table space contains a single table (LINEITEM), this statement will check all the indexes defined for that table.

Although the CHECK INDEX utility identifies inconsistencies between an index and the data it indexes and places the index in a recovery pending state if a problem is detected, it doesn't correct the inconsistencies. To do that, you need to start by analyzing the output to determine the cause of the inconsistency. Then, if the inconsistency is caused by a problem with the index, you can use the RECOVER INDEX utility to correct the index. Alternatively, you can delete the index using the DROP INDEX statement and recreate it using the CREATE INDEX statement.

The syntax of the CHECK INDEX control statement

```
CHECK INDEX
    {(index-name [PART integer] [,index-name [PART integer]]…) |
    (ALL) TABLESPACE [database-name.]tablespace-name [PART integer]}
```

Explanation

index-name	The name of an index you want to check, qualified by the ID of the creator. If you omit the creator-id, the user-id for the utility is used. If you specify two or more indexes, they must all belong to the same table space.
PART	Specifies the partition number of the physical partition you want to check in a partitioned index or the partition number of the logical partition you want to check in a nonpartitioned type 2 index.
ALL	Indicates that you want to check all the indexes in the specified table space or partition.
database-name	The name of the database that contains the table space you want to check. The default is DSNDB04.
tablespace-name	The name of the table space you want to check.

A CHECK INDEX statement that checks the indexes in the LINEITEM table space

```
CHECK INDEX (ALL) TABLESPACE MMADBV.LINEITEM
```

Note

- You should use CHECK INDEX before you use CHECK DATA to be sure that the indexes used by CHECK DATA are consistent with the data they index.

Figure 11-9   How to use the CHECK INDEX utility

How to use the RECOVER INDEX utility

Figure 11-10 presents the basic syntax of the control statement for the RECOVER INDEX utility. This utility rebuilds the specified indexes or index partitions in a table space. Alternatively, it can rebuild all the indexes in a table space. If the utility completes successfully, it also resets the recovery pending status of the rebuilt indexes.

If you compare the syntax of the RECOVER INDEX control statement with the syntax of the CHECK INDEX control statement in the previous figure, you'll see that they're almost identical. The only difference is that RECOVER INDEX has one more option: REUSE. If you include this option, the existing data sets for the specified indexes are reset and reused. Otherwise, the data sets are deleted and redefined.

Also notice that you can code the REBUILD keyword in place of RE-COVER. This is new to version 5 of DB2. In version 6 of DB2, you'll have to use REBUILD to rebuild an index. If you code RECOVER, the index will be recovered by applying log records to a copy of the index. To prepare for that change, you may want to start using REBUILD INDEX right away.

The syntax of the RECOVER INDEX control statement

```
{RECOVER | REBUILD} INDEX
   {(index-name [PART integer] [,index-name [PART integer]]…) |
    (ALL) TABLESPACE [database-name.]tablespace-name [PART integer]}
    [REUSE]
```

Explanation

index-name	The name of an index you want to rebuild, qualified by the ID of the creator. If you omit the creator-id, the user-id for the utility is used. If you specify two or more indexes, they must all belong to the same table space.
PART	Specifies the partition number of the physical partition you want to rebuild in a partitioned index or the partition number of the logical partition you want to rebuild in a nonpartitioned type 2 index.
REUSE	Indicates that the data sets that contain the index should be reset and reused. If you omit this option, the data sets are deleted and redefined.
ALL	Indicates that you want to rebuild all the indexes in the specified table space or partition.
database-name	The name of the database that contains the table space you want to rebuild. The default is DSNDB04.
tablespace-name	The name of the table space you want to rebuild.

A RECOVER INDEX statement that rebuilds the XLITEM index

```
RECOVER INDEX (MM01.XLITEM)
```

Figure 11-10   How to use the RECOVER INDEX utility

How to use the CHECK DATA utility

Figure 11-11 presents the basic syntax of the control statement for the CHECK DATA utility. This utility checks one or more table spaces or partitions for rows that violate referential or table check constraints. It can also copy violating rows to an *exception table*, and it can delete the original rows. If the violating rows are deleted, this utility resets the check pending status of the table space that contained the rows. If violating rows aren't deleted, the utility places the table space in the check pending state.

Usually, you'll run the CHECK DATA utility when you're not sure if the parent and dependent tables are synchronized. If you load a table without checking for referential or check constraints, for example, you'll want to run the CHECK DATA utility on that table before you use it. You may also want to run this utility after recovering one or more tables to a previous state.

Although you can use the DELETE YES option of CHECK DATA to delete violating rows, you'll want to be sure that you know what the cause of the problem is before you do that. Before you run the CHECK DATA utility, then, you'll want to run the CHECK INDEX utility to be sure that the problem isn't with the indexes. Then, you'll want to run CHECK DATA with the DELETE NO option to identify the violating rows.

Based on that information, you should be able to determine what is causing the violation. If you determine that the problem is with the violating rows in the dependent table, you can then run the CHECK DATA utility again with the DELETE YES option. If you want to save the violating rows in another table, you can also code the FOR EXCEPTION option. This option names a table that's being checked and the exception table that any rows deleted from that table will be written to. Note that you can code a FOR EXCEPTION option for each table in the table spaces you're checking. If a table you're checking has dependent rows in another table, for example, you'll want to code the FOR EXCEPTION option for both tables. That's because if DB2 deletes rows from the parent table, it may cascade the deletes to the dependent table if the foreign key is defined with the CASCADE option.

Before you can use the FOR EXCEPTION option, you must create the exception table it names. The easiest way to do that is to use the CREATE TABLE statement with the LIKE option to base the exception table on the original table. Note that you don't have to create a new exception table each time you run CHECK DATA. Instead, you can add rows to an existing exception table.

Although an exception table must include the same columns as the original table, it can also include two optional columns at the end of the table. DB2 will place the value of the RID field of the deleted row in the first column, which should be defined as CHAR(4) for a standard table space or CHAR(5) for a LARGE table space. DB2 will place the time that the CHECK DATA utility started in the second column, so it should be defined as TIMESTAMP. You can use these columns to identify specific rows and the execution of CHECK DATA that created them. You can give these columns any name you like.

The syntax of the CHECK DATA control statement

```
CHECK DATA
     TABLESPACE [database-name.]tablespace-name [PART integer]
    [TABLESPACE [database-name.]tablespace-name [PART integer]]…
    [SCOPE {PENDING | ALL}]
    [FOR EXCEPTION IN table-name USE exception-table-name
                   [IN table-name USE exception-table-name]…]
    [DELETE {NO | YES}]
```

Explanation

database-name	The name of the database that contains the table space you want to check. The default is DSNDB04.
tablespace-name	The name of the table space you want to check.
PART	Specifies the partition number you want to check in a partitioned table space. If you omit this option, all partitions are checked.
SCOPE	Indicates what rows you want to check. If you specify SCOPE ALL, the rows in all dependent tables in the specified table spaces are checked. If you specify SCOPE PENDING, only the rows in the tables, partitions, and table spaces that are in a check pending state are checked. SCOPE PENDING is the default.
FOR EXCEPTION	Indicates that any row that violates a referential constraint or a table check constraint should be copied to an exception table. The IN and USE options specify the name of the table that contains the error and the name of the exception table that should be used for that table.
DELETE	Indicates whether or not rows that violate referential or table check constraints should be deleted from the table space. If you specify DELETE YES, any rows that violate constraints are deleted along with any dependent rows. DELETE NO is the default. This option can only be used in conjunction with FOR EXCEPTION.

A CHECK DATA statement that checks the LINEITEM table space, writes errors to an exception table, and deletes the violating rows

```
CHECK DATA TABLESPACE MMADBV.LINEITEM
     FOR EXCEPTION IN MM01.LINEITEM USE MM01.ELINEITEM
     DELETE YES
```

Notes

- You must create any exception tables to be used by this utility before you run it. Each exception table must be defined identically to the table it's used with.

- If constraint violations are detected and the violating rows aren't deleted, the table space or partition is placed in the check pending state.

- If the CHECK DATA utility completes without detecting any constraint violations, the check pending status of the table space or partition is reset.

- CHECK DATA issues a message for each row that contains a referential or table check constraint. The row is identified by its RID, the name of the table that contains it, and the name of the constraint that it violates.

Figure 11-11   How to use the CHECK DATA utility

After you run CHECK DATA to delete violating rows and copy them to an exception table, the check pending status of the table is reset so that table can be accessed again. Then, if necessary, you can correct the rows in the exception table and insert them back into the original table using the INSERT INTO statement. This is a common technique used by DB2 programmers.

How to use the LOAD utility

Figure 11-12 presents the basic syntax of the control statement for the LOAD utility. You can use this utility to load data from an input data set into one or more tables or partitions of a table space. If you use it to load data into a table space or partition that already contains data, this utility can add the data to the end of the existing data or it can replace the existing data. This utility also builds or extends any indexes defined on the tables that are loaded.

To load a specific partition in a partitioned table space, you code the PART clause. On this clause, you code RESUME YES if you want to add to existing data, and you code RESUME NO if the partition doesn't contain any data. If the partition contains data but you want to replace the existing data instead of adding to it, you code RESUME NO REPLACE. You can also code the RE-SUME option at the table space level to indicate whether or not the table space contains data and whether you want to add to the existing data or replace it.

If you want to load only selected records from the input data set into a table, you can code the WHEN clause of the LOAD control statement. On this clause, you identify a field in the input data set and a string value that the field must equal for a record to be loaded. If the fields in the input data set are specified on the LOAD statement, you can identify the field by the name given on that specification. Otherwise, you can identify it by its position within the record. This will make more sense when you see the examples in the next figure.

Although it's not required, you can code field specifications on the LOAD statement for each field in the input data set to be loaded into the output table. You might want to do that, for example, to include only some of the fields from the input data set in the output table. You may also want to do that if the fields will be in a different order in the output table or if the fields in the input data set have different data types than the columns in the output table. Or, you may want to include the field specifications for documentation purposes. If you don't include field specifications, DB2 maps the data in the input data set into the columns in the output table using the column definitions.

To identify a field you want to load, you code the name of the column it will be loaded into in the output table followed by the POSITION option. This option indicates the location of the field in the input data set. You can also specify the data type of the field in the input table. If you omit the data type, DB2 assumes that it has the same type as the corresponding field in the output table.

By default, the LOAD utility checks that the data that's loaded into the output table satisfies the referential and check constraints defined for the table.

The syntax of the LOAD control statement

```
LOAD [DATA] [INDDN ddname]
    INTO TABLE table-name [PART integer [RESUME {YES | NO [REPLACE]}]]
        [WHEN {field-name | (start[:end])} = string]
        [(field-name POSITION(start[:end] [data-type]
        [,field-name POSITION(start[:end] [data-type]]…)]
    [[RESUME] {YES | NO [REPLACE]}]
    [ENFORCE {CONSTRAINTS | NO}]
```

Explanation

INDDN	Specifies the ddname for the data set that contains the records you want to load. The default is SYSREC.
table-name	The name of a table you want to load.
PART	Specifies the partition number of the partitioned table space you want to load.
RESUME	Indicates whether the records will be loaded into an empty table space or partition (RESUME NO) or a table space or partition that contains data (RESUME YES). RESUME NO is the default.
REPLACE	When coded on the PART clause, indicates that you only want to replace the contents of the specified partition and not the entire table space. When coded separately, indicates that you want to replace all the data in all the tables spaces, not just the data in the tables you're loading.
WHEN	Specifies a condition that determines which records are loaded. The condition compares the value of a field in the input data set with a string value. You can identify the field using a *field-name* defined on the LOAD statement or by specifying the starting and ending column of the field in the input data set.
field-name	The name of a column in *table-name* that you want to load data into, or the name of a field you want to use in the WHEN condition.
POSITION	Specifies the starting and ending column numbers of a field in the input data set. If *end* is omitted, the field extends to the beginning of the next field.
data-type	The type of data contained in the input field. Can be any of the DB2 data types. Some data types allow additional options, such as EXTERNAL and the length and scale of the data. If omitted, the data type of the column in the output table is assumed.
ENFORCE	Indicates whether or not referential and check constraints should be enforced. If you specify ENFORCE NO and constraints are specified for the table, the table space is placed in a check pending state. ENFORCE CONSTRAINTS is the default.

Notes

* If you don't define any fields on the INTO TABLE clause, the fields in the input data set are mapped to the columns in the output table using the column definitions.

* If one or more field specifications are included on the INTO TABLE clause, a specification must be included for each column in the output table that doesn't have a default value.

* If a field specification isn't included for a column in the output table and the column is defined as NOT NULL with no default value, the utility job will abend.

* You can also include a field specification for a field that's used in the WHEN clause, even if the field isn't loaded into the table. You can use any name you want for this field.

Figure 11-12   The syntax of the LOAD control statement

If it detects a violation, the violating row is deleted from the output table. (The constraints are checked after the records are written to the table.) If you want to load a table without checking for constraints, you can code the ENFORCE NO option. Then, violating records are left in the table, but the table space (or the partition if records are being loaded into a specific partition) is placed in the check pending state. To remove the check pending status, you can run the CHECK DATA utility.

In addition to checking for referential and check constraints, the LOAD utility also checks to be sure that duplicate keys don't exist for unique indexes. If duplicate keys are found, the records aren't written to the output table. So you'll want to be sure that duplicate keys don't exist in the input data set before you run the LOAD utility.

Although it's not indicated in the syntax for the LOAD statement in figure 11-12, you can load data into two or more tables with a single LOAD statement. To do that, you code an INTO TABLE clause for each table that identifies the records and fields to be written to that table. In most cases, though, you'll load each table using a separate LOAD statement.

Figure 11-13 presents three LOAD control statement examples. The first statement loads data into the customer table. Because the INDD option is omitted, the data will be loaded from the data set specified by the SYSREC DD statement. And since no field specifications are included, the data in the input data set will be mapped into the columns in the customer table using the column definitions in that table. For this to work, the fields in the input data set must be in the same sequence and have the same number of characters as their corresponding column definitions. This statement also includes the RESUME YES option so the data is added to the data already in the customer table. And it includes the ENFORCE CONSTRAINTS option so the referential and check constraints defined for the table will be checked.

The second LOAD statement in this figure loads records only for customers who live in California. To do that, it includes a WHEN clause that checks columns 77 and 78 for a value of "CA". Because this statement doesn't include the RESUME option, the customer table must be empty when it's executed.

The third LOAD statement loads data into an employee table that's defined as shown in this figure from an input data set that contains the data shown in this figure. In this example, the input data set is identified by the EMPREC DD statement. Because the REPLACE option is included, the data in this data set replaces any existing data in the employee table. Notice that this LOAD statement includes field specifications for all the fields in the input data set, and the field names are the same as the names of the columns they'll be loaded into. The exception is the STCODE field, which doesn't have a corresponding column in the employee table. It's included here so that the WHEN clause can refer to the name of the field instead of its position. Also notice that the last field, SALARY, is defined with a data type of DECIMAL EXTERNAL (9). That means that the length of the field in the input data set (the external length) is nine characters. Finally, notice that because no data is included for the last column in the table, NOTES, it's initialized with a null value.

A LOAD statement that loads all the fields and records in an input data set into the customer table

```
LOAD DATA
    ENFORCE CONSTRAINTS
    RESUME YES
    INTO TABLE MM01.CUSTOMER
```

A LOAD statement that loads selected records into the customer table

```
LOAD DATA
    ENFORCE CONSTRAINTS
    INTO TABLE MM01.CUSTOMER
    WHEN (77:78) = 'CA'
```

A LOAD statement that loads selected fields and records in the MM01.EMPLOYEE.DATA data set into the MM01.EMPLOYEE table

```
LOAD DATA INDD EMPREC
    ENFORCE CONSTRAINTS
    REPLACE
    INTO TABLE MM01.EMPLOYEE
      ( EMPNO      POSITION(1:4)      CHAR(4),
        FNAME      POSITION(5:19)     CHAR(15),
        LNAME      POSITION(20:39)    CHAR(20),
        STCODE     POSITION(40:41)    CHAR(2),
        SALARY     POSITION(42:50)    DECIMAL EXTERNAL(9) )
    WHEN STCODE = 'CA'
```

The CREATE TABLE statement for the MM01.EMPLOYEE table

```
CREATE TABLE MM01.EMPLOYEE
  ( EMPNO           CHAR(4)       NOT NULL,
    FNAME           CHAR(15)      NOT NULL,
    LNAME           CHAR(20)      NOT NULL,
    SALARY          DECIMAL(9,2)  NOT NULL,
    NOTES           VARCHAR(254),
    PRIMARY KEY (EMPNO) )
    IN MMADBV.MMASEGTS;
```

The contents of the MM01.EMPLOYEE.DATA data set

```
3001LOU          DESANTIS          CA007500.00
3002CURT         STEDMAN           MI008500.00
3003JEFF         JOLLIFF           CA002250.00
3004DEBBIE       VASQUEZ           RI009575.00
3005MIKE         PRICE             CA004400.00
3006RENE         ZOLEZZI           TX012000.00
3007JANET        RALSTON           CA006425.00
```

Figure 11-13   LOAD statement examples

Perspective

As an application programmer, you may not have the authority to use all of the commands and utilities that DB2 provides. If you're responsible for testing your applications in a quality assurance environment, however, you're likely to at least have the authority to use the commands and utilities presented in this chapter.

But even if you're not responsible for quality assurance testing, you may have the authority to use some of these commands and utilities. To change the definition of a DB2 object in your test environment, for example, you'll need to use the STOP command before making the change, and you'll need to use the START command after making the change. And you may need to use the LOAD utility to load data into the tables you use for testing.

With the information that's presented in this chapter, you should be able to perform all the data management functions you need to test your applications. Keep in mind, though, that the syntax of most of the commands and utilities presented here has been simplified. So if you need to do some processing that's not indicated in the syntax diagrams, you can refer to the IBM manuals *DB2 for OS/390 V5 Command Reference* and *DB2 for OS/390 V5 Utility Guide and Reference* for more information. You can also refer to these manuals to find out about the commands and utilities that aren't presented in this chapter.

12

How to extract information from DB2's catalog tables

The *DB2 catalog* is a set of related tables, called *catalog tables*. DB2 records a variety of information in these tables, including information about objects, application plans and packages, and user privileges. For the programmer, this catalog provides a valuable source of information about DB2 objects. This chapter shows you how to get the most useful information.

An introduction to the DB2 catalog tables

Figure 12-1 lists all of the catalog tables for versions 4 and 5 of DB2 and presents a brief description of each. Note that the full name of each catalog table starts with the authorization-id SYSIBM as a high-level qualifier. So, the complete name of the first table in this figure, SYSCHECKDEP, is actually SYSIBM.SYSCHECKDEP.

Many of the catalog tables are associated with one another in parent/dependent relationships, also known as parent/child relationships. For example, SYSTABLESPACE is the parent of SYSTABLES. That makes sense, because tables "belong" to table spaces. Similarly, SYSTABLES is the parent of SYSCOLUMNS.

Although catalog tables have structures like non-catalog tables, you can't issue DELETE, INSERT, and UPDATE statements to make changes to their contents. Instead, DB2 makes changes to these tables when you issue DDL statements, like the ones in chapter 10. However, DB2 does allow direct access for retrieval operations. So if you have the proper authorizations, you can issue SELECT statements through SPUFI to retrieve data from the catalog tables. This data can help you design and manage the objects you use as you test your programs.

Catalog tables for DB2 version 4

Table name	Contents
SYSCHECKDEP	One row for each reference to a column in a table check constraint
SYSCHECKS	One row for each table check constraint
SYSCOLAUTH	Privileges held by users over columns for updates
SYSCOLDIST	One or more rows for the first key column of an index key
SYSCOLDISTSTATS	Zero or more rows per partition for the first key column of a partitioned index
SYSCOLSTATS	Partition statistics for selected columns
SYSCOLUMNS	One row for each column in every table and view
SYSCOPY	DB2 recovery information
SYSDATABASE	One row for each database
SYSDBAUTH	Privileges held by users over databases
SYSDBRM	One row for each database request module in every application plan
SYSFIELDS	One row for every column defined with a field procedure
SYSFOREIGNKEYS	One row for each column of every foreign key
SYSINDEXES	One row for each index
SYSINDEXPART	Components of partitioned and unpartitioned indexes
SYSINDEXSTATS	One row for each partition of a partitioned index
SYSKEYS	One row for each column of every index key
SYSPACKAGE	One row for every package
SYSPACKAUTH	Privileges held by users over packages
SYSPACKDEP	Dependencies of packages on local tables, views, synonyms, table spaces, indexes, and aliases
SYSPACKLIST	Unique entries in each plan's package list
SYSPACKSTMT	One or more rows for each statement in a package
SYSPKSYSTEM	Connections to each environment where a package can be used
SYSPLAN	One row for each application plan
SYSPLANAUTH	Privileges held by users over application plans
SYSPLANDEP	Dependencies of application plans on objects
SYSPLSYSTEM	Connections to each environment where a plan can be used
SYSPROCEDURES	One row for each stored procedure
SYSRELS	One row for each referential constraint
SYSRESAUTH	Privileges held by users over storage resources
SYSSTMT	Information about each SQL statement in every DBRM
SYSSTOGROUP	One row for each storage group
SYSSTRINGS	Character conversions
SYSSYNONYMS	One row for each synonym

Figure 12-1   DB2 catalog tables (part 1 of 2)

The second table in part 2 of this figure lists the catalog tables that were added in DB2 version 5. Actually, all of these tables except for IPNAMES and SYSDUMMY1 were included in DB2 version 4. They just weren't part of the DB2 catalog. Instead, they were stored in a separate database called the *communications database*. As its name implies, the tables in this database contain information about how DB2 communicates with remote servers.

The names of the tables within the communications database in version 4 are the same as those shown for version 5 except they include the SYS prefix like all of the other tables in the catalog. For example, the LOCATIONS table in version 5 was named SYSLOCATIONS in version 4. (You learned how DB2 uses these tables to access distributed data in chapter 4.) For some reason, the SYS prefix was dropped in version 5.

The two tables that are actually new to version 5 are IPNAMES and SYSDUMMY1. The IPNAMES table was added for version 5 to implement the TCP/IP protocol you learned about in chapter 4. SYSDUMMY1 is a dummy table that can be used in an SQL statement that requires a table refer-ence, but where the actual contents of the table aren't important. For example, you could use this table to extract the system date and time using a SELECT statement like this:

```
SELECT CURRENT DATE AS CURR_DATE, CURRENT TIME AS CURR_TIME
    FROM SYSIBM.SYSDUMMY1
```

Without this table, you'd have to refer to some other system or user table even though you don't need any of the information it contains.

In this chapter, you'll be introduced to the six tables you're most likely to use. They're the ones that are shaded in figure 12-1: SYSCOLUMNS, SYSFOREIGNKEYS, SYSINDEXES, SYSKEYS, SYSRELS, and SYSTABLES. As you read about these tables, you'll get an idea of the kind of information the other tables contain and how the tables are related to each other. If you'd like more information about any of the tables listed in this figure, you can find it in the IBM manual *DB2 for OS/390 V5 SQL Reference*.

Catalog tables for DB2 version 4 (continued)

Table name	Contents
SYSTABAUTH	Privileges held by users over tables and views
SYSTABLEPART	Components of partitioned and unpartitioned table spaces
SYSTABLES	One row for each table, view, or alias
SYSTABLESPACE	One row for each table space
SYSTABSTATS	One row for each partition of a partitioned table space
SYSUSERAUTH	Privileges held by users for system operation and use
SYSVIEWDEP	Dependencies of views
SYSVIEWS	One or more rows for each view
SYSVOLUMES	One row for each volume of every storage group

New catalog tables for DB2 version 5

Table name	Contents
IPNAMES	Remote DRDA servers DB2 can access using TCP/IP
LOCATIONS	One row for every accessible remote server
LULIST	Remote DB2 data sharing groups
LUMODES	Conversation limits
LUNAMES	One row for each remote SNA client or server that communicates with DB2
MODESELECT	Mode names for conversations created to support outgoing SQL requests
SYSDUMMY1	One row for a dummy table
USERNAMES	ID translations

Notes

- The full name of each catalog table starts with the authorization-id SYSIBM as a high-level qualifier.
- The information in the LOCATIONS, LULIST, LUMODES, LUNAMES, MODESELECT, and USERNAMES tables that are new to version 5 was stored in tables in the *communications database* in version 4.

Figure 12-1   DB2 catalog tables (part 2 of 2)

How to extract column information from the SYSCOLUMNS catalog table

The SYSCOLUMNS table contains information about every column in every table and view defined in your DB2 subsystem. As you can imagine, this table can be huge. So you should issue queries against it only when it's absolutely necessary. And then, be sure to include a WHERE clause so that only the rows you need are retrieved.

The structure of the SYSCOLUMNS table

Figure 12-2 presents the structure of the SYSCOLUMNS table. The columns that are shaded in this figure are the ones I think you'll find most useful. These columns contain basic information about how the columns in each table or view are defined. The NAME column, for example, contains the name of the column, the COLTYPE column contains the data type of the column, and the NULLS column contains an indication of whether or not the column can contain null values. You're most likely to use this table if you forget how a column or a group of columns are defined.

One column you can use for a special purpose is the LABEL column, which can contain a string of up to 30 characters. Many programmers use this column to specify the header to be used for the column in report programs. That makes it easy to keep the column header consistent from one report to another.

To add a label to a column, you use the LABEL ON statement. For example, to add a label to the PCODE column of the product table, you use a statement like this:

```
LABEL ON COLUMN MM01.PRODUCT.PCODE
    IS 'PRODUCT CODE'
```

And to add a label to both columns in the product table, you use a statement like this:

```
LABEL ON MM01.PRODUCT
    (PCODE IS 'PRODUCT CODE', PDESC IS 'DESCRIPTION')
```

For a complete description of the LABEL ON statement, see the manual *DB2 for OS/390 V5 SQL Reference*.

The columns in the SYSCOLUMNS table

Column	Type	Contents
NAME	VARCHAR(18)	Name of the column
TBNAME	VARCHAR(18)	Name of the table or view that contains the column
TBCREATOR	CHAR(8)	Authorization-id of the table or view's owner
COLNO	SMALLINT	Position of the column in the table or view
COLTYPE	CHAR(8)	Type of data in the column
LENGTH	SMALLINT	Length of the data component of the column; precision for a DECIMAL column
SCALE	SMALLINT	Scale for a DECIMAL column
NULLS	CHAR(1)	"Y" if the column can contain nulls; "N" if it can't
COLCARD	INTEGER	Estimated number of distinct values in the column (version 4 only)
HIGH2KEY	CHAR(8)	Second highest value stored in the column
LOW2KEY	CHAR(8)	Second lowest value stored in the column
UPDATES	CHAR(1)	"Y" if the column can be updated; "N" if it can't
IBMREQD	CHAR(1)	"Y" if the row came from an IBM tape; "N" if it didn't
REMARKS	VARCHAR(254)	Character string specified by the user with a COMMENT ON statement
DEFAULT	CHAR(1)	"Y" if the column has a default value; "N" if it doesn't
KEYSEQ	SMALLINT	Position of the column in the table's primary key
FOREIGNKEY	CHAR(1)	"B" if the column contains foreign-key related bit data
FLDPROC	CHAR(1)	"Y" if the column has a field procedure; "N" if it doesn't
LABEL	VARCHAR(30)	Character string specified by the user with a LABEL ON statement
STATSTIME	TIMESTAMP	The date and time when RUNSTATS last updated the statistics
DEFAULTVALUE	VARCHAR(512)	The default value of the column
COLCARDF	FLOAT	Estimated number of distinct values in the column (version 5 only)

Figure 12-2   The structure of the SYSCOLUMNS table

A query against the SYSCOLUMNS table

Figure 12-3 shows two screens from a SPUFI session that display information about the columns in the tables related to invoicing. You can see the SELECT statement at the top of the SPUFI output in part 1 of this figure. Notice that this statement retrieves columns from a table named MM01.SYSCOLUMNS rather than from SYSIBM.SYSCOLUMNS. Actually, MM01.SYSCOLUMNS is a view that includes all the rows in SYSIBM.SYSCOLUMNS for tables I created. The system administrator for the system I'm using created this view, and similar views for the other system tables, to limit my access to those tables. This is common in many IBM shops, particularly those that rent space to other users.

If you look at the WHERE clause for this statement, you'll notice that one of the conditions checks for rows that I created (TBCREATOR = 'MM01'). Although this is redundant since the view used in this statement contains only the rows I created, I included this condition here and in the following examples so you can see the names of the columns that identify the creator. If you have direct access to the system tables, you'll want to be sure to include this condition to look at just the rows you created.

The WHERE clause in this example also includes a condition that specifies that rows should be selected only when their table-name value starts with the letters INV (TBNAME LIKE 'INV%'). That way, only the columns in tables related to invoicing are selected. This SELECT statement also includes an ORDER BY clause that sorts the output by column number within table name.

As you can see in the result table, three tables have names that start with INV: INVOICE, INVHIST, and INVMSTR. If you examine the displays, you'll see that all three tables consist of eight columns, and corresponding columns in each table have the same names, data types, and lengths.

Part 1

The first half of the SPUFI output for a query against the SYSCOLUMNS table that
retrieves information about columns in tables whose names start with INV

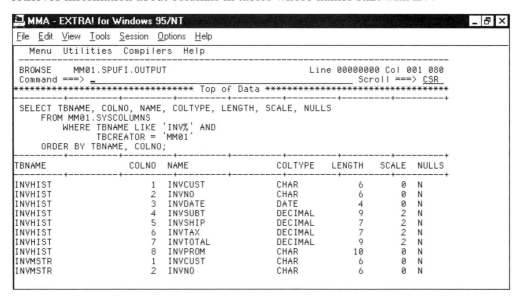

Part 2

The second half of the SPUFI output for a query against the SYSCOLUMNS table

Figure 12-3   A query against the SYSCOLUMNS table

How to extract table information from the SYSTABLES catalog table

The SYSTABLES table contains one row for each table, alias, and view in your DB2 subsystem. You're most likely to use it to retrieve general information about a table, alias, or view or about a table's relationship with other tables in the subsystem.

The structure of the SYSTABLES table

Figure 12-4 presents the structure of the SYSTABLES table. Once again, I've shaded the columns I think you'll find most useful. Although I've shaded both the CARD and CARDF columns, you should note that you can only use one or the other depending on whether you're using version 4 or version 5 of DB2. You use the CARD column for version 4, which is defined as an integer. And you use the CARDF column for version 5, which is defined as a floating-point number. In either case, the column contains the number of rows in the table.

Another difference between version 4 and version 5 is the values that can be stored in the TYPE column. For version 4, this column can contain the letters T, A, or V to indicate that the row is for a table, alias, or view. For version 5, this column can also contain a G to indicate that the row is for a temporary table. If you read chapter 10, you know that temporary tables exist only during the execution of the application that creates them. When that application ends, the temporary table, along with the row in the SYSTABLES table that contains information about it, is deleted.

The columns in the SYSTABLES table

Column	Type	Contents
NAME	VARCHAR(18)	Name of the table, view, or alias
CREATOR	CHAR(8)	Authorization-id of the owner of the table, view, or alias
TYPE	CHAR(1)	"T" for a table, "A" for an alias, "V" for a view, or "G" for a temporary table
DBNAME	CHAR(8)	Name of the database that contains the table space for the object
TSNAME	CHAR(8)	Name of the table space that contains the table or one of the tables in a view
DBID	SMALLINT	Internal identifier for the database
OBID	SMALLINT	Internal identifier for the table
COLCOUNT	SMALLINT	Number of columns in the table or view
EDPROC	CHAR(8)	Name of the edit procedure specified for the table, if any
VALPROC	CHAR(8)	Name of the validation procedure specified for the table, if any
CLUSTERTYPE	CHAR(1)	"Y" if RESTRICT ON DROP applies: blank if it doesn't
	INTEGER	Not used
CARD	INTEGER	Number of rows in the table (version 4 only)
NPAGES	INTEGER	Number of storage pages that contain rows for this table
PCTPAGES	SMALLINT	Percent of the total number of pages in the table space that contain rows for this table
IBMREQD	CHAR(1)	"Y" if the row came from an IBM tape; "N" if it didn't; other values indicate version and release dependencies
REMARKS	VARCHAR(254)	Character string specified by the user with a COMMENT ON statement
PARENTS	SMALLINT	Number of relationships in which the table is a dependent
CHILDREN	SMALLINT	Number of relationships in which the table is a parent
KEYCOLUMNS	SMALLINT	Number of columns in the table's primary key
RECLENGTH	SMALLINT	Maximum length in bytes of the data for a row
STATUS	CHAR(1)	Blank if the table doesn't have a parent index; "X" if the table does have a parent index; "I" if the definition of the table is incomplete because a parent index hasn't been created
KEYOBID	SMALLINT	Internal identifier for the table's primary key index
LABEL	VARCHAR(30)	Character string specified by the user on a LABEL ON statement
CHECKFLAG	CHAR(1)	"C" if the table contains rows that violate referential or table check constraints; blank if it doesn't
CHECKRID	CHAR(4)	RID of the first row of the table that can violate referential or table check constraints (version 4 only)
AUDITING	CHAR(1)	Audit option
CREATEDBY	CHAR(8)	Authorization-id of the user who created the table, view, or alias
LOCATION	CHAR(16)	Blank, except for an alias defined for a remote object
TBCREATOR	CHAR(8)	Blank, except for an alias, when it contains the authorization-id or the owner of the referenced table or view
TBNAME	VARCHAR(18)	Blank, except for an alias, when it contains the name of the referenced table or view
CREATEDTS	TIMESTAMP	Time when the table, view, or alias was created
ALTEREDTS	TIMESTAMP	Time when the table was last altered
DATACAPTURE	CHAR(1)	Value of the DATA CAPTURE option for the table
RBA1	CHAR(6)	Log RBA when the table was created
RBA2	CHAR(6)	Log RBA when the table was last altered
PCTROWCOMP	SMALLINT	Percentage of rows compressed in the table
STATSTIME	TIMESTAMP	Date and time when RUNSTATS last updated the statistics
CHECKS	SMALLINT	Number of check constraints defined on the table
CARDF	FLOAT	Number of rows in the table (version 5 only)
CHECKRID5B	CHAR(5)	RID of the first row of the table that can violate referential or table check constraints (version 5 only)
ENCODING_SCHEME	CHAR(1)	"E" for EBCDIC; "A" for ASCII; blank for remote aliases (version 5 only)

Figure 12-4   The structure of the SYSTABLES table

A query against the SYSTABLES table

Figure 12-5 shows a SPUFI session where I issued a SELECT statement against SYSTABLES. In this figure, I retrieved information about all the tables I created that are involved in parent/child relationships. To do that, I specified the six columns you can see in the SELECT statement at the top of the display: NAME, TYPE, COLCOUNT, PARENTS, CHILDREN, and KEYCOLUMNS. Then, I coded a compound selection condition that retrieves data only for my tables (CREATOR = 'MM01') and for tables that are a parent, a child, or both (PARENTS > 0 OR CHILDREN > 0).

As you can see, the SELECT statement returned four rows: one each for the CUSTOMER, INVOICE, LINEITEM, and PRODUCT tables I've used for the examples in this book. The "T" values in the TYPE column report that all four rows are for tables rather than for aliases or views. The COLCOUNT value shows how many columns each table contains.

The information in the result table also shows that the CUSTOMER table has no parents, but one child; that INVOICE has one parent and one child; that LINEITEM has two parents, but no children; and that PRODUCT, like CUS-TOMER, has one child, but no parents. The last column in this output, KEYCOLUMNS, shows how many columns comprise the primary key for each table. All of the tables in this figure have single-column keys except LINEITEM; its primary key is a composite of two columns.

Although this query shows that the CUSTOMER, INVOICE, LINEITEM, and PRODUCT tables are all involved in parent/child relationships of some kind, it doesn't list the specifics of the relationships. For example, although the query reports that the CUSTOMER table is a parent and the INVOICE table is a child, it doesn't show that CUSTOMER and INVOICE have a parent/child relationship with each other. For that information, you can look to another catalog table: SYSRELS.

A query that retrieves information about parent/child relationships from the SYSTABLES table

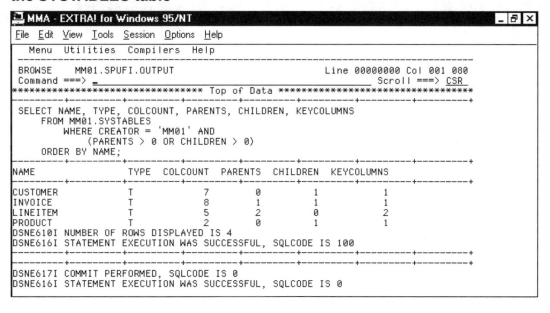

```
┌─────────────────────────────────────────────────────────────────────────────────┐
│ 🖳 MMA - EXTRA! for Windows 95/NT                                    _ ░ X        │
├───────────────────────────────────────────────────────────────────────────────────┤
│ File  Edit  View  Tools  Session  Options  Help                                   │
│ ─────────────────────────────────────────────────────────────────────────────── │
│    Menu   Utilities   Compilers   Help                                            │
│ ───────────────────────────────────────────────────────────────────────────────── │
│   BROWSE      MM01.SPUFI.OUTPUT                       Line 00000000 Col 001 080    │
│   Command ===> _                                            Scroll ===> CSR       │
│ ****************************** Top of Data ****************************************│
│ ─────────+──────────+──────────+──────────+──────────+──────────+──────────+──────────+│
│   SELECT NAME, TYPE, COLCOUNT, PARENTS, CHILDREN, KEYCOLUMNS                       │
│       FROM MM01.SYSTABLES                                                          │
│           WHERE CREATOR = 'MM01' AND                                               │
│              (PARENTS > 0 OR CHILDREN > 0)                                         │
│        ORDER BY NAME;                                                              │
│ ─────────+──────────+──────────+──────────+──────────+──────────+──────────+──────────+│
│ NAME                TYPE  COLCOUNT  PARENTS  CHILDREN  KEYCOLUMNS                  │
│ ─────────+──────────+──────────+──────────+──────────+──────────+──────────+──────────+│
│ CUSTOMER            T         7        0        1        1                         │
│ INVOICE             T         8        1        1        1                         │
│ LINEITEM            T         5        2        0        2                         │
│ PRODUCT             T         2        0        1        1                         │
│ DSNE610I NUMBER OF ROWS DISPLAYED IS 4                                             │
│ DSNE616I STATEMENT EXECUTION WAS SUCCESSFUL, SQLCODE IS 100                        │
│ ─────────+──────────+──────────+──────────+──────────+──────────+──────────+──────────+│
│ ─────────+──────────+──────────+──────────+──────────+──────────+──────────+──────────+│
│ DSNE617I COMMIT PERFORMED, SQLCODE IS 0                                            │
│ DSNE616I STATEMENT EXECUTION WAS SUCCESSFUL, SQLCODE IS 0                          │
│                                                                                   │
└───────────────────────────────────────────────────────────────────────────────────┘
```

Figure 12-5   A query against the SYSTABLES table

How to extract parent/child relationship information from the SYSRELS catalog table

The SYSRELS table contains information about the relationships among the tables in the subsystem. In other words, it contains information about referential constraints. As you'll see, however, this table doesn't include information about what columns define the constraints. To get that information, you have to combine the information in the SYSRELS tables with information from other catalog tables.

The structure of the SYSRELS table

The table at the top of figure 12-6 lists the columns in the SYSRELS table. You shouldn't have any trouble understanding the contents of most of the shaded columns in this figure. However, the last two, IXOWNER and IXNAME, deserve some additional explanation.

In most cases, a referential constraint is defined by the relationship between a foreign key in one table and the primary key of another table. If you read chapter 10, however, you know that with DB2 version 5, a foreign key can also be related to a unique key other than the primary key. In that case, the name and owner of the non-primary index that enforces the unique key is stored in the IXNAME and IXOWNER columns of the SYSRELS table. If these columns are blank, it indicates that the index for the primary key is used.

DB2 version 5 also added another possible value for the DELETERULE column. The value in this column determines what happens when DB2 receives a request to delete a row in the parent table whose primary key value matches the foreign key value of one or more rows in the child table. In addition to C (cascade), R (restrict), and N (set to null), this column can contain A (no action). A has the same effect as R: The delete operation isn't performed.

A query against the SYSRELS table

The screen at the bottom of figure 12-6 shows the results of a query that retrieves the names of child tables (TBNAME) and their parents (REFTBNAME). The query also includes the RELNAME column, which specifies the name of the referential constraint for the parent/child relationship.

As you learned in chapter 10, you can specify your own constraint name when you define a foreign key. In this example, you can see that I named the constraints after the primary keys in the parent tables that enforce the constraints. So, for example, you can read the data in the first line of the result table as "the CUSTNO column in the CUSTOMER table enforces the referential constraint with the foreign key of the INVOICE table." Note, however, that the columns in the foreign keys aren't listed in this figure. To get that information, you can use the SYSFOREIGNKEYS table.

The columns in the SYSRELS table

Column	Type	Contents
CREATOR	CHAR(8)	Authorization-id of the owner of the child table
TBNAME	VARCHAR(18)	Name of the child table
RELNAME	CHAR(8)	Referential constraint name
REFTBNAME	VARCHAR(18)	Name of the parent table
REFTBCREATOR	CHAR(8)	Authorization-id of the owner of the parent table
COLCOUNT	SMALLINT	Number of columns in the foreign key
DELETERULE	CHAR(1)	"C" if the delete rule is cascade; "R" if it's restrict; "N" if it's set to null; "A" if no action is taken
IBMREQD	CHAR(1)	"Y" if the row came from an IBM tape; "N" if it didn't
RELOBID1	SMALLINT	Internal identifier for the database that contains the parent table
RELOBID2	SMALLINT	Internal identifier for the database that contains the child table
TIMESTAMP	TIMESTAMP	Date and time the constraint was defined
IXOWNER	CHAR(8)	Owner of the unique non-primary index used for the parent key (version 5 only)
IXNAME	VARCHAR(18)	Name of the unique non-primary index used for the parent key (version 5 only)

A query that retrieves information about parent/child relationships from the SYSRELS table

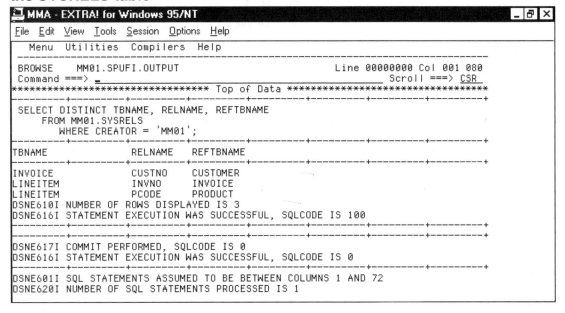

Figure 12-6   How to extract information from the SYSRELS catalog table

How to extract foreign key information from the SYSFOREIGNKEYS table

The SYSFOREIGNKEYS table contains information about the foreign keys that are defined for the tables in the subsystem. This information is most useful when used in conjunction with the information in the SYSRELS table.

The structure of the SYSFOREIGNKEYS table

The table at the top of figure 12-7 describes the contents of the columns in the SYSFOREIGNKEYS table. Each row in this table describes one foreign key column. If a foreign key consists of two columns, then, this table will contain two rows for it. Each row contains information such as the name of the column, the name of the table that contains the column, the name of the referential constraint that the column is a part of, and the position of the column within the foreign key of that referential constraint.

A query that joins data in the SYSRELS and SYSFOREIGNKEYS tables

The query in figure 12-7 combines information from the SYSRELS and SYSFOREIGNKEYS tables. If you compare the results of this query with the results of the query in figure 12-6, you'll see that this query gives a more complete picture of the columns that are used to enforce referential constraints. For example, you can see from the output in this figure that the column named INVCUST in the INVOICE table is a foreign key, and it's related to the CUSTNO column in the CUSTOMER table.

The technique shown in this figure works only because the referential constraints were given the same names as the primary key columns that enforce the constraints. If the constraints had been given other names, you'd have to use another technique to retrieve the names of the primary key columns. That technique would involve using information in the SYSKEYS and SYSINDEXES tables, which are presented next.

The columns in the SYSFOREIGNKEYS table

Column	Type	Contents
CREATOR	CHAR(8)	Authorization-id of the owner of the table that contains the column
TBNAME	VARCHAR(18)	Name of the table that contains the column
RELNAME	CHAR(8)	Referential constraint name for the foreign key that the column is a part of
COLNAME	VARCHAR(18)	Name of the column
COLNO	SMALLINT	Position of the column in the row
COLSEQ	SMALLINT	Position of the column in the foreign key
IBMREQD	CHAR(1)	"Y" if the row came from an IBM tape; "N" if it didn't

A query that retrieves information about parent/child relationships from the SYSRELS and SYSFOREIGNKEYS tables

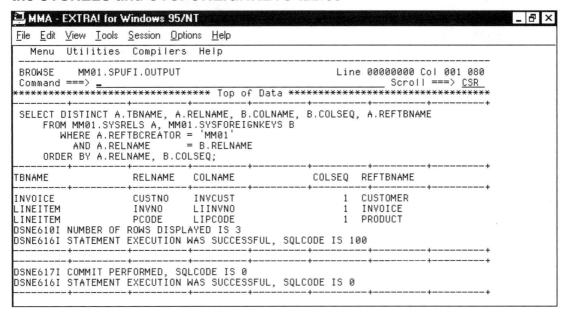

Figure 12-7 How to extract information from the SYSFOREIGNKEYS table

How to extract column information for index keys from the SYSKEYS catalog table

You may remember from chapter 10 that for every primary or unique key you define, you must also create an index that DB2 uses to enforce the uniqueness of those keys. In addition, you can create indexes for other columns that you use frequently to access the rows in a table. To get information about the keys for those indexes, you use the SYSKEYS catalog table.

The structure of the SYSKEYS table

The table at the top of figure 12-8 presents the contents of the SYSKEYS table. As you can see, each row contains information about one column in one index key. So for an index like LITEMX that consists of two key columns, the SYSKEYS table contains two rows. Each row contains information such as the name of the column, the name of the index that the column is part of, and the position of the column in the row and key.

A query against the SYSKEYS table

The screen at the bottom of figure 12-8 shows a SELECT statement that extracts column information for index keys from the SYSKEYS table. The result table includes the name of the index, the name of each column that makes up an index key, and the position of that column in the key. Notice that I sorted the output by column sequence for each index. So the two columns that make up the key for the XLITEM index are in the same order as they are in the LINEITEM table.

The columns in the SYSKEYS table

Column	Type	Contents
IXNAME	VARCHAR(18)	Name of the index
IXCREATOR	CHAR(8)	Authorization-id of the owner of the index
COLNAME	VARCHAR(18)	Name of the key column
COLNO	SMALLINT	Position of the column in the row
COLSEQ	SMALLINT	Position of the column in the key
ORDERING	CHAR(1)	"A" if the order of the column values in the index is ascending; "D" if the order is descending
IBMREQD	CHAR(1)	"Y" if the row came from an IBM tape; "N" if it didn't

A query that retrieves information about the columns that make up index keys

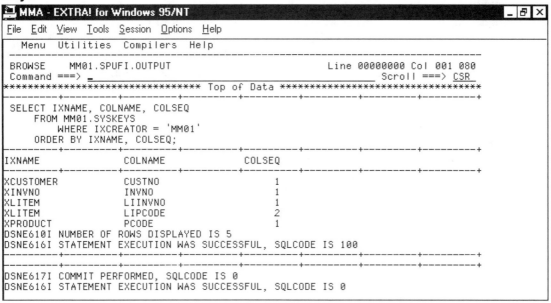

Figure 12-8   How to extract information from the SYSKEYS catalog table

How to extract index information from the SYSINDEXES catalog table

The SYSINDEXES table contains information about every index that's defined for every table in the DB2 subsystem. Like many of the other tables, it contains a lot of technical information—like the number of leaf pages it uses and the number of levels it consists of—that is probably more useful to DBAs. However, it also contains some general information that can be useful to you as a programmer.

The structure of the SYSINDEXES table

Figure 12-9 presents the contents of the SYSINDEXES table. As you can see by the shading in this figure, you'll probably use only a few of the columns in this table. These are the columns that provide general information about an index, such as the number of columns it contains, whether or not it's unique, and whether it's a type 1 or type 2 index.

As I mentioned earlier in this chapter, DB2 version 5 lets you define a referential constraint based on a foreign key in one table and a unique, non-primary key in another table. When that's the case, the UNIQUERULE column of the SYSINDEXES table contains an R to indicate that the index is for a non-primary parent key. This option isn't available with version 4 since it doesn't support non-primary parent keys.

Version 5 also added several new columns, as you can see at the bottom of the table in this figure. Two of these columns, FIRSTKEYCARDF and FULLKEYCARDF, replace the FIRSTKEYCARD and FULLKEYCARD columns that were used with version 4. The version 5 columns are defined as floating-point numbers instead of integers.

The columns in the SYSINDEXES table

Column	Type	Contents
NAME	VARCHAR(18)	Name of the index
CREATOR	CHAR(8)	Authorization-id of the owner of the index
TBNAME	VARCHAR(18)	Name of the table the index is related to
TBCREATOR	CHAR(8)	Authorization-id of the owner of the related table
UNIQUERULE	CHAR(1)	"D" if duplicates are allowed; "U" if the index is unique; "P" if the index is a unique primary index; "C" if it is used to enforce a unique constraint; "N" if it is defined with UNIQUE WHERE NOT NULL; "R" if it is used to enforce the uniqueness of a non-primary parent key
COLCOUNT	SMALLINT	Number of columns in the key
CLUSTERING	CHAR(1)	"Y" if clustering was specified for the index; "N" if it wasn't
CLUSTERED	CHAR(1)	"Y" if most of the table's rows are clustered; "N" if they aren't
DBID	SMALLINT	Internal identifier for the database that contains the index
OBID	SMALLINT	Internal identifier for an index component
ISOBID	SMALLINT	Internal identifier for an index component
DBNAME	CHAR(8)	Name of the database that contains the index
INDEXSPACE	CHAR(8)	Name of the index space that contains the index
FIRSTKEYCARD	INTEGER	Number of distinct values in the first key column (version 4 only)
FULLKEYCARD	INTEGER	Number of distinct values in the entire key (version 4 only)
NLEAF	INTEGER	Number of leaf pages in the index
NLEVELS	SMALLINT	Number of levels in the index
BPOOL	CHAR(8)	Name of the buffer pool used for the index
PGSIZE	SMALLINT	Size of subpages in the index
ERASERULE	CHAR(1)	"Y" if index data sets should be erased when dropped; "N" if they shouldn't
DSETPASS	CHAR(8)	Password for index data sets
CLOSERULE	CHAR(1)	"Y" if the index sets can be closed when the limit on the number of open data sets is reached; "N" if they can't
SPACE	INTEGER	Amount of disk storage allocated to the index
IBMREQD	CHAR(1)	"Y" if the row came from an IBM tape; "N" if it didn't; other values indicate version and release dependency
CLUSTERRATIO	SMALLINT	Percent of rows that are in clustering order
CREATEDBY	CHAR(8)	Authorization-id of the creator of the index
	SMALLINT	Not in use
	SMALLINT	Not in use
STATSTIME	TIMESTAMP	The date and time when RUNSTATS last updated the statistics
INDEXTYPE	CHAR(1)	"2" for type 2 index; blank for type 1 index
FIRSTKEYCARDF	FLOAT	Number of distinct values in the first key column (version 5 only)
FULLKEYCARDF	FLOAT	Number of distinct values in the key (version 5 only)
CREATEDTS	TIMESTAMP	Time when the index was created (version 5 only)
ALTEREDTS	TIMESTAMP	Time when the index was last altered (version 5 only)
PIECESIZE	INTEGER	Maximum size of data set storage pieces to be used for non-partitioned indexes (version 5 only)

Figure 12-9   The structure of the SYSINDEXES table

Two queries that use the SYSINDEXES table

The first screen in figure 12-10 shows a SELECT statement that lists the indexes for the test tables I created for this book. This statement retrieves five columns from the SYSINDEXES table: NAME, TBNAME, INDEXTYPE, UNIQUERULE, and COLCOUNT. As you can see, the only indexes I created were for the primary key for each table. That's what the P in the UNIQUE-RULE column indicates. The result table also indicates that all the indexes are type 2 indexes, and all the indexes except for the one for the LINEITEM table consist of a single key column. The index for LINEITEM consists of two key columns.

The second screen in figure 12-10 shows a SELECT statement that joins data from the SYSTABLES, SYSINDEXES, and SYSKEYS tables. This statement retrieves the name of each table I created from SYSTABLES, and the names and positions of the columns that make up that table's primary key from SYSKEYS. To identify the primary key columns, the query checks the UNIQUERULE column in SYSINDEXES for a value of "P." Then, it uses the NAME column in those rows to select only the primary key columns from SYSKEYS. The result is a list that includes the name of each table, the name of each column in the primary key of each table, and the sequence of each column in the primary key.

A query that retrieves information about existing indexes from the SYSINDEXES table

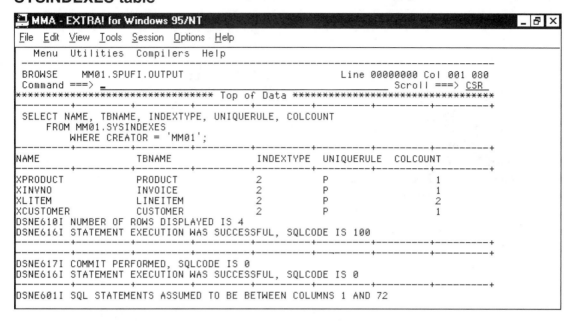

A query that retrieves information about keys from the SYSKEYS, SYSINDEXES, and SYSTABLES tables

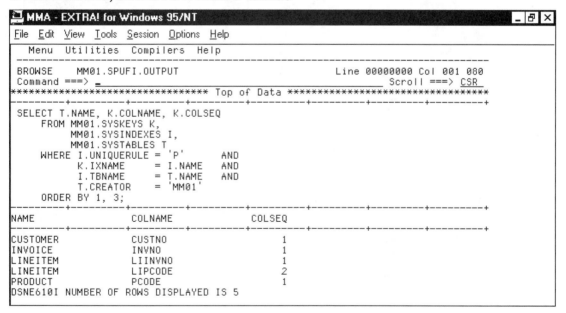

Figure 12-10   Two queries that use the SYSINDEXES table

Perspective

The SELECT statement examples presented in this chapter should give you an idea of the type of information you can extract from the DB2 catalog tables. With only minor changes, you'll be able to use these statements as models for queries of your own. If you want to find out more about the information that's available from these tables, though, you can refer to the *DB2 for OS/390 V5 SQL Reference* manual. In most cases, you'll find that this information is more appropriate for DBAs than for application programmers.

In addition to the DB2 catalog tables, some shops use other tables that provide extensions to the catalog tables. For example, a shop might use a set of tables its staff has defined to store information for database design or administration. Information about the nature of objects, their dependencies, and their relationships to business rules might also fall into this category. So be sure to check with your DBA to see if your shop uses any additional tables.

13

How to get performance analysis data using the EXPLAIN statement

The application plan for a program specifies how DB2 will access the data to process the program's SQL statements. The approach DB2 takes to processing an SQL statement is called an *access path*. When more than one access path is possible, a component of DB2 called the *optimizer* tries to select the best one. The first part of this chapter gives you some insight into how the optimizer selects an access path.

Then, the second part of this chapter shows you how to use the EXPLAIN statement to display information about the access paths DB2 uses as it executes your I/O requests. Although this information is commonly used by system administrators as they fine-tune the performance of a DB2 system, some of it can also be useful to the application programmer. So that's the information this chapter presents.

How DB2 selects an access path

To select an access path, the optimizer estimates the processing costs of the I/O operations each will require. These costs depend on many factors, including whether indexes are available for the affected tables and whether a join operation is required. After it assesses each possible access path, the optimizer chooses the one that seems like it will have the lowest cost.

Usually, indexes improve performance. So, when an appropriate index is available, the optimizer will typically use it. But that isn't always the case. If a table is small, for example, the optimizer may determine that it would cost less to look at all the data directly. The same is true if a selection is to be done on a key column that has duplicate values.

Any time DB2 accesses the data in a table, it does a *table space scan* to locate the requested rows. The first table in figure 13-1 summarizes the processing DB2 must do for a table space scan depending on the type of table space the data is stored in. As you can see, DB2 must read every page in a simple table space to locate the requested rows. If the table is stored in a segmented table space, though, DB2 can read just the segments that contain rows from the table. And if the table is stored in a partitioned table space, DB2 may be able to read just the partitions that contain rows from the table depending on the selection conditions that are specified.

If DB2 can satisfy a statement by looking only at the index for a table and not the related table, it does what's called an *index scan*. The second table in figure 13-1 lists some of the possible access paths DB2 can take when using an index. Although it's not critical that you understand how these access paths work, they can help you understand why some queries can be processed more efficiently than others. Keep in mind that to use an index scan, all the data the statement refers to must be part of the index. In many cases, DB2 must access both the index and the table to retrieve the requested data.

As you might guess, a statement that joins data from two or more tables can be costly. DB2 can use three different methods to perform a join operation: a *merge scan join*, a *nested loop join*, or a *hybrid join*. Because the details of how these methods work are complicated, I won't describe them here. If you want more information, you can refer to the IBM manual, *DB2 for OS/390 V5 Administration Guide*.

Table space scans

Table space type	How it's scanned
Simple	DB2 reads every page in the table space.
Segmented	DB2 reads only the segments in the table space that contain rows from the specified table.
Partitioned	DB2 reads only the partitions in the table space that contain rows that match the selection condition if the condition contains the first key column of the index that's used to partition the rows. This is called a *limited partition scan*.

Index access paths

Type	When it's used
Matching index scan	Selection conditions are specified on the first key column of the index or all key columns.
Index screening	Selection conditions are specified on index key columns, but the columns aren't part of the matching columns. Those conditions improve the index search by reducing the number of qualifying rows.
Non-matching index scan	The selection conditions contain no matching columns in the index, so all the index keys must be scanned. This is an efficient access path when there is more than one table in a simple table space.
IN-list index scan	A special case of the matching index scan where the IN phrase is used in the selection condition for one of the key columns.
Multiple index access	Two or more indexes are used to access the table. DB2 constructs a list that includes a union or intersection of the qualified rows and then uses that list to retrieve the rows from the table.
One-fetch access	The statement contains a MIN or MAX column function, and the matching index column is sorted in ascending (MIN) or descending (MAX) sequence. Only one row is retrieved.
Index-only access	The index contains all the necessary access information, so no data pages are read.
Equal unique index	The selection conditions specify equal conditions for all index key columns in a unique index. Only one row is retrieved.

Figure 13-1   DB2 table space scans and index access paths

How to use the EXPLAIN statement

The EXPLAIN statement lets you "ask" DB2 to explain the access paths it will use to process SQL statements. The factors that EXPLAIN reports for a given statement depend on the nature of the data the statement will access and on the availability of indexes. Those factors are usually outside your control, so you probably won't be able to do much with the information you collect with EXPLAIN. However, you may be expected to supply EXPLAIN output for some SQL statements you create. And, at the least, looking at what EXPLAIN does will give you some insight into how DB2 works.

DB2 stores the output produced by an EXPLAIN statement in a *plan table*. Before you use EXPLAIN for the first time, you need to create this table. You'll learn how to do that next. Then, I'll show you the format of the EXPLAIN statement and present some sample output.

How to create a plan table

Figure 13-2 presents a CREATE TABLE statement you can use to define your plan table. Note that the name of the table must be PLAN_TABLE, and it must be qualified by your user-id. In addition, the columns for the table must be defined exactly as shown in this figure. If they're not, the EXPLAIN statement won't work properly.

Although you must code the column definitions as shown, you should know that you can omit the last three columns if you don't need the information they contain. You should also know that you can include additional columns that aren't shown in this figure. For more information, see the description of the CREATE TABLE statement in *DB2 for OS/390 V5 SQL Administration Guide*.

To save you the time of entering the statement shown in this figure, we've made this statement available from our web site (www.murach.com). Note that the statement on our web site includes all of the columns that are available for the plan table, not just the ones shown in this figure. After you download this statement and before you run it, be sure to change the names of the database, table space, and table so they're suitable for your shop.

A CREATE TABLE statement that creates PLAN_TABLE

```
CREATE TABLE MM01.PLAN_TABLE
        (QUERYNO              INTEGER       NOT NULL,
         QBLOCKNO             SMALLINT      NOT NULL,
         APPLNAME             CHAR(8)       NOT NULL,
         PROGNAME             CHAR(8)       NOT NULL,
         PLANNO               SMALLINT      NOT NULL,
         METHOD               SMALLINT      NOT NULL,
         CREATOR              CHAR(8)       NOT NULL,
         TNAME                CHAR(18)      NOT NULL,
         TABNO                SMALLINT      NOT NULL,
         ACCESSTYPE           CHAR(2)       NOT NULL,
         MATCHCOLS            SMALLINT      NOT NULL,
         ACCESSCREATOR        CHAR(8)       NOT NULL,
         ACCESSNAME           CHAR(18)      NOT NULL,
         INDEXONLY            CHAR(1)       NOT NULL,
         SORTN_UNIQ           CHAR(1)       NOT NULL,
         SORTN_JOIN           CHAR(1)       NOT NULL,
         SORTN_ORDERBY        CHAR(1)       NOT NULL,
         SORTN_GROUPBY        CHAR(1)       NOT NULL,
         SORTC_UNIQ           CHAR(1)       NOT NULL,
         SORTC_JOIN           CHAR(1)       NOT NULL,
         SORTC_ORDERBY        CHAR(1)       NOT NULL,
         SORTC_GROUPBY        CHAR(1)       NOT NULL,
         TSLOCKMODE           CHAR(3)       NOT NULL,
         TIMESTAMP            CHAR(16)      NOT NULL,
         REMARKS              VARCHAR(254)  NOT NULL,
         PREFETCH             CHAR(1)       NOT NULL,
         COLUMN_FN_EVAL       CHAR(1)       NOT NULL WITH DEFAULT,
         MIXOPSEQ             SMALLINT      NOT NULL WITH DEFAULT)
IN DATABASE MMADBV;
```

Description

- DB2 stores output produced by the EXPLAIN statement in a special table named PLAN_TABLE. You must create this table before you use EXPLAIN for the first time.

- DB2 stores one row in PLAN_TABLE for each access path that's required to satisfy a statement. Usually, one access path is required for each table the statement refers to.

Figure 13-2   How to create a plan table

The columns in a plan table

Figure 13-3 describes the plan table columns shown in figure 13-2. As you review this information, keep in mind that DB2 adds a row to this table for each access path it uses to process a statement. In most cases, that means one row is added for each table the statement refers to. However, additional rows may be added for more complex statements.

The columns you're most likely to use as you analyze statements are the ones that are shaded in this figure. You'll use the QUERYNO column, for example, to retrieve the rows added for a particular statement. You specify that number on the EXPLAIN statement as you'll see in a moment. You'll use the other columns to determine the name of the table that's being processed (TNAME), the type of access that's used to retrieve data from the table (ACCESSTYPE), the name of the index that's used for an index scan (ACCESSNAME), whether or not only the index was used (INDEXONLY), and the method that was used to join tables (METHOD). You'll see examples of most of these columns later in this chapter.

PLAN_TABLE column descriptions

Column	Contents
QUERYNO	A number that identifies the statement that was explained. You can assign this number using the SET option of the EXPLAIN statement. Otherwise, DB2 assigns a number.
QBLOCKNO	A number that identifies the position of the query in the statement (1 for the outermost query, 2 for the next query, and so on).
APPLNAME	The name of the application plan that contains the statement; blank if the statement wasn't embedded in a program and executed from a plan or explained when binding the plan.
PROGNAME	The name of the program or package that contains the statement; blank if the statement wasn't embedded in a program or explained when the plan or package was bound.
PLANNO	A number that identifies the step that the query indicated in QBLOCKNO was executed in.
METHOD	A number that indicates the join method used for the current step of the plan: 0 for the first table accessed, a continuation of the previous table accessed, or no join used; 1 for a nested loop join; 2 for a merge scan join; 3 not for accessing a new table, but for sorting a table to meet the requirements of ORDER BY, GROUP BY, or DISTINCT; and 4 for a hybrid join.
CREATOR	The creator of a table accessed for the first time in the current step of the statement.
TNAME	The name of a table, temporary table, materialized view, table expression, or an intermediate result table for an outer join that's accessed for the first time in the current step of the statement.
TABNO	A number that identifies references to tables. For IBM use only.
ACCESSTYPE	The method used to access a table: "I" for an index, "I1" for a one-fetch index scan, "N" for an IN-list index scan, "R" for a table space scan, "M" for a multiple-index scan (followed by "MX", "MI", or "MU"), "MX" for an index scan on the index named in ACCESSNAME, "MI" for an intersection of multiple indexes, and "MU" for a union of multiple indexes; blank if not applicable.
MATCHCOLS	The number of index keys used in an index scan.
ACCESSCREATOR	The creator of an index used in an index scan.
ACCESSNAME	The name of an index used in an index scan.
INDEXONLY	"Y" if only the index was accessed; "N" if the table had to be accessed.
SORTN_UNIQ	"Y" if an intermediate sort was required on the new table to remove duplicate rows; "N" if it wasn't.
SORTN_JOIN	"Y" if an intermediate sort was required on the new table in a merge scan or hybrid join; "N" if it wasn't.
SORTN_ORDERBY	"Y" if an intermediate sort was required on the new table to process an ORDER BY clause; "N" if it wasn't.
SORTN_GROUPBY	"Y" if an intermediate sort was required on the new table to process a GROUP BY CLAUSE; "N" if it wasn't.
SORTC_UNIQUE	"Y" if an intermediate sort was required on the composite table to remove duplicate rows; "N" if it wasn't.
SORTC_JOIN	"Y" if an intermediate sort was required on the composite table in a merge scan or hybrid join; "N" if it wasn't.
SORTC_ORDERBY	"Y" if an intermediate sort was required on the composite table to process an ORDER BY clause; "N" if it wasn't.
SORTC_GROUPBY	"Y" if an intermediate sort was required on the composite table to process a GROUP BY clause; "N" if it wasn't.
TSLOCKMODE	The lock mode to be acquired on the new table or its table space or partitions.
TIMESTAMP	The date and time the row was processed.
REMARKS	Text that can be supplied by the user.
PREFETCH	The prefetch method used to retrieve data.
COLUMN_FN_EVAL	Indicates when column functions are processed.
MIXOPSEQ	The sequence number of a step in a multiple-index operation.

Figure 13-3   Columns in the PLAN_TABLE table

How to code the EXPLAIN statement

Figure 13-4 presents the syntax of the EXPLAIN statement. Notice that I included the EXEC SQL and END-EXEC delimiters you use if you code this statement in a program. Since this statement isn't particularly useful in a program, though, you're more likely to issue it interactively under SPUFI. When you do, you omit the EXEC SQL and END-EXEC delimiters.

You can supply two variable items when you invoke EXPLAIN. The first is an integer that will identify the explanation it produces. DB2 stores this number in the QUERYNO column for each row it adds to the plan table. Note that the number you specify should be a number that's not already used in that table. If it's not, you'll have no way to identify the rows for a particular statement. To avoid duplicate values in the QUERYNO column, you should delete rows from the plan table regularly.

The second variable of EXPLAIN is the SQL statement to be explained. It may be a SELECT, INSERT, UPDATE, or DELETE statement coded as a literal. Note that you can use EXPLAIN with UPDATE and DELETE only if the statement doesn't use a cursor. In other words, the statement must not contain the CURRENT OF clause.

The screen in this figure shows the results of an EXPLAIN statement that analyzes a SELECT statement. As you can see, this SELECT statement retrieves all the columns from the customer table for rows that have customer numbers in the range 400001 to 400005. Notice that this EXPLAIN statement specifies that the rows that are added to the plan table should be identified with the number 1.

After the EXPLAIN statement is a SELECT statement that retrieves information that was added to the plan table by EXPLAIN. This statement includes a WHERE condition that specifies that only those rows with a value of 1 in the QUERYNO column should be retrieved. You can see the results immediately following this statement.

The results show that a single access path will be used to retrieve the requested data. The "I" in the ACCESSTYPE column indicates that DB2 will use an index to locate the matching rows. That's appropriate since the range of records to be retrieved is small. The name of the index it will use is XCUSTOMER, as you can see in the ACCESSNAME column. Since the index doesn't contain all the requested columns, however, DB2 will also have to retrieve data from the base table. That's why the value in the INDEXONLY column is "N". The other column that's displayed, METHOD, contains a value of zero since the statement being explained doesn't require a join operation.

The syntax of the EXPLAIN statement

```
EXEC SQL
    EXPLAIN {ALL | PLAN} [SET QUERYNO = query-number] FOR
        sql-statement
END-EXEC.
```

Explanation

ALL | PLAN	Inserts a row into the plan table for each step in the execution of sql-statement. The steps for enforcing referential constraints are not included. PLAN and ALL perform the same functions.
query-number	An integer you want EXPLAIN to assign to the rows it adds to the plan table for the current run. The value is stored in the QUERYNO column of the plan table.
sql-statement	A SELECT or INSERT statement, or an UPDATE or DELETE statement that doesn't use a cursor. If EXPLAIN is embedded in a program, sql-statement may not be a host variable. If EXPLAIN is dynamically prepared, sql-statement may not be the name of a prepared statement.

The results of an EXPLAIN statement that analyzes a simple SELECT statement

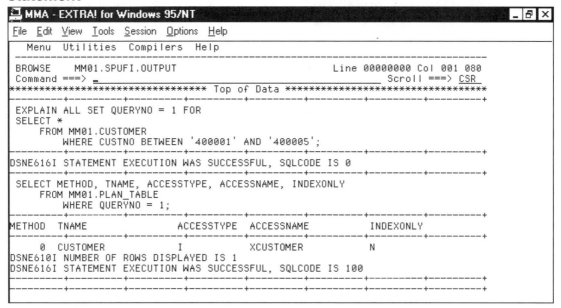

Note

- The EXPLAIN statement can be used only to get information about objects at the current server.

Figure 13-4   How to code the EXPLAIN statement

EXPLAIN analysis of SELECT statements that retrieve data from a single table

Figure 13-5 presents two more EXPLAIN statements. They analyze SELECT statements that retrieve data from the customer table just like the one in figure 13-4. In fact, the SELECT statement in the first example is identical to the one in figure 13-4 except that it retrieves rows from a larger range: 400000 to 499999. Because this range includes a large number of records, the index isn't used to locate those records. That's indicated by the "R" in the ACCESSTYPE column of the EXPLAIN results and the blank in the ACCESSNAME column. Again, this approach makes sense. DB2 figured out that it will have to read most of the rows in the table to satisfy this SELECT statement. So working through the index doesn't offer any benefit.

The second EXPLAIN statement in this figure analyzes a SELECT statement that retrieves rows from the customer table for the same range of customer numbers as in the first example. In this case, though, only the customer number is retrieved from each row. Because that column is contained in the XCUSTOMER index for the table, the requested data can be retrieved using just that index. That's indicated by the "I" in the ACCESSTYPE column and the "Y" in the INDEXONLY column.

EXPLAIN analysis of a SELECT statement that retrieves data only from the customer table

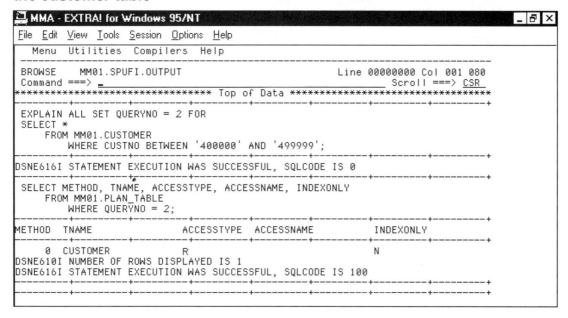

EXPLAIN analysis of a SELECT statement that retrieves data only from the customer index

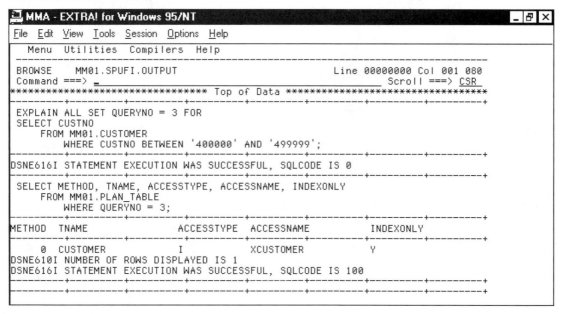

Figure 13-5   EXPLAIN analysis of SELECT statements that retrieve data from a single table

EXPLAIN analysis of SELECT statements that retrieve data from multiple tables

Figure 13-6 presents two more EXPLAIN examples. Unlike the examples presented so far, these EXPLAIN statements analyze SELECT statements that retrieve data from more than one table. Because of that, more than one row is added to the plan table for each statement.

The SELECT statement in the first example retrieves data from a view named V_CUSTPROD. This is the view you saw in chapter 10. It includes data from four tables: CUSTOMER, INVOICE, LINEITEM, and PRODUCT.

The four rows DB2 added to the plan table for this statement represent the steps it will go through as it does the join necessary to create the view. The values in the METHOD column indicate that DB2 will use a nested loop join to combine data from the PRODUCT table with data from the LINEITEM table and hybrid joins to combine data from the CUSTOMER and INVOICE tables with the data from the LINEITEM and PRODUCT tables. Notice that all four tables are accessed through their indexes, and all require access to data in the base tables.

The second example in this figure shows a simpler join that names the tables it will process explicitly: CUSTOMER, INVOICE, and LINEITEM. Notice that the only information required from the LINEITEM table is the product code value (LIPCODE). Because this column is part of the table's primary key, DB2 can retrieve its value from the index; it doesn't need to access the table. To retrieve the requested data from the customer and invoice tables, both the index and the base table must be accessed. As in the first example, hybrid joins are used to combine the data in the INVOICE and CUSTOMER tables with the data from the LINEITEM table.

EXPLAIN analysis of a SELECT statement that retrieves data from a view that names four tables

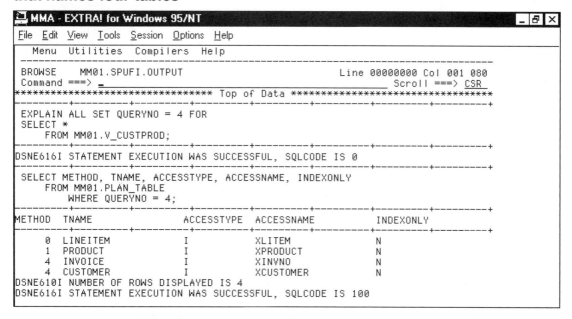

EXPLIAN analysis of a SELECT statement that joins data from three tables

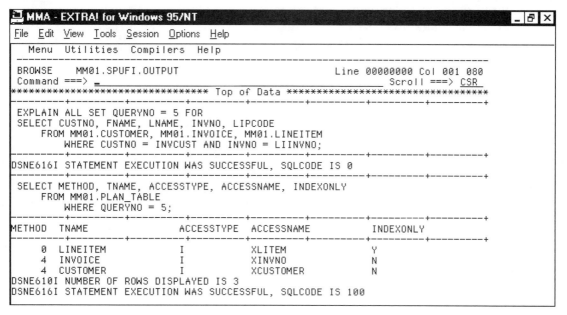

Figure 13-6   EXPLAIN analysis of SELECT statements that retrieve data from multiple tables

Perspective

If you need to dig into the details of DB2 internals, EXPLAIN is a good place to start. For example, you can determine when sorts are necessary to process a statement and what locking a statement can cause. If you use EXPLAIN, though, keep in mind that a statement can incur costs that EXPLAIN doesn't report. In particular, EXPLAIN doesn't report the processing DB2 has to do to enforce referential constraints. And it can only return information about access to data stored at the local site. You can't get an explanation of access paths for data stored at remote sites.

In addition to the EXPLAIN statement, DB2 provides two other tools you may be able to use to analyze your SQL statements. The DB2 Performance Monitor combines information from the EXPLAIN statement and the DB2 catalog tables, and it presents the information in a dialog box rather than in a table. Unfortunately, this tool isn't usually made available to application programmers.

With DB2 version 5, you can also use a new program called DB2 Visual Explain to analyze your SQL statements. Visual Explain is a separate product that comes with DB2 version 5 and that runs on an OS/2 workstation. (Version 6 of this product will also run on Windows NT workstations.) If you have access to an OS/2 workstation, then, you can use this program to display EXPLAIN information in a graphical format. For information on how to use Visual Explain, see the online help that's available on the Visual Explain CD-ROM that comes with DB2.

A

SQLCODE and SQLSTATE values

This appendix lists all of the SQLCODE and SQLSTATE values for version 5.0 along with a detailed description of each error. The SQLCODE is set by DB2 after each SQL statement is executed. DB2 conforms to the ISO/ANSI SQL standards as follows:

If SQLCODE = 0, the execution was successful.
If SQLCODE > 0, the execution was successful with a warning.
If SQLCODE < 0, the execution was not successful.

The SQLSTATE value is also set by DB2 after the execution of each SQL statement. As a result, application programs can check the execution of SQL statements by testing the SQLSTATE value instead of the SQLCODE value. SQLSTATE is a 5-byte character-string variable in the SQL communication area. Often, one SQLSTATE value is equivalent to two or more SQLCODE values.

In the pages that follow, you'll first see a table of all the SQLCODE and SQLSTATE values in SQLCODE sequence. Then, you'll see a table of all the SQLSTATE values along with their SQLCODE equivalents in SQLSTATE sequence. In both tables, the descriptions are the same. Within these descriptions, an item in parentheses is an item that shows when the IBM error message for that code is displayed or printed.

Because these tables include all of the possible codes that can occur, some of the descriptions refer to terms and facilities that aren't presented in this book. Our goal, however, was to make a complete list, so you shouldn't encounter a code that you can't find in this appendix. If you need more information about these codes, please refer to *DB2 for OS/390 V5 Messages and Codes*.

Warning SQLCODE values

SQLCODE	SQLSTATE	Description
+012	01545	The unqualified column name (column-name) was interpreted as a correlated reference.
+098	01568	A dynamic SQL statement ends with a semicolon.
+100	02000	Row not found for FETCH, UPDATE, or DELETE, or the result of a query is an empty table.
+110	01561	The SQL update to a data capture table was not signaled to the originating subsystem.
+111	01590	The subpages option is not supported for type 2 indexes.
+117	01525	The number of insert values is not the same as the number of object columns.
+162	01514	The table space (database-name.tablespace-name) has been placed in check pending mode.
+203	01552	The qualified column (column-name) was resolved using a non-unique or unexposed name.
+204	01532	(Name) is an undefined name.
+206	01533	(Column-name) is not a column of an inserted table, updated table, or any table identified in a FROM clause.
+218	01537	The SQL statement referencing a remote object can't be explained.
+219	01532	The required explanation table (table-name) doesn't exist.
+220	01546	The column (column-name) in explanation table (table-name) isn't defined properly.
+304	01515	A value with data type (data-type1) can't be assigned to a host variable because the value isn't within the range of the host variable in position (position-number) with data type (data-type2).
+331	01520	The null value has been assigned to a host variable because the string can't be translated. The reason is (reason-code), character (code-point), host variable (position-number).
+339	01569	The SQL statement has been successfully executed, but there may be some character conversion inconsistencies.
+402	01521	The location (location) is unknown.
+403	01522	The local object referenced by the CREATE ALIAS statement doesn't exist.
+464	01609	The procedure (proc) returned (num) query result sets, which exceeds the defined limit (integer).
+466	01610	The procedure (proc) returned (num) query result sets.
+494	01614	The number of result sets is greater than the number of locators.
+535	01591	The result of the positioned update or delete may depend on the order of the rows.
+541	01543	The referential or unique constraint (name) has been ignored because it is a duplicate.
+551	01548	The (auth-id) doesn't have the privilege to perform operation (operation) on object (object-name).
+552	01542	The (auth-id) doesn't have the privilege to perform operation (operation).
+558	01516	The WITH GRANT option is ignored.
+561	01523	The ALTER, INDEX, and REFERENCES privileges can't be granted to public at all locations.
+562	01560	A grant of a privilege was ignored because the grantee already has the privilege from the grantor.
+610	01566	The INDEX (index-name) has been placed in recover pending mode.
+625	01518	The definition of table (table-name) has been changed to incomplete.
+626	01529	Dropping the index terminates enforcement of the uniqueness of a key that was defined when the table was created.
+645	01528	The WHERE NOT NULL is ignored because the index key can't contain null values.

+650	01538	The table being created or altered can't become a dependent table.
+653	01551	Table (table-name) in partitioned table space (tspace-name) isn't available because its partitioned index hasn't been created.
+658	01600	The SUBPAGES value is ignored for the catalog index (index-name).
+664	01540	The internal length of the limit-key fields for the partitioned index (index-name) exceeds the length imposed by the index manager.
+738	01530	The definition change of object (object-name) may require similar change on read-only systems.
+802	01519	An exception error (exception-type) has occurred during (operation-type) operation on (data-type) data, and in position (position-number).
+806	01553	The bind isolation level RR conflicts with table space LOCKSIZE PAGE or LOCKSIZE ROW and LOCKMAX 0.
+807	01554	The result of decimal multiplication may cause an overflow.
+863	01539	The connection was successful but only SBCS will be supported.
+2000	56094	Type 1 indexes with subpages greater than 1 can't become group buffer pool dependent in a data sharing environment.
+30100	01558	The operation completed successfully but a distribution protocol violation has been detected. The original SQLCODE = (original-sqlcode) and original SQLSTATE = (original-sqlstate).

Error SQLCODE values

SQLCODE	SQLSTATE	Description
-007	42601	The statement contains the illegal character (character).
-010	42603	The string constant beginning (string) is not terminated properly.
-029	42601	The INTO clause is required.
-060	42815	An invalid (type) specification: (spec) where "type" is either LENGTH or SCALE, and "spec" is the specified length or scale. Length or scale must be specified by an unsigned integer constant and the value must be in the range allowed by the data type.
-084	42612	An unacceptable SQL statement was executed due to one of the following: (1) an attempt to PREPARE or EXECUTE IMMEDIATE an SQL statement that can't be prepared; (2) the embedded SQL statement isn't an SQL statement supported by DB2; or (3) the statement referenced an undeclared cursor.
-101	54001	The statement is too long or too complex.
-102	54002	A literal string is too long. The string begins (string).
-103	42604	The (literal) is an invalid numeric literal.
-104	42601	Illegal symbol "token." Some symbols that might be legal are: (token-list).
-105	42604	The statement contains an invalid string.
-107	42622	The name (name) is too long. The maximum allowable size is (size).
-108	42601	The name (name) is qualified incorrectly.
-109	42601	The (clause) clause isn't permitted in the context in which it appears in the SQL statement for the following reasons: (1) a subselect can't have an INTO clause; (2) a CREATE VIEW statement can't have INTO, ORDER BY, or FOR UPDATE clauses; (3) an embedded SELECT statement can't have ORDER BY or FOR UPDATE clauses; (4) SELECT statements used in cursor declarations can't have an INTO clause; (5) A CREATE TABLESPACE statement can't specify the LARGE clause without the NUMPARTS option; (6) a CREATE TABLESPACE statement can't specify LOCKPART without the NUMPARTS option; (7) an ALTER TABLESPACE statement can't specify LOCKPART for a non-partitioned table space; (8) a table space with LOCKPART YES can't be altered to LOCKSIZE TABLESPACE; (9) or a table space with LOCKSIZE TABLESPACE can't be altered to LOCKPART YES.

-110	42606	The literal beginning with (string) contains one or more characters that aren't valid hexadecimal digits.
-111	42901	A column function doesn't include a column name.
-112	42607	The operand of a column function is another column function.
-113	42602	An invalid character was found in (string), reason code –nnn.
-114	42961	A three-part SQL procedure name was provided in an SQL CALL, ASSOCIATE LOCATORS, or DESCRIBE PROCEDURE statement. The first part of the SQL procedure name, which specifies the location where the stored procedure resides, didn't match the value of the SQL CURRENT SERVER special register.
-115	42601	A predicate is invalid because the comparison operator (operator) is followed by a parenthesized list or by ANY or ALL without a subquery.
-117	42802	The number of insert values isn't the same as the number of object columns.
-118	42902	The object table or view of the INSERT, DELETE, or UPDATE statement is also identified in a FROM clause.
-119	42803	A column identified in a HAVING clause isn't included in the GROUP BY clause.
-120	42903	A WHERE clause or SET clause includes a column function.
-121	42701	The column (name) is identified more than once in the INSERT or UPDATE statement.
-122	42803	A SELECT statement with no GROUP BY clause contains a column name and a column function in the SELECT clause or a column name is contained in the SELECT clause but not in the GROUP BY clause.
-125	42805	An integer in the ORDER BY clause doesn't identify a column of the result.
-126	42829	The SELECT statement contains both an UPDATE clause and an ORDER BY clause.
-127	42905	The keyword DISTINCT is specified more than once in a subselect.
-128	42601	Invalid use of null in a predicate.
-129	54004	The statement contains too many table names.
-130	22019/22025	The ESCAPE clause consists of more than one character (SQLSTATE value 22019), or the string pattern contains an invalid occurrence of the ESCAPE character (SQLSTATE value 22025).
-131	42818	A statement with the LIKE predicate has incompatible data types.
-132	42824	A LIKE predicate is invalid because the second operand isn't a string.
-133	42906	A column function in a subquery of a HAVING clause is invalid because all column references in its argument aren't correlated to the GROUP BY result that the HAVING clause is applied to.
-134	42907	Improper use of a long string column (column-name) or a host variable of maximum length greater than 254.
-136	54005	The SORT can't be executed because the sort key length is greater than 4000 bytes.
-137	54006	The length of the result of a concatenation exceeds 32,764 (if character operands) or 16,382 (if graphic operands).
-138	22011	The second or third argument of the SUBSTR function is out of range.
-144	58003	Invalid section number (number).
-148	42809	The source table (source-name) can't be renamed because it is a view or an active RLST table or has a synonym defined on it.
-150	42807	The object of the INSERT, DELETE, or UPDATE statement is a view for which the requested operation isn't permitted.
-151	42808	The UPDATE statement is invalid because the catalog description of column (column-name) indicates that it can't be updated.
-152	42809	The DROP clause (clause) in the ALTER statement is invalid because (constraint-name) is a (constraint-type).
-153	42908	The CREATE VIEW statement doesn't include a required column list.
-154	42909	The CREATE VIEW failed because the view definition contains a UNION, a UNION ALL, or a remote object.

-156	42809	The statement doesn't identify a table.
-157	42810	Only a table name can be specified in a foreign key clause; (object-name) isn't the name of a table.
-158	42811	The number of columns specified for the view isn't the same as the number of columns specified by the SELECT clause.
-159	42809	The object specified in the DROP VIEW statement, DROP ALIAS statement, or COMMENT ON ALIAS statement identifies a table instead of a view or an alias.
-160	42813	The WITH CHECK OPTION doesn't apply to a view definition under either of the following circumstances: the view is read-only (for example, the view definition includes DISTINCT, GROUP BY, or JOIN) or the view definition includes a subquery.
-161	44000	The INSERT or UPDATE isn't allowed because a resulting row doesn't satisfy the view definition.
-164	42502	The authorization ID (auth-id) doesn't have the authority necessary to create views with qualifiers other than its own authorization ID. Specifically, the attempt to create a view with qualifier (authorization ID) is rejected.
-170	42605	An SQL statement includes the scalar function (function-name) with either too many or too few arguments.
-171	42815	Either the data type, the length, or the value of argument (nn) of scalar function (function-name) is incorrect.
-173	42801	The cursor is not a read-only cursor. WITH UR can be specified only if DB2 can determine that the cursor is read-only.
-180	22007	The length or string representation of a DATE, TIME, or TIMESTAMP value doesn't conform to any valid format.
-181	22007	The string representation of a datetime value isn't a valid datetime value.
-182	42816	The specified arithmetic expression contains an improperly used datetime value or labeled duration.
-183	22008	The result of an arithmetic operation is a date or timestamp that isn't within the valid range of dates, which is between 0001-01-01 and 9999-12-31.
-184	42610	The specified arithmetic expression contains a parameter marker improperly used with a datetime value.
-185	57008	The local format option has been used with a date or time and no local exit has been installed.
-186	22505	The logical format option has been used with a datetime value and DB2 has discovered that the datetime exit routine has been changed to produce a longer local format.
-187	22506	A reference to a CURRENT DATE/TIME special register is invalid because the MVS time-of-day (TOD) clock is bad or the PARMTZ is out of range.
-188	22503	The host variable reference in the DESCRIBE TABLE statement doesn't contain a valid string representation of a name.
-189	22522	CCSID (ccsid) is unknown or invalid for the data type or subtype.
-191	22504	A string can't be used because it is invalid mixed data.
-197	42877	A SELECT statement that specifies both the union of two or more tables and the ORDER BY clause can't use qualified column names in the ORDER BY clause.
-198	42617	The operand of the PREPARE or EXECUTE IMMEDIATE statement is blank or empty.
-199	42601	Illegal use of keyword (keyword). Token (token-list) was expected.
-203	42702	A reference to column (column-name) is ambiguous.
-204	42704	The object identified by (name) isn't defined in the DB2 subsystem.
-205	42703	No column with the specified (column-name) occurs in the table or view (table-name).
-206	42703	(Column-name) isn't a column of an inserted table, updated table, or any table identified in a FROM clause.

-208	42707	The ORDER BY clause is invalid because column (name) isn't part of the result table.
-219	42704	The required explanation table (table-name) doesn't exist.
-220	55002	The column (column-name) in an explanation table (table-name) isn't defined properly.
-221	55002	"SET OF OPTIONAL COLUMNS" in the explanation table (table-name) is incomplete. Optional column (column-name) is missing.
-240	428B4	The PART clause of a LOCK TABLE statement is invalid.
-250	42718	A three-part object name (table, view, or alias) can't be used until the local location name is defined.
-251	42602	Token (name) isn't valid. A location name can't contain alphabetic extenders. (The standard alphabetic extenders in the United States are #, @, $.)
-300	22024	The C string variable contained in host variable or parameter (position-number) isn't NUL-terminated.
-301	42895	The value of input host variable or parameter number (position-number) can't be used as specified because of its data type.
-302	22001/22003	The value of an input variable or parameter number (position-number) is invalid or too large for the target column or the target value. The SQLSTATE value is 22003 if the value is too large. Otherwise, it's 22001.
-303	42806	A value can't be assigned to output host variable number (position-number) because the data types aren't comparable.
-304	22003	A value with data type (data-type1) can't be assigned to a host variable because the value isn't within the range of the host variable in position (position-number) with data type (data-type2).
-305	22002	The null value can't be assigned to output host variable number (position-number) because no indicator variable is specified.
-309	22512	A predicate is invalid because a referenced host variable has the null value.
-310	22023	Decimal host variable or parameter (number) contains non-decimal data.
-311	22501	The length of input host variable number (position-number) is negative or greater than the maximum.
-312	42618	The host variable (variable-name) appears in the SQL statement, but the SQL statement is a prepared statement; the attributes of the variable are inconsistent with its usage in the static SQL statement; or the variable is not declared in the application program.
-313	07001	The number of host variables specified isn't equal to the number of parameter markers.
-314	42714	The statement contains an ambiguous host variable reference.
-327	22525	The row can't be inserted because it's outside the bound of the partition range for the last partition.
-330	22021	A string can't be used because it can't be translated. The reason is (reason-code), character (code-point), host variable (position-number).
-331	22021	A string can't be assigned to a host variable because it can't be translated. The reason is (reason-code), character (code-point), position (position-number).
-332	57017	The operation required the translation of a string to a different coded character set, but the particular translation isn't described in the SYSSTRINGS catalog table. The first (ccsid) identifies the coded character set of the string and the second (ccsid) identifies the coded character set to which it must be translated.
-333	56010	The subtype of a string variable isn't the same as the subtype known at bind time and the difference can't be resolved by translation.
-338	42972	An ON clause is invalid. This return code reports a violation of one of the following: (1) one expression of the predicate must only reference columns of one of the operand tables of the associated join operator, and the other expression of the predicate must only reference columns of the other operand table; (2) a VALUE or COALESCE function is allowed in the ON clause only when the join operator is a FULL OUTER JOIN or FULL JOIN; or (3) an

		operator other than equals (=) isn't allowed in a FULL OUTER JOIN or FULL JOIN.
-339	56082	The SQL statement can't be executed from an ASCII based DRDA application requestor to a V2R2 DB2 subsystem.
-351	56084	An unsupported SQLTYPE was encountered in position (position-number) on a PREPARE or DESCRIBE operation. Some SQL data types aren't supported by DB2 version 4. Position (position-number) is the position of the first element with an invalid data type in the SQLDA. A common reason why this error occurs is when DB2 attempts to describe large object data residing on a non-DB2 server. Some of the SQLTYPEs that can cause this error are: LOB, BLOB, CLOB, and DBLOB.
-400	54027	The catalog has the maximum number of user defined indexes (100).
-401	42818	An arithmetic operation appearing within the SQL statement has a mixture of numeric and non-numeric operands, or the operands of a comparison operation aren't compatible.
-402	42819	A non-numeric operand has been specified for the arithmetic function or operator (arith-fop).
-404	22001	An INSERT or UPDATE statement specifies a value that is longer than the maximum-length string that can be stored in column (column-name).
-405	42820	The numeric literal (literal) can't be used as specified because it is out of range.
-406	22003	A calculated or derived numeric value isn't within the range of its object column.
-407	23502	An UPDATE or INSERT value is null, but the object column (column-name) can't contain null values.
-408	42821	An UPDATE or INSERT value isn't comparable with the data type of its object column (column-name).
-409	42607	The operand of the COUNT function in the SQL statement violates SQL syntax. A common error is a column name or other expression without DISTINCT.
-410	42820	The specified floating point literal (literal) is more than 30 characters in length.
-411	56040	A reference to the CURRENT SQLID special register is invalid in a statement that contains the three-part name or alias of an object that is remote to the remote server.
-412	42823	The SELECT clause of a subquery specifies multiple columns.
-413	22003	An overflow occurred during a numeric data type conversion.
-414	42824	A LIKE predicate is invalid because the first operand isn't a string.
-415	42825	The corresponding columns (column-name) of the operands of a UNION or a UNION ALL don't have comparable column descriptions.
-416	42907	The UNION specified in the SQL statement couldn't be performed because one of the tables participating in the union contains a long string column (for example, a VARCHAR column with length greater than 254). The operands of a UNION can't contain long string columns.
-417	42609	A statement string to be prepared includes parameter markers as the operands of the same operation.
-418	42610	A statement string to be prepared contains an invalid use of parameter markers.
-419	42911	The decimal divide operation is invalid because the result would have a negative scale.
-420	22018	The value of a character string argument wasn't acceptable to the (function-name) function.
-421	42826	The operands of a UNION or UNION ALL don't have the same number of columns.
-423	0F001	An invalid result set locator value.
-426	2D528	An application using DRDA protocols has attempted to issue a dynamic

		COMMIT statement while connected to a location where updates aren't allowed.
-427	2D529	An application using DRDA protocols has attempted to issue a dynamic ROLLBACK statement while connected to a location where updates aren't allowed.
-440	42884	The number of parameters in the parameter list doesn't match the number of parameters expected for stored procedure (name), AUTHID (authid), LUNAME (luname). The (number) parameters were expected.
-444	42724	DB2 received an SQL CALL statement for a stored procedure and found the row in the SYSIBM.SYSPROCEDURES catalog table associated with the requested procedure name. However, the MVS load module identified in the LOADMOD column of the SYSIBM.SYSPROCEDURES row couldn't be found.
-450	39501	While returning parameters from a stored procedure to an application, DB2 detected an overlay of one of the parameters. A stored procedure overwrote storage beyond a parameter's declared length.
-469	42886	DB2 received an SQL CALL statement for a stored procedure. DB2 found the row in the SYSIBM.SYSPROCEDURES catalog table associated with the requested procedure name. However, parameter (number) was identified in the PARMLIST column of the SYSIBM.SYSPROCEDURES table as an OUT or INOUT parameter. A host variable must be supplied on the SQL CALL statement for parameters defined as OUT or INOUT.
-470	39002	DB2 received an SQL CALL statement for a stored procedure and found a null value in the incoming parameter list. The DB2 stored procedure was defined in the SYSIBM.SYSPROCEDURES catalog table with LINKAGE=, which specifies that the DB2 stored procedure doesn't accept null values.
-471	55023	The SQL CALL for stored procedure (name) failed due to reason (reason-code). See *DB2 for OS/390 V5 Messages and Codes* for the definition of the reason-codes.
-480	51030	The procedure (procedure-name) has not yet been called.
-482	51030	The procedure (procedure-name) returned no locators.
-496	51033	The SQL statement can't be executed because it references a result set that wasn't created by the current server.
-497	54041	An attempt was made to create an object in database (database-name), but the limit of 32,767 OBIDs has been exceeded for that database.
-499	24516	The cursor (cursor-name) has already been assigned to this result set or another result set from procedure (procedure-name).
-500	24501	The FETCH, UPDATE, DELETE, or CLOSE statement identifies a closed cursor that was defined with the WITH HOLD option. The cursor was closed when the connection where it was dependent was destroyed during a commit operation. The connection was destroyed because the application process placed it in the released state, or the application plan was bound with the DISCONNECT(AUTOMATIC) option.
-501	24501	The cursor identified in a FETCH or CLOSE statement isn't open.
-502	24502	The cursor identified in an OPEN statement is already open.
-503	42912	The application program attempted to update (using a cursor) a value in a column of the object table that wasn't identified in the FOR UPDATE clause in the cursor declaration.
-504	34000	The cursor name (cursor-name) isn't defined.
-507	24501	The cursor identified in the UPDATE or DELETE statement isn't open.
-508	24504	The cursor identified in the UPDATE or DELETE statement isn't positioned on a row.
-509	42827	The application program attempted to execute an UPDATE or DELETE WHERE CURRENT OF cursor statement where the table named in that statement didn't match the name of the table specified in the declaration for that cursor.

-510	42828	The application program attempted to execute an UPDATE or DELETE WHERE CURRENT OF cursor statement against a table or view that can't be updated or deleted. This can occur for a delete from a read-only view or for an update in which the cursor wasn't defined with the FOR UPDATE clause.
-511	42829	The result table of the SELECT statement can't be updated. This can occur if the SELECT specifies more than one table or view in the FROM clause, if the SELECT list contains a built-in function or DISTINCT, or if the statement contains an ORDER BY, GROUP BY or HAVING clause. This can also occur if a view is specified in the FROM clause and the view can't be updated.
-512	56023	The statement reference to a remote object is invalid. One of the following conditions exists: (1) the statement refers to multiple locations; (2) a statement with a remote reference is being EXPLAINED either by a dynamic EXPLAIN statement or the EXPLAIN(YES) option; (3) an alias is used incorrectly; or (4) a three-part name is implicitly or explicitly used in a statement that is not supported by the DB2 private protocols.
-513	42924	The alias (alias-name) must not be defined on another local or remote alias.
-514	26501	The application program has tried to use a cursor (cursor-name) that is not in a prepared state. The cursor is associated with a statement that either (1) has never been prepared, or (2) has been invalidated by a commit or rollback operation.
-516	26501	The DESCRIBE statement doesn't identify a prepared statement.
-517	07005	Cursor (cursor-name) can't be used because its statement name doesn't identify a prepared SELECT statement.
-518	07003	The EXECUTE statement doesn't identify a valid prepared statement. One of the following conditions exists: (1) the statement named in the EXECUTE statement has not been prepared; (2) the statement named in the EXECUTE statement identifies a SELECT statement; or (3) the statement named in the EXECUTE IMMEDIATE statement identifies a SELECT statement.
-519	24506	The application program has attempted to PREPARE (actually, re-PREPARE) the SELECT statement for the specified cursor when that cursor was already open.
-525	51015	The SQL statement can't be executed because it was in error at bind time for section (sectno) package (pkgname) consistency token X('contoken').
-526	42995	The requested function doesn't apply to global temporary tables.
-530	23503	The INSERT or UPDATE value of foreign key (constraint-name) is invalid.
-531	23504	The parent key in a parent row can't be updated because it has one or more dependent rows in relationship (constraint-name).
-532	23504	The relationship (constraint-name) restricts the deletion of row with RID X('rid-number').
-533	21501	An INSERT operation with a subselect attempted to insert multiple rows into a self-referencing table. The subselect of the INSERT operation should return no more than one row of data.
-534	21502	An UPDATE operation attempted to update a primary key on multiple rows of the object table. This code will be issued only for plans and packages bound prior to version 5.
-536	42914	The DELETE statement is invalid due to referential constraints for table (table-name).
-537	42709	The PRIMARY KEY clause, a FOREIGN KEY clause, or a UNIQUE clause identifies column (column-name) more than once.
-538	42830	The FOREIGN KEY (name) doesn't conform to the description of the parent key of table (table-name).
-539	42888	The CREATE or ALTER TABLE statement can't be executed because the indicated table (table-name) doesn't have a primary key. So, the primary key can't be dropped, or the table can't be defined as a parent in a referential constraint.

-540	57001	The definition of table (table-name) is incomplete because it lacks a primary key index or a required unique index.
-542	42831	(Column-name) can't be a column of a primary key or a unique constraint because it can contain null values.
-543	23511	A row in a parent table can't be deleted because the check constraint (check-constraint) restricts the deletion.
-544	23512	The check constraint specified in the ALTER TABLE statement can't be added because an existing row violates the check constraint.
-545	23513	The requested operation isn't allowed because a row doesn't satisfy the check constraint (check-constraint).
-546	42621	The check constraint (check-constraint) is invalid.
-548	42621	The check constraint that is defined with (column-name) is invalid.
-549	42509	The (statement) statement isn't allowed for (object_type1 object_name) because the bind option DYNAMICRULES(BIND) in the (object_type2) is in effect.
-551	42501	(Auth-id) doesn't have the privilege to perform operation (operation) on object (object-name). Beginning with version 5, SQLCODE -551 will be returned instead of SQLCODE -204 for the runtime error where an object does not exist and the CURRENT RULES special register is set to 'STD'.
-552	42502	(Auth-id) doesn't have the privilege to perform operation (operation).
-553	42503	(Auth-id) isn't one of the valid authorization IDs.
-554	42502	An authorization ID can't grant a privilege to itself.
-555	42502	An authorization ID can't revoke a privilege from itself.
-556	42504	(Authid2) can't have the (privilege) privilege (on_object) revoked by (authid1) because the revokee doesn't possess the privilege or the revoker didn't make the grant.
-557	42852	Inconsistent GRANT/REVOKE keyword (keyword). Permitted keywords are (keyword-list).
-558	56025	Invalid clause or combination of clauses on a GRANT or REVOKE statement.
-559	57002	The authorization mechanism has been disabled in the DB2 subsystem. Consequently, GRANT and REVOKE statements are ignored.
-567	42501	(Bind-type) authorization error using (auth-id) authority package = (package-name) privilege = (privilege).
-571	25000	The statement would result in a multiple site update. This SQLCODE is issued in the following situations: (1) when an application program operating in an IMS or CICS environment attempts to modify data at a remote location where multi-site update capabilities aren't supported; or (2) when an application has explicit SQL statements within a commit scope that would result in updates at multiple sites where one of the sites where data is being updated doesn't support multi-site updates.
-573	42890	The table (table-name) doesn't have a unique key with the specified column names.
-574	42894	The specified default value conflicts with the column definition.
-580	42625	The result expressions of a case expression can't all be NULL.
-581	42804	The data types of the result expressions of a case expression are not compatible.
-582	42625	The search condition in a SEARCHED WHEN clause can't be a quantified predicate, an IN predicate, or an EXISTS predicate.
-601	42710	The CREATE statement tried to create an object (name) of type (obj-type), but an object of that type with the same name is already defined in the DB2 subsystem.

-602	54008	The number of columns specified in the CREATE INDEX statement exceeds 64, the maximum permitted by DB2.
-603	23515	The index defined in the CREATE INDEX statement couldn't be created as unique because the specified table already contains rows that are duplicates with respect to the values of the identified columns.
-604	42611	A column definition in the CREATE or ALTER TABLE statement contains an invalid length, precision, or scale attribute specification.
-607	42832	The operation or option (operation) can't be performed on the catalog object specified in the SQL statement.
-611	53088	Only LOCKMAX 0 can be specified when the lock size of the table space is TABLESPACE or TABLE.
-612	42711	The column (column-name) is a duplicate column name.
-613	54008	The primary key or a unique constraint is too long or has too many columns.
-614	54008	The index can't be created because the sum of the internal lengths of the identified columns is greater than the allowable maximum.
-615	55006	The operation (operation-type) can't be performed because the package is in use by the same application process.
-616	42893	The object (obj-type1 obj-name1) can't be dropped because it is referenced by object (obj-type2 obj-name2). Some types of objects can't be dropped if there are other objects that are dependent on them. For example, a storage group can't be dropped if there are one or more existing table spaces that use that storage group.
-617	56089	All indexes defined for a table within a table space with LOCKSIZE ROW must be defined as type 2 indexes.
-618	42832	Operation (operation) isn't allowed on system databases.
-619	55011	The statements CREATE, ALTER, or DROP for a table space in the work file database can't be processed unless the work file database is stopped (using the STOP command).
-620	53001	The keyword (keyword) in (stmt-type) statement isn't permitted for a table space in the work file database.
-621	58001	A duplicate DBID (dbid) was detected and previously assigned to (database-name). An inconsistency exists between the DB2 catalog and directory.
-622	56031	FOR MIXED DATA is specified in a column description of a CREATE or ALTER TABLE statement, but the MIXED DATA install option is set to NO.
-623	55012	A clustering index already exists on table (table-name). A given table can have only one cluster index.
-624	42889	Table (table-name) already has a primary key.
-625	55014	Table (table-name) doesn't have an index to enforce the uniqueness of the parent key.
-626	55015	An ALTER statement specifies a BUFFERPOOL, USING, PRIQTY, SECQTY, ERASE, or GBPCACHE clause, but the page set isn't stopped.
-627	55016	The ALTER statement is invalid because the page set has user-managed data sets.
-628	42613	Mutually exclusive clauses were specified in one or more of the following ways: (1) a CREATE TABLESPACE statement contains both the SEGSIZE and NUMPARTS clauses; (2) a CREATE TABLESPACE statement contains both the SEGSIZE and LARGE clauses; (3) a CREATE or ALTER TABLESPACE statement contains both the LOCKPART YES and LOCKSIZE TABLESPACE clauses; (4) a (column-definition) contains both NOT NULL and DEFAULT NULL clauses; (5) a (column-definition) contains both FIELDPROC and DEFAULT clauses; (6) a SELECT statement contains both the UPDATE clause and the FOR FETCH ONLY clause; (7) an ALTER TABLE statement contains both a DROP CONSTRAINT clause and either a DROP FOREIGN KEY clause or a DROP CHECK clause; or (8) a CREATE or ALTER TABLESPACE statement contains both the LOCKPART YES and LOCKSIZE TABLESPACE clauses.

-629	42834	SET NULL can't be specified because FOREIGN KEY (name) can't contain null values.
-630	56089	The WHERE NOT NULL specification is invalid for type 1 indexes.
-631	54008	The FOREIGN KEY (name) is too long or has too many columns.
-632	42915	The table can't be defined as a dependent of (table-name) because of delete rule restrictions.
-633	42915	The (delete-rule) specified in a FOREIGN KEY clause of the ALTER TABLE statement is invalid. The indicated (delete-rule) is required because a self-referencing constraint must have a (delete-rule) of CASCADE or NO ACTION or the relationship would cause the table to be delete-connected to the same table through multiple paths and such relationships must have the same (delete-rule).
-634	42915	The CASCADE delete rule specified in the FOREIGN KEY clause of an ALTER TABLE statement is invalid because the relationship would form a cycle that would cause a table to be delete-connected to itself or the relationship would cause another table to be delete-connected to the same table through multiple paths with different delete rules or with a delete rule equal to SET NULL.
-635	42915	The delete rules can't be different or can't be SET NULL.
-636	56016	The partitioning keys for partition (part-num) aren't specified in ascending or descending order.
-637	42614	Duplicate (keyword) keyword.
-638	42601	The table (table-name) can't be created because the CREATE TABLE statement doesn't contain any column definitions.
-639	56027	A partition key of the clustering index can't be updated. Therefore, a foreign key column with a delete rule of SET NULL can't be a column of a partition key if that column is nullable. If this error occurs for an ALTER TABLE operation, the foreign key can't be created. If this error occurs for a CREATE INDEX operation, the index can't be created.
-640	56089	LOCKSIZE ROW can't be specified because a table in this table space has a type 1 index.
-642	54021	There is a limit to the total number of columns that can be used in UNIQUE constraints in a CREATE TABLE statement. The statement exceeds that limit.
-643	54024	The check constraint definition exceeds the maximum allowable limit of 3800 characters. The redundant blank spaces are excluded from this limit.
-644	42615	The value specified for the keyword (keyword) parameter in the (stmt-type) SQL statement isn't a permitted value.
-646	55017	Table (table-name) can't be created in partitioned/default table space (tspace-name) because it already contains a table. Only one table may reside in a partitioned or default table space.
-647	57003	Buffer pool (bp-name) can't be specified because it hasn't been activated.
-650	56090	The ALTER INDEX statement can't be executed, reason (reason-code).
-651	54025	The CREATE TABLE or ALTER TABLE statement causes the table descriptor (record OBD) to exceed the object descriptor size limit of 32KB.
-652	23506	The result of the SQL statement has been rejected by the installation defined edit or validation procedure (proc-name) for the object table.
-653	57004	Table (table-name) in partitioned table space (tspace-name) isn't available because its partitioned index hasn't been created.
-655	56036	The CREATE or ALTER STOGROUP statement is invalid because the storage group would have both specific and nonspecific volume IDs.
-660	53035	Index (index-name) can't be created on a partitioned table space (tspace-name) because key limits aren't specified.
-661	53036	Index (index-name) can't be created on a partitioned table space (tspace-name) because the number of PART specifications isn't equal to the number of partitions of the table space.

-662	53037	A partitioned index can't be created on a non-partitioned table space (tspace-name).
-663	53038	The number of key limit values is either zero or greater than the number of columns in the key of index (index-name).
-665	53039	The PART clause of an ALTER statement is omitted or invalid.
-666	57005	The (stmt-verb object) can't be executed because function (function) is in progress.
-667	42917	The DROP INDEX statement attempted to drop the cluster index for a table residing in a partitioned table space. The cluster index for such a table can't be dropped explicitly with the DROP INDEX statement.
-668	56018	The ALTER TABLE statement attempted to add a column to a table that has an edit procedure. If a table has an edit procedure, no column can be added to it.
-669	42917	A table in a partitioned table space can't be dropped by the DROP TABLE statement. It can only be dropped implicitly when the table space is dropped.
-670	54010	The record length of the table exceeds the page size limit.
-671	53040	The buffer pool attribute of the table space can't be altered as specified because it would change the page size of the table space.
-672	55035	The DROP operation failed for table (table-name) because the table being dropped has the RESTRICT ON DROP attribute, or the table space or database being dropped contains the specified table, which has the RESTRICT ON DROP attribute.
-676	53041	A 32K page buffer pool may not be used for an index. Only 4KB buffer pools (BP0, BP1, and BP2) can be specified for indexes.
-677	57011	An attempt to either open (create) or expand a buffer pool has failed because insufficient virtual storage was available.
-678	53045	The literal (literal) specified for the index limit key must conform to the data type (data-type) of the corresponding column (column-name).
-679	57006	The object (name) can't be created because a drop is pending on the object.
-680	54011	Too many columns are specified for a table. The maximum number of columns permitted per table is 750.
-681	23507	Column (column-name) is in violation of an installation defined field procedure. RT: (return-code), RS: (reason-code), MSG: (message-token).
-682	57010	Field procedure (procedure-name) couldn't be loaded.
-683	42842	Invalid column type for fieldproc, BIT DATA, SBCS DATA, or MIXED DATA option, (column-name).
-684	54012	The length of literal list beginning (string) is too long.
-685	58002	Invalid field type, (column-name).
-686	53043	A column defined with a field procedure can't be compared with another column with a different field procedure.
-687	53044	One column can't be compared with another column that has incompatible field types.
-688	58002	Incorrect data returned from field procedure, (column-name), (msgno).
-689	54011	Too many columns defined for a dependent table. The maximum number of columns allowed for a dependent table is 749.
-690	23508	The statement is rejected by data definition control support. The reason is (reason-code).
-691	57018	The required registration table (table-name) doesn't exist.
-692	57018	The required unique index (index-name) for DDL registration table (table-name) doesn't exist.
-693	55003	The column (column-name) in DDL registration table or index (table-name) (index-name) isn't defined properly.
-694	57023	The DDL statement can't be executed because a drop is pending on the DDL registration table (table-name).
-713	42815	The value specified in the SET (special-register) statement is not a valid value of the indicated special register.

-715	56064	Program (program-name) depends on a function of DB2 that is not supported by the current active release.
-716	56065	Program (program-name) was precompiled under a release not supported by the current level of DB2, or the contents of the DBRM have been modified after the precompilation phase.
-717	56066	The (bind-type) for (object-type) (object-name) with mark (release-dependency-mark) failed because (object-type) depends on functions of the release from which fallback has occurred. The plan or package indicated depends on a function of DB2 not supported by the currently active release.
-718	56067	The REBIND for package (package-name) failed because IBMREQD of (ibmreqd) is invalid. The IBMREQD column of the SYSIBM.SYSPACKAGE catalog table for the named package contains an unrecognizable character.
-719	42710	An attempt is made to add a package that already exists. The combination of 'location.collection.package.version' must be unique in the SYSIBM.SYSPACKAGE table. In addition, the combination of 'location.collection.package.consistency-token' must be unique.
-720	42710	An attempt is made to create a version of a package that already exists. Package name = (package-name), version = (version2).
-721	42710	An attempt is made to add or replace a package with a consistency token that is not unique for that package. Package name = (pkg-id), consistency token = (contoken).
-722	42704	The indicated subcommand was issued against a package that doesn't exist. Bind type = (bind-type), authorization ID = (auth-id), package = (package-name).
-726	55030	Bind error attempting to replace package = (package-name). There are ENABLE or DISABLE entries currently associated with the package.
-730	56053	The parent of a table in a read-only shared database must also be a table in a read-only shared database.
-731	56054	User-defined data set (dsname) must be defined with SHAREOPTIONS(1,3). The VSAM SHAREOPTIONS must be (1,3) for all of the indexes and table spaces in the database.
-732	56055	The database is defined on this subsystem with the ROSHARE READ attribute, but the table space or index space hasn't been defined on the owning subsystem.
-733	56056	The description of a table space, index space, or table in a ROSHARE READ database must be consistent with its description in the owner system.
-734	56057	The ROSHARE attribute of a database can't be altered from ROSHARE READ.
-735	55004	Database (dbid) can't be accessed because it is no longer a shared database.
-736	53014	Invalid OBID (obid) specified. An invalid OBID value was given on the CREATE statement.
-737	56056	A CREATE TABLE statement was issued using an implicit table space. An implicit table space may not be used in a database that has been defined as a read-only shared database.
-741	55020	A work file database is already defined for member (member-name).
-742	53004	The WORKFILE clause can't be used on a CREATE DATABASE statement to create a work file database for a DB2 subsystem that isn't a member of a DB2 data sharing group. The system database, DSNDB07, is the implicit work file database.
-750	42986	The source table (source-name) can't be renamed because it is referenced in existing view definitions.
-751	42987	A stored procedure has been placed in MUST_ROLLBACK state due to SQL operation (name).
-752	0A001	The CONNECT statement is invalid because the process isn't in the connectable state.

-802	22012/22003	Exception error (exception-type) has occurred during (operation-type) operation on (data-type) data, position (position-number). The processing of an SQL arithmetic function or arithmetic expression that was either in the SELECT list of an SQL SELECT statement, in the search condition of a SELECT, UPDATE, or DELETE statement during the evaluation of a column function, or in the SET clause of the UPDATE statement has encountered an exception error, possibly indicated by (exception-type). The SQLSTATE is 22012 if ZERO DIVIDE, and 22003 if other than ZERO DIVIDE.
-803	23505	An inserted or updated value is invalid because the index in INDEX SPACE (indexspace-name) constrains columns of the table so no two rows can contain duplicate values in those columns. RID of existing row is X(rid).
-804	07002	An error was found in the application program input parameters for the SQL statement. The reason is (reason-code). The following is a list of reason codes: (01) Open issued for non-cursor; (02) Close issued for non-cursor; (03) prepare of EXECUTE IMMEDIATE; (04) statement isn't recognized; (05) no statement string present; (06) bad SQLDA format in parameter list; (07) SQLDA length is invalid; (08) unrecognized input data type; (09) invalid length for input variable; (10) invalid data length for output variable; (11) the value of SQLDABC is not consistent with the value of SQLD; (12) invalid input data pointer; (13) invalid output data pointer; (14) SQLN has too many items for SQLDABC; (15) input RDI pointer is invalid.
-805	51002	DBRM or PACKAGE NAME (location-name.collection-id.dbrm-name.consistency) token not found in plan (plan-name). The reason is (reason-code). See *DB2 for OS/390 V5 Messages and Codes* for the definition of the reason-codes.
-807	23509	Access denied: Package (package-name) isn't enabled for access from (connection-type connection-name).
-808	08001	The CONNECT semantics that apply to an application process are determined by the first CONNECT statement executed (successfully or unsuccessfully) by the application process.
-811	21000	Execution of an embedded SELECT statement has resulted in a result table containing more than one row. Alternatively, a subquery contained in a basic predicate has produced more than one value.
-812	22508	The SQL statement can't be processed because a blank collection-ID was found in the current PACKAGESET special register while trying to form a qualified package name for program (program-name.consistency-token) using plan (plan-name).
-815	42920	An embedded SELECT statement of a subquery of a basic predicate either (1) directly contains a GROUP BY or HAVING clause, or (2) specifies as its object a view having a definition that includes a GROUP BY or HAVING clause. Neither construct is permitted.
-817	25000	The SQL statement can't be executed because the statement will result in a prohibited update operation.
-818	51003	The precompiler-generated timestamp (x) in the load module is different from the bind timestamp (y) built from the DBRM (z). This problem can occur if you: (1) precompile, compile, and link, without doing a BIND of the application; (2) precompile and BIND, without doing the compile and link for the application program; or (3) BIND the application using a DBRM that resulted from a different precompile of the application program than that which produced the object module that is linked into the application module.
-819	58004	SYSIBM.SYSVTREE.VTREE is a varying-length string column that contains the parse trees of views. In processing a view, the length control field of its parse tree was found to be zero.
-820	58004	The SQL statement can't be processed because (catalog-table) contains a value that isn't valid in this release.

-822	51004	The SQLDA contains an invalid data address or indicator variable address.
-840	54004	The number of items returned in the select list or presented in an insert list exceeds the allowable maximum of 750.
-842	08002	A connection to (location-name) already exists.
-843	08003	The SET CONNECTION or RELEASE statement must specify an existing connection.
-870	58026	The number of host variables in the statement isn't equal to the number of descriptors.
-872	51032	A valid CCSID has not yet been specified for this MVS/ESA subsystem.
-873	53090	Data encoded with different CCSIDs can't be referenced in the same SQL statement.
-874	53091	The encoding scheme specified for the table isn't the same as that for the table space containing this table.
-875	42988	The operand (operand) can't be used with the ASCII data that's referenced.
-876	53092	The object ('object') can't be created for reason ('reason').
-877	53093	CCSID ASCII isn't allowed for this database or table space.
-878	53094	The PLAN_TABLE used for EXPLAIN can't be ASCII.
-879	53095	A column can't be created as GRAPHIC, VARGRAPHIC, or LONG VARGRAPHIC in an ASCII table.
-900	08003	The SQL statement can't be executed because the application process isn't connected to an application server.
-901	58004	Unsuccessful execution caused by a system error that doesn't preclude the successful execution of subsequent SQL statements.
-902	58005	The pointer to the essential control block, either the CT or the RDA, is zeroes. This precludes the successful execution of the current SQL statement, as well as any subsequent SQL statements. A rebind is required.
-904	57011	Unsuccessful execution caused by an unavailable resource. The reason is (reason-code), type of resource (resource-type), and resource name (resource-name).
-905	57014	Unsuccessful execution due to resource limit being exceeded, resource name = (resource-name) limit = (limit-amount1) CPU seconds ((limit-amount2) service units) derived from (limit-source).
-906	51005	The SQL statement can't be executed because this function is disabled due to a prior error.
-908	23510	(Bind-type) error using (auth-id) authority. The BIND, REBIND, or AUTO-REBIND operation isn't allowed.
-910	57007	The SQL statement can't access an object on which a DROP or ALTER is pending.
-911	40001	The current unit of work has been rolled back due to a deadlock or timeout. The reason is (reason-code), type of resource (resource-type), and resource name (resource-name).
-913	57033	Unsuccessful execution caused by a deadlock or timeout. The reason is (reason-code), type of resource (resource-type), and resource name (resource-name).
-917	42969	Bind package failed. An error has occurred that prevents the package from being created. This SQLCODE can be issued during bind or commit processing.
-918	51021	Execution of the SQL statement failed because a communication link between the local DB2 and at least one remote server no longer exists. A previous failure caused this condition.
-919	56045	A rollback operation is required.
-922	42505	Authorization failure: (error-type) error. The reason is (reason-code).
-923	57015	Connection not established: DB2 (condition), reason (reason-code), type (resource-type), name (resource-name).
-924	58006	DB2 connection internal error, (function-code), (return-code), (reason-code).
-925	2D521	COMMIT not valid in IMS or CICS environment.

-926	2D521	ROLLBACK not valid in IMS/VS or CICS environment.
-927	51006	The language interface (LI) was called when the connecting environment wasn't established. The program should be invoked under the DSN command.
-929	58002	Failure in a data capture exit: (token).
-939	51021	ROLLBACK required due to unrequested ROLLBACK of a remote server.
-947	56038	The SQL statement failed because it will change a table defined with data capture changes, but the data can't be propagated.
-948	56062	The unit of work was initiated before DDF was started, and the application attempted to perform a distributed operation. The unit of work must be terminated by a rollback operation.
-950	42705	The location name specified in the CONNECT statement is invalid or not listed in the communications database.
-965	51021	Stored procedure (procname) terminated abnormally.
-981	57015	The SQL statement failed because the RRSAF connection isn't in a state that allows SQL operations for reason (reason-code).
-991	57015	CALL ATTACH was unable to establish an implicit CONNECT or OPEN to DB2. RC1= rc1, RC2= rc2.
-2001	53089	The number of host variable parameters for a stored procedure isn't equal to the number of expected host variable parameters. Actual number (sqldanum), expected number (opnum).
-30000	58008	Execution failed due to a distribution protocol error that will not affect the successful execution of subsequent commands or SQL statements: Reason (reason-code) (sub-code).
-30020	58009	Execution failed due to a distribution protocol error that caused deallocation of the conversation: Reason (reason-code) (sub-code).
-30021	58010	Execution failed due to a distribution protocol error that will affect the successful execution of subsequent commands or SQL statements: Manager (manager) at level (level) not supported error.
-30030	58013	Commit request was unsuccessful, a distribution protocol violation has been detected, or the conversation has been deallocated. Original SQLCODE= (original-sqlcode) and original SQLSTATE=(original-sqlstate).
-30040	57012	Execution failed due to unavailable resources that will not affect the successful execution of subsequent commands or SQL statements. Reason (reason-code) type of resource (resource-type) resource name (resource-name) product ID (pppvvrrm) RDBNAME (rdbname).
-30041	57013	Execution failed due to unavailable resources that will affect the successful execution of subsequent commands and SQL statements. Reason (reason-code) type of resource (resource-type) resource name (resource-name) product ID (pppvvrrm) RDBNAME (rdbname).
-30050	58011	(Command-or-SQL-statement-type) command or SQL statement invalid while BIND process in progress.
-30051	58012	Bind process with specified package name and consistency token not active.
-30052	42932	Program preparation assumptions are incorrect.
-30053	42506	An authorization failure encountered for the package owner.
-30060	08004	The user isn't authorized to access an RDB.
-30061	08004	An attempt was made to access an RDB that can't be found.
-30070	58014	(Command) command not supported error.
-30071	58015	(Object-type) object not supported error.
-30072	58016	(Parameter) : (subcode) parameter not supported error.
-30073	58017	(Parameter) : (subcode) parameter value not supported error.
-30074	58018	Reply message with (codepoint) SVRCOD not supported error.
-30080	08001	Communication error (code) (subcode). A SNA communication error was detected. Appendix A in *VTAM FOR MVS/ESA Programming for LU 6.2* contains the valid 'code' and 'subcode' values that can appear in this message.
-30081	58019	(Prot) communication error detected. API=api, LOCATION=loc, func, ERROR CODES=rc1 rc2 rc3.

-30082	08001	The connection failed for security reason (reason-code (reason-string)).
-30090	25000	An update operation or a dynamic commit or rollback was attempted at a server that was supporting an application that was in a read-only execution environment (IMS or CICS).
-30104	56095	Error in bind option (option) or bind value (value).
-30105	56096	Bind option (option1) isn't allowed with bind option (option2).

Warning SQLSTATE values

SQLSTATE	SQLCODE	Description
01003	n/a	Null values were eliminated from the argument of a column function.
01004	n/a	The value of a string was truncated when assigned to a host variable.
01503	n/a	The number of result columns is larger than the number of host variables provided.
01504	n/a	The UPDATE or DELETE statement does not include a WHERE clause.
01505	n/a	The statement was not executed because it is unacceptable in this environment.
01506	n/a	An adjustment was made to a DATE or TIMESTAMP value to correct an invalid date resulting from an arithmetic operation.
01507	n/a	One or more non-zero digits were eliminated from the fractional part of a number used as the operand of a multiply or divide operation.
01514	+162	The table space (database-name.tablespace-name) has been placed in check pending mode.
01515	+304	A value with data type (data-type1) can't be assigned to a host variable because the value isn't within the range of the host variable in position (position-number) with data type (data-type2).
01516	+558	The WITH GRANT option is ignored.
01517	n/a	A character that could not be converted was replaced with a substitute character.
01518	+625	The definition of table (table-name) has been changed to incomplete.
01519	+802	An exception error (exception-type) has occurred during (operation-type) operation on (data-type) data, and in position (position-number).
01520	+331	The null value has been assigned to a host variable because the string can't be translated. The reason is (reason-code), character (code-point), host variable (position-number).
01521	+402	The location (location) is unknown.
01522	+403	The local object referenced by the CREATE ALIAS statement doesn't exist.
01523	+561	The ALTER, INDEX, and REFERENCES privileges can't be granted to public at all locations.
01524	n/a	The result of a column function does not include the null values that were caused by evaluating the arithmetic expression implied by the column of the view.
01525	+117	The number of insert values is not the same as the number of object columns.
01528	+645	The WHERE NOT NULL is ignored because the index key can't contain null values.
01529	+626	Dropping the index terminates enforcement of the uniqueness of a key that was defined when the table was created.
01530	+738	The definition change of object (object-name) may require similar change on read-only systems.
01532	+204	(Name) is an undefined name.
	+219	The required explanation table (table-name) doesn't exist.
01533	+206	(Column-name) is not a column of an inserted table, updated table, or any table identified in a FROM clause.
01537	+218	The SQL statement referencing a remote object can't be explained.
01538	+650	The table being created or altered can't become a dependent table.

01539	+863	The connection was successful but only SBCS will be supported.
01540	+664	The internal length of the limit-key fields for the partitioned index (index-name) exceeds the length imposed by the index manager.
01542	+552	The (auth-id) doesn't have the privilege to perform operation (operation).
01543	+541	The referential or unique constraint (name) has been ignored because it is a duplicate.
01545	+012	The unqualified column name (column-name) was interpreted as a correlated reference.
01546	+220	The column (column-name) in explanation table (table-name) isn't defined properly.
01548	+551	The (auth-id) doesn't have the privilege to perform operation (operation) on object (object-name).
01551	+653	Table (table-name) in partitioned table space (tspace-name) isn't available because its partitioned index hasn't been created.
01552	+203	The qualified column (column-name) was resolved using a non-unique or unexposed name.
01553	+806	The bind isolation level RR conflicts with table space LOCKSIZE PAGE or LOCKSIZE ROW and LOCKMAX 0.
01554	+807	The result of decimal multiplication may cause an overflow.
01558	+30100	The operation completed successfully but a distribution protocol violation has been detected. The original SQLCODE = (original-sqlcode) and original SQLSTATE = (original-sqlstate).
01560	+562	A grant of a privilege was ignored because the grantee already has the privilege from the grantor.
01561	+110	The SQL update to a data capture table was not signaled to the originating subsystem.
01566	+610	The INDEX (index-name) has been placed in recover pending mode.
01568	+098	A dynamic SQL statement ends with a semicolon.
01569	+339	The SQL statement has been successfully executed, but there may be some character conversion inconsistencies.
01590	+111	The subpages option is not supported for type 2 indexes.
01591	+535	The result of the positioned update or delete may depend on the order of the rows.
01600	+658	The SUBPAGES value is ignored for the catalog index (index-name).
01609	+464	The procedure (proc) returned (num) query result sets, which exceeds the defined limit (integer).
01610	+466	The procedure (proc) returned (num) query result sets.
01612	n/a	The part clause of a LOCK TABLE statement is not valid.
01614	+494	The number of result sets is greater than the number of locators.
02000	+100	Row not found for FETCH, UPDATE, or DELETE, or the result of a query is an empty table.
56094	+2000	Type 1 indexes with subpages greater than 1 can't become group buffer pool dependent in a data sharing environment.

Error SQLSTATE values

SQLSTATE	SQLCODE	Description
07001	-313	The number of host variables specified isn't equal to the number of parameter markers.
07002	-804	An error was found in the application program input parameters for the SQL statement. The reason is (reason-code). The following is a list of reason codes: (01) Open issued for non-cursor; (02) Close issued for non-cursor; (03) prepare of EXECUTE IMMEDIATE; (04) statement isn't recognized; (05) no statement string present; (06) bad SQLDA format in parameter list; (07)

		SQLDA length is invalid; (08) unrecognized input data type; (09) invalid length for input variable; (10) invalid data length for output variable; (11) the value of SQLDABC is not consistent with the value of SQLD; (12) invalid input data pointer; (13) invalid output data pointer; (14) SQLN has too many items for SQLDABC; (15) input RDI pointer is invalid.
07003	-518	The EXECUTE statement doesn't identify a valid prepared statement. One of the following conditions exists: (1) the statement named in the EXECUTE statement has not been prepared; (2) the statement named in the EXECUTE statement identifies a SELECT statement; or (3) the statement named in the EXECUTE IMMEDIATE statement identifies a SELECT statement.
07005	-517	Cursor (cursor-name) can't be used because its statement name doesn't identify a prepared SELECT statement.
08001	-808	The CONNECT semantics that apply to an application process are determined by the first CONNECT statement executed (successfully or unsuccessfully) by the application process.
	-30080	Communication error (code) (subcode). A SNA communication error was detected. Appendix A in *VTAM FOR MVS/ESA Programming for LU 6.2* contains the valid 'code' and 'subcode' values that can appear in this message.
	-30082	The connection failed for security reason (reason-code (reason-string)).
08002	-842	A connection to (location-name) already exists.
08003	-843	The SET CONNECTION or RELEASE statement must specify an existing connection.
	-900	The SQL statement can't be executed because the application process isn't connected to an application server.
08004	-30060	The user isn't authorized to access an RDB.
	-30061	An attempt was made to access an RDB that can't be found.
0A001	-752	The CONNECT statement is invalid because the process isn't in the connect able state.
0F001	-423	An invalid result set locator value.
21000	-811	Execution of an embedded SELECT statement has resulted in a result table containing more than one row. Alternatively, a subquery contained in a basic predicate has produced more than one value.
21501	-533	An INSERT operation with a subselect attempted to insert multiple rows into a self-referencing table. The subselect of the INSERT operation should return no more than one row of data.
21502	-534	An UPDATE operation attempted to update a primary key on multiple rows of the object table. This code will be issued only for plans and packages bound prior to version 5.
22001	-404	An INSERT or UPDATE statement specifies a value that is longer than the maximum-length string that can be stored in column (column-name).
22001/22003	-302	The value of an input variable or parameter number (position-number) is invalid or too large for the target column or the target value. The SQLSTATE value is 22003 if the value is too large. Otherwise, it's 22001.
22002	-305	The null value can't be assigned to output host variable number (position-number) because no indicator variable is specified.
22003	-304	A value with data type (data-type1) can't be assigned to a host variable because the value isn't within the range of the host variable in position (position-number) with data type (data-type2).
	-406	A calculated or derived numeric value isn't within the range of its object column.
	-413	An overflow occurred during a numeric data type conversion.
22007	-180	The length or string representation of a DATE, TIME, or TIMESTAMP value doesn't conform to any valid format.
	-181	The string representation of a datetime value isn't a valid datetime value.
22008	-183	The result of an arithmetic operation is a date or timestamp that isn't within the valid range of dates, which is between 0001-01-01 and 9999-12-31.

22011	-138	The second or third argument of the SUBSTR function is out of range.
22012/22003	-802	Exception error (exception-type) has occurred during (operation-type) operation on (data-type) data, position (position-number). The processing of an SQL arithmetic function or arithmetic expression that was either in the SELECT list of an SQL SELECT statement, in the search condition of a SELECT, UPDATE, or DELETE statement during the evaluation of a column function, or in the SET clause of the UPDATE statement has encountered an exception error, possibly indicated by (exception-type). The SQLSTATE is 22012 if ZERO DIVIDE, and 22003 if other than ZERO DIVIDE.
22018	-420	The value of a character string argument wasn't acceptable to the (function-name) function.
22019/22025	-130	The ESCAPE clause consists of more than one character, or the string pattern contains an invalid occurrence of the ESCAPE character.
22021	-330	A string can't be used because it can't be translated. The reason is (reason-code), character (code-point), host variable (position-number).
	-331	A string can't be assigned to a host variable because it can't be translated. The reason is (reason-code), character (code-point), position (position-number).
22023	-310	Decimal host variable or parameter (number) contains non-decimal data.
22024	-300	The C string variable contained in host variable or parameter (position-number) isn't NUL-terminated.
22501	-311	The length of input host variable number (position-number) is negative or greater than the maximum.
22503	-188	The host variable reference in the DESCRIBE TABLE statement doesn't contain a valid string representation of a name.
22504	-191	A string can't be used because it is invalid mixed data.
22505	-186	The logical format option has been used with a datetime value and DB2 has discovered that the datetime exit routine has been changed to produce a longer local format.
22506	-187	A reference to a CURRENT DATE/TIME special register is invalid because the MVS time-of-day (TOD) clock is bad or the PARMTZ is out of range.
22508	-812	The SQL statement can't be processed because a blank collection-ID was found in the current PACKAGESET special register while trying to form a qualified package name for program (program-name.consistency-token) using plan (plan-name).
22512	-309	A predicate is invalid because a referenced host variable has the null value.
22522	-189	CCSID (ccsid) is unknown or invalid for the data type or subtype.
22525	-327	The row can't be inserted because it's outside the bound of the partition range for the last partition.
23502	-407	An UPDATE or INSERT value is null, but the object column (column-name) can't contain null values.
23503	-530	The INSERT or UPDATE value of foreign key (constraint-name) is invalid.
23504	-531	The parent key in a parent row can't be updated because it has one or more dependent rows in relationship (constraint-name).
	-532	The relationship (constraint-name) restricts the deletion of row with RID X('rid-number').
23505	-803	An inserted or updated value is invalid because the index in INDEX SPACE (indexspace-name) constrains columns of the table so no two rows can contain duplicate values in those columns. RID of existing row is X(rid).
23506	-652	The result of the SQL statement has been rejected by the installation defined edit or validation procedure (proc-name) for the object table.
23507	-681	Column (column-name) is in violation of an installation defined field procedure. RT: (return-code), RS: (reason-code), MSG: (message-token).
23508	-690	The statement is rejected by data definition control support. The reason is (reason-code).
23509	-807	Access denied: Package (package-name) isn't enabled for access from (connection-type connection-name).

23510	-908	(Bind-type) error using (auth-id) authority. The BIND, REBIND, or AUTO-REBIND operation isn't allowed.
23511	-543	A row in a parent table can't be deleted because the check constraint (check-constraint) restricts the deletion.
23512	-544	The check constraint specified in the ALTER TABLE statement can't be added because an existing row violates the check constraint.
23513	-545	The requested operation isn't allowed because a row doesn't satisfy the check constraint (check-constraint).
23515	-603	The index defined in the CREATE INDEX statement couldn't be created as unique because the specified table already contains rows that are duplicates with respect to the values of the identified columns.
24501	-500	The FETCH, UPDATE, DELETE, or CLOSE statement identifies a closed cursor that was defined with the WITH HOLD option. The cursor was closed when the connection where it was dependent was destroyed during a commit operation. The connection was destroyed because the application process placed it in the released state, or the application plan was bound with the DISCONNECT(AUTOMATIC) option.
	-501	The cursor identified in a FETCH or CLOSE statement isn't open.
	-507	The cursor identified in the UPDATE or DELETE statement isn't open.
24502	-502	The cursor identified in an OPEN statement is already open.
24504	-508	The cursor identified in the UPDATE or DELETE statement isn't positioned on a row.
24506	-519	The application program has attempted to PREPARE (actually, re-PREPARE) the SELECT statement for the specified cursor when that cursor was already open.
24516	-499	The cursor (cursor-name) has already been assigned to this result set or another result set from procedure (procedure-name).
25000	-571	The statement would result in a multiple site update. This SQLCODE is issued in the following situations: (1) when an application program operating in an IMS or CICS environment attempts to modify data at a remote location where multi-site update capabilities aren't supported; or (2) when an application has explicit SQL statements within a commit scope that would result in updates at multiple sites where one of the sites where data is being updated doesn't support multi-site updates.
	-817	The SQL statement can't be executed because the statement will result in a prohibited update operation.
	-30090	An update operation or a dynamic commit or rollback was attempted at a server that was supporting an application that was in a read-only execution environment (IMS or CICS).
26501	-514	The application program has tried to use a cursor (cursor-name) that is not in a prepared state. The cursor is associated with a statement that either (1) has never been prepared, or (2) has been invalidated by a commit or rollback operation.
	-516	The DESCRIBE statement doesn't identify a prepared statement.
2D521	-925	COMMIT not valid in IMS or CICS environment.
	-926	ROLLBACK not valid in IMS/VS or CICS environment.
2D528	-426	An application using DRDA protocols has attempted to issue a dynamic COMMIT statement while connected to a location where updates aren't allowed.
2D529	-427	An application using DRDA protocols has attempted to issue a dynamic ROLLBACK statement while connected to a location where updates aren't allowed.
34000	-504	The cursor name (cursor-name) isn't defined.
39002	-470	DB2 received an SQL CALL statement for a stored procedure and found a null value in the incoming parameter list. The DB2 stored procedure was

		defined in the SYSIBM.SYSPROCEDURES catalog table with LINKAGE=, which specifies that the DB2 stored procedure doesn't accept null values.
39501	-450	While returning parameters from a stored procedure to an application, DB2 detected an overlay of one of the parameters. A stored procedure overwrote storage beyond a parameter's declared length.
40001	-911	The current unit of work has been rolled back due to a deadlock or timeout. The reason is (reason-code), type of resource (resource-type), and resource name (resource-name).
42501	-551	(Auth-id) doesn't have the privilege to perform operation (operation) on object (object-name). Beginning with version 5, SQLCODE -551 will be returned instead of SQLCODE -204 for the runtime error where an object does not exist and the CURRENT RULES special register is set to 'STD'.
	-567	(Bind-type) authorization error using (auth-id) authority package = (package-name) privilege = (privilege).
42502	-164	The authorization ID (auth-id) doesn't have the authority necessary to create views with qualifiers other than its own authorization ID. Specifically, the attempt to create a view with qualifier (authorization ID) is rejected.
	-552	(Auth-id) doesn't have the privilege to perform operation (operation).
	-554	An authorization ID can't grant a privilege to itself.
	-555	An authorization ID can't revoke a privilege from itself.
42503	-553	(Auth-id) isn't one of the valid authorization IDs.
42504	-556	(Authid2) can't have the (privilege) privilege (on_object) revoked by (authid1) because the revokee doesn't possess the privilege or the revoker didn't make the grant.
42505	-922	Authorization failure: (error-type) error. The reason is (reason-code).
42506	-30053	An authorization failure encountered for the package owner.
42509	-549	The (statement) statement isn't allowed for (object_type1 object_name) because the bind option DYNAMICRULES(BIND) in the (object_type2) is in effect.
42601	-007	The statement contains the illegal character (character).
	-029	The INTO clause is required.
	-104	Illegal symbol "token." Some symbols that might be legal are: (token-list).
	-108	The name (name) is qualified incorrectly.
	-109	The (clause) clause isn't permitted in the context in which it appears in the SQL statement for the following reasons: (1) a subselect can't have an INTO clause; (2) a CREATE VIEW statement can't have INTO, ORDER BY, or FOR UPDATE clauses; (3) an embedded SELECT statement can't have ORDER BY or FOR UPDATE clauses; (4) SELECT statements used in cursor declarations can't have an INTO clause; (5) A CREATE TABLESPACE statement can't specify the LARGE clause without the NUMPARTS option; (6) a CREATE TABLESPACE statement can't specify LOCKPART without the NUMPARTS option; (7) an ALTER TABLESPACE statement can't specify LOCKPART for a non-partitioned table space; (8) a table space with LOCKPART YES can't be altered to LOCKSIZE TABLESPACE; or (9) a table space with LOCKSIZE TABLESPACE can't be altered to LOCKPART YES.
	-115	A predicate is invalid because the comparison operator (operator) is followed by a parenthesized list or by ANY or ALL without a subquery.
	-128	Invalid use of null in a predicate.
	-199	Illegal use of keyword (keyword). Token (token-list) was expected.
	-638	The table (table-name) can't be created because the CREATE TABLE statement doesn't contain any column definitions.
42602	-113	An invalid character was found in (string), reason code –nnn.
	-251	Token (name) isn't valid. A location name can't contain alphabetic extenders. (The standard alphabetic extenders in the United States are #, @, $.)

42603	-010	The string constant beginning (string) is not terminated properly.
42604	-103	The (literal) is an invalid numeric literal.
	-105	The statement contains an invalid string.
42605	-170	An SQL statement includes the scalar function (function-name) with either too many or too few arguments.
42606	-110	The literal beginning with (string) contains one or more characters that aren't valid hexadecimal digits.
42607	-112	The operand of a column function is another column function.
	-409	The operand of the COUNT function in the SQL statement violates SQL syntax. A common error is a column name or other expression without DISTINCT.
42609	-417	A statement string to be prepared includes parameter markers as the operands of the same operation.
42610	-184	The specified arithmetic expression contains a parameter marker improperly used with a datetime value.
	-418	A statement string to be prepared contains an invalid use of parameter markers.
42611	-604	A column definition in the CREATE or ALTER TABLE statement contains an invalid length, precision, or scale attribute specification.
42612	-084	An unacceptable SQL statement was executed due to one of the following: (1) an attempt to PREPARE or EXECUTE IMMEDIATE an SQL statement that can't be prepared; (2) the embedded SQL statement isn't an SQL statement supported by DB2; or (3) the statement referenced an undeclared cursor.
42613	-628	Mutually exclusive clauses were specified in one or more of the following ways: (1) a CREATE TABLESPACE statement contains both the SEGSIZE and NUMPARTS clauses; (2) a CREATE TABLESPACE statement contains both the SEGSIZE and LARGE clauses; (3) a CREATE or ALTER TABLESPACE statement contains both the LOCKPART YES and LOCKSIZE TABLESPACE clauses; (4) a (column-definition) contains both NOT NULL and DEFAULT NULL clauses; (5) a (column-definition) contains both FIELDPROC and DEFAULT clauses; (6) a SELECT statement contains both the UPDATE clause and the FOR FETCH ONLY clause; (7) an ALTER TABLE statement contains both a DROP CONSTRAINT clause and either a DROP FOREIGN KEY clause or a DROP CHECK clause; or (8) a CREATE or ALTER TABLESPACE statement contains both the LOCKPART YES and LOCKSIZE TABLESPACE clauses.
42614	-637	Duplicate (keyword) keyword.
42615	-644	The value specified for the keyword (keyword) parameter in the (stmt-type) SQL statement isn't a permitted value.
42617	-198	The operand of the PREPARE or EXECUTE IMMEDIATE statement is blank or empty.
42618	-312	The host variable (variable-name) appears in the SQL statement, but the SQL statement is a prepared statement; the attributes of the variable are inconsistent with its usage in the static SQL statement; or the variable is not declared in the application program.
42621	-546	The check constraint (check-constraint) is invalid.
	-548	The check constraint that is defined with (column-name) is invalid.
42622	-107	The name (name) is too long. The maximum allowable size is (size).
42625	-580	The result expressions of a case expression can't all be NULL.
	-582	The search condition in a SEARCHED WHEN clause can't be a quantified predicate, an IN predicate, or an EXISTS predicate.
42701	-121	The column (name) is identified more than once in the INSERT or UPDATE statement.
42702	-203	A reference to column (column-name) is ambiguous.
42703	-205	No column with the specified (column-name) occurs in the table or view (table-name).

	-206	(Column-name) isn't a column of an inserted table, updated table, or any table identified in a FROM clause.
42704	-204	The object identified by (name) isn't defined in the DB2 subsystem.
	-219	The required explanation table (table-name) doesn't exist.
	-722	The indicated subcommand was issued against a package that doesn't exist. Bind type = (bind-type), authorization ID = (auth-id), package = (package-name).
42705	-950	The location name specified in the CONNECT statement is invalid or not listed in the communications database.
42707	-208	The ORDER BY clause is invalid because column (name) isn't part of the result table.
42709	-537	The PRIMARY KEY clause, a FOREIGN KEY clause, or a UNIQUE clause identifies column (column-name) more than once.
42710	-601	The CREATE statement tried to create an object (name) of type (obj-type), but an object of that type with the same name is already defined in the DB2 subsystem.
	-719	An attempt is made to add a package that already exists. The combination of 'location.collection.package.version' must be unique in the SYSIBM.SYS-PACKAGE table. In addition, the combination of 'location.collection.pack-age.consistency-token' must be unique.
	-720	An attempt is made to create a version of a package that already exists. Package name = (package-name), version = (version2).
	-721	An attempt is made to add or replace a package with a consistency token that is not unique for that package. Package name = (pkg-id), consistency token = (contoken).
42711	-612	The column (column-name) is a duplicate column name.
42714	-314	The statement contains an ambiguous host variable reference.
42718	-250	A three-part object name (table, view, or alias) can't be used until the local location name is defined.
42724	-444	DB2 received an SQL CALL statement for a stored procedure and found the row in the SYSIBM.SYSPROCEDURES catalog table associated with the requested procedure name. However, the MVS load module identified in the LOADMOD column of the SYSIBM.SYSPROCEDURES row couldn't be found.
42801	-173	The cursor is not a read-only cursor. WITH UR can be specified only if DB2 can determine that the cursor is read-only.
42802	-117	The number of insert values isn't the same as the number of object columns.
42803	-119	A column identified in a HAVING clause isn't included in the GROUP BY clause.
	-122	A SELECT statement with no GROUP BY clause contains a column name and a column function in the SELECT clause or a column name is contained in the SELECT clause but not in the GROUP BY clause.
42804	-581	The data types of the result expressions of a case expression are not compatible.
42805	-125	An integer in the ORDER BY clause doesn't identify a column of the result.
42806	-303	A value can't be assigned to output host variable number (position-number) because the data types aren't comparable.
42807	-150	The object of the INSERT, DELETE, or UPDATE statement is a view for which the requested operation isn't permitted.
42808	-151	The UPDATE statement is invalid because the catalog description of column (column-name) indicates that it can't be updated.
42809	-148	The source table (source-name) can't be renamed because it is a view or an active RLST table or has a synonym defined on it.
	-152	The DROP clause (clause) in the ALTER statement is invalid because (constraint-name) is a (constraint-type).

	-156	The statement doesn't identify a table.
	-159	The object specified in the DROP VIEW statement, DROP ALIAS statement, or COMMENT ON ALIAS statement identifies a table instead of a view or an alias.
42810	-157	Only a table name can be specified in a foreign key clause; (object-name) isn't the name of a table.
42811	-158	The number of columns specified for the view isn't the same as the number of columns specified by the SELECT clause.
42813	-160	The WITH CHECK OPTION doesn't apply to a view definition under either of the following circumstances: the view is read-only (for example, the view definition includes DISTINCT, GROUP BY, or JOIN) or the view definition includes a subquery.
42815	-060	An invalid (type) specification: (spec) where "type" is either LENGTH or SCALE, and "spec" is the specified length or scale. Length or scale must be specified by an unsigned integer constant and the value must be in the range allowed by the data type.
	-171	Either the data type, the length, or the value of argument (nn) of scalar function (function-name) is incorrect.
	-713	The value specified in the SET (special-register) statement is not a valid value of the indicated special register.
42816	-182	The specified arithmetic expression contains an improperly used datetime value or labeled duration.
42818	-131	A statement with the LIKE predicate has incompatible data types.
	-401	An arithmetic operation appearing within the SQL statement has a mixture of numeric and non-numeric operands, or the operands of a comparison operation aren't compatible.
42819	-402	A non-numeric operand has been specified for the arithmetic function or operator (arith-fop).
42820	-405	The numeric literal (literal) can't be used as specified because it is out of range.
	-410	The specified floating point literal (literal) is more than 30 characters in length.
42821	-408	An UPDATE or INSERT value isn't comparable with the data type of its object column (column-name).
42823	-412	The SELECT clause of a subquery specifies multiple columns.
42824	-132	A LIKE predicate is invalid because the second operand isn't a string.
	-414	A LIKE predicate is invalid because the first operand isn't a string.
42825	-415	The corresponding columns (column-name) of the operands of a UNION or a UNION ALL don't have comparable column descriptions.
42826	-421	The operands of a UNION or UNION ALL don't have the same number of columns.
42827	-509	The application program attempted to execute an UPDATE or DELETE WHERE CURRENT OF cursor statement where the table named in that statement didn't match the name of the table specified in the declaration for that cursor.
42828	-510	The application program attempted to execute an UPDATE or DELETE WHERE CURRENT OF cursor statement against a table or view that can't be updated or deleted. This can occur for a delete from a read-only view or for an update in which the cursor wasn't defined with the FOR UPDATE clause.
42829	-126	The SELECT statement contains both an UPDATE clause and an ORDER BY clause.
	-511	The result table of the SELECT statement can't be updated. This can occur if the SELECT specifies more than one table or view in the FROM clause, if the SELECT list contains a built-in function or DISTINCT, or if the statement contains an ORDER BY, GROUP BY or HAVING clause. This can also occur if a view is specified in the FROM clause and the view can't be updated.

42830	-538	The FOREIGN KEY (name) doesn't conform to the description of the parent key of table (table-name).
42831	-542	(Column-name) can't be a column of a primary key or a unique constraint because it can contain null values.
42832	-607	The operation or option (operation) can't be performed on the catalog object specified in the SQL statement.
	-618	Operation (operation) isn't allowed on system databases.
42834	-629	SET NULL can't be specified because FOREIGN KEY (name) can't contain null values.
42842	-683	Invalid column type for fieldproc, BIT DATA, SBCS DATA, or MIXED DATA option, (column-name).
42852	-557	Inconsistent GRANT/REVOKE keyword (keyword). Permitted keywords are (keyword-list).
42877	-197	A SELECT statement that specifies both the union of two or more tables and the ORDER BY clause can't use qualified column names in the ORDER BY clause.
42884	-440	The number of parameters in the parameter list doesn't match the number of parameters expected for stored procedure (name), AUTHID (authid), LUNAME (luname). The (number) parameters were expected.
42886	-469	DB2 received an SQL CALL statement for a stored procedure. DB2 found the row in the SYSIBM.SYSPROCEDURES catalog table associated with the requested procedure name. However, parameter (number) was identified in the PARMLIST column of the SYSIBM.SYSPROCEDURES table as an OUT or INOUT parameter. A host variable must be supplied on the SQL CALL statement for parameters defined as OUT or INOUT.
42888	-539	The CREATE or ALTER TABLE statement can't be executed because the indicated table (table-name) doesn't have a primary key. So, the primary key can't be dropped, or the table can't be defined as a parent in a referential constraint.
42889	-624	Table (table-name) already has a primary key.
42890	-573	The table (table-name) doesn't have a unique key with the specified column names.
42893	-616	The object (obj-type1 obj-name1) can't be dropped because it is referenced by object (obj-type2 obj-name2). Some types of objects can't be dropped if there are other objects that are dependent on them. For example, a storage group can't be dropped if there are one or more existing table spaces that use that storage group.
42894	-574	The specified default value conflicts with the column definition.
42895	-301	The value of input host variable or parameter number (position-number) can't be used as specified because of its data type.
428B4	-240	The PART clause of a LOCK TABLE statement is invalid.
42901	-111	A column function doesn't include a column name.
42902	-118	The object table or view of the INSERT, DELETE, or UPDATE statement is also identified in a FROM clause.
42903	-120	A WHERE clause or SET clause includes a column function.
42905	-127	The keyword DISTINCT is specified more than once in a subselect.
42906	-133	A column function in a subquery of a HAVING clause is invalid because all column references in its argument aren't correlated to the GROUP BY result that the HAVING clause is applied to.
42907	-134	Improper use of a long string column (column-name) or a host variable of maximum length greater than 254.
	-416	The UNION specified in the SQL statement couldn't be performed because one of the tables participating in the union contains a long string column (for example, a VARCHAR column with length greater than 254). The operands of a UNION can't contain long string columns.

42908	-153	The CREATE VIEW statement doesn't include a required column list.
42909	-154	The CREATE VIEW failed because the view definition contains a UNION, a UNION ALL, or a remote object.
42911	-419	The decimal divide operation is invalid because the result would have a negative scale.
42912	-503	The application program attempted to update (using a cursor) a value in a column of the object table that wasn't identified in the FOR UPDATE clause in the cursor declaration.
42914	-536	The DELETE statement is invalid due to referential constraints for table (table-name).
42915	-632	The table can't be defined as a dependent of (table-name) because of delete rule restrictions.
	-633	The (delete-rule) specified in a FOREIGN KEY clause of the ALTER TABLE statement is invalid. The indicated (delete-rule) is required because a self-referencing constraint must have a (delete-rule) of CASCADE or NO ACTION or the relationship would cause the table to be delete-connected to the same table through multiple paths and such relationships must have the same (delete-rule).
	-634	The CASCADE delete rule specified in the FOREIGN KEY clause of an ALTER TABLE statement is invalid because the relationship would form a cycle that would cause a table to be delete-connected to itself or the relationship would cause another table to be delete-connected to the same table through multiple paths with different delete rules or with a delete rule equal to SET NULL.
	-635	The delete rules can't be different or can't be SET NULL.
42917	-667	The DROP INDEX statement attempted to drop the cluster index for a table residing in a partitioned table space. The cluster index for such a table can't be dropped explicitly with the DROP INDEX statement.
	-669	A table in a partitioned table space can't be dropped by the DROP TABLE statement. It can only be dropped implicitly when the table space is dropped.
42920	-815	An embedded SELECT statement of a subquery of a basic predicate either (1) directly contains a GROUP BY or HAVING clause, or (2) specifies as its object a view having a definition that includes a GROUP BY or HAVING clause. Neither construct is permitted.
42924	-513	The alias (alias-name) must not be defined on another local or remote alias.
42932	-30052	Program preparation assumptions are incorrect.
42961	-114	A three-part SQL procedure name was provided in an SQL CALL, ASSOCIATE LOCATORS, or DESCRIBE PROCEDURE statement. The first part of the SQL procedure name, which specifies the location where the stored procedure resides, didn't match the value of the SQL CURRENT SERVER special register.
42969	-917	Bind package failed. An error has occurred that prevents the package from being created. This SQLCODE can be issued during bind or commit processing.
42972	-338	An ON clause is invalid. This return code reports a violation of one of the following: (1) one expression of the predicate must only reference columns of one of the operand tables of the associated join operator, and the other expression of the predicate must only reference columns of the other operand table; (2) a VALUE or COALESCE function is allowed in the ON clause only when the join operator is a FULL OUTER JOIN or FULL JOIN; or (3) an operator other than equals (=) isn't allowed in a FULL OUTER JOIN or FULL JOIN.
42986	-750	The source table (source-name) can't be renamed because it is referenced in existing view definitions.
42987	-751	A stored procedure has been placed in MUST_ROLLBACK state due to SQL operation (name).

42988	-875	The operand (operand) can't be used with the ASCII data that's referenced.
42995	-526	The requested function doesn't apply to global temporary tables.
44000	-161	The INSERT or UPDATE isn't allowed because a resulting row doesn't satisfy the view definition.
51002	-805	DBRM or PACKAGE NAME (location-name.collection-id.dbrm-name.consistency) token not found in plan (plan-name). The reason is (reason-code). See *DB2 for OS/390 V5 Messages and Codes* for the definition of the reason-codes.
51003	-818	The precompiler-generated timestamp (x) in the load module is different from the bind timestamp (y) built from the DBRM (z). This problem can occur if you: (1) precompile, compile, and link, without doing a BIND of the application; (2) precompile and BIND, without doing the compile and link for the application program; or (3) BIND the application using a DBRM that resulted from a different precompile of the application program than that which produced the object module that is linked into the application module.
51004	-822	The SQLDA contains an invalid data address or indicator variable address.
51005	-906	The SQL statement can't be executed because this function is disabled due to a prior error.
51006	-927	The language interface (LI) was called when the connecting environment wasn't established. The program should be invoked under the DSN command.
51015	-525	The SQL statement can't be executed because it was in error at bind time for section (sectno) package (pkgname) consistency token X('contoken').
51021	-918	Execution of the SQL statement failed because a communication link between the local DB2 and at least one remote server no longer exists. A previous failure caused this condition.
	-939	ROLLBACK required due to unrequested ROLLBACK of a remote server.
	-965	Stored procedure (procname) terminated abnormally.
51030	-480	The procedure (procedure-name) has not yet been called.
	-482	The procedure (procedure-name) returned no locators.
51032	-872	A valid CCSID has not yet been specified for this MVS/ESA subsystem.
51033	-496	The SQL statement can't be executed because it references a result set that wasn't created by the current server.
53001	-620	The keyword (keyword) in (stmt-type) statement isn't permitted for a table space in the work file database.
53004	-742	The WORKFILE clause can't be used on a CREATE DATABASE statement to create a work file database for a DB2 subsystem that isn't a member of a DB2 data sharing group. The system database, DSNDB07, is the implicit work file database.
53014	-736	Invalid OBID (obid) specified. An invalid OBID value was given on the CREATE statement.
53035	-660	Index (index-name) can't be created on a partitioned table space (tspace-name) because key limits aren't specified.
53036	-661	Index (index-name) can't be created on a partitioned table space (tspace-name) because the number of PART specifications isn't equal to the number of partitions of the table space.
53037	-662	A partitioned index can't be created on a non-partitioned table space (tspace-name).
53038	-663	The number of key limit values is either zero or greater than the number of columns in the key of index (index-name).
53039	-665	The PART clause of an ALTER statement is omitted or invalid.
53040	-671	The buffer pool attribute of the table space can't be altered as specified because it would change the page size of the table space.
53041	-676	A 32K page buffer pool may not be used for an index. Only 4KB buffer pools (BP0, BP1, and BP2) can be specified for indexes.
53043	-686	A column defined with a field procedure can't be compared with another column with a different field procedure.

53044	-687	One column can't be compared with another column that has incompatible field types.
53045	-678	The literal (literal) specified for the index limit key must conform to the data type (data-type) of the corresponding column (column-name).
53088	-611	Only LOCKMAX 0 can be specified when the lock size of the table space is TABLESPACE or TABLE.
53089	-2001	The number of host variable parameters for a stored procedure isn't equal to the number of expected host variable parameters. Actual number (sqldanum), expected number (opnum).
53090	-873	Data encoded with different CCSIDs can't be referenced in the same SQL statement.
53091	-874	The encoding scheme specified for the table isn't the same as that for the table space containing this table.
53092	-876	The object ('object') can't be created for reason ('reason').
53093	-877	CCSID ASCII isn't allowed for this database or table space.
53094	-878	The PLAN_TABLE used for EXPLAIN can't be ASCII.
53095	-879	A column can't be created as GRAPHIC, VARGRAPHIC, or LONG VARGRAPHIC in an ASCII table.
54001	-101	The statement is too long or too complex.
54002	-102	A literal string is too long. The string begins (string).
54004	-129	The statement contains too many table names.
	-840	The number of items returned in the select list or presented in an insert list exceeds the allowable maximum of 750.
54005	-136	The SORT can't be executed because the sort key length is greater than 4000 bytes.
54006	-137	The length of the result of a concatenation exceeds 32,764 (if character operands) or 16,382 (if graphic operands).
54008	-602	The number of columns specified in the CREATE INDEX statement exceeds 64, the maximum permitted by DB2.
	-613	The primary key or a unique constraint is too long or has too many columns.
	-614	The index can't be created because the sum of the internal lengths of the identified columns is greater than the allowable maximum.
	-631	The FOREIGN KEY (name) is too long or has too many columns.
54010	-670	The record length of the table exceeds the page size limit.
54011	-680	Too many columns are specified for a table. The maximum number of columns permitted per table is 750.
	-689	Too many columns defined for a dependent table. The maximum number of columns allowed for a dependent table is 749.
54012	-684	The length of literal list beginning (string) is too long.
54021	-642	There is a limit to the total number of columns that can be used in UNIQUE constraints in a CREATE TABLE statement. The statement exceeds that limit.
54024	-643	The check constraint definition exceeds the maximum allowable limit of 3800 characters. The redundant blank spaces are excluded from this limit.
54025	-651	The CREATE TABLE or ALTER TABLE statement causes the table descriptor (record OBD) to exceed the object descriptor size limit of 32KB.
54027	-400	The catalog has the maximum number of user defined indexes (100).
54041	-497	An attempt was made to create an object in database (database-name), but the limit of 32,767 OBIDs has been exceeded for that database.
55002	-220	The column (column-name) in an explanation table (table-name) isn't defined properly.
	-221	"SET OF OPTIONAL COLUMNS" in the explanation table (table-name) is incomplete. Optional column (column-name) is missing.
55003	-693	The column (column-name) in DDL registration table or index (table-name) (index-name) isn't defined properly.
55004	-735	Database (dbid) can't be accessed because it is no longer a shared database.

55006	-615	The operation (operation-type) can't be performed because the package is in use by the same application process. The type of bind operations are BIND, REBIND, and DROP.
55011	-619	The statements CREATE, ALTER, or DROP for a table space in the work file database can't be processed unless the work file database is stopped (using the STOP command).
55012	-623	A clustering index already exists on table (table-name). A given table can have only one cluster index.
55014	-625	Table (table-name) doesn't have an index to enforce the uniqueness of the parent key.
55015	-626	An ALTER statement specifies a BUFFERPOOL, USING, PRIQTY, SECQTY, ERASE, or GBPCACHE clause, but the page set isn't stopped.
55016	-627	The ALTER statement is invalid because the page set has user-managed data sets.
55017	-646	Table (table-name) can't be created in partitioned/default table space (tspace-name) because it already contains a table. Only one table may reside in a partitioned or default table space.
55020	-741	A work file database is already defined for member (member-name).
55023	-471	The SQL CALL for stored procedure (name) failed due to reason (reason-code). See *DB2 for OS/390 V5 Messages and Codes* for the definition of the reason-codes.
55030	-726	Bind error attempting to replace package = (package-name). There are ENABLE or DISABLE entries currently associated with the package.
55035	-672	The DROP operation failed for table (table-name) because the table being dropped has the RESTRICT ON DROP attribute, or the table space or database being dropped contains the specified table, which has the RESTRICT ON DROP attribute.
56010	-333	The subtype of a string variable isn't the same as the subtype known at bind time and the difference can't be resolved by translation.
56016	-636	The partitioning keys for partition (part-num) aren't specified in ascending or descending order.
56018	-668	The ALTER TABLE statement attempted to add a column to a table that has an edit procedure. If a table has an edit procedure, no column can be added to it.
56023	-512	The statement reference to a remote object is invalid. One of the following conditions exists: (1) the statement refers to multiple locations; (2) a statement with a remote reference is being EXPLAINED either by a dynamic EXPLAIN statement or the EXPLAIN(YES) option; (3) an alias is used incorrectly; or (4) a three-part name is implicitly or explicitly used in a statement that is not supported by the DB2 private protocols.
56025	-558	Invalid clause or combination of clauses on a GRANT or REVOKE statement.
56027	-639	A partition key of the clustering index can't be updated. Therefore, a foreign key column with a delete rule of SET NULL can't be a column of a partition key if that column is nullable. If this error occurs for an ALTER TABLE operation, the foreign key can't be created. If this error occurs for a CREATE INDEX operation, the index can't be created.
56031	-622	FOR MIXED DATA is specified in a column description of a CREATE or ALTER TABLE statement, but the MIXED DATA install option is set to NO.
56036	-655	The CREATE or ALTER STOGROUP statement is invalid because the storage group would have both specific and nonspecific volume IDs.
56038	-947	The SQL statement failed because it will change a table defined with data capture changes, but the data can't be propagated.
56040	-411	A reference to the CURRENT SQLID special register is invalid in a statement that contains the three-part name or alias of an object that is remote to the remote server.

56045	-919	A rollback operation is required.
56053	-730	The parent of a table in a read-only shared database must also be a table in a read-only shared database.
56054	-731	User-defined data set (dsname) must be defined with SHAREOPTIONS(1,3). The VSAM SHAREOPTIONS must be (1,3) for all of the indexes and table spaces in the database.
56055	-732	The database is defined on this subsystem with the ROSHARE READ attribute, but the table space or index space hasn't been defined on the owning subsystem.
56056	-733	The description of a table space, index space, or table in a ROSHARE READ database must be consistent with its description in the owner system.
	-737	A CREATE TABLE statement was issued using an implicit table space. An implicit table space may not be used in a database that has been defined as a read-only shared database.
56057	-734	The ROSHARE attribute of a database can't be altered from ROSHARE READ.
56062	-948	The unit of work was initiated before DDF was started, and the application attempted to perform a distributed operation. The unit of work must be terminated by a rollback operation.
56064	-715	Program (program-name) depends on a function of DB2 that is not supported by the current active release.
56065	-716	Program (program-name) was precompiled under a release not supported by the current level of DB2, or the contents of the DBRM have been modified after the precompilation phase.
56066	-717	The (bind-type) for (object-type) (object-name) with mark (release-dependency-mark) failed because (object-type) depends on functions of the release from which fallback has occurred. The plan or package indicated depends on a function of DB2 not supported by the currently active release.
56067	-718	The REBIND for package (package-name) failed because IBMREQD of (ibmreqd) is invalid. The IBMREQD column of the SYSIBM.SYSPACKAGE catalog table for the named package contains an unrecognizable character.
56082	-339	The SQL statement can't be executed from an ASCII based DRDA application requestor to a V2R2 DB2 subsystem.
56084	-351	An unsupported SQLTYPE was encountered in position (position-number) on a PREPARE or DESCRIBE operation. Some SQL data types aren't supported by DB2 version 4. Position (position-number) is the position of the first element with an invalid data type in the SQLDA. A common reason why this error occurs is when DB2 attempts to describe large object data residing on a non-DB2 server. Some of the SQLTYPEs that can cause this error are: LOB, BLOB, CLOB, and DBLOB.
56089	-617	All indexes defined for a table within a table space with LOCKSIZE ROW must be defined as type 2 indexes.
	-630	The WHERE NOT NULL specification is invalid for type 1 indexes.
	-640	LOCKSIZE ROW can't be specified because a table in this table space has a type 1 index.
56090	-650	The ALTER INDEX statement can't be executed, reason (reason-code).
56095	-30104	Error in bind option (option) or bind value (value).
56096	-30105	Bind option (option1) isn't allowed with bind option (option2).
57001	-540	The definition of table (table-name) is incomplete because it lacks a primary key index or a required unique index.
57002	-559	The authorization mechanism has been disabled in the DB2 subsystem. Consequently, GRANT and REVOKE statements are ignored.
57003	-647	Buffer pool (bp-name) can't be specified because it hasn't been activated.
57004	-653	Table (table-name) in partitioned table space (tspace-name) isn't available because its partitioned index hasn't been created.

57005	-666	The (stmt-verb object) can't be executed because function (function) is in progress.
57006	-679	The object (name) can't be created because a drop is pending on the object.
57007	-910	The SQL statement can't access an object on which a DROP or ALTER is pending.
57008	-185	The local format option has been used with a date or time and no local exit has been installed.
57010	-682	Field procedure (procedure-name) couldn't be loaded.
57011	-677	An attempt to either open (create) or expand a buffer pool has failed because insufficient virtual storage was available.
	-904	Unsuccessful execution caused by an unavailable resource. The reason is (reason-code), type of resource (resource-type), and resource name (resource-name).
57012	-30040	Execution failed due to unavailable resources that will not affect the successful execution of subsequent commands or SQL statements. Reason (reason-code) type of resource (resource-type) resource name (resource-name) product ID (pppvvrrm) RDBNAME (rdbname).
57013	-30041	Execution failed due to unavailable resources that will affect the successful execution of subsequent commands and SQL statements. Reason (reason-code) type of resource (resource-type) resource name (resource-name) product ID (pppvvrrm) RDBNAME (rdbname).
57014	-905	Unsuccessful execution due to resource limit being exceeded, resource name = (resource-name) limit = (limit-amount1) CPU seconds ((limit-amount2) service units) derived from (limit-source).
57015	-923	Connection not established: DB2 (condition), reason (reason-code), type (resource-type), name (resource-name).
	-981	The SQL statement failed because the RRSAF connection isn't in a state that allows SQL operations for reason (reason-code).
	-991	CALL ATTACH was unable to establish an implicit CONNECT or OPEN to DB2. RC1= rc1, RC2= rc2.
57017	-332	The operation required the translation of a string to a different coded character set, but the particular translation isn't described in the SYSSTRINGS catalog table. The first (ccsid) identifies the coded character set of the string and the second (ccsid) identifies the coded character set to which it must be translated.
57018	-691	The required registration table (table-name) doesn't exist.
	-692	The required unique index (index-name) for DDL registration table (table-name) doesn't exist.
57023	-694	The DDL statement can't be executed because a drop is pending on the DDL registration table (table-name).
57033	-913	Unsuccessful execution caused by a deadlock or timeout. The reason is (reason-code), type of resource (resource-type), and resource name (resource-name).
58001	-621	A duplicate DBID (dbid) was detected and previously assigned to (database-name). An inconsistency exists between the DB2 catalog and directory.
58002	-685	Invalid field type, (column-name).
	-688	Incorrect data returned from field procedure, (column-name), (msgno).
	-929	Failure in a data capture exit: (token).
58003	-144	Invalid section number (number).
58004	-819	SYSIBM.SYSVTREE.VTREE is a varying-length string column that contains the parse trees of views. In processing a view, the length control field of its parse tree was found to be zero.
	-820	The SQL statement can't be processed because (catalog-table) contains a value that isn't valid in this release.
	-901	Unsuccessful execution caused by a system error that doesn't preclude the successful execution of subsequent SQL statements.

58005	-902	The pointer to the essential control block, either the CT or the RDA, is zeroes. This precludes the successful execution of the current SQL statement, as well as any subsequent SQL statements. A rebind is required.
58006	-924	DB2 connection internal error, (function-code), (return-code), (reason-code).
58008	-30000	Execution failed due to a distribution protocol error that will not affect the successful execution of subsequent commands or SQL statements: Reason (reason-code) (sub-code).
58009	-30020	Execution failed due to a distribution protocol error that caused deallocation of the conversation: Reason (reason-code) (sub-code).
58010	-30021	Execution failed due to a distribution protocol error that will affect the successful execution of subsequent commands or SQL statements: Manager (manager) at level (level) not supported error.
58011	-30050	(Command-or-SQL-statement-type) command or SQL statement invalid while BIND process in progress.
58012	-30051	Bind process with specified package name and consistency token not active.
58013	-30030	Commit request was unsuccessful, a distribution protocol violation has been detected, or the conversation has been deallocated. Original SQLCODE= (original-sqlcode) and original SQLSTATE=(original-sqlstate).
58014	-30070	(Command) command not supported error.
58015	-30071	(Object-type) object not supported error.
58016	-30072	(Parameter) : (subcode) parameter not supported error.
58017	-30073	(Parameter) : (subcode) parameter value not supported error.
58018	-30074	Reply message with (codepoint) SVRCOD not supported error.
58019	-30081	(Prot) communication error detected. API=api, LOCATION=loc, func, ERROR CODES=rc1 rc2 rc3.
58026	-870	The number of host variables in the statement isn't equal to the number of descriptors.

SQLCA and SQLDA fields

Part 1 of this series presented the most useful fields in the SQL communication area (SQLCA). Now, this appendix presents all of the fields in the SQLCA. In addition, it presents the fields in the SQL Descriptor Area (SQLDA) and shows you how to define an area for these fields in a COBOL program. For more information on how to use the SQLDA, see the IBM manual *DB2 for OS/390 V5 Application Programming and SQL Guide*.

SQLCA fields

The SQLCA is an area that DB2 uses to communicate with an application program. Specifically, the SQLCA contains information about the result of the last SQL statement issued by the application program. You can use the fields in the SQLCA to determine if specific errors occurred during the processing of a statement so that your program can proceed accordingly.

Figure B-1 describes the fields in the SQLCA. To include these fields in a COBOL program, you code an SQL INCLUDE statement as shown in the programs throughout this book.

The two fields in the SQLCA you're most likely to use are SQLCODE and SQLSTATE. Both contain a return code that indicates the status of the most recent SQL statement. The difference between the two is that SQLCODE is unique to DB2 for MVS, and SQLSTATE can be used across DB2 (and ANSI-compliant SQL) platforms. So if your DB2 application runs on DB2 for MVS, DB2 for OS/2, and DB2 for Windows NT, it should check the SQLSTATE field instead of the SQLCODE field.

Some of the SQLERRD and SQLWARN fields can also be useful in a COBOL program. For example, you can use SQLERRD(3) to determine how many rows were affected by an INSERT, DELETE, or UPDATE statement. You can use SQLERRD(5) to determine the position of a syntax error in a dynamic SQL statement. And you can use SQLWARN3 to determine if the number of host variables and result columns are the same. Many of the other fields aren't useful in a COBOL program.

The fields in the SQLCA

Field	Data type	Description
SQLCAID	8-byte string	Text string that identifies the SQLCA
SQLCABC	Binary fullword	Length of the entire SQLCA
SQLCODE	Binary fullword	SQL return code
SQLERRML	Binary halfword	Length of data in SQLERRMC
SQLERRMC	70-byte string	Data items that are substituted in error messages
SQLERRP	8-byte string	DB2 diagnostic information
SQLERRD(1)	Binary fullword	Internal error code
SQLERRD(2)	Binary fullword	Internal error code
SQLERRD(3)	Binary fullword	Number of rows affected by an INSERT, DELETE, or UPDATE statement
SQLERRD(4)	Binary fullword	Estimate of resources required for a prepared SQL statement
SQLERRD(5)	Binary fullword	Location of an SQL error in a statement processed dynamically
SQLERRD(6)	Binary fullword	Internal error code
SQLWARN0	1-byte string	Contains W if any other WARN field contains W
SQLWARN1	1-byte string	Contains W if a string was truncated when stored in a host variable
SQLWARN2	1-byte string	Contains W if null values were excluded during the processing of a column function
SQLWARN3	1-byte string	Contains W if the number of result columns is larger than the number of host variables
SQLWARN4	1-byte string	Contains W if a prepared UPDATE or DELETE statement doesn't have a WHERE clause
SQLWARN5	1-byte string	Contains W if the SQL statement isn't valid in DB2 for OS/390
SQLWARN6	1-byte string	Contains W if an arithmetic operation produces an unusual date or timestamp
SQLWARN7	1-byte string	Contains a W if one or more nonzero digits were eliminated from the fractional part of a number used as the operand of a decimal multiply or divide operation
SQLWARN8	1-byte string	Contains a W if a character that couldn't be converted was replaced with a substitute character
SQLWARNA	1-byte string	Contains a W if at least one character field of the SQLCA or the SQLDA names or labels is invalid due to a character conversion error
SQLSTATE	5-byte string	A return code that indicates the status of the most recent SQL statement

Figure B-1   SQLCA fields

SQLDA fields

DB2 can use the fields in the SQLDA to share information with an application program. The SQLDA can be used in a variety of statements, and the information it contains has a different meaning depending on the statement that uses it. To use the SQLDA in a COBOL program, you must code its description in the Working-Storage Section as shown in figure B-2. You can't use the SQL INCLUDE statement.

This figure also describes the contents of each field in the SQLDA. When used in an OPEN, FETCH, EXECUTE, or CALL statement, the SQLDA provides information to DB2 about the host variables or output buffers used by the application program. For OPEN or EXECUTE, the fields in each occurrence of SQLVAR describe the input value that's substituted for a parameter marker in the prepared statement. For FETCH, these fields describe a host variable or buffer in the application program that will contain a column from each row in the result table. And for CALL, these fields describe a host variable that corresponds to a parameter in the parameter list for the stored procedure.

When used in a PREPARE INTO or DESCRIBE statement, the SQLDA provides information to the application program about a prepared statement, and the fields in each occurrence of SQLVAR describe a row in the result table. When used with DESCRIBE TABLE, the SQLDA provides information about the columns of a table or view, and each occurrence of SQLVAR describes one column. When used with DESCRIBE CURSOR, the SQLDA provides information about the result set associated with the cursor, and each SQLVAR occurrence describes a column in the result set. And when used with DESCRIBE PROCEDURE, the SQLDA provides information about the result sets returned by a stored procedure, and each SQLVAR occurrence describes one result set.

A COBOL description for SQLDA

```
01   SQLDA.
     05   SQLDAID          PIC X(8)    VALUE 'SQLDA    '.
     05   SQLDABC          PIC S9(8)   COMP VALUE 33016.
     05   SQLN             PIC S9(4)   COMP VALUE 750.
     05   SQLD             PIC S9(4)   COMP VALUE 0.
     05   SQLVAR           OCCURS 1 to 750 TIMES
                           DEPENDING ON SQLN.
          10   SQLTYPE     PIC S9(4)   COMP.
          10   SQLLEN      PIC S9(4)   COMP.
          10   SQLDATA     POINTER.
          10   SQLIND      POINTER.
          10   SQLNAME.
               15   SQLNAMEL  PIC S9(4)   COMP.
               15   SQLNAMEC  PIC X(30).
```

The fields in the SQLDA

Field	Data type	Use in OPEN, FETCH, EXECUTE, and CALL	Use in DESCRIBE and PREPARE INTO
SQLAID	8-byte string	Indicates if SQLNAME contains an overriding CCSID.	Text string that identifies the SQLDA.
SQLDABC	Binary fullword	Not used.	Length of the SQLDA.
SQLN	Binary halfword	Occurrences of SQLVAR.	Occurrences of SQLVAR.
SQLD	Binary halfword	Number of host variables described by occurrences of SQLVAR.	Number of columns described by occurrences of SQLVAR.
SQLTYPE	Binary halfword	A code that indicates the data type of the host variable and whether an indicator variable is provided.	A code that indicates the data type of the column and whether or not it allows null values.
SQLLEN	Binary halfword	The length of the host variable.	The length of the column.
SQLDATA	Pointer	The address of the host variable.	The CCSID for character or graphic columns. Not used for other types of data. For DESCRIBE PROCEDURE, the result set locator value associated with the result set.
SQLIND	Pointer	The address of the associated indicator variable.	Set to −1 for DESCRIBE PROCEDURE. Reserved for all other uses.
SQLNAMEL	Binary halfword	The length of the data in SQLNAMEC.	The length of the data in SQLNAMEC.
SQLNAMEC	30-byte string	Can contain a CCSID.	The name or label of the column. For DESCRIBE PROCEDURE, the name of the cursor used by the stored procedure.

Figure B-2   SQLDA fields

Index

D

X

DB2 for the COBOL Programmer

Part 1 / Second Edition   **Curtis Garvin and Steve Eckols**

Written from the programmer's point of view, this book will quickly teach you what you need to know to handle DB2 data in your COBOL programs using embedded SQL. You'll learn how to: design and code programs that retrieve and update DB2 data...use joins and unions to combine data from two or more tables (that includes coverage of outer joins and the explicit syntax for inner joins)...use column functions and scalar functions...code subqueries...work with variable-length data and null values...use error handling techniques and ROLLBACK to protect DB2 data...use the locking features efficiently...use SPUFI and QMF to create test tables...and develop DB2 programs interactively (using DB2I, a TSO facility) or in batch.

So if you want to learn how to write DB2 application programs, get a copy of this book today!

DB2, Part 1, 15 chapters, 431 pages, **$45.00**
ISBN 1-890774-02-2

Murach's Beginning Visual Basic .NET

From beginner to entry-level programmer   **Anne Prince**

Learn Visual Basic .NET the Murach way, with an emphasis on professional programming practices, practical examples, and the paired-pages design that makes for faster learning and reference.

The first section gets you going with VB.NET right away. Here, you'll learn the language essentials you'll use every day, and you'll gain experience in working in the development environment. You'll also be introduced to the object-oriented programming practices that underlie the language. Then, section 2 builds on that base by teaching you more about working with Windows forms and controls. And section 3 teaches you the essential skills that a professional needs to have, such as working with dates, strings, arrays, collections, structures, files, inheritance, class libraries, and XML.

Once you have the essentials down, section 4 introduces you to database programming, while section 5 shows you the basics of web programming. Although you'll need to learn more about these subjects before you can create full-fledged database and web applications, you'll have the foundation you need to add to your skills more easily.

Murach's Visual Basic .NET, ISBN 1-890774-15-4
Scheduled for June 2002

www.murach.com • Toll-free 1-800-221-5528 (Weekdays, 8-5 Pacific Time) • Fax 1-559-440-0963

Murach's CICS for the COBOL Programmer

Now covers up through CICS Transaction Server

Raul Menendez and Doug Lowe

Our best-selling, two-part CICS series has now been revised into a single, concise volume that presents everything today's CICS programmer needs to know.

You'll get off to a fast start learning all the CICS elements you'll use in just about every program you write. That includes:

- how to use Basic Mapping Support (BMS)
- pseudo-conversational programming…what it is and why you have to use it
- basic CICS commands for terminal handling, VSAM file handling, error handling, and program control
- how to *design* a CICS program using event-driven design so it's easier to code, test, and maintain
- how to use IBM-supplied transactions like CEMT, CECI, and EDF to simplify testing and debugging

Then, you'll move on to the CICS features you'll use regularly, though you won't need all of them for every program. Like temporary storage queues...browse

commands for file processing...DB2 access...CICS control features for specialized functions...and the intercommunication features of CICS.

Beyond the coding details, though, you'll see how to design, code, and test a CICS program whose presentation logic (that is, all the functions related to sending data to and receiving data from the terminal) is separated from the business logic (the functions that process the data). This is a growing trend as tools like Java are used to handle the user interface while CICS still gets the data and does the backend processing. Then, you'll see how this approach influences another trend: programming for the Web using CICS.

So whether you're a CICS trainee who needs to start from scratch or an experienced CICS programmer who's ready to master advanced skills, this is the book for you!

Murach's CICS, 22 chapters, 633 pages, **$54.00**
ISBN 1-890774-09-X

Murach's Beginning Java 2

Includes versions 1.3 & 1.4

Andrea Steelman

If you're ready to add Java programming to your skill set, this book gets you to a professional level in record time. In fact, by the end of chapter 2, you'll be writing programs that use Java classes. By chapter 4, you'll be developing your own classes. And by chapter 6, you'll be starting to design, code, test, and debug the kind of object-oriented Java applications that businesses rely on.

But that's just Section 1. Section 2 teaches you about the features you'll use in your Java programs every day. That includes working with dates, coding loops, manipulating arrays and strings, handling exceptions, and more.

Figuring out how to create a graphical user interface can be a nightmare with other books. But this one has you create your first GUI, complete with Swing components, from start to finish in chapter 11. Then, the

remaining 4 chapters in Section 3 show you how to enhance that interface and how to convert it to an applet.

Because stored data is critical to most business applications, Section 4 teaches you how to use Java to handle text and binary files. Then, in Section 5, chapter 19 introduces you to using JDBC to store the data for business objects in a database instead of a file. Finally, chapter 20 teaches you how to use threads to optimize the performance of your Java applications.

So whether you're completely new to Java or know the basics but haven't yet mastered subjects like building GUIs with Swing components or using JDBC or threads, *Murach's Beginning Java 2* gives you the professional training you need.

Murach's Beginning Java 2, 20 chapters, 712 pages, **$49.50**
ISBN 1-890774-12-X

 www.murach.com · Toll-free 1-800-221-5528 (Weekdays, 8-5 Pacific Time) · Fax 1-559-440-0963

Murach's OS/390 and z/OS JCL

For training and reference   **Raul Menendez and Doug Lowe**

Anyone who's worked in an IBM mainframe shop knows that JCL is tough to master. You learn enough to get by...but then you stick to that. It's just too frustrating to try to put together a job using the IBM manuals. And too time-consuming to keep asking your co-workers for help...especially since they're often limping along with the JCL they know, too.

That's why you need a copy of *Murach's OS/390 and z/OS JCL*. It zeroes in on the JCL you need for everyday jobs...so you can learn to code significant job streams in a hurry.

You'll learn how to compile, link-edit, load, and execute programs. Process all types of data sets.

Manage job and program execution, data set allocation, and SYSOUT processing. Create and use JCL procedures. Execute general-purpose utility programs. Access files designed for UNIX systems. And much more.

But that's not all this book does. Beyond teaching you JCL, it explains the basics of how the mainframe works so you can apply that understanding as you code JCL. That's the kind of perspective that's missing in other JCL books and courses, but it makes you a more confident and valuable programmer.

Murach's OS/390 and z/OS JCL, 21 chapters,
559 pages, **$62.50**
ISBN 1-890774-14-6

MVS TSO

Part 1: Concepts and ISPF   **Doug Lowe**

Now you can quickly master ISPF with this practical book. Chapter 1 introduces you to MVS...good background no matter how much MVS experience you've had. It also shows you how TSO/ISPF relates to MVS, so you'll understand how to use ISPF to control the operating system functions.

The remaining 7 chapters teach you all the specifics of using ISPF for everyday programming tasks. You'll learn how to edit and browse data sets; use the ISPF utilities to manage your data sets and libraries; compile, link, and execute programs interactively; use the VS

COBOL II or OS COBOL interactive debugger; process batch jobs in a background region; manage your background jobs more easily using the Spool Display & Search Facility (SDSF) to browse JES2 queues; use member parts lists to track the use of subprograms and COPY members within program libraries; use two library management systems that support hierarchical libraries—the Library Management Facility (LMF) and the Software Configuration and Library Manager (SCLM); and more!

MVS TSO, Part 1, 8 chapters, 467 pages, **$42.50**
ISBN 0-911625-56-9

MVS TSO

Part 2: Commands and Procedures (CLIST and REXX)   **Doug Lowe**

If you're ready to expand your skills beyond ISPF and become a TSO user who can write complex CLIST and REXX procedures with ease, this is the book for you. It starts by teaching you how to use TSO commands for common programming tasks like managing data sets and libraries, running programs in foreground mode, and submitting jobs for background execution. Then, it

shows you how to combine those commands into CLIST or REXX procedures for the jobs you do most often...including procedures that you can use as edit macros under the ISPF editor and procedures that use ISPF dialog functions to display full-screen panels.

MVS TSO, Part 2, 10 chapters, 450 pages, **$42.50**
ISBN 0-911625-57-7

 www.murach.com · Toll-free 1-800-221-5528 (Weekdays, 8-5 Pacific Time) · Fax 1-559-440-0963